SOUTHERN CALIFORNIA METROPOLIS

SOUTHERN CALIFORNIA METROPOLIS *A Study in*

Development of Government for a

Metropolitan Area

BY WINSTON W. CROUCH
AND BEATRICE DINERMAN

UNIVERSITY OF CALIFORNIA PRESS | BERKELEY AND
LOS ANGELES 1963

654699

UNIVERSITY OF CALIFORNIA PRESS
BERKELEY AND LOS ANGELES, CALIFORNIA
CAMBRIDGE UNIVERSITY PRESS, LONDON, ENGLAND
© 1963 BY THE REGENTS OF THE UNIVERSITY OF CALIFORNIA
LIBRARY OF CONGRESS CATALOG CARD NUMBER: 63-21640
PRINTED IN THE UNITED STATES OF AMERICA

Preface

THIS BOOK is about the Los Angeles metropolitan area. The central theme focuses upon the process by which organized groups have sought to identify public issues and reach decisions on them. It has a long and dynamic cast of characters, composed of the numerous interest groups who have attempted, throughout the years, to influence this decision-making process within the context of a rapidly changing, fluid environment. There are no heroes; there are no villians.

This story does not carry a "message." It deals with issues and events whose social significance cannot be questioned. If there is a message to be gleaned from this volume, it is that greater knowledge of the philosophical, legal, political and social forces that have shaped the present system of local government must precede any successful adjustment of the status quo. This book attempts to clarify the nature of these forces and to assess their present and potential impact on the structure of local government in the Los Angeles metropolitan area.

The concept of the metropolitan area has tended to highlight two contradictory characteristics of the current urban scene: the dispersion of political power among a number of centers, and the presence of issues and problems whose impact transcends the jurisdiction of any one local government. These metropolitan "facts of life" have limited traditional institutions of local government in their responses to the demands of an ever-growing metropolitan community. How can public decisions be made in a setting in which political power is so diffused? How can areawide issues be identified? How can conflicts be resolved? How can decisions be implemented, if made? These questions continue to plague metropolitan areas.

In the Los Angeles area, political authority is even more widely dispersed than in most other metropolitan regions. Despite this fragmentation, decisions affecting urban growth have been made and implemented. A large and mobile population has been accommodated. Industry, commerce and cultural activities have prospered. However, the continuing economic progress and the absence of chaotic conditions under present governmental arrangements have not been sufficient inducements to still the voices of students of metropolitan affairs. Would a restructuring of local governmental institutions produce more effective public decisions with less expenditure of resources? What types of realignments among institutions of local government would expedite action on public issues? How can local government best be organized to meet the ever-increasing challenges of metropolitan growth?

In this volume, we have looked upon the present governmental structure as the product of significant decisions made by former generations that have established political and legal constraints upon the decisions made today. Such constraints represent built-in features of the present system, which tend to slow down the rate of change and to guide the direction in which change takes place. Power is thereby viewed within the institutional framework. We were interested in examining the manner in which a political system, created during a time when there were few municipalities and no great clusters of urban dwellers, has adjusted to new conditions heralded by the development of a metropolitan aggregation. We were equally interested in the consequences of the revisions in the California political system fashioned by the Progressive movement during the 1910–1916 era.

On the basis of the collected information, we have posed the hypothesis that democratic ideology and group interests have combined to produce competing power centers from which countervailing forces operate. No one center or force has had sufficient resources to dominate decision-making in the metropolitan area. Each is represented by a set of public officials, supported by public and private interests that have a stake in the outcome of the decisions to be made. From time to time, others enter the contest and attract sufficient support to alter a decision on a particular issue. Because there are several forces in competition, each is induced to expand resources in order to secure a part of the negotiation. This process of negotiation is a dynamic one characterized by frequent change and modification. However, the rate of change and its direction are largely influenced by predetermined legal and political constraints inherent in the present system.

In the final section of the book, we analyze several alternative directions in which changes in the governance of the metropolitan area might be brought about. In doing this, we seek to assess the consequences of interaction between various sets of competitors. What developments could conceivably upset the present balance? What direction would these changes take? What will be the nature of the new realignment?

This study was made possible by a generous grant from the John R. Haynes and Dora Haynes Foundation to the Bureau of Governmental Research at the University of California, Los Angeles. For several years the Bureau centered its research interest upon several aspects of metropolitan government; and a number of staff studies from this particular project have already been published in limited editions. In preparing this book we have drawn heavily upon the investigations made by several staff members. We gladly acknowledge the assistance given by Richard Bigger, Ross Clayton, George Frederickson, Robert Giordano, Evan Iverson, Kenneth Johnson, James Kitchen, Jack Meisner, Edward Staniford, Nils Wagenhals, Robert Warren, and Richard Yerby. Wherever possible, we have cited their publications or manuscripts. Special thanks are due to Belmont Brice, Jr. for his help with Chapter Two; to Eugene Dvorin for the preliminary work on governmental decentralization; and to Miss Judith N. Jamison for her painstaking study of newspapers in the metropolitan community.

Innumerable city, county, and state officials have given us information and cooperated in many ways. Arthur Will, of Los Angeles County, and Jay Michael, of the League of California Cities, responded especially helpfully to our many requests for data.

The cartography is the work of Mordecai Albert, who meticulously and understandingly transformed the general information we were able to supply. Miss Dorothy V. Wells, the Bureau librarian, ably assisted us at all times with bibliographical and documentary problems. Mrs. Jean Eberhart and Mrs. Beverly Stewart helped immeasurably in typing and preparing the manuscript.

Stanley Scott, assistant director of the Institute of Governmental Studies at the University of California, Berkeley, Professors John C. Bollens and J. A. C. Grant, colleagues at UCLA, and Dean Gordon Watkins, University of California, Santa Barbara, very kindly read parts of the manuscript and offered suggestions that were very helpful. All these, however, in accordance with custom and fact, we hold blameless for errors of fact or interpretation that occur in the book.

WINSTON W. CROUCH
BEATRICE DINERMAN

Contents

II. CONTENDERS FOR LEADERSHIP

III. DECENTRALIZATION—MANY DECISION CENTERS

IV. ALTERNATIVE COURSES

TEXT TABLES

APPENDIX TABLES

FIGURES

PART I
THE SETTING AND FRAMEWORK

ONE

The Los Angeles Metropolitan Area:
Background for Analysis

MOBILITY AND CHANGE IN THE METROPOLIS

Los Angeles, the second largest metropolitan area in the United States, is literally the product of the technological age—the era of the automobile, the airplane, and the rocket. Although the community has a long recorded history, of which many residents are actively conscious, its development as a vast, complex urban center has been achieved within the lifetime of persons now active in the political and commercial life of the metropolis. Mobility and change characterize the scene here. The community has grown in human resources as a consequence of a series of tremendous population migrations; its people have experience with movement and relocation. Here industries that were new to the national economy have flourished and matured and have struggled to maintain their position in the economic firmament in competition with new industries born of technological change. The motion picture industry grew from an infant industry to a world-leading giant. As television developed, it drew upon the talent resources mobilized by the movie industry and forced numerous changes in the commercial entertainment world. Similarly, airframe manufacturing developed in southern California from pioneering origins to make the Los Angeles metropolitan area one of the principal national centers of this industry. As missiles replaced manned aircraft in military operations, and as development and production of space vehicles became a major preoccupation of national policy, the airframe industry partly shifted its resources to the new activities. The new fed upon the old for manpower, technical skill, and organizational bases. Organization of new firms for research, development, and manufacturing and the construction of new physical facilities caused shifts in the centers of influence and activity as well as in manpower.

Inasmuch as the physical facilities of the metropolitan area are still developing to accommodate a growing population, changes are constantly taking place in the area's appearance. Visible signs of mobility and change are constantly in evidence.

ASPECTS OF MOBILITY

Residential mobility is well known. The United States Bureau of the Census reports that between March, 1959, and March, 1960, the rates of residential mobility were higher for the Los Angeles–Long Beach Standard Metropolitan Statistical Area than were those for any other standard metropolitan statistical area.[1] The great growth in this area's population has been produced by the movement of large numbers of people from other parts of the United States into the southern California coastal region.[2]

Once here, people demonstrate a tendency to move their residence in search of more advantageous conditions. The Bureau of the Census reports that 18.9 per cent of the civilian population in the Los Angeles area moved their residence within the county in 1959–1960, whereas only 8.4 per cent moved in New York and only 14.4 per cent in Chicago.[3] Movement within the county appears not to be influenced entirely by a desire to locate residence near employment; climatic conditions and social customs are also important factors.

Social mobility, the movement of individuals and families within the ranks of community social structure, although less often noted than residential mobility, is high in Los Angeles. The American cultural thesis that the poor but industrious boy (and girl) can rise to high economic and social status is supported here by numerous cases, although few fortunes of vast magnitude have been accumulated solely within the metropolitan area. The motion picture, oil, real estate, construction, airframe, and electronic industries have contributed many examples of persons who rose from low to high economic and social status in the course of a relatively few years. Furthermore, many out-

---

[1] U.S. Bureau of the Census, *Current Population Reports*, Series P-20, no. 113 (Jan. 27, 1962), p. 2.

[2] Warren S. Thompson, *Growth and Changes in California's Population* (Los Angeles: Haynes Foundation, 1955).

[3] U.S. Bureau of the Census, *op. cit.*, p. 13. Figures are given in terms of standard metropolitan statistical areas.

standing elective office holders, professional people, engineers, and scientists, as well as several Nobel prize winners, have risen from humble origins in this metropolitan area.

INNOVATIONS IN ACTIVITIES AND INSTITUTIONS

Although mobility and innovation are separate phenomena, they tend to interact. Several types of innovation have characterized public and private activity in this area. Conditions in Los Angeles were different from those in older sections of the country; hence, new methods and new institutions had to be created. Many transplanted institutions were modified as well. Foresight was required to transform the natural desert environment of southern California to, first, an agricultural economy featuring subtropical agriculture and, later, an urban industrial economy. The development of water supply systems needed by both economies required the inventive skill and the talents of engineers, scientists, and business enterprisers.

Innovation has been demonstrated in the art of governance as well as in science and technology and in the skills of economic production. Administrative institutions, as well as legal arrangements, facilitating the organization and management of water supply systems are in point. The irrigation district, the municipal water district, the mutual water company, the quasi-independent municipal water department, and the metropolitan water district were devised to solve problems of accumulating, managing, and distributing a scarce commodity, water, for the benefit of the community. Institutions and procedures created to cope with air pollution problems were similarly novel: a science policy was developed for local government at a time when public opinion demanded immediate action, and a physical-science research program was organized on a relatively large scale, involving a local government in the operation of research facilities and in contracting with private groups for research information. The new situation demanded application of such familiar administrative-legal processes as licensing, inspection, and administrative adjudication. Community relations had to be kept smooth and public opinion had to be kept satisfied in the first difficult stage of scientific investigation of the physical sources of air pollution.

The county Sanitation Districts system was a new type of institution when it was developed in 1923. It provided an arrangement by which numerous cities and unincorporated fringe areas could work together to form a metropolitan waste-disposal system. This plan produced functional integration in fact, although the participants were determined to preserve local self-government whenever possible.

The intergovernmental contract has been given extensive use in this metropolitan area, altering traditional relationships between local governments. The multiple-service type of contract negotiated between the county and numerous cities under the Lakewood Plan is completely different from any other agreement between local governments.

Southern California pioneered in other aspects of local government as well. The initiative, the referendum, and the recall—processes for registering the public will in local governmental affairs—were employed in Los Angeles early in the American history of direct legislation. Likewise, municipal and county home-rule charters constituted significant experiments in local government. Because Los Angeles County and several of its cities were among the first to adopt home-rule charters, they were able also to be pioneers in such matters as budgeting, fiscal control, administrative organization and methods, and administrative management. Furthermore, the chief administrative officer concept of organization has been developed extensively among the local governments in the Los Angeles metropolitan area.

A GOVERNMENTAL CONCEPT OF THE METROPOLITAN AREA

The metropolitan area has been defined in a number of ways. The sociologist, the economist, the political scientist, and the governmental specialist are each likely to conceive of the metropolitan area in a different manner. A common starting point, however, is the definition given by the Bureau of the Census. The Census identifies a Los Angeles–Long Beach Standard Metropolitan Area, encompassing Los Angeles and Orange counties. It sets apart the urban area adjacent to this Standard Metropolitan Area on the east as the San Bernardino–Riverside Standard Metropolitan Area, although the latter has many economic and political ties with the Los Angeles–Long Beach area.

The region serviced by the Metropolitan Water District of Southern California includes large portions of six counties: Los Angeles, San Bernardino, Riverside, Orange, Ventura, and San Diego. In a study of metropolitan airport requirements, beginning in 1961, representatives from Imperial County joined those from the six counties served by the water district. A study of outdoor recreational requirements of the population in the Los Angeles metropolitan area considered six counties as the primary base for study.[4]

---

[4] Outdoor Recreation Requirements Review Commission, *Impact of Growth of the Los Angeles Metropolitan Region on the Demand for Outdoor Recreation Facilities in Southern California*, vol. 3, Report 21 (Washington, D.C.: Government Printing Office, 1963).

At the present time, the Metropolitan Water District is the only governmental agency operating under state law that encompasses an area greater than one county.[5] Los Angeles County alone serves as the general political and administrative unit comprising most of the metropolitan area. Although Orange County has many associations with Los Angeles, the communities are still sufficiently distinct to justify their operating as separate governmental entities. Problems of local government, other than those relating to water supply, have been treated acceptably by the governments of the two counties, and of the several cities and numerous special districts within them. For the purpose of this study, we shall consider Los Angeles County as comprising the Los Angeles metropolitan area.

The formal structure of government in Los Angeles gives the appearance of being simpler than that which operates in several of the larger metropolitan areas of the United States. As Los Angeles lies entirely in California, it avoids the interstate problems that afflict Greater New York, Philadelphia, Chicago, Washington, D.C., or St. Louis. It operates within the framework of one legal system. Beyond this point, however, the simplicity of the formal structure is illusory.

Within the one county there are seventy-four cities, although one city scarcely figures in the metropolitan analysis. Avalon is situated on Santa Catalina Island twenty-eight miles off the mainland. All incorporated cities have the same organic constitutional status, although they vary in size of population, in taxable wealth, and in type of internal governmental mechanisms. Under California law there are no villages, towns, boroughs, or townships.

A variety of single- and multiple-purpose special districts complicates the governmental pattern, however. School districts administer elementary and secondary schools, including junior colleges—which are legally considered parts of the secondary school system. Some simplification of the school administrative system has been achieved by combining school districts in urban areas to produce unified jurisdictions coterminous with city boundaries, although school units are independent of the city governments. Numerous other special districts provide services in the areas outside cities. A few districts, such as the county flood control and air pollution control districts, provide a single functional service for city areas as well as for unincorporated territory. Although the county Tax Assessor lists 244 special districts that levied taxes in 1961, two hundred of those listed were under the jurisdiction

---

[5] Administrative areas established by state and federal agencies for convenience in conducting administrative business are differentiated here from the instruments of local or regional government.

of the county Board of Supervisors, thereby simplifying the governmental pattern to some degree.[6] Forty-four special districts operate under their own independently chosen governing bodies.[7]

THE FORMAL STRUCTURE OF GOVERNMENT

There is considerable uniformity among the local governments in the metropolitan area in formal structure. The county and all the cities, except Los Angeles, operate under an elective board or council and have no independently elected executive officer. Members of the county Board of Supervisors and the councils in a minority number of cities are elected from districts, thereby emphasizing local community interests in the selection of policy determining officers. The special districts, like their counterparts in other sections of the country, are governed by boards of directors. No district has an independently elected executive officer. Two districts having metropolitan proportions, the Metropolitan Water District and the County Sanitation Districts system, are confederations governed by boards composed of representatives from their constituent local government units.

Los Angeles City is the exception to the common pattern of formal local governmental structure. It has a city council composed of fifteen members elected by districts, and a mayor and controller, each elected by the voters of the city at large. The mayor does not have extensive executive powers. By the city charter's prescription, he is compelled to share power with the city council and with administrative boards and commissions. The controller is confined to the fiscal field.

Local governments make extensive use of professional administrators. The larger suburban cities, such as Glendale, Pasadena, and Long Beach, have employed the city manager plan for approximately forty years. The county has had a chief administrative officer and staff since 1938, the city of Los Angeles since 1945. In the period comprising 1949–1961, all except five of the other cities employed either a manager or an administrative officer. Professionalism also has grown in such functional fields as public health, planning, personnel, and engineering.

This element of professionalism, together with the relatively stable local bureaucracies, has given a significant continuity and strength to local government. The combination of a full-time, professionally oriented administrative corps and a part-time elective officer body

---

[6] Los Angeles County, Auditor-Controller, *Taxpayers' Guide 1961* (Los Angeles: County of Los Angeles, 1961).

[7] These districts include those for cemetery, hospital, library, mosquito abatement, recreation and park, sanitation, and soil conservation functions.

has given a distinctive style to local government. In the climate of opinion that has resulted, matters tend to be resolved quietly by informal methods in semiprivacy rather than by public display of controversy, compromise, and adjustment. The manager or the chief administrative officer attempts to allay tension and resolve disputes before matters become open public controversies.

Local governmental officialdom has been assigned an unusually complex array of functions in Los Angeles. Numerous functions that in many sections of the United States are placed in the sphere of private responsibility are here performed by public bodies. These include activities relating to art galleries, art schools, sports stadia, outdoor symphonies, and historical centers. Civil service laws, designed primarily to stabilize a public-employment situation, have been applied in such a manner as to require local governments to utilize public employees rather than contract with private concerns to perform construction work, repair and maintain equipment, and operate parking lots, employee cafeterias, and auditoriums. Architectural design work on city and county buildings is a major exception to this practice. The remarkable point about this situation is not the extent to which these activities have become public ones, but that they have been public for so long a time. Although there are privately endowed libraries and privately supported music and art organizations, the public activities have been the predominant ones in the area. Cultural and recreational activities have been placed in the public category in order to ensure a steady support base from tax funds. The public bodies governing many of these activities, for example, the Hollywood Bowl, the County Art Museum, the Music Center, the Griffith Park planetarium, the Greek Theater, the zoo, the marinas and yacht anchorages, the municipal and county golf courses, have sought to foster the concept that they are supplying regional needs. The Coliseum and Sports Arena clearly are regional facilities. Although not all of the activities are administered by public employees, public local bodies made the decisions to create the facilities or programs and to control their use. These types of activities have become accepted so thoroughly as public functions that sets of local officials compete to devise, offer, and control programs expected to have public appeal.

THE NATURE OF POLITICS IN THE
METROPOLITAN AREA

In the absence of a formal governmental structure encompassing the entire area, speculation arises concerning the existence of an informal organization with power to obtain decisions on truly areawide matters. Political systems tend to develop around specific governmental jurisdictions because political contests between organized groups are designed to control government actions. Inasmuch as the Los Angeles metropolitan area is organized currently as a series of local units, one would expect to find a series of political systems operating therein. Does an areawide group exist in fact? Are there several groups competing at the area level? Is the number of power groups roughly equal to the number of formal governments, or is the number considerably larger because some other formula may govern the distribution of power?

In this chapter some general features of the local political systems are set forth in order to provide a framework for discussion. We propose to develop this framework in later chapters by examining the factors that relate to the large parts of the area's government. It is possible to make several generalizations about local politics in the Los Angeles metropolitan area which are helpful in setting the frame of reference.

In much of American government, political parties function as informal agents to facilitate operation of the formal structure. They recruit and select candidates for elective office. They articulate issues. Under some circumstances they facilitate intergovernmental coördination.[8] In California, however, the political parties are unable to perform this function for metropolitan areas and are replaced by other political instruments.

The basic characteristics of local politics in California were shaped by decisions made during the second decade of this century. These decisions, which were influenced by the ideology of the Progressive movement, removed political parties from direct involvement in the local governmental process and substituted *ad hoc* combinations of private groups that are less easily identified by the voters. The Progressive movement emphasized nonpartisanship in local government policy making. As a corollary, it also emphasized the value of a nonpartisan corps of civil servants capable of administering an ever-increasing variety of governmental services and guided by standards determined by professional groups rather than political considerations.

CANDIDATE RECRUITMENT AND SELECTION

Changes in the methods of recruiting and selecting candidates for local elective offices have produced especially significant consequences.

---

[8] Roscoe C. Martin, Frank J. Munger, *et al., Decisions in Syracuse*, Metropolitan Action Studies, no. 1 (Bloomington: Indiana University Press, 1961), illustrate how a political party becomes a significant element in providing intergovernmental coördination in a metropolitan area.

The change began in 1909, when the city of Berkeley abolished the party convention as a method for nominating local candidates. Other chartered cities in various parts of the state quickly followed this example.[9] In 1911, state legislation applied the nonpartisan ballot to school elections, and in 1913, the same method was extended to county and chartered city elections. The doctrine of the Progressives was epitomized by the slogan, "Concentrate on the man, not on the party." By emphasizing the candidate, they sought to open election contests to persons who were impatient with or repelled by the control techniques exercised by political parties in nominating conventions. Under the nonpartisan system, anyone who was legally eligible was free to be a candidate in the primary elections. The basic resources required were the support of a small number of electors who would sign the nominating petition and a relatively small amount of money for the filing fee.

Nonpartisanship tends to deprecate the importance of campaign organization in mobilizing support on behalf of candidates in order to win elections. This system places a heavy responsibility upon the candidate to build an *ad hoc* organization for promotion of his candidacy, and to recruit workers and funds with which to support his campaign.

The Progressive reforms also sought to prevent the candidate, incumbent and challenger alike, from capturing the local civil services and using them as nuclei of campaign organizations. Civil service laws were adopted widely in local governments and were drawn in a manner calculated to neutralize the local public services in matters relating to the selection of local officials.

As Professor Eugene Lee reports in his study of nonpartisan elections in selected California cities, "local elections more often center on personalities than issues." [10] Campaigns are focused therefore on individuals, and although candidate slates are frequently presented, individual campaigns, separately financed, organized, and administered, are the rule.[11]

Although the costs of local election campaigns vary widely, depending upon tradition, geographical locations, and personalities, money is important for the successful conduct of a contested local election campaign. The money is supplied by those interested in the outcome of the election. Individual contributions are usually in small sums. Organization contributions come largely from utilities, contractors, property owners who desire zoning changes, land develop-

---

[9] Eugene C. Lee, *The Politics of Nonpartisanship* (Berkeley and Los Angeles: University of California Press, 1960), p. 23.

[10] *Ibid.*, p. 128.

[11] *Ibid.*, p. 131.

ers, and those who seek to sell goods or services to the local government.

The politics of group mobilization, as Professor Lee calls it, also demands publicity for the candidate, inasmuch as he must seek to attract persons who are not personally acquainted with him. Hence much of the expense of campaigning for city, county, and district offices consists of obtaining campaign materials, newspaper advertising, and local radio and television time. The candidate who has the active editorial support of newspapers holds a great advantage over other candidates because he is able to have a favorable image of himself presented to the voters at no cost to himself. In his statewide study, Lee estimates that the groups most favored by nonpartisanship are:

> those segments of the community which are characterized by formal or informal organization and patterns of communications. Among these groups are the business community, along with, and often complemented by, the local press. . . . Yet a great variety of other groups are active and influential: veterans' organizations, women's clubs, service clubs and lodges, improvement associations, labor unions, and lay church groups. . . .[12]

Although instruments of mass communication are especially influential factors in local nonpartisan elections, the candidate who has a wide acquaintanceship among a substantial bloc of voters by participating in organizations or through some specially publicized activity may escape dependence upon news media.

In the Los Angeles metropolitan area, one newspaper, the Los Angeles *Times,* has been unusually influential in local matters over a long period of years. The *Times* makes active endorsements of candidates for mayor and councilmen in Los Angeles City, Los Angeles County, and Los Angeles City School District Board elections. It also expresses vigorously its editorial views on issues arising within these three jurisdictions as well as within the Metropolitan Water District, Flood Control District, and Air Pollution Control District. Although it reports local news of the suburban cities, this paper does not endorse candidates for local office in other portions of the metropolitan area. Other daily papers having a metropolitan circulation seldom endorse local candidates. Periodically they take editorial positions on local issues. Daily newspapers in the suburban cities are often active in endorsing council candidates or taking sides on local issues in their respective cities. However, the *Times* has remained consistently the most influential news medium at the metropolitan level.

---

[12] *Ibid.,* p. 163.

In sum, the nonpartisan method of nominating and selecting candidates for local offices makes the media of mass news communication and the sources of campaign funds crucial to the political process. Most candidates must negotiate with those who are influential with such resources in order to project themselves and their ideas to the electorate. If a candidate does not choose to enlist the support of those who control these resources, he must either seek the support of some previously organized group that desires to have a champion in local office or build a personal following that will supply the necessary resources to conduct a successful campaign.

Consensus Negotiation among Officeholders

Inasmuch as nonpartisan nomination and election procedures tend to produce individual candidacies for local office, the successful candidate tends to respond to the suggestions and urgings of those who assisted his election. Hence, he sees little reason to vote consistently with any specific set of associates in office. One of the chief goals of the Progressives was to free elected policy makers from the constraints of party cohesion when voting on issues in city councils and boards of supervisors. The available evidence suggests that this goal has been achieved.

Information regarding the voting behavior of local officials is meager. The authors of a study of voting splits in city councils in Los Angeles County conclude that party affiliation does not play a significant role in determining the lineup of council members on controversial issues.[13] Nevertheless, this same study indicates that councils composed of registered members of the two major political parties are more apt to split than are councils composed entirely of members registered in one party. It remains to be established whether this situation is owing to ideological differences that may extend to community issues or to a tendency to relate city policy matters to matters at the state level that have a definite partisan tinge. Lee concludes that one reason for intrusion of partisanship into local politics is that many county chairmen look to the city hall or county courthouse as sources of candidates for state and national offices.[14]

The authors of the article on city councils find some correlation between the occupations of the council members and their lineup on controversial matters. Data on the occupational groupings of council

---

[13] Robert J. Huckshorn and Charles E. Young, "Study of Voting Splits in City Councils in Los Angeles County," *Western Political Quarterly*, XIII (June, 1960), 479–497.

[14] Lee, *op. cit.*, p. 117.

members indicate that the largest number are engaged in personally owned business enterprises, and the second largest group, in real estate and insurance sales. Among professional persons, lawyers composed the largest group. Councils in which lawyers were numerically predominant tended to show the smallest number of divisions in voting.

The types of issues over which divisions arise in city councils seem to have nothing in common with issues that divide the parties in state and national politics. The most controversial issues in city council politics relate to zoning, personnel matters, and public works. The study cited found only one council that consistently split on a subject involving intergovernmental relations, and that subject related more to metropolitan problems than to state party issues.

Intergovernmental relationships in the Los Angeles metropolitan area do not seem to be influenced by partisan considerations of state-wide political parties. Overtones of partisanship that appear in some communities at election time are not usually carried over into voting on city councils or the board of supervisors. Relationships among official groups from two or more cities or between a city government and the county seem to be governed by considerations other than state political party advantage or loyalty. We must look elsewhere than to political party leaders for a source of influence that will cut across local governmental boundary lines to coördinate decision-making on matters of metropolitan significance.

INFLUENCE GROUPS IN LOCAL POLITICS

In the absence of political parties at the local governmental level, special-interest groups have tended to prevail. The groups have generally devoted their attention to aggregating those persons concerned with a single dominant interest and articulating that interest. Examples include those engaged in real estate development and sales, veterans, and lay church members. Unlike political parties, these groups do not attempt to organize persons holding several different predominant interests into a united political endeavor. Frequently the groups are *ad hoc* in nature, coming into being to express an interest on one issue at one particular time.

Few general-purpose political action groups have survived for long in southern California local politics.[15] In the early 1920's a City Club flourished in Los Angeles for a time. Over a somewhat longer period, a Municipal League, devoted to supporting municipal ownership of

---

[15] See Lorin Peterson, *The Day of the Mugwump* (New York: Random House, 1962), pp. 234–247, for an interesting journalistic analysis of political organization in Los Angeles.

business enterprises supplying electricity and water and to several
other issues of municipal policy, exercised considerable influence in
Los Angeles City politics. It passed from the scene in the late 1930's.
A few years later, Clifford Clinton and his Citizens' Independent Vice
Investigating Committee played an active role in the city's politics for
a short time. A municipal-league-type of organization operated in
Long Beach for several years. Municipal reform groups, community
improvement societies, and taxpayers' leagues have started up and then
have expired after a few years of activity in the larger municipalities.
A substantial number of such organizations have been protest groups,
formed to combat a zoning proposal, the routing of a state freeway or
local road, or the location of a type of building that allegedly failed
to conform to prevailing neighborhood standards; or to object to sharp
rises in assessed valuation of property for tax purposes. In the absence
of on-going organizations that can identify issues and act as inter-
mediaries between citizens who have a stake in occasional policy decisions of local governments and the policy deciders, this type of special-interest group is formed to mobilize the weight of citizen numbers
to influence the policy makers.

Municipal and county government employees have become active
in organizing themselves to articulate demands upon their governmental employers with respect to wages and working conditions. Although the collective voting power of public employees has been directed rather strictly to matters pertaining to their employment, such
organizations have achieved greater prominence in the decade of the
1950's. Most of them comprise employees of the various departments
of a particular local government, and are thus general employees' units.
Police and firemen, who have usually formed their own separate organizations, have been effective in winning adoption of policies favorable to their employment interests. The interests of local employee
groups impinge upon several problems of metropolitan government,
particularly those of formal governmental organization and intergovernmental relations. Political efforts of public employees have been
directed both to exercising pressure-group influence upon councils
and to directing appeal to the voters by means of initiative petitions.
Although the employee groups have most often expressed concern regarding retirement systems, wage formulas, and employment policies,
they have also been active in matters that affect their employment less
directly. For example, employee groups in the Los Angeles Water and
Power Department have sought to protect the public-ownership system against political attacks, and to influence the formation of operational policies within the agency. In a somewhat similar way, Los

Angeles County sheriff deputies have allegedly opposed the incorporation of new cities, for fear that such incorporations would threaten
the existing county system and diminish the size of the sheriff's force.
An organization of county firemen has actively urged adoption of a
plan to integrate fire departments and form a metropolitan fire-sup-
pression system.

AREAWIDE GROUPS LIMITED

No organization has yet come forward to aggregate interests and
articulate demands relating to the full range of areawide policies, although an occasional interest-group has sought action on a particular
need. For example, the Colorado River Association mobilized political
strength to obtain decisions allocating water resources in the Colorado
River and to support the program administered by the Metropolitan
Water District of Southern California. This association continued to
exist for many years after the Colorado River Compact was formulated
and the district became an administrative reality. A similar type of
group has been active in flood control matters, particularly with reference to securing federal appropriations for dams and flood channel
works, but none has developed to focus interest on regional planning,
transportation, or like matters at the metropolitan level. Frequently
the *ad hoc* groups formed to secure action on particular issues exist
only for the purpose of financing and managing a campaign for a bond
issue for a regional storm-drain system, a major sewage-disposal
project, an airport expansion, or the like.

The Los Angeles Chamber of Commerce is often the group from
which leadership is drawn to develop consensus among public officials
and interested private bodies and to organize the *ad hoc* efforts to
secure voter consent. Throughout the years 1900–1961, this body has
stood almost alone as a continuing group that attempts to identify regional requirements and to articulate interests at that level. It is limited
in scope by the fact that its membership is drawn chiefly from the
owning and managing personnel of commercial and industrial organizations whose center of interests lies within the city of Los Angeles or
its immediate neighborhood. The chamber is not purposively structured to identify and articulate the interests of the business community
of the entire region. Consequently its influence is opposed in those
sections of the area where there is a strong conviction that the chamber and the city of Los Angeles have interrelated interests.

The chamber's usual interests have been focused upon such activities as securing public financial support for organizations that will
publicize the growth potentials of the area and urging local govern-

ments to develop public-works programs that will facilitate economic growth of the community. One interest has led the chamber to promote advertising campaigns that will publicize the attractions of the community in order to support the tourist industry and to induce persons and firms to relocate in southern California. The other interest has led to campaigns for flood control, waste disposal, airport construction, harbor development, and similar public works. Although the chamber is involved in promoting governmental action on a number of matters, it is by no means a general-purpose group, in the usual sense in which that term is used.

There are almost no general-interest groups seeking to influence the formulation or execution of policy at either the municipal level or the metropolitan area level. The grouping of aggregates of political interest is made according to a different pattern. The pattern is more nearly a grouping of interests according to functional concerns. Influence groups, composed of clusters of public and private representatives, tend to form around programs; for example, planning and zoning, harbors, air pollution control, flood control, indigent aid, and public health protection. Around each function there is a cluster of public officials and employees as well as groups of private parties that are interested in influencing the program and ensuring public support for the official programs.

PLURAL CENTERS OF INFLUENCE

Although there is some overlap in the membership of the influence groups concerned with several functions at the local and regional levels alike, there is no common aggregate. Because the membership of the influence groups surrounding functional organizations tends to vary, a pluralistic political system has developed in which competition exists among groups who covet the prizes to be bestowed through the allocation of political and economic resources. This pluralistic organization of the metropolitan community has been posited for other American metropolitan communities as well as for Los Angeles.[16]

In the Los Angeles metropolitan area there are numerous centers of power and influence contending for a share in the distribution of "goods" that go with political and economic power. The majority of these centers are oriented toward communities or local areas. A few are structured on a larger scale and seek to influence decisions relating to the area as a whole. Participants in these centers of areawide in-

[16] Wallace Sayre and Herbert Kaufman, *Governing New York City* (New York: Russell Sage Foundation, 1960); Martin, Munger, *et al., op. cit.;* Robert Dahl, *Who Governs?* (New Haven: Yale University Press, 1962).

fluence exercise their resources to support activities that will check their competitors and gain them advantage in the metropolitan scene.

SUMMARY

In a relatively short space of time, southern California, and especially the part of Los Angeles County located between the San Gabriel mountain range and the Pacific Ocean, has grown from a semiurban, semirural section to the second most populous metropolitan area in the United States. This growth has occurred during a period when technology and a high national standard of income have made transportation and communication available to an extraordinarily large percentage of urban dwellers. Mobility is a dominant element in human activity in the area. Change has also been an important conditioning influence.

Political traditions and legal institutions of the state of California, developed during this period when Los Angeles has undergone great growth, have set a pattern for local government and politics that is decentralized and fragmented. Political geography is divided among several local government jurisdictions. Similarly, political organization to mobilize persons and articulate interests has been decentralized and fragmented. Although some formal institutions of local government serve the metropolitan area, informal centers of power and influence are structured on a small scale. The scene is predominantly characterized by competition and strategic moves of countervailing forces.

TWO

Countervailing Forces
in the Metropolis

THE PATTERN of government in the Los Angeles metropolitan area is the product of a series of adjustments that have been negotiated over a period of sixty years. The negotiations that produced this pattern have been influenced by a variety of events that have taken place in the private and public sectors of the economy as well as in the political field. In both economic sectors there has been competition between varying sets of aspirants seeking to gain a preëminent role in each of certain key activities. Economic and political activities have interacted. No important set of contestants has confined itself exclusively to either the economic or the political sphere.

As one aspirant or set of aspirants has achieved a position of eminent advantage, coalitions of competitors have joined forces to check the "front-runner." These countervailing forces have adjusted the balance of power or influence among the contestants and produced a modus vivendi in which there was a wider sharing of the prizes of the contest. Competition has continued between the contestants in a variety of ways.

Since the latter part of the nineteenth century, the dominant cultural and political values in the life of the area have favored efforts by individuals and groups to seize advantage for themselves by controlling an activity or an institution that was crucial to the particular field of affairs with which the contestants were associated. Equally strong, however, has been the value judgment that no group should be per-

mitted to dominate an institution or activity for its own interest longer
than for a brief time, if at all. If the instrumentalities of the market
were not sufficient to produce a restraint upon the enterpriser that
threatened to prevail over the activity, a politically devised coun-
tervalent was developed instead. Technological inventiveness, as well
as acuity of advertising and persuasion, has been used in the effort to
cut down the leader and to produce one or more competitors.

The economic base of the Los Angeles metropolitan area has been
produced and shaped by a series of entrepreneurs in key resources
who have sought to manage economic goods and organizations to their
advantage. The particular pattern that the competition took depended
upon the unique resources of the region and the needs that demanded
fulfillment. A metropolitan area is comprised primarily of people,
which produces demands both for local government and for economic
organization to supply goods and services. Metropolitan areas are the
products of an industrial society, although cities have been common to
many societies in history. To attract and retain a large aggregation
of people at a particular location, certain resources must be available
and be organized for use. These include transportation, water, and
energy or motive power. Although other factors are also important for
the economic base of a metropolis, we will confine our analysis to the
efforts made by various sets of competitors to organize and control institutions supplying these resources. The efforts had important consequences for local governmental institutions in the Los Angeles area
and influenced much of the local political activity.

COUNTERVAILING FORCES IN
TRANSPORTATION SUPPLY

Rail transportation has been peculiarly important in the development
of Los Angeles. Between 1870 and 1915, when the Panama Canal was
opened, it determined economic development and strongly influenced
the growth of local government. Even though water, road, and air
transportation are important alternatives today, the railroads retain
their basic importance in the regional economy, as they do also in the
national field.

Soon after the first transcontinental railroad was completed, southern California land values rose in areas adjacent to the route and town
sites were surveyed in anticipation of an inflow of population.[1] The
new towns that sprang up on survey maps during that era formed the

---

[1] Richard Bigger and James D. Kitchen, *How the Cities Grew* (Los Angeles:
Bureau of Governmental Research, University of California, 1952), pp. 6–15.

base for the cities of later times. Placement of rail lines determined the basic pattern of urban location and development.

Economic opportunities made possible by one transcontinental railroad were not uniformly distributed; hence efforts were made to attract other rail enterprisers to enter southern California. Competition eventually became general.

The Transcontinental Railroads

The Southern Pacific, the first transcontinental railroad to enter southern California, followed a southerly route. In order to induce the company to construct its line into Los Angeles, the local voters agreed to transfer city and county interests in a local railroad, the Los Angeles and San Pedro Railway Company, and to issue bonds as an additional subsidy. The railroad reached the city in 1876, and by 1878 the transcontinental links were completed.

Shortly after entering the Los Angeles area, the Southern Pacific absorbed still another local line, the Los Angeles and Independence Railroad, which had been constructed in 1875 to connect both Los Angeles City and mining areas in Nevada with a pier at Santa Monica Bay. By acquiring the two lines, the Southern Pacific obtained all local transportation facilities and all existing outlets to ocean shipping adjacent to Los Angeles. It also built a branch line to Anaheim, where another small port was located. For approximately a decade, the company held a monopoly on transportation in the Los Angeles area. Economic potentialities of the region, however, offered an incentive to competitors.

The Santa Fe Railroad first entered the area over lines leased from the Southern Pacific. Almost immediately afterward, the two companies engaged in a passenger-rate war. This competition induced large numbers of persons to come to southern California and to invest in lands bordering the rail routes. By purchasing some small local lines and completing construction of its transcontinental route, the Santa Fe consolidated its system in southern California. In 1888 it sought an ocean outlet by constructing a line between Los Angeles and Redondo Beach. In the same year it extended a line southward from Los Angeles to San Diego. Shortly after completing the two extensions, the Santa Fe built other lines to connect several communities in southern California. One of these lines was the "Figure 8 loop" that connected points in Los Angeles, San Bernardino, Riverside, and Orange counties.[2] Most of these routes became important links in a transportation

---

[2] Some of these counties, notably Orange, were created by state political action detaching territory from the original body of Los Angeles County.

system supporting the southern California tourist industry as well as the movement of freight. Much of the area served by the system came to be the center of the southern California orange- and lemon-growing section. Marketing of the fruit crops depended upon having transcontinental shipping facilities available.

A third transcontinental rail system entered the area several years after the first two had established themselves. It was formed by two companies that commenced construction from opposite points. The San Pedro, Los Angeles, and Salt Lake Railroad, incorporated in 1901, began in San Pedro and built northeastward. The line paralleled the Santa Fe and Southern Pacific tracks at several points, and left the coastal plain via the Cajon Pass near San Bernardino. This company was headed by Senator W. A. Clark of Montana, who owned large land holdings in the Long Beach–San Pedro area. The Oregon Short Line, a subsidiary of the Union Pacific, began building southward from Salt Lake. By 1912, the lines joined, and for several years the two companies operated the route jointly. In 1921 the Union Pacific purchased the Clark interests, gaining direct access to the Pacific Coast and its ocean shipping for the first time.[3] Upon completion of this system, Los Angeles became the western terminus of three major rail systems.

Although competition between the railroads was the normal condition, coöperation to provide certain types of facilities proved to be equally in the public interest. The Interstate Commerce Commission approved a plan, in 1929, to unify all rail services at the Los Angeles Harbor. This arrangement made it possible for shippers to move freight to the waterfront terminals via any connecting railroad. In 1932 the state Railroad Commission approved a proposal for a Los Angeles union passenger terminal that had been advocated for many years by municipal leaders. The site selected fitted into the official civic-center plan and aided efforts to redevelop the core of the city.

The railroad corporations made additional impacts upon the pattern of industrial and business growth in the metropolitan area by developing their land holdings. Each railroad sought to encourage industrial firms to locate where they would be served by that road's transportation services. The Southern Pacific concentrated on areas between

---

[3] The Union Pacific met the Central Pacific, a subsidiary of the Southern Pacific, at Ogden, Utah, and trains from Chicago had had to proceed to San Francisco over Central Pacific lines. This arrangement had been the subject of much contention between the two major rail companies until a modus vivendi was worked out by the Interstate Commerce Commission.

Glendale and Los Angeles, along the Los Angeles River channel, and in the neighborhood of Alhambra. The Santa Fe owned large tracts in East Los Angeles that were adjacent to its lines. It organized the Los Angeles Union Stockyards Company and the Central Manufacturing

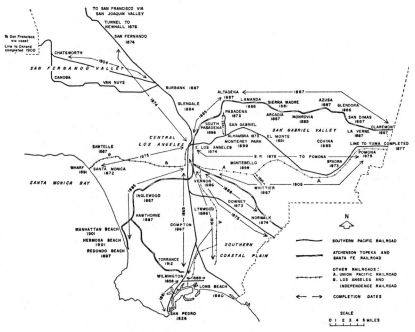

FIG. 2. Railroad development, Los Angeles County.

District to induce the businesses that would be users of its transportation facilities to locate at reciprocally advantageous sites. The Union Pacific also had interests in East Los Angeles and in areas near the Los Angeles Harbor. Subsidiaries of both the Santa Fe and the Union Pacific also controlled lands that became important oil-producers.

ELECTRIC RAILWAYS

Electric railways exercised an important influence upon the growth patterns of the Los Angeles metropolitan area between 1885 and the 1920's. Construction of interurban lines encouraged many who worked or had business in Los Angeles to live in the suburbs and commute to the central area. This development stimulated suburban subdividing activities and community promotion businesses.[4]

---

[4] Bigger and Kitchen, *op. cit.*, pp. 8–10.

Integration in the Industry. Street railways and interurban lines in a metropolitan area offer users a more effective service if formed into an areawide system. Hence, unification of small independent lines took place relatively early in the history of the industry. To prevent a unified system from exercising its economic power arbitrarily, checks were developed. Municipal regulation, unchecked by market competition, was tried. Competition of buses, both privately and municipally owned, grew in intensity. Eventually the street railway succumbed.

The history of street railways in Los Angeles was similar to that of other cities throughout the United States. In the beginning, several single-line street railway enterprises were organized. The Los Angeles Cable Railway Company was organized in 1887, and was soon joined by several other small companies. During the following ten-year period, these lines amalgamated to form the Los Angeles Railway Company, which promptly failed. At that juncture, Henry E. Huntington, nephew of one of the founders of the Central Pacific Railroad and a large stockholder in the Southern Pacific Railroad, became interested in the Los Angeles street railway situation. He reorganized the Los Angeles Railway Company in 1899 and became its sole owner.[5] The company's lines served Los Angeles, Inglewood, Eagle Rock, and Vernon. It made relatively little effort, however, to keep pace with the expansion of the city of Los Angeles during the great annexation period of 1913–1925. It made no attempt to expand into such areas as San Fernando Valley, Hollywood, and the western annexations. Hence, it became a localized passenger system. The company was further limited because its trackage was built on a gauge common to street railways that did not match the gauge used by the steam railroads. Therefore, it could not collect and distribute freight for the transcontinental railroads.

Interurban electric railways passed through organizational transitions that were remarkably parallel to those encountered by the street railways in the central area. Four interurban electric line enterprises were organized in southern California, beginning in 1876. The first connected Santa Monica with downtown Los Angeles. Another connected Wilmington and Long Beach. A third, the San Gabriel Valley Rapid Transit Electric Railway, ran between Los Angeles and Monrovia. The largest of the four connected Santa Monica, Sawtelle, Hollywood, and Los Angeles.

---

[5] California Railroad Commission, *Opinions and Orders* (1915), VI, 274–275 (hereafter cited as Railroad Commission). Sufficient stock in the Los Angeles Railway Company was owned by others to qualify them as officers of the company.

Consolidation of interurban lines began shortly after 1900 and was completed when the Pacific Electric Railway Company was formed in 1911.[6] Henry Huntington was a leader in the project, although the capital stock of the unified company was owned by the Southern Pacific Company.[7] The Pacific Electric system operated both passenger and freight services over an extensive network of standard-gauge tracks. Its interurban passenger service connected almost every incorporated city in Los Angeles County and reached the urbanized portions of Orange, San Bernardino, and Riverside counties that lay within the coastal area. It was a completely integrated system that focused upon downtown Los Angeles.

In several cities, including Los Angeles, Pasadena, and Long Beach, the Pacific Electric operated local streetcars. Although the Los Angeles Railway paralleled the Pacific Electric's tracks in some places, there was essentially no competition between the two systems. For the most part, they served different areas. Ultimately the two arranged to transfer passengers and offer wider travel opportunities.

The Pacific Electric influenced suburban development because it offered a unified system of travel that was regional in scope. By serving as a local distributor of freight and express traffic, it also enabled commerce and industry to develop in the suburban communities. The steam railroads confined their passenger activities to receiving and discharging passengers in transcontinental travel and did not attempt to provide suburban commuting services.

The Pacific Electric had an active interest in developing certain communities in southern California. Like the railroads, it had a variety of interests. In addition to its transportation services, it controlled three subsidiary land companies that held property in Glendale, Burbank, San Fernando Valley, Redondo Beach, and Newport Beach, among other communities.

Although the electric railway industry in the Los Angeles area never achieved complete vertical consolidation, several firms were linked through common ownership. For example, the Pacific Power and Light Company, in which Henry Huntington was a major stockholder, served both electric railway companies in which he was interested. Although

---

[6] The lines merged included the Los Angeles Interurban Railway Company, the Los Angeles and Redondo Railway Company, the Riverside and Arlington Railway Company, the San Bernardino Valley Traction Company, the Redlands Central Railway Company, the San Bernardino Interurban Railway Company, and the Los Angeles Pacific Company (Railroad Commission, *Opinions and Orders* [1912], I, 772).

[7] *Ibid.* (1913), II, 575.

it supplied numerous domestic and industrial power users, 78 per cent of its total business was with the electric railways.[8] The firm merged with the Southern California Edison Company in 1917.

Buses and Automobiles Challenge Electric Railways. Metropolitan growth posed serious dilemmas for the electric railways. Most of the new tract developments featured single-family dwellings on land parcels that were of a size that tended to disperse the population over the land rather than to concentrate it. Electric railways depended upon concentrations of population for passenger volume. Private automobiles, aided by the publicly provided street patterns, became effective competitors of the electric railways. Both electric railway systems sought to meet some of the challenge presented by new metropolitan growth that took place after 1925 by establishing bus lines to serve new areas and to provide feeder service to the rail lines. The Los Angeles Motor Coach Company, organized and owned jointly by the two railway corporations, served a considerable portion of the city.[9] Buses operated by the two companies—separately—served other sections. In 1930, the Railroad Commission approved the Pacific Electric's application to buy a controlling share in the Motor Transit Company, a bus company that served large parts of southern California.

Bus transportation proved attractive to new enterprisers who sought to enter the field. It possessed several advantages in comparison with electric railways. It did not depend upon a single supplier of motive power, nor did it require special rights of way or expensive trackage facilities. Privately owned bus companies used the public streets after obtaining a city franchise and a permit from the state Utilities Commission. Several bus companies were organized in the metropolitan area, and most of them served communities in which neither electric railway company had either car or bus lines. Several smaller companies served newly developed residential areas.

A few suburban municipalities organized city-owned bus systems to supply the transportation needs of suburban workers and shoppers which were not fulfilled by the established transit systems. These lines were designed chiefly to facilitate movement within the particular city and therefore tended to counteract the influence of the electric railway systems that focused upon the central shopping and industrial area of Los Angeles. It was equally true, however, that Santa Monica, Culver City, Torrance, Gardena, and Montebello routed some of their bus lines to connect with major streetcar railheads. The Santa Monica

---

[8] David H. Redinger, *The Story of Big Creek* (Los Angeles: Angelus Press, 1949), p. 35.

[9] Railroad Commission, *Opinions and Orders* (1940), XLII, 627 ff.

municipal bus system became a real competitor to both electric railway systems and to private bus companies. On two occasions it sought to extend its lines into the downtown portion of Los Angeles, but the Los Angeles city council refused permission.

A municipally owned bus system is able to set its own fare structure and to determine operating policies, subject only to the approval of its city council, when it operates within a single city. Unlike a privately owned company, it is not subject to state regulation. When a suburban city council is motivated to compete with the central city of Los Angeles to build up regional shopping centers and local industry, the municipal bus system is a convenient instrument, particularly in the absence of a metropolitan-wide transit system.

Both electric rail companies, with relatively fixed route patterns, found themselves seriously challenged by private automobiles and competing bus systems. The Los Angeles Railway sold its properties to the Metropolitan Coach Lines, a subsidiary of National City Lines, Inc., a Delaware holding company. The Pacific Electric Company moved to reduce its passenger service and become ancillary to the Southern Pacific Railroad, placing greater emphasis upon freight traffic. Its passenger lines that had no freight potential were dropped as rapidly as the state regulatory commission would permit, and its lines in Pasadena and Glendale were sold to local companies.

Metropolitan Transit Integration. Metropolitan growth overwhelmed the privately owned passenger transit industry. As rapidly as the state, cities, and counties succeeded in planning and constructing street and freeway systems to accommodate the vast numbers of private automobiles, the electric railways faded. Lack of high-speed public transportation caused streetcar and bus riders to turn to private automobiles. Therefore, the market incentives that normally spur private investment in transit systems became weaker and weaker.

In the face of this situation, a group of influential persons prevailed upon the state legislature to create a Metropolitan Transit Authority.[10] The proposal was based on the twin premises that an integrated public transportation system was essential to the economy of the metropolitan area and that it was necessary for public enterprise to supply an indispensable function when normal market incentives failed to lure private investment. It was deemed necessary to create a state agency in order to overcome the rivalries among the communities for control

---

[10] *Cal. Stats.* (1951), chap. 1668. The Authority was authorized to become an operating utility by *Cal. Stats.* (1957), chap. 547.

of transportation. The governing board of the Authority was appointed by the governor, after consultation with local leaders. Capital with which to purchase the Los Angeles Transit Lines, Metropolitan Coach Lines, and the passenger system of the Pacific Electric was provided by sale of bonds for which the revenues of the Authority were pledged in repayment. The new public agency took over the operating equipment and the employees of each company and set out to produce an integrated metropolitan system. Later, the Authority negotiated the purchase of some other small privately owned bus lines and integrated them also into the public system. The municipal systems remained independent, however.

On several occasions, locally oriented political groups have challenged the Metropolitan Transit Authority in its efforts to produce an integrated, regional transit system. In the first instance, leaders from Orange, San Bernardino, and Riverside counties insisted upon deleting sections of the enabling legislation that would have directed the MTA to plan and operate a multi-county system. They expressed fear that a transit authority would focus traffic patterns upon the central core of Los Angeles and that suburban regional centers would suffer some adverse consequences. Again, when the MTA sought legislation in 1961 that would have authorized its governing body to determine location of bus stops and to condemn property where needed for commuter parking, it met stiff opposition from municipalities. The autonomous nature of the Authority was vigorously criticized, and several proposals were introduced in the Legislature to make the MTA more directly responsible to popular influences.

COMPETITION TO CONTROL TRANSPORTATION TERMINALS

A harbor is a junction between land transportation and water transportation, and those who control the points at which transshipment takes place influence the trend of commerce. Airports are somewhat similar to harbors because they are the junctions between land and air transportation. When an airport is located in proximity to a harbor, both facilities become more significant links in the transportation system than is either acting alone.

Location of harbors depends to a considerable degree upon natural, geographic factors, although man has improved port sites to increase their usefulness. Choices of site location for airports are not limited so severely as are those for harbors. Weather conditions, such as absence of fog and presence of favorable winds, have been important. Availability of suitable large tracts of land is limited, in part, by the natural slope of the land and by the presence or absence of mountain ranges that may endanger aerial navigation. Other principal features that tend to determine the location of airports are the results of man's actions.

Ocean Harbors and Ports

The significance of harbor location for metropolitan development is indicated by the fact that most major urban centers of the world have developed around harbors. In the nineteenth century, the city of Los Angeles was in an unfavorable position due to the fact that it was at least twenty miles from a natural harbor or anchorage for ocean-going vessels. Furthermore, the natural harbor sites in the adjacent area were poor. Both Santa Monica and Redondo Beach were no more than open anchorages where ships could approach the shore safely and tie up to a pier. Depth of water at both sites, however, made dredging of approach channels unnecessary. The third site, San Pedro–Wilmington, offered more protection from storms, but the channel to the inner harbor was shallow and not overly wide.

Railroad enterprisers had realized the significance of harbors and had sought to stake claims to sites that would enhance their respective positions. The Southern Pacific had attempted to develop the Santa Monica location, and the Santa Fe had succeeded in putting its line through to tidewater at Redondo Beach. A local group, primarily the Banning family, had been active in promoting shipping at San Pedro–Wilmington for many years, but those interests had been merged with the Southern Pacific system.

Development of any really adequate harbor facilities depended upon construction of a breakwater to protect shipping from storms. It was generally accepted that it was the function of the federal government to build navigational aids, hence a decision by Congress would determine which site was to become the major harbor. Three engineering reports evaluated the features of each possible site; and the final one, made in 1896, found the San Pedro–Wilmington harbor possessed the best natural features. The Southern Pacific Railroad, under the leadership of Collis P. Huntington, who vigorously advocated the Santa Monica location, objected to the recommendation. Los Angeles business groups, allied with others in San Pedro, favored the San Pedro–Wilmington project. Senator Stephen White, a Los Angeles resident, established himself firmly in Los Angeles political history when he led the successful effort to obtain Congressional appropriations for a breakwater at San Pedro. Funds were voted later for channel dredging and harbor improvements.

Several groups seemed to gain advantage from the choice of San

Pedro–Wilmington as the harbor to be developed. The Southern Pacific Railroad and its subsidiaries controlled much of the waterfront. Others included companies belonging to the Banning family, and several lumber importing firms. The Los Angeles and Salt Lake railroad owned considerable waterfront property and controlled some wharves. The towns of San Pedro and Wilmington operated a portion of the waterfront under lease from private holders.

Completion of the breakwater in 1910 coincided with other events that gave further impetus to efforts to develop an adequate harbor. Chief among these was the building of the Panama Canal, which was to reduce voyage time between Pacific Coast ports and population centers on the Atlantic seaboard.

Municipal Administration Chosen. Los Angeles business and political leaders, anticipating the completion of the harbor project, worked to link that city with the new harbor. The Los Angeles Chamber of Commerce, which had actively supported Senator White in the Congressional controversy, provided much of the leadership. In 1906, the city of Los Angeles annexed a narrow "shoestring" of land to bring its boundaries adjacent to Wilmington and San Pedro. In 1908, the Chamber set up a committee on harbor development to head its program to obtain the annexation of the harbor area to Los Angeles. In that same year the Los Angeles City Council created a three-member city harbor commission, although the harbor lay within the boundaries of the incorporated towns of San Pedro and Wilmington!

California law did not provide specific procedures at that time to permit an incorporated city to consolidate with another. Therefore, the next step in the Los Angeles plan was to secure a change in the statutes. The Consolidation Act of 1909, sponsored by Los Angeles representatives and passed after an acrimonious legislative fight in which railroad company pressure allegedly figured in opposition, gave the city the authority it sought. A Consolidation Committee composed of representatives of the Los Angeles City Council, civic bodies in Los Angeles, and the county Board of Supervisors met in June, 1909, with leaders from San Pedro and Wilmington to discuss mutual interests in consolidation. City representatives talked of developing a major port that would serve an interior region that was estimated to include Arizona and Utah. In order to assure a degree of local autonomy for the two towns that were being asked to consolidate with Los Angeles, the committee proposed to create a borough plan of local government within the consolidated city. Out of these discussions emerged a consolidation proposal, and in August, 1909, the voters of San Pedro and

Wilmington voted to join Los Angeles. At last, Los Angeles had reached the waterfront!

The next crucial question was: Which set of contestants should control access to the water's edge, where ship transportation met land transportation? In 1908, a state legislative committee had investigated each of the state's major harbor sites relative to developing state control of harbor facilities.[11] The San Pedro and Los Angeles legislators had vigorously opposed state investment or control at San Pedro, and had advocated municipal operation.

The prospect for municipal control of the harbor did not appear particularly bright in 1909. The terminal facilities, which consisted of eighteen thousand feet of waterfrontage improved with wharves and connected with the two railway systems, were under control of private companies. About fifteen thousand feet of municipally-owned waterfrontage in the outer harbor was suitable to serve seagoing shipping needs. In the inner harbor, at Wilmington, there was about twenty-three thousand feet of municipally owned frontage, but its access channels required more dredging.

Municipal leaders, headed by the Los Angeles Harbor Commission, attacked the validity of the land patent under which the companies claimed control of waterfront lands. They alleged that the 1879 state constitution had prohibited making grants to any private party of tidelands within two miles of an incorporated town or city. Private land claimants contended that the properties had been used constructively for many years and argued that inasmuch as the state had not contested their claims previously, it had lost its rights to do so. The state Attorney General was persuaded to sue in order to test the validity of the claims, and in an opinion given in Superior Court in Los Angeles on January 3, 1911, Judge Bordwell ruled that the tidelands should revert to the state, to be held in trust for all its citizens.[12]

Immediately following the court decision a series of events occurred that resulted in placing the waterfront under municipal control, although the private claimants appealed to higher courts. On March 9, 1911, at a special municipal election, the voters of Los Angeles City approved a charter amendment that created a Harbor Department and defined its powers and duties. The Legislature convened in its regular session, and on March 19, Senator Leslie Hewitt, former City Attorney

---

[11] California Legislature, Joint Committee on Harbors, *Report and Recommendations* (Sacramento, 1908), pp. 13–15.

[12] The opinion was based both upon the wording of the act of Congress which admitted California into the Union and that of the California Constitution of 1879. *The People of the State of California* v. *Southern Pacific Railroad Company et al.* (No. 64,535 Superior Court of Los Angeles County, January 3, 1911).

of Los Angeles, introduced a bill to transfer the tidelands at San
Pedro–Wilmington to the city of Los Angeles. Timing of this move was
particularly favorable to the city because the Progressive group that
had just won control of the Legislature had based their campaign on
a platform of anti-railroad slogans. Opposition to the Los Angeles bill
was led by the San Francisco legislative delegation, who expressed the
view that the proposal would produce unfavorable results for the state-
administered Port of San Francisco. Ultimately, however, a complicated set of vote trades permitted the Los Angeles bill to pass. The
Los Angeles delegation traded support of a San Francisco state harbor
bond measure and modification of Los Angeles' claim for reapportion-
ment of legislative districts for support of the Los Angeles tidelands
bill. Additional support was also gained when legislators from Long
Beach, San Diego, and Oakland introduced bills to transfer tidelands
to the municipal governments in those communities.

The principal issue in the legislative discussion proved to be the
choice between state and municipal development and control of
the harbors. Legislators from some inland counties contended that the
state's harbors should be developed by the state government in the
interest of farming enterprises as well as those interests that were
represented by city governments. Some opponents argued that if the
state could lease the tidelands, as the court had held, the state should
lease the lands to municipalities and derive a monetary return from
the use of its resources. The cities' representatives pointed out that the
state had spent little for development of harbors. They suggested that
if the state would grant the authority to municipalities to develop and
operate ports, the local governments would raise the required capital
and would manage the facilities in a manner satisfactory to the various
interests involved. Ultimately, four separate statutes were approved
granting tidelands within the cities of Los Angeles, Long Beach, San
Diego, and Oakland to the municipalities in perpetual trust for the
purpose of developing harbors. The harbors were to remain free for
general use for navigation and commerce. Each municipality was prohibited from granting away or selling any tidelands, but it was authorized to grant leases and franchises for their use and for the use of any
wharves, buildings or improvements that it might construct upon
them. Each city was to be free to set fees and rentals. In essence, the
state delegated its interest to the four municipalities and authorized
them to become enterprisers in harbor management without subjecting
their performance to state administrative review.

Several years elapsed before Los Angeles was able to clear title to
the tidelands. Ultimately the courts sustained the Bordwell decision

and the subsequent legislation, although some claims had to be compromised.

The city has vested responsibility for harbor development in the Harbor Department, an administrative unit created by the city charter. Most of the decision-making responsibility has been assigned by the charter to a five-member Harbor Commission appointed by the mayor. Municipal bonds, which have been approved by the voters and which constitute obligations against the general tax revenues of the city, have financed construction of wharves, piers, sheds, and other harbor facilities. Earnings of the Harbor Department are devoted to repaying bond debts and meeting the operating expenses. The charter gives the commission authority to allocate and spend its income from harbor revenues for objects specified in the charter. Commission actions are subject to council review only if revenues prove inadequate for harbor needs. Since 1926, the Harbor Department has been a self-financing enterprise, although the costs of police and fire protection and other municipal services in the harbor area are supported by the general city budget in the same manner as are similar services in other parts of the city. The Harbor Department does not operate wharves and warehouses but leases city-owned structures for use by private enterprises. It also leases land and grants franchises to private businesses to construct and operate facilities on the waterfront.

Business and farming groups situated in a wide area surrounding the city have been as much interested in the harbor operation as commercial and industrial firms within Los Angeles. The area served by the port extends throughout most of southern California and parts of Arizona, Nevada, and Utah. The metropolitan city, however, is responsible for developing facilities, determining rates, and governing access to the waterfront.

Discovery of oil in the harbor area has altered the uses made of the port and therefore has caused the facilities to change. Three major petroleum fields, Signal Hill, Wilmington, and Dominguez, are located in close proximity to the inner harbor. Crude petroleum has overshadowed agricultural products and manufactured items, in gross tonnage and value of commerce handled at the port, for several years. As a consequence of this shift in activity, local interests have tended to outweigh regional ones, although shippers in the hinterlands continue to have a stake in the harbor.

Municipal Rivalry. During the initial stages of public-port development, Long Beach set out to rival Los Angeles in providing harbor service. Although its first attempt to annex a portion of Terminal

Island, a long, sandy land-tongue that extended into the harbor area, proved to be legally faulty, it succeeded before Los Angeles consolidated San Pedro and Wilmington. Long Beach voters approved a $245,000 bond issue that enabled their city to purchase waterfront lands, to construct a pier, a wharf, and some sheds. The Long Beach harbor, located on Terminal Island, was not particularly well situated. It was separated physically from the main portion of the city by the Los Angeles River channel, and it was less protected from adverse weather than was San Pedro–Wilmington.

Discovery of oil in 1936 had a most important impact upon the Long Beach harbor development. The city has carried on an intensive drilling program on city-owned lands in the harbor district, chiefly on tidelands that have been reclaimed or filled. Revenues derived from the sale of oil have been devoted to harbor improvements, including the filling of additional tidelands and the construction of piers, wharves, and storage sheds. In the 1950's the city of Long Beach began a large-scale reconstruction of its port facilities to produce a major port.

Harbor administration is vested in a commission composed of five members nominated by the City Manager and appointed by the City Council. This body has jurisdiction over the Harbor District, an area that is defined in the charter. Within that district, the commission has sole responsibility for managing municipally owned lands and facilities. It is responsible for constructing and maintaining harbor facilities and for leasing them to private concerns for specific periods of time. It is in charge of oil drilling on city property within the district and manages the revenues derived from this source for harbor purposes.

The Long Beach harbor development has been aided by federal construction of breakwaters since the Navy decided to establish its major shore facilities at Long Beach. During the 1920's, large units of the Pacific Fleet were stationed at San Pedro as well as Long Beach. A change in strategic plans in 1935 caused the fleet to shift to the Hawaiian Islands, but upon the outbreak of World War II Long Beach again became a center of naval activity. The San Pedro breakwater, extended towards Long Beach, made it possible for even the largest naval ships to operate from a fleet anchorage. A naval shipyard and a naval station, constructed on Long Beach harbor lands, have continued to be two of the principal defense installations on the Pacific Coast.

Suggestions have been made from time to time, largely by interests favorable to Los Angeles, that the two harbor authorities be combined. Similar proposals have been made when labor-management disputes

have interrupted cargo handling. Political rivalry has continued between the two cities, however. Each has a considerable investment in
physical facilities. The oil revenue received by Long Beach makes that
city particularly strong and enables it to provide very modern types of
port facilities. It has maintained an aggressive policy in expanding its
port facilities, in spite of a serious problem of subsidence that results
from pumping oil from beneath harbor lands. Los Angeles harbor,
however, continues to handle the larger portion of the goods moved in
the total harbor area.

AIRPORTS

Owing to conditions that are peculiar to airport management and to
aviation, municipal ownership of airports has tended to gain ascend-
ancy over private ownership, and the number of private airports has
declined. Prior to 1929, there were approximately thirty airports under
private operation in the Los Angeles area. Air-transport terminals, as
well as fields serving instructional and private flying, were privately
owned during that period. Since 1930, private fields have gradually
disappeared, leaving the function to municipal enterprise. Hughes and
Lockheed aircraft manufacturing companies each maintains a field
adjacent to its plants and the latter's field is also used for commercial
flights. Municipal fields are maintained by Los Angeles, Long Beach,
Santa Monica, Torrance, and Hawthorne; the Los Angeles International Airport is the major terminal for the metropolitan area.

Reasons for the near-disappearance of privately owned airfields are
numerous, but the major one is the rise in land values. As the demand
for land for residential and commercial development has increased,
smaller flying fields have become too valuable to use for either pleas-
ure or commercial aircraft. Pressure from residents annoyed by aircraft
noises caused some city councils to close small private fields. Public
agencies, supported politically by strong groups that have an economic
interest in the air-travel and aircraft manufacturing industries, seem
to be the only instruments capable of retaining the large amounts of
land needed for a modern airport in the midst of metropolitan developments.

The federal government has also fostered municipal ownership of
airports. Congress has generally favored municipal ownership in its
legislation providing federal funds for airport development and flight
control systems to ensure safety of operations. Federal administrative
agencies have implemented these policies, assisting public authorities
to develop landing facilities and installing navigational-control equipment at airports that have been selected as major terminals.

Municipal Administration Prevails. Although several local governments have sought to provide airport facilities for the Los Angeles metropolitan area, the city of Los Angeles has been in the preëminent position, especially since 1947. The Long Beach and Santa Monica municipal airports have existed almost as long as Los Angeles International, but neither has been able to challenge the latter's position. For a number of years, the county government made tentative efforts to play a major role by acquiring and maintaining airports, in accordance with its regional plan. It has turned its attention more recently to other matters. Hawthorne and Torrance municipal airports are chiefly for local services and are not regional facilities.

Los Angeles entered the airport activity in 1928 when it leased a portion of a private field operated by William Mines located in the vicinity of El Segundo and Hyperion. It had already annexed the area around that airport in 1920. The city council created a Department of Airports by ordinance and retained supervision of the program, passing upon all financial matters and leases. In 1934 and 1935, the federal Works Progress Administration assisted the city to improve and extend the runway. Additional federal funds were made available to complete improvements, on the condition that the city secure title to the land. In 1936, the city acquired 640 acres and became sole owner of Mines' field. In 1940, the mayor and council agreed to form a Board of Airport Commissioners to supervise administration and maintain liaison with groups interested in the program. When the city voters approved a $3,500,000 bond issue to finance construction of an airport terminal, Los Angeles was prepared to bid for the privilege of operating the main regional airport. The commercial airlines were preparing to shift from a privately owned terminal in Glendale when the war intervened. It was not until December, 1946, that the municipal terminal became the major airlines' facility for the Los Angeles metropolitan area.

The airport's administrative organization was strengthened when a charter amendment, adopted in 1947, gave the department a semi-independent status that was similar to that already enjoyed by the Harbor and Water and Power departments. The amendment vested responsibility for airport matters in a five-member commission, appointed by the mayor. The commission was authorized to appoint staff, construct terminals and landing fields, and lease sites for hangars, offices, and manufacturing plants on the municipally owned lands. City construction was to be financed by bonds, subject to approval by city voters, and the city general-tax revenues were pledged as guarantee of repayment. Funds derived from leases and other transactions were to be devoted to airport purposes.

With the development of jet propelled aircraft, the Los Angeles municipal airport became the only field in the area large enough to accommodate landing and take-off. Presently it enjoys a virtual monopoly of transcontinental and international air travel in the southern California region. It continues also to be a center around which firms manufacturing aircraft and related equipment, as well as businesses dealing with passenger and air-freight travel, tend to locate.

Competitors for Metropolitan Service. As air travel increased in volume and economic importance, tensions began to develop between Los Angeles and others interested in regional development. The location of the airport is a handicap to communities in San Fernando Valley, the east side of Los Angeles, and Orange County. The street and highway pattern does not provide the outlying areas rapid and convenient access to the airport, and even the central district of Los Angeles has relatively poor access. Other communities have witnessed the remarkable growth of the Westchester area surrounding the municipal airport and have desired to achieve similar growth. Manufacturing and service businesses in the vicinity of the airport provide employment opportunities for large numbers of people and contribute substantially to the financial strength of Los Angeles City and the area adjacent to the airport.

Potential competitors have been handicapped by two factors, however. One was lack of land for sites suitably adjacent to existing population centers, and the other was availability of capital in sufficient amount to finance the huge cost of a modern major airport.

Los Angeles County tentatively entered the competition when it acquired a surplus military airfield at Lancaster, in the northern portion of the county. Land for expansion was available, although announcement of the county's decision, plus the decision of Lockheed Aircraft Company to lease portions of the county field for an assembly plant and testing facilities, touched off a realty boom in the area that absorbed some of the land adjacent to the field. Lack of agreement on regional airport needs, plus the fact that Lancaster was excessively distant from existing population centers, caused the county to go slow on development plans.

Because only a few airports can be developed in a region to accommodate transcontinental and international travel, the ones that do survive become focal points for a large service area. The area served by the Los Angeles municipal airport includes Los Angeles, Ventura, Orange, San Bernardino, and Riverside counties. The city of Ontario, located near the border between Los Angeles and San Bernardino counties, has developed an alternate to the Los Angeles airport. This facility has been constructed on the site of a former military air base. Several manufacturing establishments have located plants at this field. Transcontinental and international traffic uses the facility to some extent, although the chief occasions have been when the Los Angeles field was closed by weather conditions.

In 1960, the Los Angeles Chamber of Commerce initiated a study of future airport needs in southern California. A coördinating committee composed of representatives of county boards of supervisors and chambers of commerce in Los Angeles, Orange, Ventura, San Bernardino, and Riverside counties sponsored preliminary studies. In addition to considering airport requirements and criteria for site selection, the committee also investigated means for financing additional ports of various types and administering a program. It was generally agreed that the function of supplying these facilities had become regional in scope. No one city or county could meet the entire need. Whether unified control of an airport system comprising several facilities would be politically acceptable remained an unresolved question. Among the interests that will have to be reconciled in order to have a regional airport system are those represented by cities and counties, the federal Civil Aeronautics Board, and numerous airlines companies and businesses having direct financial involvement in air transportation. The future of this matter remains unclear.

COUNTERVAILING FORCES IN ENERGY RESOURCE SUPPLY

Development of a modern metropolis depends upon availability of natural resources for the supply of energy. The industrial revolution that produced the modern urban complexes came about when inventions made possible the harnessing of energy resources for the large-scale production of goods. In the Los Angeles area, a series of competitors has appeared on the scene to organize energy-distributing systems. Attempts to monopolize any one source of energy have been met by countervailing efforts. In some instances, a rival organization has developed; in others, competitors seek to develop a substitute source of energy. Municipal governments have often entered the economic field to counter a potential monopoly by private corporate enterprises.

Energy resources that have been controlled and put to industrial use thus far include coal, water power, electricity, petroleum, and natural gas. Historically, the principal industrial developments in the United States were located where one or more of these resources were readily available. Until recently, each source of energy was limited in some manner in its adaptability to being packaged and shipped from one location to another. Such shipment increases the cost of the delivered energy and therefore the cost of manufacturing, so industrial development tended to take place where the sources of energy were nearby. All mining and some industrial activities, such as metal production and plating, are intensive users of energy resources and place great demands upon the total resource supply. Such activities tend to locate where they can obtain most economically the large amount of energy supplies they need. Development of methods and means for transporting economically various types of energy-producing commodities has had much to do with the wider site-location of industrial plants. The kind of energy available at relatively low cost in a particular area tends to determine the type of economic development that will take place there. An area that is deficient in coal but possesses petroleum, for example, will develop economic activities that can successfully use petroleum for their energy base. The ability to substitute an energy resource that possesses a price advantage for others that are in deficit supply or are more expensive will also influence the economic development of a region.

A Deficit Area Seeks Resources

When the Los Angeles area began to expand in population shortly after 1900, it lacked sufficient energy-resources to support an industrial development that would, in turn, sustain further population growth. Compared to many older centers of population and industry in the United States, it was a deficit area. Coal was completely lacking within the area; known deposits of commercial value were situated so far distant that transportation costs made any activity dependent upon coal a highcost operation. Nevertheless, coal and coke were imported and used for enterprises for which no adequate substitute was available at the time. Water power was lacking also as a direct source of energy. Streams were neither large nor constant in flow. Although some hydroelectric energy had been generated at plants on the Santa Ana and San Gabriel rivers and on Mill Creek, deficient storage capacity caused the plants to depend upon seasonal rainfall. Petroleum was known to exist in the area, and the developed sources were beginning to show some promise. The Los Angeles–Salt Lake field was one of the state's leading producers at the time, with a production of two million barrels per year.[13] Natural gas was in moderate supply.

[13] Edwin Higgins, *California's Oil Industry* (Los Angeles: Chamber of Mines and Oil, 1928), p. 13. In 1941 Dr. John Parke Young, an outstanding economics

Electric energy offered a reasonably attractive source for lighting and industrial power. Sufficient petroleum was available locally to serve as a primary source of energy for generating plants. Although water power for generators was limited in the local area, it was adequate to supplement other sources. Influx of population and development of cities in southern California produced a rising demand for electric energy for urban street lighting, household uses, and for increasingly varied commercial and industrial developments. Organization of electric railway systems for local and interurban travel also spurred the demand for electric energy. To supply these urban demands, numerous local companies were organized to produce electric power by steam generating plants that were supplied by petroleum, and also to produce commercial gas from coal and coke supplies that were brought in by rail transportation. These enterprises were capable of meeting the demands of lighting and transportation, but they were unable to supply a substantial amount of manufacturing. In 1904, the Los Angeles Gas and Electric Company was organized by San Francisco investors. Similar enterprises were formed in the suburban communities by local enterprisers. The Southern California Edison Company, a concern that was interested originally both in electric power and in other forms of energy, was incorporated in 1909. The Pacific Light and Power Company was interested exclusively in electrical energy, which it supplied by means of steam plants.

Consolidation of companies began in 1909, the Southern California Edison Company acquiring the Edison Electric Company which, in its turn, had produced a consolidation of several local companies.[14] This particular action integrated a major portion of the electric industry in the suburbs outside the city of Los Angeles. Almost concurrently with the Edison consolidation, additional smaller mergers took place in other suburban areas located to the east and south of Los Angeles. The Southern California Gas Company, organized in 1910, acquired the Domestic Gas Company of Los Angeles, and the San Bernardino

---

scholar, wrote: "Production of oil in Los Angeles County goes back over sixty years, but only during the past twenty years has it been such a major factor in the city's economic life" (Los Angeles: Preface to a Master Plan, ed. L. Deming Tilton and George W. Robbins [Los Angeles: Pacific Southwest Academy, 1941], pp. 66–67).

[14] Included in the Edison merger were Pasadena Electric Light and Power Company, Santa Ana Gas and Electric Company, Redlands Electric Light and Power Company, United Electric Gas and Power Company, Mountain Power Company, California Power Company, Southern California Power Company, Pomona and Ontario Light and Fuel Company, Whittier Light and Fuel Company, Riverside Light and Fuel Company, Colton Gas Company, and People's Gas Company of Monrovia.

Gas and Electric Company. The Southern Counties Gas Company, organized in 1911, also began to acquire other companies, chiefly in the San Gabriel Valley of Los Angeles County and in Orange County.

Municipal ownership of electric utilities began to appear on the scene at the same time that privately owned firms sought to integrate and to divide customer territory. On May 3, 1906, the city of Pasadena voted the first of a series of bond issues to finance construction of a generating plant that was supplied by fuel oil.[15] The city system competed with the Southern California Edison Company. In 1909 the city offered to buy energy from the company for a period of years if the latter would relinquish its distribution system within the municipality. The company made a counteroffer to purchase the city system, but both plans came to naught. The city ultimately succeeded in replacing the company.

The city of Glendale established a municipal electrical generating plant in 1909 and voted bonds to finance the purchase of the Glendale Light and Power Company's distributing system. The city of Burbank, adjacent to Glendale on the west, set up a municipal electric system in 1913, purchasing the properties of the Burbank Light and Power Company.[16] Each municipal system was organized chiefly to supply street lighting. However, controversies over rates charged by local privately owned companies led to municipal ownership of plants supplying homes and industries.

HYDROELECTRIC ENERGY SUPPLY

California's mountains, with their numerous streams and lakes in the higher reaches, presented the state with a potential source of hydro-electric power. The area adjacent to Los Angeles, however, was deficient in water-power generating sites. Early hydro developments located near Ontario and Redlands aided primarily irrigation and agricultural developments, although some of the energy developed was devoted to urban uses. Lack of sites capable of developing large quantities of electric power effectively limited the significance of hydroelectric energy until economically advantageous means for transporting power from other sections of the state were perfected.

A *Municipally Administered System.* The city of Los Angeles developed a municipally owned electric system as a by-product of its municipal water project in the Owens Valley. So long as the munici-

---

[15] C. Wellington Koiner, *History of Pasadena's Municipal Light and Power Plant* (Pasadena: City of Pasadena, 1925).

[16] Railroad Commission, *Opinions and Orders* (1913), III, 389.

pality had derived its water supply from the Los Angeles River, there was no possibility of establishing a municipal electricity enterprise, because the water was obtained by pumping from underground pools rather than from running streams. When it acquired water rights in the Owens Valley section of Inyo County and built an aqueduct to bring the water to the city, it also obtained water-power sites. The aqueduct had a sufficient drop in elevation at certain places to permit hydroelectric generating plants to be built as ancillary projects of the water system. At other locations, pumping was required to lift the water over high points. Early in the life of the water project, municipal authorities decided to build, acquire, and operate an electricity distributing system in the city, in competition with the privately owned utilities. A municipal organization, titled the Bureau of Los Angeles Aqueduct Power, was created in 1909 to build the generating plants. The project was approved by the city voters in 1910, when they authorized a $3,500,000 bond issue to finance it. A charter amendment approved in 1911 created the Department of Public Service and the Public Service Commission. Within this organization, the Bureau of Power and Light became the entity to administer the electricity system.

Municipal distribution of hydroelectric power began in Los Angeles in 1916. Between that date and 1927, many large areas were annexed and several small cities consolidated with Los Angeles. Not all additions of city territory expanded the municipal electric system's service area, however. Nevertheless, market competition between the municipal system and the private utilities, the Los Angeles Gas and Electric and the Southern California Edison Company, existed chiefly in the older portions of the city.

An Integrated Private System. The privately owned electricity companies began building hydroelectric plants in 1911 to supplement their supply from steam-powered generating plants. The Pacific Light and Power Corporation selected the Big Creek–San Joaquin section of the high Sierras in central California for its principal water-power project. Shortly thereafter, the Mt. Whitney Power and Electric Company built in the mountains near Visalia. The Los Angeles municipal system had obtained most of the sites on the eastern slope of the mountains; therefore the private companies turned to the western slopes. The initial work in the Big Creek area consisted of three dams that formed the Huntington Lake reservoir, two power houses, and a 248-mile high-tower transmission line to Los Angeles.[17] In June, 1917, the Southern

---

[17] David H. Redinger, *The Story of Big Creek* (Los Angeles: Angelus Press, 1949).

California Edison Company acquired the properties of both companies, including the Big Creek project.[18] Completion of the two

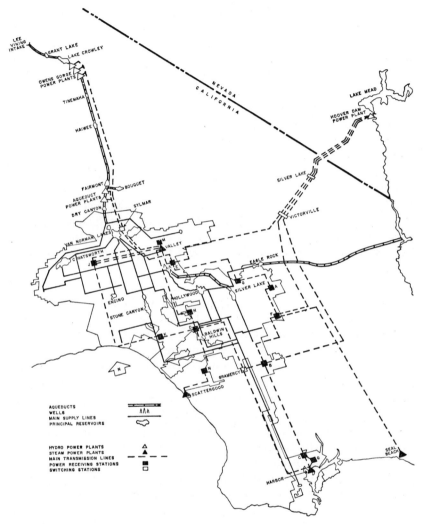

FIG. 3. Los Angeles city water and electric system.

mergers made the Southern California Edison Company the major private corporate supplier of electricity in southern California and in the lower San Joaquin Valley.

[18] Railroad Commission, *Opinions and Orders*, XIII, 263; Railroad Commission, *Report of the Railroad Commission of California, 1916–1917*, I, 95–97.

Municipal-Private System Rivalry. Competition between the Los
Angeles municipal system and the private companies took many forms
and occurred in a variety of places. The private utilities were subject
to regulation by the State Railroad Commission[19] in regard to rates,
conditions of service, territory served, and corporate financing. The
city could appear before the Railroad Commission as an interested
party when that body considered matters pertaining to the private
utilities within the city. It could complain to the commission regarding
utility operations and cause investigations to be made. Furthermore,
it could issue or withhold franchises for the utility companies to place
their poles, lines, and other distribution equipment in city streets or
on other municipal property. The city's franchise jurisdiction was assured by the state constitution.

A different set of conditions controlled the municipal utility enterprises. The state constitution sanctioned municipal ownership of electric power systems and exempted them from supervision by the state
Railroad Commission. Local political processes were given full reign
over all municipal enterprises. In these circumstances, the privately
owned utilities were not backward about taking an active role in local
politics.

The municipal electric system was organized within the municipal
bureaucracy as a unit of the Department of Water and Power. A
Public Service Commission, composed of five persons appointed by the
mayor for fixed terms, determined policies for the power system.[20]
Rates, level of service, and general management policies were established by the commission, although rate increases required City Council approval. Municipal voters had a hand in deciding policy for the
municipal electric system when they were given the opportunity to
approve or disapprove bond issues for the expansion of the system.
Basic legal constraints upon the municipal electric system were set
forth in the city charter, and amendments to the charter could only be
made with the approval of the municipal electorate.

The municipal power system was deeply involved in the local political processes from the start. Groups associated with or friendly to the
private system opposed the establishment of the municipal distributing
system. This opposition continued for a number of years and used
several means of attack. The power bureau's legal authority was questioned in the courts. Charter amendments extending or clarifying the
bureau's powers and responsibilities were vigorously opposed in the
press and in election campaigns. Similarly, municipal ownership and

---

[19] Later renamed the Public Utilities Commission.
[20] The commission was later known as the Water and Power Commission.

power-bureau operations were made issues in most mayoral and councilmanic elections during the 1920's and 1930's. In defense of its position, the municipal system developed a comprehensive and vigorous campaign organization.

The first major step to resolve the competition between the municipal and the private systems was made in 1922, when the Edison Company sold its distributing system within the city to the Water and Power Department. This fulfilled an agreement reached in December, 1916. The delay had been due, in part, to a dispute over the valuation of the properties. For a considerable period previous to this, the power bureau's generating plants had had the capacity to produce more than could be sold by means of its own lines, and the Edison Company had purchased the surplus power, distributing it at rates determined by the city.

Municipal ownership of facilities for producing and distributing electrical energy was firmly established in southern California by 1920. Los Angeles, Pasadena, Glendale, and Burbank had approved this form of municipal activity. Pasadena completed negotiations to purchase the Edison Company's distributing system within its borders in 1920; Los Angeles acquired the company's lines in 1922.

For a time it appeared that the state might enter the power production field. A group of public power advocates presented an initiative statute to the state voters in 1922 that would have placed the state in the generating hydroelectric power business. This proposal was defeated in one of the most energetically fought campaigns of the decade. The privately owned utility companies conducted an expensive and successful campaign to defeat the measure.

The federal government proved to be a major force in the determination of electric-power policies, and it consistently assisted the municipal enterprises. Inasmuch as many of the streams arose on federal lands and generating plant sites were often to be found in national forest areas, Congress and federal administrative agencies were involved in the basic decisions. The federal government aided the city of Los Angeles to develop a municipally controlled water and electricity program on the eastern slope of the Sierra Nevada mountains. The private power companies were granted permits to construct plants on the western slopes. The government's decision to construct a high dam at Boulder Canyon on the Colorado River proved to be a major event in policy-making relating to the supply of electric energy and water to southern California. Initially the Boulder Canyon project was a reclamation undertaking to assist agriculture. States in the Colorado River basin joined with the federal government in an interstate compact to apportion water within the multi-state river basin. The federal government undertook to build the dam and other works. The Metropolitan Water District of Southern California, organized under California law to build and operate an aqueduct and a wholesale water distributing system to supply the area around Los Angeles, was allocated a portion of the water. The government also agreed to develop hydroelectric power at the dam, and it decided to make the power available to both publicly and privately owned distributing systems, mostly in the Los Angeles area. Federally owned generating plants were leased to the Los Angeles Department of Water and Power and the Southern California Edison Company.

Arrangements for transporting Colorado River power from the generating site to the consuming area fostered coöperation between the four municipal systems that had been established in the Los Angeles metropolitan area. The city of Los Angeles became the prime enterpriser to construct and operate high-tension transit lines between the river site and the metropolis. The Glendale, Burbank, and Pasadena systems agreed to purchase specific quantities of power. Inasmuch as the three suburban systems depended primarily upon steam plants, the Colorado River power gave them a supplemental energy source that they greatly needed to meet increased demands resulting from urban growth. Los Angeles received the first power from the Boulder Canyon project on October 9, 1936. At an election held two months later, the city's voters approved a charter amendment authorizing the Bureau of Power and Light to issue revenue bonds in the amount of $46,340,000 and to purchase the electric system of the Los Angeles Gas and Electric Corporation, the one remaining privately owned system. This purchase was completed on January 29, 1937.

Further adjustments between suppliers of energy to the metropolitan market determined the corporate pattern that prevailed for a long period thereafter. One adjustment resulted from decisions that produced further specialization in the energy-supply industry. The Los Angeles Gas and Electric Company merged its remaining properties with the Southern California Gas Company, which shared the Los Angeles metropolitan area gas industry with the Southern Counties Gas Company. Both firms had been acquired previously by the Pacific Lighting Company, a holding company with headquarters in San Francisco. Electric systems that had been acquired by the two gas companies were sold to the Southern California Edison Company; and, thereafter, the gas and electricity industries virtually drew apart and formed separate competing enterprises.

The second adjustment involved the division of territory between the Edison Company and the Los Angeles Water and Power Department. With the completion of negotiations, in 1939, by which the city purchased the private companies within its borders, the Water and Power Department became the large central city's sole supplier of electricity. The Edison Company supplied the unincorporated areas within Los Angeles County and all other municipalities except Pasadena, Glendale, and Burbank.[21] The extensive growth of population and industry that has taken place in the suburban areas since the conclusion of World War II has given the Edison Company a substantial domain, equalling or exceeding that won by the municipal systems.

In view of the fact that the two major systems, Los Angeles municipal and Edison, had negotiated a division of territory, rivalry between them ended, in a sense, and a degree of equilibrium was achieved. In another sense, however, the two systems merely took new postures. Any extended effort on the part of the city to annex new areas, or to consolidate with other municipalities to achieve metropolitan governmental integration, would disturb the modus vivendi established in 1939. To extend the municipal boundaries, except to annex uninhabited territory, would be to invade the company's service territory and reopen the rivalries of previous years.

PETROLEUM AND GAS RIVAL HYDROELECTRIC ENERGY

Both electric systems found the gas industry to be their principal competitor. Territories granted to the two gas companies by the state Utilities Commission overlapped those served by the city and the Edison Company. Although the privately owned utilities' rates and service-levels were regulated by the state, competition between the industries consisted of seeking to win customers by emphasizing the advantages of one energy source as compared with those of the other. Price differences figured to some extent, but competition depended chiefly upon such matters as the ability of each to meet seasonal peak-load demands.

Natural gas had been available in limited quantity in the Los Angeles area from local petroleum fields since the early part of the century. It had also been imported from the Midway field in southern San Joaquin Valley since 1913.[22] The gas industry became an important supplier in southern California only after petroleum was discov-

---

[21] The city of Azusa maintained a municipal distributing system which purchased electricity from the Edison Company. The city of Vernon leased its generating plant to the Edison Company.

[22] Railroad Commission, *Opinions and Orders* (1913), II, 940–941.

ered at Huntington Beach in 1920 and at Signal Hill in 1921. The
Signal Hill and other discoveries, located chiefly in the southern and
southwestern sections of Los Angeles County, opened a complete new
chapter in the area's energy-resource story. The combined petroleum
and gas discoveries made possible greater industrial development
throughout the entire region.

Natural gas distribution was controlled by a unified corporate structure. The Pacific Light and Gas Supply Company controlled the gas
supplies that were distributed by the Southern California and Southern
Counties companies. All three firms were owned by a single holding
corporation, the Pacific Lighting. As demands for natural gas in the
metropolitan area exceeded the local supply, the Pacific Light and Gas
Supply Company imported from additional fields in San Joaquin Valley, and when these supplies proved inadequate to meet ever-mounting
demands, it acquired additional supplies from fields in Texas and
Oklahoma.

New orders of priority in importance developed among the area's
energy-supplying industries. None was crowded out, but relative levels
of importance fluctuated. Hydroelectric energy, which had been a
leader in the early 1920's, lagged, as compared to petroleum and gas.
After 1945, for example, both the Los Angeles Water and Power Department and the Edison Company found it necessary to construct
several additional generating plants, each powered by steam produced
from consumption of petroleum. This type of generating plant was
more economical than additional water-powered plants. Furthermore,
the latter were subject to seasonal fluctuations, resulting from changes
in water-supply levels. Petroleum-supplied plants could be relied upon
to provide a firm amount of power; they were also necessary for
stand-by and support purposes in the total supply system.

Expansion of the petroleum-processing industry, together with increased consumption of petroleum and petroleum products, produced
new problems in the Los Angeles metropolitan area, however. Concurrent with the increase in use of petroleum, air pollution increased.
Reduction of air pollution became a major political issue and groups
seeking to prevent pollution made the petroleum industry their prime
target. Chief among these were leaders in the tourist industry, who
became fearful in the early 1950's that air pollution would affect their
business adversely.

Early proponents of hydroelectric power had claimed that this
energy source was a "clean" one that would not produce the polluted
atmospheric conditions associated with industrialization exemplified
by Pittsburgh, Chicago, and St. Louis. So long as hydroelectric power

had been a major source of industrial energy the Los Angeles region had been relatively free of smoke or gases. The situation changed radically after 1945, when petroleum was called upon to bear a much greater portion of the total energy supply.

When efforts by individual cities proved inadequate to cope with air pollution, state legislation was sought and a special Air Pollution Control District was organized to regulate plants and equipment and gases or smoke discharged into the atmosphere. The district was given jurisdiction over an area that was equal to that of the county. By code enforcement and securing the voluntary coöperation of industry, the district produced a number of changes in industrial plant operation. It induced many firms that used petroleum to produce heat and energy to shift to natural gas when the atmospheric pollution reached a specified level. Finally, in order to emphasize this policy, the district adopted an order directing plants to shift to gas or other nonpolluting bases of energy when atmospheric conditions made severe air pollution highly probable. Experience indicated that periods of high pollution probability covered approximately half the year. Therefore, the district's policy requiring a shift of fuel produced a major dislocation in the energy-supply industries. The Southern California Edison Company and the Los Angeles Department of Water and Power were affected in the same manner as other industries that relied upon petroleum for an energy source. Both systems found it necessary to become large-scale customers of the gas companies.

All public suppliers of energy are faced with the problem of supplying peak demands. Reserves, in the form of supplementary generating equipment and storage facilities, must be planned to meet the requirements of peak periods. Nevertheless, the cost of supplementary equipment and the ability to store energy sets limits upon the ability of each supplier to meet its peak-load requirements. Both industries, gas and electricity, have chosen to work out a system of priorities among their customers. Those with a low priority must be prepared to switch to alternative sources of power or to close their operations when the supplier finds it necessary to limit supplies to higher priority purchasers. The gas industry, for example, places industrial users lower on its priority list than domestic users, because the former usually have a greater ability to switch to alternative sources of power. For political and customer-relations purposes, an energy-supply utility must be prepared to serve domestic purchasers without interruption.

When a power supplier, such as the Southern California Edison Company, finds itself in danger of having its basic source reduced or cut off by another supplier, such as the gas industry, it must arrange substitutes or alternates. In 1963, the Edison Company and the Water and Power Commission negotiated contracts with the Tennessee Gas Transmission Company to ensure a firm quantity of gas to supplement their petroleum stocks. The proposal met strong opposition from the local gas companies, which alleged that this was a needless and expensive duplication of services. A decision depends upon the Federal Power Commission's approval of a new interstate pipeline.

A Municipal Gas Competitor. Natural-gas distribution is not completely the domain of the private companies. One municipal system serves a significant portion of the metropolitan area. The city of Long Beach enjoys a unique position in that it has been able to exploit petroleum and gas resources existing under its tidelands. The city has leased numerous tidelands sites to private companies for drilling and exploitation. It receives royalties from petroleum extraction, and it operates a municipal gas system to distribute gas to purchasers throughout the city. The city acquired its distribution system from the Southern Counties Gas Company in 1924,[23] in order to control the sale of gas for both municipal and commercial uses.

Division of territory between the municipal and private gas distributing agencies has produced a situation comparable to that existing between Los Angeles and the Edison Company. Larger annexations to the city cut into the private utility's territory. City-company contests over annexation are illustrated by the Lakewood incident. In 1951, the city of Long Beach strove to persuade the residents of the Lakewood section, which lies adjacent to the city on the north, to annex. Among the inducements offered was the opportunity to purchase gas from the municipal gas system at rates purported to be lower than those charged by the private firm. In the campaigns that ensued, the company became an influential supporter of the successful effort to incorporate Lakewood as a separate city. The incorporation action thwarted Long Beach's aim to expand northward and kept the area within the company's service domain.

COUNTERVAILING FORCES IN WATER SUPPLY

Water supply in the southern California coastal plain, upon which the city of Los Angeles and the surrounding metropolitan area have developed, been limited by nature largely to sources that are available in underground basins. There are no continuously flowing

---

[23] *Ibid.* (1924), XXIV, 916.

streams, nor are there substantial lakes within the area or immediately adjacent to it.[24] Basically the region is a desert in its surface characteristics. Rainfall is limited, seldom exceeding fifteen inches per year, so that agriculture and urban planting alike depend upon irrigation. Three river systems, the Los Angeles, San Gabriel, and Santa Ana, provide natural drainage channels from the mountain canyons to the ocean. Although these rivers are often raging streams in the winter season, necessitating extensive flood control programs, they are dry during much of the year. Water percolates, however, through the alluvial fans that have built up at the mouths of the various mountain canyons in geologic time periods, and the water thus percolated gathers in underground basins at lower elevations. Subterranean rock barriers form the natural boundaries of these basins and control the underground flow.

In the geological and meteorological environment of southern California, surface-property owners have a special interdependence with regard to water rights. These owners have a recognized legal right to sink well-shafts on their land and to pump water for reasonable beneficial use on their properties. So long as the supply of underground water equals or exceeds the demands made upon it by surface owners, there is no problem. Drought conditions or marked increases in pumping, however, produce several types of conflict. Property owners situated at a higher elevation may deprive those at a lower location of water or make it more expensive for the latter to obtain supplies. Overpumping at any point in a basin lowers the water table in the underground reservoir and makes problems for all users. Such a situation has been particularly serious in the coastal areas, because overdrafts upon underground fresh-water supplies have resulted in salt-water intrusion.

CONFLICTING CLAIMS ON WATER RESOURCES

The nature of the water situation is such that not only is there a built-in conflict created between urban areas and agriculture for the possession of water as well as land, but also competition between the several urban areas for the local ground-water resources is predictable. From an early date it was evident that the supply of water for urban purposes would be limited. Competition between sets of municipal leaders for water supplies that could ensure future urban development began shortly after 1900, the same time period in which other sets of

---

[24] Some streams do flow over a portion of their channels but "go underground" and percolate into subsurface channels and basins as the result of damming or other blockages.

competitors sought to organize transportation and energy resources for an expanding community.

Several types of action were taken. In the period immediately after 1900, those cities in which the drive for municipal expansion and urban development was most pronounced sought to integrate their control of ground water by organizing municipally owned systems. This was done either by purchasing or condemning privately owned water companies or by acquiring lands overlying water basins and percolated streams. Municipal water systems thereafter became instruments of municipal policy, to assist in promoting territorial expansion or to

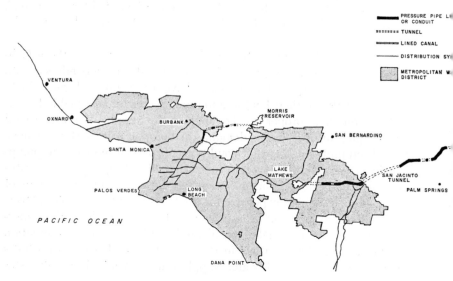

FIG. 4. Metropolitan Water District of Southern California.

protect the city against merger with other municipalities. The cities that succeeded as bastions of municipal independence or as contenders for metropolitan leadership shored up their positions early by gaining control of their domestic water systems.

Creation of public agencies to finance and manage the importation of water from other areas, to supplement the local ground-water resources, was a second major development. Two systems have been created to accomplish this purpose. The Los Angeles Municipal Water System was the first to do this, partly because its municipal leaders had the imagination and the drive to accomplish such a huge undertaking, and partly because it was the only city possessing sufficient financial resources to undertake the task. The other agency is the

Metropolitan Water District of Southern California, in which the city of Los Angeles joins with several cities and municipal water districts to mobilize sufficient taxable wealth to finance the importing of water from the Colorado River. At no time has imported water completely replaced local ground water as the basic resource for urban development in the Los Angeles metropolitan area, however (see table 1). The imported water has been treated as a supplement and a guarantee of supplies to meet future demands.

As urban development has intensified, the contest for underground water has grown keener. A pattern has unfolded in this competition

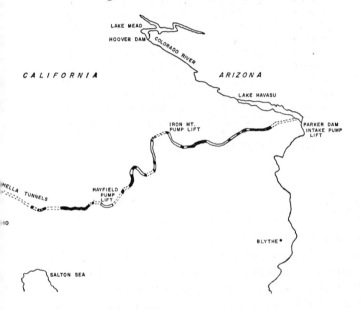

and a method for allocating claims has been developed. Lowered water levels within each of the natural basins have forced cities, mutual water companies, private concerns and individuals to sink ever deeper wells or to search for other, supplemental sources. At the same time there has been need to establish order and stability in ground-water rights. The technique used has been to bring all ground-water users in a basin into litigation to determine priorities and apportion rights. The Raymond Basin area, comprising a forty square mile portion of the San Gabriel Valley in which several cities, such as Pasadena, South Pasadena, and San Marino, and numerous unincorporated communities are located, was the first to seek this type of adjustment. The city of Pasadena filed a complaint in superior court, in 1937, but

TABLE 1

WATER PRODUCTION OF CONSTITUENT UNITS
OF THE METROPOLITAN WATER DISTRICT, 1958–1959

Units	Local production (in acre-feet)	MWD acre-feet delivered	Total	Per cent of total	
				Local	MWD
Beverly Hills	9,146.8	2,722.3	11,869.1	77.1	22.9
Burbank	20,565.9	3,849.6	24,515.5	84.3	15.7
Central Basin[a]	194,419.4	6,623.5	201,042.9	96.7	3.3
Coastal[a]	1,901.0	11,803.3	13,704.3	13.9	86.1
Compton	7,367.8	178.4	7,546.2	97.7	2.3
Eastern[a]	123,806.0	28,700.6	152,506.6	81.2	18.8
Glendale	21,372.1	1,806.9	23,179.0	92.2	7.8
Long Beach	28,922.1	18,547.8	47,469.9	60.9	39.1
Los Angeles City	428,689.0[b]	82,817.0	511,506.0	83.8	16.2
Pasadena	16,421.8	16,322.4	32,744.2	50.2	49.8
Pomona Valley[a]	39,397.6	6,444.3	45,841.9	85.9	14.1
San Marino	5,186.6	0.0	5,186.6	100.0	0.0
Santa Monica	877.8	14,019.7	14,897.5	5.9	94.1
Torrance	924.2	14,913.2	15,837.4	5.8	94.2
West Basin[a]	54,380.0	65,273.9	119,653.9	45.4	54.6

SOURCE: Metropolitan Water District of Southern California, *Twenty-first Annual Report* (1959), p. 40.

[a] Municipal Water District.

[b] Local production figures for Los Angeles City include water from Owens Valley–Mono Basin as well as local ground water. Of the 428,689 acre-feet listed as "local," 320,783 acre-feet came from the Owens–Mono source, and 99,906 acre-feet from local ground water sources.

the case did not come to formal trial until May, 1944. Parties to the suit stipulated facts and issues and turned to the court to confirm a plan to allocate water resources in the basin. The decision of the trial court was modified and confirmed by the state Supreme Court in 1949.[25] It allocated water rights among a considerable number of users and designated a water master to enforce the provisions of the judgment.

Public agencies have tended to supplant private firms as the chief suppliers of ground water in the metropolitan area. Private land and water companies played significant roles in developing a number of communities but many gave way to public units after the initial development period passed, and as costs of producing water increased. A total of thirty-nine commercial water companies continue to operate in Los Angeles County,[26] although the long-range tendency has been for

[25] *City of Pasadena* v. *City of Alhambra et al.*, 33 Cal. 2d 908, 207 P. 2d 17 (1949).

[26] State Water Resources Board, *Water Utilization and Requirements of California*, II (Sacramento, 1955), 268.

small water companies to integrate into larger firms, in a manner similar to that followed in other utility services.

Mutual water companies, a type of semipublic organization to join the land owners in small communities, have been formed to pool the land owners' water interests and to pump and distribute water from underground sources. This type of company has often been formed by land developers to supply housing tracts situated outside areas served by municipal or other public systems. In many instances, mutual water companies have leased their facilities to private water firms to manage.

County waterworks districts have been employed in unincorporated territory to finance distributing systems serving water at retail to householders. These districts are primarily special assessment districts, inasmuch as the county Board of Supervisors acts as the governing board and the county engineer's department serves as the administrative agent for all districts. There were eight such districts in Los Angeles County in 1955. A county water district is a slightly different type of organization. It is distinguished from its waterworks counterpart by the fact that it has its own locally elected governing board. In 1955, there were ten districts of this type in operation. Three irrigation districts were also listed as providing water for domestic users, in addition to serving their primary purpose.[27]

Water service is provided in the Los Angeles area by the following array of public agencies:[28]

    1 metropolitan water district
  33 municipal water departments
    5 municipal water districts
    8 county waterworks districts
  10 county water districts
    3 irrigation districts
283 mutual water companies

The suburban water-supply organization, outside the few large cities, is a most complex one. There seems to be a tendency for each municipality to try to integrate the various water systems within its boundaries by forming a municipal water department. Lakewood, for example, purchased the properties of the Lakewood Land and Water Company shortly after the city was incorporated in 1954. Several cities are faced with a difficult situation because a number of mutual water companies exist within their municipal area, complicating efforts to establish a unified water system.

---

[27] *Ibid.*
[28] *Ibid.*

CITY OF LOS ANGELES

When the race for urban development began in the early 1900's, the city of Los Angeles discovered that it possessed a unique advantage for control of water supplies capable of supporting a major urban community. That advantage was based upon the Spanish governmental institution of the *pueblo*, through which the royal government had vested the water rights in the Los Angeles River in the Pueblo de Los Angeles, the legal ancestor of the American city. Inasmuch as Los Angeles was the only pueblo ever established in the area that is being discussed, this city possessed a peculiar advantage that was to become especially significant when ground-water supplies became relatively scarce.

The Spanish-California pueblo was a reservation of royal domain that covered four square leagues. Land within the pueblo was granted by the royal government to individuals for use, but certain features, including water, were reserved for common purpose.[29] During the Mexican regime, attempts to challenge this legal system, with respect to water, were defeated and the pueblo's interest was upheld. Challenges made in early years of the American period were successful at first, but the Legislature reënacted the city's charter and reaffirmed the city's interest in the river's flow.[30] This action was sustained and protected by the California Supreme Court and by the federal courts.[31]

The California courts have extended the city's influence in the Los Angeles river basin by supporting its contention that the pueblo right applied to the subterranean flow of the river as well as to the water in the flowing stream. By supporting the priority of the pueblo rights over the riparian rights of owners of lands that overlay the subterranean flow, the courts favored the city water system against other municipal and agricultural claimants that were located at points in the river basin above Los Angeles. The decisions permitted riparian land owners to withdraw water by pumping only so long as the water was surplus of the needs of the city of Los Angeles. Los Angeles could, however, reclaim the surplus to its use whenever its needs increased. For example, the cities of Glendale and Burbank, both of which were located in the same basin with Los Angeles, could withdraw under-

---

[29] Vincent Ostrom, *Water and Politics* (Los Angeles: Haynes Foundation, 1953), pp. 27–40.

[30] *Cal. Stats.* (1873–74), p. 633.

[31] *City of Los Angeles* v. *Pomeroy,* 124 Cal. 597, 57 P. 585 (1899); *Hooker* v. *Los Angeles,* 188 U.S. 314 (1902).

ground water supplies only so long as the needs of the city of Los Angeles did not require the water.[32]

Los Angeles residents debated, for a period between 1898 and 1901, whether to authorize a private water company to develop the local resources and distribute water to the city area, or to establish a municipal water department. A train of decisions, ratified by the municipal voters, concluded in the choice of municipal operation. They approved a bond issue in August, 1901, to finance a municipal program. In February, 1902, a Board of Water Commissioners began to operate the waterworks system that the city acquired from the private company; and the voters adopted a charter amendment in 1903, clinching the determination that municipal operation would be the basic policy.

City leaders began immediately to plan for acquisition of additional water resources in the Owens River, located in Inyo County, more than two hundred miles north of Los Angeles. In September, 1905, the voters approved a bond issue to finance purchase of the water rights in the Owens River. An aqueduct, by which the water was brought to the city, was constructed by the city's own work force, directed by William Mulholland, superintendent of the water department.

Water Supply and Territorial Growth. The imported water arrived in the Los Angeles area in 1913 and promptly touched off debates on the policy to govern distribution. This new supply was expected to be five times as great as the local resources that had been available previously;[33] therefore the city's total water supply was deemed to be well in excess of its needs for a considerable period of time.

Central to the policy question of water use and distribution was the interpretation of the city's legal powers to dispose of the surplus water. This surplus might comprise water from the pueblo interest in the Los Angeles River system as well as from the Owens River importation. The legal background for this policy decision had been established by a number of state court decisions in the period preceding arrival of the Owens Valley water. Litigation in 1895 had determined that the city could not sell pueblo water to supply lands outside the city, and that the long-standing practice of selling such water to individuals and commercial companies beyond the city borders did not create a legal right to do so.[34] Three communities that had no resources of their

[32] *City of Los Angeles* v. *City of Glendale; City of Los Angeles* v. *City of Burbank,* 23 Cal. 2d 68, 142 P. 2d 289 (1943).

[33] Ostrom, *op. cit.,* p. 148.

[34] *Vernon Irrigation Company* v. *City of Los Angeles,* 106 Cal. 237, 252, 39 P. 762 (1895).

own and had depended upon buying water from Los Angeles voted to annex to the city following that court decision.[35] Annexation of water-deficit communities was further encouraged by another state supreme court decision, *City of Los Angeles* v. *Pomeroy*, given in 1899.[36] In this instance the court said that pueblo water rights were not limited to use by lands or householders in the original city but could be applied also to annexed areas, regardless of when annexation took place. The court also held that the needs of the enlarged city took priority over the claims of riparian lands above Los Angeles on the Los Angeles River. This decision set off a flurry of annexations. Between the time the decision was given and the Owens Valley water arrived, communities such as Hollywood, East Hollywood, Colgrove, and Arroyo Seco joined the city of Los Angeles.

The city government considered several plans for marketing the imported water, among which was a proposal to sell to deficit areas that would bid the highest price. In April, 1913, the City Council submitted to the electorate several proposals to finance conduits through which water would be distributed on a wholesale basis to areas outside the city. This plan was opposed by William Mulholland, superintendent of the city's water system, who argued that the only legal method by which those areas could be assured city water was for them to annex to the city. All but one of the bond issues failed.

A policy based upon the Mulholland proposal began to crystallize. The Public Service Commission urged a three point policy: (1) that the city sell water only to areas that were likely to come into the city by annexation or consolidation, (2) that the property owners in the areas desiring water be required to finance distributing systems that would be constructed under the supervision of the city's water engineers, and (3) that each distributing system thus constructed should become part of the city-owned system when annexation was achieved. At Mayor Rose's suggestion, the City Council created an Annexation Commission to investigate the problem of surplus-water disposal.[37] This commission approved the Public Service Commission's proposals, with a few slight modifications. The annexation group expressed the opinion that the legal situation generally made annexation the only satisfactory method by which the city could dispose of its surplus water and that areas proposing to finance distribution systems could not obtain sound legal backing for their plans unless they annexed to the city. The proposal that water be made available only to land within the city

---

[35] Highland Park, Garvanza, and University districts.

[36] 124 Cal. 597, 57 P. 585.

[37] Martin F. Betkouski, chairman; Miles Gregory, George Dunlap, George Harrison, Ora Monette, Ralph Criswell, Leslie Hewitt, and J. A. Anderson.

was adopted by the City Council and became the guiding principle for the city's actions.

During a period of twelve years after the adoption of this policy, the city of Los Angeles underwent an enormous expansion that ultimately made it the largest city in the United States, in point of territory. Annexation of the San Fernando Valley in 1915 more than doubled the city's area, increasing it from 107.62 square miles to 284.81 square miles. This action was followed by annexations of the Westgate, Palms, West Adams, West Coast, and Bairdstown areas. Most of the annexations were situated westward of the central (or original) portion of the city. In the northeast area, Eagle Rock, Occidental, and Annandale sections were added. In the southern portion, only Watts was added. However, substantial tracts were annexed in the southwest: West Coast, Angeles Mesa, Hyde Park and Wagner sections. In general, the annexation movement pointed toward the ocean.

Annexation of the San Fernando Valley involved several unique situations. When this action was contemplated the valley was largely devoted to agricultural uses, and large tracts were owned by a few influential people who were also prominent in the Los Angeles business community. Enhancement of the land values in the valley by the guarantee of a water supply that would also be adequate for urban development touched off a political controversy within the city that delayed adoption of the annexation policy. Another unique feature was the location of the valley with reference to the original city, the Los Angeles River, and the terminal point of the Owens Valley aqueduct. It lay below the Chatsworth reservoir, the terminal for the Owens Valley aqueduct. Water placed upon the land in the San Fernando Valley by irrigation tended to percolate into the natural underground reservoirs and flow downstream in the river basin where much of it could be captured for reuse. This percolation condition was the basis for one of the plans to justify bringing the valley area into the city.

Other areas annexed to the city of Los Angeles were in other water basins and hence presented different situations. The Westgate addition, for example, was outside the area related to the Los Angeles River. The West Los Angeles Water Company had served a portion of this area, but after the court decisions had ruled out sale of pueblo water supplies to outside agencies, the company sold its facilities to the city. In 1915, the Los Angeles voters defeated a proposal to sell water to the cities of Sawtelle and Santa Monica and to certain mutual water companies. Not long after this action, Sawtelle agreed to consolidate with Los Angeles.

The Los Angeles City water policy, compounded from judge-made law, City Council actions, plebescites of the municipal electorate, and administrative acts of the city water bureaucracy, produced widespread annexation. This consequence soon stimulated the development of two countering elements that sought to slow down or terminate the great land-expansion activity. One element arose within the city's administration and sought to temper the enthusiasm of the expansionists. The second arose among Los Angeles' neighbors. As early as 1922, the Public Service Commission of the city began to warn against the tendency to spread the city's boundaries over too much land area.[38] William Mulholland, the city water superintendent, also warned that the area already absorbed into the city was commensurate with the available water supply. In 1925, the Public Service Commission formally advised the City Council that it was no longer possible to provide an adequate supply of water for the areas that were then seeking annexation. In 1927, the commission stated its position even more emphatically, that no more land should be added to the city until an additional water supply was available.

Although Los Angeles has continued to annex territory periodically since 1927, most of the later additions have been relatively small compared to the San Fernando Valley and Westgate additions. The great period of expansion took place between 1915 and 1927.

OTHER CITIES

The annexation drive that expanded the territorial borders of the city of Los Angeles inevitably caused much resentment and fear in cities adjacent to it. Small cities, such as Sawtelle, Eagle Rock, Hyde Park, and Barnes City, capitulated and consolidated with Los Angeles in order to secure adequate water for their land owners. Other cities that were more fortunately located or were more forehanded organized municipal water departments and sought to develop adequate groundwater resources. These escaped the pressure to join Los Angeles, although agitation in many communities produced spirited contests in councilmanic elections and, in several instances, brought the consolidation issue to a referendum vote.

Evidence in table 2 indicates that almost every city adjacent to Los Angeles that remained independent of the larger city organized a municipal water department prior to or during the period when the most frantic annexation and consolidation activity took place (1915–1927). Culver City was the principal exception. It has no municipal water department, and is supplied by commercial companies.

---

[38] Ostrom, *op. cit.*, p. 159.

TABLE 2

SUBURBAN MUNICIPAL WATER DEPARTMENTS

Municipality	Date works acquired
Alhambra	1916
Beverly Hills	1924
Burbank	1913
Glendale	1914
Hawthorne	1924
Huntington Park	1920
Inglewood	1919
Lynwood	1921
Manhattan Beach	1913
Monterey Park	1921
Pasadena	1912
San Fernando	1920
Santa Monica	1916
South Gate	1925
South Pasadena	1922
Vernon	1924

SOURCE: State Controller, *Financial Transactions of Municipalities and Counties for the Year 1948* (Sacramento, 1948), pp. 136–141.

Long Beach, Pasadena, and Glendale, the principal rivals of Los Angeles for territory, population, and economic base, each developed municipal water systems shortly after Los Angeles began to seek the Owens Valley source. Initially each of these cities depended upon ground-water sources. Pasadena annexed the Arroyo Seco to protect a major source of its local ground water.[39] Glendale extended its boundaries into the Verdugo Hills to obtain and protect its water sources. Long Beach began a municipal water system in 1911 that drew upon wells in areas surrounding the city.

Mere existence of a municipal water department did not guarantee, however, that a city could secure sufficient water to supply municipal needs from local sources. In the 1920's, almost every city with a population of more than twenty-five thousand felt a need to secure additional sources. Periodic droughts, coupled with a population boom, caused municipal leaders to be concerned. Importation of water appeared to be the feasible alternative, and the proposal by William Mulholland of Los Angeles, that the Colorado River be tapped, proved to be the accepted action.

[39] It is interesting to note that, although the Arroyo Seco is a tributary of the Los Angeles River system, the city of Los Angeles has never pressed a pueblo water claim against the city of Pasadena.

A METROPOLITAN WATER DISTRICT

Importation of water on the scale possible in the Colorado River plan proved to be a most important check upon Los Angeles' annexation politics. In order to organize an institution capable of financing and managing the distribution of the Colorado River supply, many cities had to be brought together. This action was accomplished by creating the Metropolitan Water District of Southern California. Initial members of the district were Los Angeles, Pasadena, Glendale, Burbank, Beverly Hills, Santa Monica, and San Marino, in Los Angeles County; and Anaheim, Colton, San Bernardino, and Santa Ana, in other counties. It was formally incorporated and began existence in December, 1928.

The purpose of this district was to construct an aqueduct, storage reservoirs, and treatment plants, and to sell water to its constituent territories at wholesale rates. Retail distribution continued to be the function of municipal water departments and water districts. The district's operations were to be financed by property taxes and by sale of water to its members.

The state statute that set up the district provided for a governing board to be composed of persons appointed by the chief executive of each member-municipality. Each representative was to cast one vote for each $10,000,000 of assessed value of property within the constituent municipality, although no local unit was permitted to have more than 50 per cent of the district's voting strength. This provision was to serve as a limit upon the strength of Los Angeles on the district board, inasmuch as that municipality had more than half the assessed valuation represented in the original district organization. On the other hand, a city's delegation was permitted to cast its votes as a bloc in accordance with the wishes of its majority. By casting its combined vote the Los Angeles delegation was able to exercise a dominant role in the controversies that divided the district board from time to time.

Municipalities not originally members of the metropolitan district are permitted to join upon petition and agreement to pay a proportionate share of the capital outlay of the district. It is also possible for municipalities to join municipal water districts that in turn may petition for membership in the metropolitan district. Each member municipality is entitled to water for domestic and municipal purposes in the same ratio that the municipality's assessed valuation for tax purposes bears to the district's total. This formula determines the maximum amount to which the municipality is entitled and any member can decide the amount of water it chooses to draw. Although member municipalities have drawn varying percentages of their entitlements, and few have reached their maximum, the guarantee has had a stabilizing effect upon intermunicipal relations.

SUMMARY

The pattern of local government in the Los Angeles metropolitan area has been affected by the struggles between sets of competitors that have sought to control significant segments of the economic base of the area. Competition has not been confined, however, to groups in the private sector of the economy. Municipal corporations have been utilized as vehicles in the contest. In some instances, public policy has called for the use of municipal corporations as instruments to counter monopolistic efforts by private groups to gain control of a sector of the region's economic base. At the same time, there have been deliberate efforts by suburban municipalities to counter the tendencies of the central city to press its advantages in the competition to determine the governmental-economic pattern.

In some instances, as in the provision of hydroelectric power, a kind of equilibrium is reached between two great competitors; yet, activity is renewed when competitors of a different type offer alternatives and thereby seek to gain new advantages over the previously entrenched groups. Among the municipal corporations, Los Angeles has been aggressive in seeking advantages that would make that city the most influential in the region and bring within its borders large amounts of land and population. Lesser polarities, such as Long Beach and Pasadena, have arisen to challenge the central city.

The type of contest that has taken place in the Los Angeles metropolitan area has been determined in part by the region's particular deficiencies and strengths in natural resources. It has been determined also by the legal and political constraints of California government that have given municipalities great opportunities for maneuver.

THREE

Legal Constraints on Government for the Metropolitan Area

GOVERNMENT of the metropolitan area is carried on by a variety of agencies, each with its own jurisdiction, its own public to be served, its own financial resources, and its own set of officers and employees. Doctrines and practices of American public law require each unit of local government to be tied to a definite piece of territory that constitutes the unit's jurisdiction. In a metropolitan area, however, the interests and influences of a particular unit frequently range beyond the legal boundaries. Rivalry and competition between various units are ever present, although the particular sets of rivals and antagonists vary from time to time according to the stakes being sought. Some participants in this contest are inclined to be more active than others, but few remain quiescent and satisfied with the status quo.

The rivalries between local governments in the Los Angeles metropolitan area are conducted in accordance with sets of rules that indicate certain probabilities for action. Although no war game is plotted here, the grand strategies and tactical moves of this contest are influenced by these rules. While the rules governing the actions relevant to the emergence of metropolitan government may vary, from time to time, the basic ones stem initially from the state. These are to be found largely in the state constitution, in session statutes and codes enacted by the Legislature. Decisions of the state's courts interpreting and applying them contribute significantly to the core of legal rules by which those who seek to guide the local governments may operate.

In several important phases the constitution and statutes are silent; hence the courts have searched the judicial precedents and legal commentaries and have produced theories to fill those gaps in the law.

By nature, law is a continuous fabric whose strands stretch back in history. The American legal system is such that a complete legal concept is seldom scrapped and a totally new one inaugurated. A constant adjustment takes place, as new facts present themselves.

One of the most interesting features of these legal rules is that many, although written initially to cover a specific problem or situation, or to express a theory of government, have been applied to a totally different set of facts at a later time. As new conditions arise, the existing rules are examined by both official and private parties to determine how they may be adapted to fit the changed situation. In numerous instances rules that were written with one objective in mind may be plausibly interpreted to supply quite a different type of result under differing circumstances. Legislative bodies are seldom able to predict the long-range consequences of their decisions. Yet, although the written rules may be changed from time to time, the original concept often remains the same.

When examining the governmental pattern in a metropolitan area, one need not look exclusively to the state constitution, statutes, and judicial decisions in order to identify the rules by which the various participants have sought to achieve their demands or to fend off the maneuvers of their rivals. One will also find them in the assumptions upon which the written words are based.

SPECIFICATIONS AND ASSUMPTIONS IN THE STATE CONSTITUTION

California's second constitution, adopted in 1879, continued some of the specifications and assumptions regarding local government that had been established in the first, which had been put in force in 1850.[1] It specified a relatively simple structure. It continued the counties that had existed at the time and directed the Legislature to provide for a system of county government that was to be uniform throughout the

---

[1] The first constitution had been extremely sketchy in its statements regarding local governments. It had directed the Legislature to establish a system of county and town governments which were to be as nearly uniform as practicable throughout the state. Also it had directed the Legislature to provide for the organization of cities and incorporated villages. The constitution writers' chief preoccupation with respect to the subject seemed to have been to ensure that the Legislature would restrict the powers of local governing bodies to imposing taxes, levying assessments, incurring indebtedness, and lending credit. They feared that municipal corporations would abuse the authority granted in those matters!

state. All territory within the state was to be included in one county or another. The few city governments that had been created under the previous constitution were continued. Local governmental powers and responsibilities were divided between the counties and the cities.

Separate Urban and Rural Governments

Neither the first nor the second constitution made any explicit statement about the distinction between city government and county government. Neither set forth any concept regarding the role that these units were expected to perform in the state's local-government system. Evidently the constitutional writers believed that there was a common understanding of these matters in American government and law, and that the Legislature needed no guidance in establishing local governmental institutions in California. It may be inferred that the constitutional founding fathers assumed that county governments were to act as agents of the state in performing a range of functions that the Legislature would allocate from time to time, and that these governments would be concerned chiefly with affairs of the rural areas. It may also be assumed that cities were to govern urban areas and that their boundaries would have some relevance to urban settlement, although some California cities, for example, San Diego, had territorial boundaries extending far beyond their urban settlement in 1879. Another assumption that seems to have been built into the thinking about local government was that municipal boundaries should not extend across county lines. This is neither affirmed nor denied in specific language in the constitution; yet, the assumption is valid that its writers believed the relationship between a city and a county to be so close that a city must of necessity be confined to territory within one county.

There was no definite provision for a level of government intermediate between the county and the city. Some states have established villages and towns for the government of small communities that are neither rural nor strictly urban. Although the California constitution made reference to towns and townships, neither term found a meaningful place in this state's local government structure. Towns have been regarded as equivalent to cities and not as parts of a class of municipal governments having smaller populations and possibly fewer powers.[2] The Legislature went no further with townships than to per-

---

[2] *Ex parte Wall* (1874), 48 Cal. 279. The designation "town" has been dropped from legislative wording.

mit counties to opt for the election of justices of the peace and constables as township officers.[3]

The concept of the modern metropolis, a vast concentration of population governed by a variety of local governments, was beyond the imagination or experience of the writers of the 1879 constitution. There were no clusters of cities because there was no concentration of urban population. Most counties had but one city, many had none. San Francisco was the major center of urban population in the state at that time, having a population of 233,959. That community possessed a special form of government, a consolidated city-county. Because of this precedent, and to legitimize its continuance, the constitution provided that a city and a county might be merged and consolidated into one municipal government with one set of officers.[4] This precedent was to linger as a will-o'-the-wisp luring political leaders of other areas from time to time when metropolitan areas appeared on the California scene.

Local Home Rule Origins

The 1879 constitution made two innovations in local governmental policy that were to have vast significance for the entire pattern of California government in later years. It forbade the Legislature to create municipal corporations (cities) by special laws and directed it instead to provide by general laws for the creation, organization, and classification of these entities.[5] It also authorized any city possessing more than one hundred thousand population to prepare a charter for its own government, consistent with the constitution and laws of the state.[6] These provisions laid the foundation for a system of municipal home rule that was to become highly meaningful when the state became heavily populated. California was the second state to adopt home rule, Missouri having preceded it by four years.

Introduction of the municipal home-rule concept brought into being several closely related ideas. The larger cities were to be permitted some degree of freedom from state legislative tutelage. Yet, because local governments were in many respects subordinate to the state, it was necessary to provide some process by which the state and local spheres of authority could be reconciled. The courts were thrust into the gap left by the Legislature. Municipal home rule substituted rule by the courts for rule by the Legislature.

[3] *Kenyon* v. *Johnson*, 97 Cal. App. 552, 276 P. 110 (1929).
[4] *California Constitution*, Art. XI, sec. 7.
[5] *Ibid.*, Art. XI, sec. 6.
[6] *Ibid.*, Art. XI, sec. 8.

Legislative interference in the affairs of local governments that were already organized and in operation was prohibited on several specific points. The Legislature could not impose specific tax systems upon cities or counties, but could only provide authority by general law for local bodies to levy and collect taxes for local purposes.[7] It was also directed not to delegate authority to any special commission, private corporation, or individual to supervise or interfere in any way with any county or city improvement or property.[8] Furthermore, no county or city was to be created or its powers altered by special legislative act.[9]

To give local governing authorities the opportunity to carry out responsibilities vested in them, the constitution authorized all counties and cities to make and enforce within their limits all such local, police, sanitary, and other regulations as the local governing body deemed necessary and which were not in conflict with general laws enacted by the state.[10] Thereafter, of course, the significant problem became one of determining the extent to which local law conflicted with general state laws. The courts, by the exercise of their authority to construe statutes, interpret the constitution, and review local ordinances and charters, became the principal determinant in this problem.

POPULAR CHECKS UPON REPRESENTATIVE INSTITUTIONS

The shift away from state legislative control over local government also brought the local electorate into an active role as a counterweight to local legislative bodies. It caused the state to exchange the previously established system of representative government in cities for a mixed system of democratic and representative principles. In the new system, the voters were given some decision-making tasks that had belonged previously to the state Legislature and some that had been exercised by local legislative bodies, that is, by city councils and county boards of supervisors.

Referral of major policy matters to the electorate usually represents a lack of confidence in the ability of the elected representative body to reflect popular views and to make wise decisions. Often, proponents of referenda in local government anticipate that the electorate will reject the proposition submitted, thus preserving the status quo. Analysis of the direct government process tends to lend weight to that estimate. The mechanics of the referendum are so inflexible by nature that compromise is almost impossible. In the Legislature, proponents

---

[7] *Ibid.*, Art. XI, sec. 12.
[8] *Ibid.*, Art. XI, sec. 13.
[9] *Ibid.*, Art. IV, sec. 25.
[10] *Ibid.*, Art. XI, sec. 11.

of a bill may agree to amendments at various stages of progress through the law-making machinery in order to pick up sufficient votes to secure adoption. In the referendum process, however, once a proposal is scheduled for the ballot, it is irrevocably committed to the language in which it is phrased, and passes or fails in that form.

Considering a different aspect of the problem, it has been argued that those policy matters that have long-range consequences for the community should be submitted to the electorate and not be decided entirely by a legislative body that has been elected to transact a wide range of routine business. It is difficult, however, to categorize satisfactorily the subjects that must, according to the California constitution, be submitted to a vote of local electorates.

Two matters made subject to electoral vote by the 1879 constitution had been within the jurisdiction of local legislative bodies previously. Consequences of decisions taken on these matters might be long-range ones, although the subjects did not relate to fundamentals in the system of government. The approval of a majority of the electors in the county was required for the transfer of the county seat from one community to another. Proponents of the referendum requirement may have anticipated that the votes of the town losing the center of county government, coupled with those from areas that might find the shift inconvenient, would override those of the town that stood to gain. At least the record shows only one removal of a county seat after 1879.[11] Also any county, city, or school district that wished to incur indebtedness was required to secure consent of a two-thirds majority of its qualified electors who voted at an election. Certainly the extraordinary majority required for approval of bond issues particularly indicated the restrictive intent of the referendum. This was a larger majority than that required for adoption of state bond issues.

The local electorate was given an important role in two other matters that more nearly concerned fundamentals of the local government system. One dealt with the creation of new municipalities, the other with adopting a locally prepared city charter. Previously the state Legislature had had the exclusive authority to create municipal corporations by special enactment. The new constitution did not specifically require that local voters should pass upon proposals to incorporate a municipality. However, the assumption that direct voting was intended was sufficiently strong that the Legislature did require this procedure when it wrote the Municipal Corporation Act of 1883, the first general statute implementing the policies set forth in the new constitution.

---

[11] In 1888 Shasta County voters approved the transfer of the county seat from Shasta City to Redding. *California Government Code,* Sec. 23645.

Indications of the partially developed democratic theories held by the writers of the 1879 constitution appear specifically in two places. One, the local government article of the constitution provided that cities and towns previously incorporated by a special act should organize under the new general laws "whenever a majority of the electors voting at a general election shall so determine." [12] Two, cities that were eligible to write a municipal charter were required to submit the document to a referendum of local electors. The procedure for writing a municipal charter comprised three distinct steps. The city council had the exclusive prerogative to initiate proceedings. After a board of freeholders had been elected and had drafted a charter document, the city's qualified voters were to be given an opportunity to accept or reject it. If the voters approved it, the matter then was to be laid before the Legislature for approval or rejection, without amendment.

In view of the widespread distrust of representative bodies, both state and local, that existed in California in the 1870's, it is understandable that the members of the constitutional convention turned to the popular veto (referendum) to obtain a counterbalance in those matters that appeared to be significant in the experience of their era. Members of the Constitutional Convention of 1878 were strongly antagonistic to the Legislature and wrote into the new constitution numerous restrictions upon legislative discretion. In his admirable monograph entitled *Motivation and Technique in the California Constitutional Convention, 1878–79,* Professor Swisher narrates the political events that produced this antagonism toward the Legislature and explains several of the restrictive provisions in the document.[13]

Legislative manipulation of city government had been only one of the abuses. From 1850 to 1879 the Legislature had authority to create or abolish municipalities by special law and to change the structure of any municipality or alter its powers at will. Some of the difficulties encountered may be illustrated by the experience of Oakland.[14] This community was incorporated as a town on May 4, 1852, by a special act that included a grant of title to the municipality of the tidelands on its waterfront. Shortly thereafter the town trustees bestowed the waterfront lands upon a private individual. In 1854, the Legislature enacted a new law changing the town to a city and making a new grant of powers. Later, after a turnover in the membership of the city council, the city began suit to set aside the town's gift of the water-

---

[12] *California Constitution,* Art. XI, sec. 6.

[13] Carl B. Swisher, *Motivation and Technique in the California Constitutional Convention, 1878–79* (Claremont: Pomona College, 1930).

[14] Winston W. Crouch, *State Aid to Local Government in California* (Berkeley: University of California Press, 1939), p. 379.

front lands. Before the case came to trial, the Legislature amended the city charter, attempting to confirm the town trustees' action and redefining the boundaries of the city's tidelands. Ultimately the courts reorganized the private titles to portions of the lands. Other localities had similar difficulties with legislative meddling. Numerous communities in the Mother Lode mining area experienced the Legislature's whimseys in creating and abolishing municipal corporations for factional political reasons.

LOCAL GOVERNMENT AS PROTECTOR OF PUBLIC INTERESTS

Some features of the 1879 constitution touched upon public policy relating to services or land-uses that have been important to local governments. Water rights and water uses were declared to be public matters and subject to state control. Where water was supplied to city inhabitants by private suppliers, the city was given responsibility to regulate the rates to be charged.[15] The constitution also empowered cities to regulate the conditions under which private enterprisers supplying water, gas, or light might use the city's streets for utility purposes, thus establishing the basis for local public-utility franchises.

In an effort to block the state and local legislative bodies from diverting potential harbor sites from public control, the constitution barred the transfer of tidelands located within two miles of city boundaries to private persons or corporations. The state had acquired title to the tidelands from the national government through the terms of the treaty transferring California from Mexico. No expression of policy was made in 1879, however, as to whether such tidelands should be developed by the state or by municipalities or other public bodies. Apparently the constitutional writers were content to anticipate that both the state and municipal governments would encourage harbor developments. Proscription of private development of harbors was rooted in the anti-corporation politics that prevailed in the constitutional convention.[16]

SPECIFICATIONS AND ASSUMPTIONS IN CONSTITUTIONAL AMENDMENTS

Unlike the fundamental law of some states, such as Rhode Island and Tennessee, the California constitution has been amended on numerous occasions. As the state's population grew and urban centers developed, it was possible to change the basic rules concerning local government. Instead of producing changes in the concepts and assumptions about

---

[15] *California Constitution*, Art. XIV, sec. 1.
[16] Swisher, *op. cit.*

the local government system, however, the people of California added more details to the constitution. Concepts and assumptions remained essentially as they were in 1879, but were extended in greater specificity in order to apply them to new situations.

HOME RULE AND DIRECT GOVERNMENT EXTENDED

Municipal home rule was comparatively limited in the 1879 constitution; it was a lodgement, inviting further efforts to enlarge the area of municipal autonomy. Only cities having more than 100,000 population could draft a charter and escape from whatever limitations existed in general statutes pertaining to municipalities. At that time, San Francisco was the only city that could qualify. A series of constitutional amendments soon expanded the application of home rule, however. In 1892, the population requirement for local-charter cities was reduced sharply: from more than one hundred thousand to more than thirty-five hundred. This action really opened the way for a drive toward municipal freedom.

A new reference to democratic theory was made in 1902, when citizen groups were authorized to petition to have charter amendments submitted to the voters. Previously, the elected city council alone could determine whether a city would seek a home-rule charter and whether it would amend one. In many instances, groups that were dominant in a city council opposed the policies advocated by others for inclusion in a home rule charter. Often this opposition related to proposed additions of new functions. In many instances, it revolved around municipal ownership and operation of a utility, for example, water or electricity. To provide an opportunity to circumvent blockades in a city council, a constitutional amendment authorized the proposing of charter amendments by initiative petitions signed by 15 per cent of the qualified voters of the city. The ancient privilege of petitioning the government was thus injected into the formal procedure of charter drafting. Determined groups could thereby circumvent the defenders of a status quo entrenched in the representative council.

In 1911, the initiative petition process was pushed one step further when a constitutional amendment was adopted that made it possible to petition to prepare a charter. A petition, signed by 15 per cent of the qualified voters of the city, would force calling an election to select a board of freeholders whose duty it would be to prepare a charter. The initiative petition method, as well as the home-rule charter procedure, were heartily advocated by the partisans of the Progressive movement in California. The movement or group sought to inject greater democracy into state and local governments as a means for breaking the control that political organizations allegedly exercised over such representative bodies as the state Legislature, city councils, and county boards of supervisors. It was particularly effective in this state between 1910 and 1916. In the general state election in 1910, the movement elected its slate of state officers, headed by Governor Hiram Johnson, and secured a majority in both houses of the Legislature. The 1911 Legislature adopted a number of constitutional amendments, including the one extending the municipal home-rule process. Although only a small number of cities, including Piedmont, San Mateo, Santa Clara, and Redondo Beach, made use of the initiative to inaugurate charters, the existence of an alternative to council action opened up the strategy of charter adoption.

Municipal Affairs Concept Strengthened

Those who were interested in developing local self-government suffered several disappointments, but eventually they were able to overcome those frustrations by means of constitutional amendments. The basic theory that they sought to realize was that a municipality's affairs would be best determined by those most closely affected by the results of the policy. This theory was developed at a time when the state was most unresponsive to pressures seeking to promote public services. Municipal home rule was a means to achieve experimentation in governmental institutions and procedures to serve newly intensified demands for governmental services.

Frustration of efforts to achieve municipal home rule was grounded in the constitutional formula that the city might not adopt regulations that were in conflict with general state law. The state had but to adopt a general regulation pertaining to a subject to nullify municipal efforts. Cities were in peril of having the standards of municipal regulation lowered by a state law that rested upon a common denominator conditioned by the political feasibility of statewide enforcement. The problem for those who were most interested in municipal efforts was to devise some formula that would give to a chartered city a reasonably wide latitude to develop local policy without colliding with the legitimate interests of the state. A constitutional amendment in 1896 sought to provide this formula by exempting municipal charters from control by general law when "municipal affairs" were involved. This proved to be a very limited victory for the home-rule proponents. The constitutional wording was so very unspecific that the courts ruled against the cities on numerous occasions. A direct, but only partially foreseen, outcome of the amendment was to force charter cities to amend their charters frequently to spell out in detail the powers and duties that were to be included in "municipal affairs." A chartered city could claim the municipal affairs protection only if the charter clearly specified the legal basis.[17]

A more successful effort was made in 1914. Chartered cities were empowered to make and enforce all laws and regulations in respect to municipal affairs, subject only to the restrictions and limitations laid down in their own charters. In respect to other affairs, they were to be controlled by general state laws.[18] The courts have generally accepted the view that the adoption of this amendment "declares an entirely new scheme for the granting of municipal charters, the effect of which places cities organized thereunder entirely beyond the interference of general laws in regard to the administration of municipal affairs." [19] The Supreme Court has consistently held that if no restrictions or limitations are found in the city charter, the power of the city in municipal affairs is full and complete.[20] Certainly the record is consistent and clear that the courts have interpreted "municipal affairs" in a manner to assist the cities.[21]

INTERNAL ADJUSTMENTS FOR METROPOLITAN CITIES

The concept of a two-level government has been considered in several plans for restructuring the governments of large metropolitan centers in various countries. Essentially the concept is based upon the idea that a central government will have jurisdiction over the larger area and will share powers and responsibilities with a number of subunits that will have a clearly recognized status in the organization. The borough plan is one variation on this concept.

In 1911, the California constitution was amended to authorize chartered cities to establish a borough system of government. This amendment resulted from the negotiations between representatives of Los Angeles, Wilmington, and San Pedro with respect to the harbor-area consolidation plan. The city charter of Los Angeles had been amended in 1909 to establish a procedure whereby areas within the city could organize a borough government,[22] and it was thought necessary to have a constitutional amendment to reënforce the city charter provi-

---

[17] John C. Peppin, "Municipal Home Rule in California," California Law Review, XXX (Nov., 1941), 1–45.

[18] California Constitution, Art. XI, sec. 6, as amended Nov. 3, 1914.

[19] Storke v. City of Santa Barbara, 76 Cal. App. 40, 244 P. 158 (1925).

[20] Pasadena v. Charleville, 215 Cal. 384, 10 P. 2d 745 (1932).

[21] Peppin, op. cit., and continuation in California Law Review, XXXI (March, 1942), XXXII (Dec., 1944), XXXIV (Dec., 1946).

[22] Wendell Maccoby, "The Borough System of Government for Metropolitan Areas," in California Legislature, Assembly, Report of Subcommittee to Assembly Interim Committee on State and Local Taxation (Sacramento, 1951), pp. 60–61.

sion. This plan was soon nullified, however. When Article XI, section 8, of the constitution was revised to strengthen the "municipal affairs" clause, the sentence pertaining to the borough plan was reworded in such a manner as to require a city wishing to establish a plan to divide the entire city into boroughs.[23]

Interest in the borough plan revived in the Los Angeles area during the post–World War II period when the central city was being pressed to provide public works and improved services for several areas that were experiencing great population growth. In 1950, Assemblyman Vincent Thomas of San Pedro persuaded the Assembly Interim Committee on State and Local Taxation to make a study of the borough plan and negotiated a constitutional amendment that was adopted in 1952. This amendment restored the 1911 plan and permitted chartered cities to amend their charters to create a borough system for the whole or any part of the city. As yet, no city has made use of this provision.

EXTRATERRITORIAL POWERS OF CITIES

Inasmuch as the constitution recognizes both counties and cities, it may be reasoned that those who wrote the Constitution of 1879 assumed that a city would exercise jurisdiction solely within its borders; that it would not be a general-enterprise corporation offering services to or enforcing regulations upon those who resided outside. This was the assumption or frame of reference that was commonly expressed in legal commentaries on city government in the United States. Evidently it never occurred to the members of the constitutional convention that California cities might, a short time later, seek to go far beyond their borders to acquire water-bearing lands and to construct dams, aqueducts, power stations, and other works to bring water and electricity to the city's inhabitants. Nor did it occur to them that a city might wish to establish sewer treatment and disposal plants outside the city in order to place a nuisance as far away from its citizens and residents as possible. In any case, the constitution was silent on the subject. When a city was first challenged on extraterritorial exercise of powers, the courts ruled that if a power were clearly given a city for the benefit of its inhabitants, it might exercise the power outside its territorial limits in order to accomplish the purpose.[24] Two tests were to be applied: did the city clearly have power to perform the function, and was the performance for the benefit of the city's inhabitants?

---

[23] *Crose* v. *Los Angeles*, 175 Cal. 774, 167 P. 386 (1917). Wilmington residents had sought to force the Los Angeles City Council to implement a petition requesting an election on the establishment of a borough.

[24] *McBean* v. *City of Fresno*, 112 Cal. 159, 44 P. 358 (1896).

When the Progressives obtained an amendment in 1911 to clarify and strengthen the power of municipalities to acquire and operate utility works, the question of extraterritorial power became extremely important. One problem was to give constitutional approval to municipalities that wished to acquire and operate light, water, power, heat, transportation, telephone, and communications systems for the benefit of their own inhabitants. The companion question was: should municipal corporations be permitted to become enterprisers for the supply of these services to persons or businesses located outside but adjacent to the undertaking cities? A city that acquired water-bearing lands outside its limits might wish to sell some of its water to farmers and to residents of neighboring small towns. To deny such authority might create great hardships and disturbances in the economy of the area from which the water was to be taken. Conceivably, a city that generated hydroelectric power at its plants located in thinly populated rural areas might sell it to local inhabitants without undertaking to sell power generally in other, more developed areas in competition with private firms. The constitutional amendment gave broad authority to any municipality to "furnish such services to inhabitants outside its boundaries," and left it tacitly to the Legislature and the courts to determine if curbs on this broad grant of authority were desirable. The home-rule principle had become so thoroughly established, however, that this amendment recognized one curb: a municipality seeking to supply utility services within another's borders would be required to obtain the consent of the other city's council.

Municipal Utilities Exempt from State Regulation

The Progressive-sponsored amendment in 1911 that authorized municipal operation of public utilities was tender toward municipal home rule in several respects. Although the Progressives strengthened the power of the state Railroad Commission to supervise public utilities and fix their rates, this amendment clearly exempted municipally owned utilities from state regulation.[25] This exemption was interpreted by the courts to release a municipality from obtaining a certificate of convenience and necessity from the Railroad Commission for construction and maintenance of electric plants and distributing systems.[26] After 1911 the municipalities were largely free of all state control regarding utilities. Local policy-making machinery determined the extent to which the municipality would compete with the private sector of the economy or with other public agencies. Disputes between pub-

---

[25] *California Constitution*, Art. XII, sec. 23.
[26] *Gas etc. Corporation* v. *Department of Public Service*, 52 Cal. App. 27, 197 P. 962 (1921).

licly owned utilities over territory to be served were to be settled by negotiation between cities. Rates and service policies were to be governed by local political processes.

COUNTIES GIVEN HOME RULE

California was the first state to extend to counties some of the home-rule opportunities that had been given to municipalities. Although county home rule does not permit the same expansiveness in regard to local government functions and powers as does the municipal type, it gives counties that choose to accept it an opportunity to strengthen themselves by reshaping their governmental structure. In California, home rule permits counties to simplify the traditionally cumbersome governmental structure and to determine the salaries for most of their officers and employees. California first extended this authority to counties at a time when interest in local government was running high, and it enabled some urban counties to compete with the municipalities with some degree of equality.

County home rule was championed initially by the Progressive wing of the Republican party. In the 1909 session of the Legislature, they were defeated in their effort to sponsor a constitutional amendment authored by Assemblyman Drew of Fresno.[27] However, they succeeded in placing a county home-rule plank in the 1910 Republican party platform. The statement urged the state to adopt "A county government act which shall provide an improved system of county government, with the greatest possible measure of home rule compatible with necessary uniformity." [28] This proposal was supported further by Governor Hiram Johnson in his inaugural address in 1911.[29] The Governor quoted State Controller Nye with approval, citing the large number of county salary schedules and changes in general laws pertaining to details of county affairs that came routinely before the Legislature. Both officials urged that each county be permitted "to draft its own county government act, subject to ratification by the Legislature." The legislative session that followed immediately after the inauguration drafted a constitutional amendment permitting any county, regardless of its size, to prepare a charter in which it could choose the method of selecting all officers excepting the board of supervisors, provide for consolidation of offices, determine local salaries, and accomplish a miscellany of other matters. Chartered counties remained subject to general state laws, however, in regard to their

---

[27] Franklin Hichborn, *Story of the Session of the California Legislature of 1911* (San Francisco: James H. Barry, 1911), pp. 327–328.

[28] *Ibid.*, p. xxi.

[29] *Ibid.*, p. xiii.

powers and functions. The voters ratified the amendment in November, 1911.

COUNTIES AUTHORIZED TO PERFORM MUNICIPAL FUNCTIONS

County governments were further strengthened and given a more prominent role in metropolitan affairs by constitutional amendments adopted in 1914 permitting them to undertake municipal functions for cities within their boundaries. The amendments were worded in permissive language and depended upon city and county charter revision and state general legislation for implementation.[30] Enabling legislation was adopted at the same session, pending approval of the constitutional policy by the voters.[31] Thus two significant procedures for metropolitan simplification—functional consolidation and the intergovernmental contract—were launched with constitutional approval.

THE ELECTORAL VETO: THE REFERENDUM

No subjects were added to the list of constitutionally required local government referenda between 1879, when the second constitution was adopted, and the legislative session in 1911. Several were added at that and succeeding sessions and elections. First, the amendment that gave counties the opportunity to prepare home rule charters required a referendum before a charter could be adopted, amended, or surrendered. Another amendment authorized chartered cities to establish a borough plan, subject to approval by a majority of voters in the affected area.

Local political skirmishes over proposed metropolitan government adjustments that took place throughout the state between 1914 and 1922 produced marked interest in the use of the referendum as a device to retard or halt formal coördination or integration of local governments. First, any city council that sought to arrange for the county to perform a municipal function was required to submit the proposal to a local referendum. Two different procedures for bringing about metropolitan integration by means of city-county consolidation were added to the constitution in 1918. Approval of either plan was contingent upon a referendum in each county and city involved in the consolidation. Finally, in 1922, a specification was added that no city could be consolidated with another without the approval of a majority

---

[30] *California Constitution*, Art. XI, secs. 6 and 7½, paragraph 4½.

[31] *Cal. Stats.* (1913), chap. 329, p. 667. The statute limited the scope of this authorization to counties that had adopted a charter. At the time of adoption, this applied only to Los Angeles County, the only county that had prepared a freeholder county charter.

of the voters of the city being annexed. Prior to that date, eight cities had consolidated with Los Angeles. Some had acted by council action only, and some had also obtained approval of a popular majority. Los Angeles used the new procedure successfully on a few occasions, but in general, interest in municipal consolidation throughout the state waned after the referendum was required.

The most recent addition to the referendum list is clearly based upon distrust of the elected local council. An amendment adopted in 1933 required any general-law city or county that desired to appropriate from its general funds a sum larger than 105 per cent of its expenditures in the previous year, to secure the approval of a majority of those voting in an election held for the purpose.

Analysis of the constitutional requirements for local referenda indicates no consistent pattern or theory. Why, for example, should the constitution require a referendum on the question of consolidating one municipality with another, yet be silent with regard to creating or disincorporating a city? One would seem to be no more fundamental a question than the other. One explanation is that statute law has required a referendum for incorporation and dissolution of municipalities for so many years that it did not seem important to add those procedural requirements to the constitution. On the other hand, consolidation, which is a more recent subject of contention, was not covered by statutory specification until after the constitution was amended. By giving it a place in constitutional law, greater emphasis was given to this subject.

Constant additions to constitutional and statute law have produced a complicated set of rules that will condition any set of strategies for adjustment of government in metropolitan areas in this state. Both sources of the rules, the constitution and statutes, must be looked at together. In the next chapter, we consider the elaboration and expansion of the rules made by statutory enactments.

FOUR

Legal Constraints: Legislation

THE CALIFORNIA CONSTITUTION has left much of the law-making regarding local government and intergovernmental relations to the Legislature. The Constitution of 1879 made certain prohibitions upon legislative action, but it charged the Legislature with responsibility for enacting general statutes that would mark out policy and establish a framework of local government for the state. This the Legislature proceeded to do in 1883 when it enacted the first omnibus legislation on municipal government.

LEGISLATIVE ACTIONS ROUNDING OUT THE LEGAL FRAMEWORK FOR CITIES

Legislation for local government has not been kept in the framework of all-encompassing omnibus statutes. Soon after the adoption of the second state constitution, the Legislature followed a constitutional suggestion by classifying both cities and counties according to population and enacting legislation for classes of local governments. Furthermore, the legislation for a particular class of cities or counties was not confined to comprehensive statutes for each group. In the larger cities, one-city classes often resulted. In counties, each county was assigned to a separate class. Statutes pertaining entirely to one element of subject matter were often adopted without any reference to other statutes that related to the same city or county. Because no effort was made to treat the subjects of local government systematically and exhaustively in codes or comprehensive statutes, the pattern of legislation was often inconsistent and spotted.

As details were added to the constitution, legislation often filled in their substance. Because the constitutional sections were often legislative in nature, distinctions between basic, constitutional principles and statutory matters became blurred. Neither the constitutional sections relating to local government nor the numerous statutory enactments reflected an internally consistent theory of the nature and characteristics of local governments. Both represented the piecemeal growth of policy statements. Neither had as its basic guide a statement of concepts as to what local government was expected to be or to do. Both were based upon assumptions that were made when the state was thinly populated and when its economy was largely based upon cattle raising, farming, and mining. Implications of the growth of urban areas into vast metropolitan complexes were reflected only by attempts to provide isolated statutory approvals for some local efforts.

The statutory framework for local government in California has been dominated by the philosophy, expressed in the Constitution of 1879, that the state should abdicate from its central role of determining public interest and expressing policies for the benefit of the state as a whole. By so abdicating for a considerable period of time, it threw local elements upon their own devices and encouraged them to Balkanize the state. As the implications of changes in the economy and social structure became more evident, the state was urged by some to reassert a role of leadership. However, the legislative and executive branches found themselves confronted with sets of local interests that had become accustomed to a theory of government that emphasized localism. Furthermore, this localism was based upon a system of government that had relatively few substantive rules. It was a political system, characterized by struggle and competition.

DETERMINING STANDARDS FOR INCORPORATION OF CITIES

The pattern of action by which cities have been organized since the second constitution became effective was established by the Municipal Corporation Act of 1883.[1] Two basic principles in this pattern have continued without modification. First, a municipal corporation is considered to be a voluntary creation, brought into being only at the request of local inhabitants rather than at the instigation of the state. Second, the process by which this action is accomplished is political in the basic sense of the term. It is one in which contending forces negotiate a decision by argument, persuasion, and the use of influence and political power. The two principles tend to interact.

---

[1] Later, the Municipal Corporation Act was made a part of the state's *Government Code*.

Undoubtedly the creation of a governmental entity is a political act, whether the end product created is a nation-state or a municipality. The term "political act," however, is broad, and it is possible to create a governmental entity in a variety of ways, some of which may contain "built-in" elements that will invite contentions and struggles. Viewed in the light of conditions that existed in 1883, California's Municipal Corporation Act probably did not appear to its sponsors to contain such elements of contention. Yet by the mid-twentieth century, conditions existing in the state's metropolitan areas demonstrated that the act contained several built-in elements. Inasmuch as the initiative to organize a city must come from local leaders, those leaders will not begin action unless they believe that there is an advantage to be gained, vis-à-vis some other group, whether it be those governing the county or those who lead another unit of government, such as another city. Furthermore, there is usually a lively political operation involved in determining which set of local residents and property owners will be assembled to initiate the process of creating a municipal corporation.

The Legislature has established certain substantive and procedural standards that must be met by those who seek to create a municipal corporation, and it has delegated the administration of incorporation proceedings to county boards of supervisors. The substantive standard that was spelled out in statute law required the proposed area to have a minimum of five hundred inhabitants.[2] No specification was made as to the extent of territory to be included, density of population on the land, resources to finance a city government, or shape of the city boundaries that would encompass the required minimum population.

The bulk of the requirements were procedural in nature, specifying steps that the proponents of an incorporation and the board of supervisors must take, as well as the manner in which they must take them. As responsibility for administering the law was delegated to the county board of supervisors in the respective counties, the process of incorporation became an exercise in tactical maneuvers within the local political area, governed by a few ground rules laid down by the state.

The procedural rules are fairly specific and limiting upon the proponents of incorporation and the county board of supervisors alike. Action may be started by a local group giving formal notice in writing to the board of supervisors of intention to circulate a petition. A valid petition must bear the signatures of at least 25 per cent of the qualified

[2] This was altered in 1957 to require a minimum of 500 registered voters for incorporation in counties having more than 2 million inhabitants (Los Angeles).

voters and represent at least 25 per cent of the land value in the area proposed for incorporation. Signers must be land owners, but the principle of "one owner, one signature" prevails, regardless of the amount of land owned. The petition must describe the boundaries of the proposed area accurately and set forth the estimated number of inhabitants. Failure to comply accurately with these requirements stops the proceeding as a legal transaction. The board of supervisors is without legal authority to proceed if petition procedures are violated at any point by the board, by its clerk, or by the petition's proponents. If the board does proceed in such circumstances, opponents of the transaction have a basis for filing a suit in the courts to invalidate the incorporation.

The board of supervisors is strictly controlled by state law at all points of the incorporation process, except one. The board may alter the boundaries of the proposed city in any manner it chooses, although it may not add property that had not been described in the petition. At one point in the procedure, property owners may file written protests against the proposal. If owners of 51 per cent of the property so protest, the proposal automatically fails. If less than 51 per cent file written protests, the board of supervisors must hold a public hearing, at which time the property owners may make protests orally. After the matter has been heard, the board of supervisors may accept or reject the protests, or accept some and reject others. This phase of the proceedings is deemed to be legislative in nature and the courts decline to interfere with or review the actions of the supervisors. In exercising its discretion to exclude parcels of property from a proposed city, the board acquires a significant political leverage. Inasmuch as members of boards of supervisors are elected by districts, the supervisor in whose district an incorporation action develops is drawn to the eye of the storm. Whether the remainder of the board members defer to that supervisor's wishes in the matter depends upon the political relationships that exist between members of the board.

At first consideration it would appear that incorporation of a city represents a compact between property owners in a given area for the purpose of creating a local government, using the machinery of the board of supervisors and the rules established by the state to accomplish this purpose. However, a property owner is not entirely a free agent in choosing to join or reject such a compact. His land may be included in the description of the proposed city by action of other persons, the sponsors of the petition, and if the board of supervisors believes that the property belongs within the boundaries they may reject the owner's protest. Such a decision may appear to be in the interest of the public good because the interests of the individual should give way to the greater interests of the community. In some instances, however, the board of supervisors leaves newly incorporated cities with irregularly shaped boundaries, by excluding some properties on the outer margin of the city but declining to exclude other properties. The decision is political, made without explicit basis or standard. Owners of unimproved property have often raised the point that they would receive no benefits of fire protection, police protection, schools, and health administration, if included in a city. Their demands have been brushed aside, in some instances, by boards of supervisors and they have received no comfort from the courts. Yet cities have been formed with "islands" of unincorporated property completely surrounded by city territory, presumably because the owner was able to prevail upon the board of supervisors.[3]

Inasmuch as no reviewing body has authority to require that property additional to that included in the petition be brought into the city in order to produce an optimum area for municipal purposes, the strategic ideas of the self-selected group of petition sponsors prevail in this matter. A sponsoring group may choose to avoid certain areas, because they estimate that the sentiments of voters in those areas will be opposed to their own on certain issues once the city is organized. A variety of other reasons peculiar to the individual community situation may motivate a group of incorporation sponsors.

The last significant stage in the political process of creating a municipal corporation is the election that is held within the area to be organized. The county is responsible for conducting the election and the board of supervisors is required to canvass the returns. Although the incorporation petition must be signed by property owners, the election is determined by registered voters who are on the voter rolls at the time the petition is circulated. A simple majority of those who participate in the election determines the result. Upon completion of the canvass, and if a majority is found to favor the incorporation, the county must file the results of the election with the secretary of state. This filing completes the procedure, and the municipal corporation begins its legal existence at that time.

Activities engaged in by some partisans in a number of emotionally charged incorporation struggles produced a reaction that caused the

---

[3] Prior to 1951 it was possible to exclude parcels of land that lay within the heart of the proposed city and were surrounded completely by parts of the city. A number of cities have had these "islands" in their midst. Legislation forbids exclusion of land if it will result in the formation of an unincorporated island within a city.

Legislature to adopt a number of restrictions upon the circulation of incorporation petitions. These changes have been made since 1951. A number of communities had been kept in continuous turmoil over a period of years by repeated efforts by small groups to promote incorporations. The rule now in effect directs that if an incorporation effort proceeds to the election stage and is defeated, no sponsoring group may file a new petition in the area for two years.[4]

Other restrictions have been enacted in an effort to reduce confusion arising out of competition between incorporations and annexation efforts. When a group of local citizens seeks incorporation of a populous unincorporated area that is located adjacent to or near an established city, groups opposed to this plan may make a counterproposal to annex the area to the city. In the 1950's, there were several such contests in which opposing groups were seeking to incorporate and to annex the same parcels of property at the same time. At that time the law had laid down no rules to cover such a situation or to determine priorities for the alternative actions. The lack of explicit rules caused the competitors to turn to the courts in search of support for their partisan views. In an effort to restore some orderliness to the proceedings and reduce the need for resort to the courts, the Legislature established certain priorities and required additional procedures. The rule now in effect requires that when a notice of intention to circulate an incorporation is filed, no annexation action may be started with respect to any part of the area for ninety days thereafter. In order to bring the incorporation efforts more into the open, the clerk of the county board of supervisors is also required to notify the city councils of any cities whose borders touch upon the proposed city. The adjacent cities have no official part in the proceedings, but this action by the board clerk does give them public notice, in the event that they are planning to negotiate any annexations.

A significant feature in the legal characteristics of a municipal corporation is that once it is created it has continuing legal existence until it takes steps in accordance with state law to liquidate its affairs. Mere failure to perform functions or to levy taxes does not dissolve a municipal corporation. Therefore, when one contemplates reorganizing the governmental structure in a metropolitan area, the point becomes immediately evident that the success of any action that would alter the territory or jeopardize the existence of a municipal corporation depends upon the wishes of the voters in the municipality. The electorate holds a firm veto power over dissolution proposals.

---

[4] *California Government Code,* Sec. 34325.1 as amended in 1957.

PROCEDURES FOR DISSOLVING A CITY

Action to disincorporate a city may be started only by a petition signed by 20 per cent of the qualified voters. The petition is presented to the council; upon receipt of it, the council must call a special election in which a simple majority of those voting determines the outcome. Division and liquidation of property, equipment, and accounts of a disincorporated city become tasks of the county government. A city that has employed a group of employees, constructed public buildings, acquired property with which to provide parks and recreation areas, and acquired other assets is likely to find outright dissolution too complex to be attractive. Few cities in California have dissolved their corporate status.

Consolidation with another city has proven to be a more useful method by which to alter a municipality's status. In metropolitan areas, where there are several cities with adjacent boundaries, consolidation attracts those who are interested in simplifying and integrating the governmental structure. California statute law offers two choices of legal proceedings to bring about merger of two or more cities, the Consolidation Acts of 1909 and 1913. In consolidation, as in incorporation and disincorporation, the local electorate holds a firm veto power. Action may be started only by petition. Under the 1909 act, the petition must be signed by at least one-fifth of the registered voters in each of the cities involved in the proceeding. Upon completion of such petitions, the city council of the larger city must submit the matter to an election in each city, after publishing notices in accordance with the state law.[5] Each city is responsible, however, for conducting the election within its jurisdiction. In order to canvass the results, the councils of the consolidating cities convene in joint session. If a majority of those voting in each city favors the consolidation, the proposal succeeds.

The 1913 act offers a set of procedures that differ in several particulars from those earlier and that were devised to apply in instances where group or factional rivalries are vigorously skirmishing. They are somewhat less cumbersome, in that they eliminate the requirement of a referendum in the larger city. Possibly this was eliminated because the larger city's electorate tended to exhibit a greater degree of lethargy towards the referendum. Had all the consolidation efforts with which the city of Los Angeles was involved been processed under the 1909 act, the voters of that city would have faced frequent special elections in certain years.

---

[5] *Ibid.*, Sec. 35708 *et seq.*

A group of five electors may file notice of intention to circulate a petition with the council of the city that seeks to consolidate. If the council approves the notice, no other petition for consolidation with any city may be initiated in that city for the next thirty days. Under the 1913 act, the petition must contain a slightly higher percentage of registered voters than that required by the 1909 act—one-fourth instead of one-fifth. The election under the 1913 act need take place only in the city that seeks to consolidate. If a majority of the voters approve, the proposition is put before the council of the larger city for approval. Only in the event that the council rejects the proposal does it become necessary to consult the voters of the larger city. Other procedures are approximately the same under both statutes.

Both consolidation acts were based upon the assumption that the smaller city would initiate consolidation with a larger neighbor. The city proposing the consolidation is required to pay the expenses incurred in the proceedings, and the ordinances of the smaller city are superseded by those of the larger. Debts and public property belonging to the smaller city are taken over by the larger one.

POLICIES FOR ANNEXATION

Policies governing the annexation of land to incorporated cities are chiefly the product of statutes in California. The constitution makes scarcely any specifications concerning the subject. However, the decision in 1879 to prohibit the Legislature from passing special acts transformed annexation from a matter of state policy to one chiefly local. Prior to that action, state policy prevailed, and many cities had their boundaries enlarged by state legislation. Since the proscription of this procedure, the state has determined policy only in a broad sense by establishing certain standards intended to control local actions. The initiative for local action and the direction it takes are solely the results of interplay between local political forces.

Legislative policies governing annexation revolve around four propositions. It is assumed that as land changes from rural to urban uses, owners and residents will find it desirable to bring that land within the jurisdiction of a city in order to become eligible for the type of services that a city is legally capable of providing. It follows that the initiative for bringing about annexation will be exercised by those who will benefit directly by the action, for example, the land owners and residents. The third proposition assumes that the normal pattern of city growth will be one of consecutive expansions, extending outward from a central base of territory. Therefore, it is plausibly required that territory annexed must be contiguous to the city with which it is to be joined. Finally, the state exercises its responsibility by specifying procedures that are uniform in application and detailed in prescription in order to condition the local political processes.

Change of Land Use. In a basic sense, annexation is a result of urban growth and land-use change. Inasmuch as state policy divides local governments into urban and rural instruments, it is logical to assume that when the characteristics of a community change from rural to urban, the area will transfer from a governing unit that provides rural services to one that provides urban-type services. Had the simple dichotomy of counties and cities that the 1879 constitution provided continued to prevail, this assumption would have been realistic. However, two other legislatively developed policies have tended to blur the distinction between urban and rural forms of government. First, the Legislature chose to create special districts, and that type of local unit became very attractive to residents of areas shifting from truly rural conditions towards an urban status. Many suburban areas have used a variety of special districts to fill their requirements for local services, and hence have not annexed to cities. Second, the Legislature authorized counties to undertake numerous functions that had traditionally been the prerogatives of cities. The urban county, with its sheriff-directed police force, its county library system, its health department, and its park and recreation program, tended to meet the needs of many suburban communities and slow their initiative for annexation. Often special districts were governed by the county board of supervisors, and in such cases the county government was in a particularly strong position to discourage annexation or blunt the desire for it.

Local Initiative for Governmental Change. As suggested above, annexation under California law is a process that involves negotiation. In inhabited areas, the initiative to commence annexation proceedings formally is given exclusively to the residents of the area that is outside the city. A city is unable to initiate annexation officially except where the land being sought is uninhabited. Although a city may be anxious to annex inhabited territory, it is forced either to maintain the fiction that it is a passive agency or to resort to unofficial, even covert, efforts to encourage the residents of the desired area to propose annexation.

The principle that appears to govern California statute law in this matter might be called "the local-benefit principle." So long as property owners are reasonably satisfied with the services provided by county government and special districts, they may decline to initiate annexation proceedings. Whenever they believe that they may benefit by a transfer to a city, they may initiate negotiations to accomplish that objective. However, this process of choosing or negotiating a benefit is not as free to all the interested parties as it may seem at first glance. The state law lays down no standard regarding how few or how many persons are required to be inhabitants of an area that may be proposed for annexation or what amount of land may constitute a single parcel for negotiating an annexation. In the absence of such specifications, the determination of which parcels of land and which inhabitants shall be formed into a parcel or tract for purposes of working out an annexation decision is left open to political maneuver and manipulation. It is equally possible to put together in one annexation only those parcels of land whose inhabitants may favor the move or to combine a majority known to favor the proposal with a carefully selected opposition minority whose land may be included in order to give tax strength or to round out boundaries. The range of possible combinations is extensive.

Annexation policy represents a continuation of the principle that controls incorporation, and it suffers from the same basic defect. It is based upon the principle that no agency outside the community should determine which parcels of land and which set of inhabitants shall be joined in a municipal corporation. Neither has a single property owner the power to make this decision. Annexation and incorporation actions are entirely within the province of a locally constituted electorate majority. However, as we have seen, such a majority may be manipulated to suit the interests of some local groups and thwart the desires of others.

In a metropolitan situation, where several municipalities are involved, the influences that affect the annexation process differ considerably from those that operate in a situation where a single city is surrounded chiefly by rural or suburban areas. In a metropolis, a suburban community may have a choice of more than one city with which to annex. It may also choose the alternative of incorporating as a city, if it has the prerequisite amount of population and territory. No state policy-preference is expressed in the statute. The only criterion that applies is that the annexing territory must be contiguous to the city it proposes to join. This criterion, however, often complicates the process. If the area proposed for annexation is not actually contiguous to the city, sufficient land must be included to provide a connecting link.

There are various open, official actions that a city government may take with the intent of making annexations attractive to both the residents and the property owners of adjacent unincorporated areas. A city that is planning to encourage annexation may locate fire stations and other facilities near its borders, thus exhibiting its preparation to serve an expanded area. Its municipal library may extend book-borrowing privileges to residents adjacent to the city without fee or with minimum fees. Other less formal administrative actions may demonstrate the city's preparedness to serve an adjacent area. Attitudes of the city council and key administrative officials towards annexing a particular area have much to do with developing public opinion therein. It is not unusual for city administrators to meet with residents of an area where annexation is being discussed. If the city government is interested in encouraging annexation, these informal discussions can become important determinants in the negotiations. A city council may adopt an official policy that accepts annexations without charge of an entrance fee, making available to them all city-owned facilities and services at the regular, annual municipal tax rate. Such a policy places the cost of constructing public works and of organizing the municipal services upon the property owners and taxpayers of the original city. It also creates a favorable psychological effect among residents and property owners of the annexing territory towards the transfer, because no lump-sum liabilities have to be met before the benefits of municipal services can be obtained.

Annexation charges are subject to negotiation, in a broad sense. State law permits, but does not require, the annexing area to vote upon whether it will contribute to repayment of bond debts incurred by the city previous to the annexation. A city may choose to establish such charges; it is discretionary with the city council. A few California cities have set a scale of charges for annexations, the justification being that new areas ought to contribute towards the repayment of the outlay that the city had made to create its police and fire protection systems, water plants, lighting equipment, libraries, and other public facilities.

Many suburban areas undoubtedly consider the strength of the city's government and the quality of its administration when they negotiate annexation. They also consider its political or controlling interest-group complexion. Cities that offer a high quality of administrative performance are likely to attract areas to apply for annexation. A low property-tax rate, coupled with moderately high service levels for administration, make a city most attractive.

The motivations that may induce a city governing body to seek or to accept annexation of territory may be varied indeed. In most instances it may simply be a desire to integrate newly developed areas with the older section in order to maintain a semblance of economic and political unity. The newer growth may have been made necessary by the fact that land within the city's original boundaries had been fully developed and economic trends caused those seeking housing or industrial expansion to obtain lands outside the city. It may have resulted from subdivision activities by developers in areas outside the city, making lands available for urban uses and seeking to market them in competition with property within the city. Merchants in the central area may desire to have a new residential community annexed in order to assure that the residents will become accustomed to shopping in their city rather than in a rival community.

Increasing the population total of the city appears to be a continuing goal that appeals to municipal political leaders and commercial boosters alike. Ability to cite an increasing population conceivably advertises the community's assets. Numbers alone may, of course, multiply problems by increasing the demands for municipal services without commensurately increasing the wealth of the community to support the added services. Yet, population-count does produce certain favorable results. Distribution of state subventions, such as the municipal share of the state-collected gasoline tax, is based upon population. Population, as well as municipal boundaries, is taken into consideration when districts are organized for election of county supervisors, state legislators, and members of congress. Hence, extension of municipal boundaries affects the influence of municipal political leaders and groups.

Annexation also serves defensive purposes. It may be used to prevent objectionable land uses from being established where the city has no jurisdiction. It may also prevent an area from incorporating as a city and becoming a potential rival for area influence. Similarly, it may be employed to prevent another municipality from extending its area and influence. All these commercial-political rivalries have been demonstrated in the use of the annexation process.

Contiguity of Territory. The assumption that a city will grow in an orderly fashion by annexing contiguous territory as areas around the city change from rural to urban characteristics is understandable if it is also assumed that an incorporated city represents a community of interest among those who organized it. The "doctrine of contiguity" seeks merely to ensure that the territorial base of the city will remain intact and in one continuous piece of land.

In the American law of municipal corporations, the "doctrine of contiguity" developed from judge-made theories about what an incorporated city should be.[6] In the absence of statutory specifications about the character of territory to be annexed, the courts have insisted upon contiguity as a criterion for any annexation.[7] Early cases in states other than California appear to be based upon the judges' belief that the basic nature of a municipality dictated that the territory be of one piece and therefore contiguous.[8] The point was seldom argued or elaborated. It seemed to follow from the point that a municipality was limited in its jurisdiction to those persons and parcels of property that were located within its boundaries. The thought that two or more sets of areas that were divided by intervening territory of another unit of government could operate under a single legal jurisdiction seemed to be rejected as contrary to the nature of the system.

California cases that invoke the "doctrine of contiguity" refer to "the free flow of commerce" as a criterion that controls judgment of the facts.[9] This would appear to place the whole matter on the base of commercial convenience and not upon legal jurisdiction or upon administrative convenience for city administrative officials. The growth in the number of governing units in a metropolitan area presents several situations that undermine confidence in the "doctrine of contiguity." It is difficult to understand how commerce is any more adversely affected by a situation in which a city comprises several noncontiguous parcels of territory, than it is by a situation wherein several local governments operate adjacent to each other in the same metropolitan area. Presumably the free flow of commerce is accomplished along streets and highways. It is possible, of course, that if a city annexed a noncontiguous area, streets in the intervening strip of land might be different in width or standard of paving. Yet this can scarcely be a different situation than that which exists in a metropolitan area in which more than seventy cities and a county operate. Intergovernmental coöperation and extragovernmental pressures from groups interested in transportation and related matters tend to produce uniformity in the street pattern and in maintenance standards. State construction of highways and freeways has provided a completely new influence upon the "free flow of commerce" and offers an alternative to local streets.

---

[6] John F. Dillon, *Treatise on the Law of Municipal Corporations* (Chicago: James Cockcroft, 1872), p. 167; Chester James Antieau, *Municipal Corporation Law* (New York: Matthew Bender, 1958), I, 34.

[7] *City of Denver* v. *Coulehan*, 20 Colo. 471, 39 P. 425 (1894).

[8] *Railway Co.* v. *Town of Oconto*, 50 Wis. 189, 6 N.W. 607; *Smith* v. *Sherry*, 50 Wis. 210, 6 N.W. 561 (1880).

[9] *People ex rel. Peck* v. *City of Los Angeles*, 154 Cal. 220, 97 P. 311 (1908); *People ex rel. City of Pasadena* v. *City of Monterey Park*, 40 Cal. App. 715, 181 P. 825 (1919).

If one of the purposes of a city is to support commercial and industrial activity by supplying municipal services, the doctrine of contiguity may not be necessary to accomplish that purpose. A city might supply water, sewer facilities, electric power and other services requiring pipes, lines and other fixed facilities to a noncontiguous area with no greater inconvenience than it could supply most contiguous areas. It would be necessary for the city to obtain easements along the streets in the intervening territory, but it would not be essential that the city have contiguous area in order to accomplish its purposes. For many years, the city of Los Angeles has held easements through other cities and along streets in unincorporated territory in the county, for operation of water mains, sewer lines, and power cables that serve various portions of the city. Although all territory within the city of Los Angeles is theoretically contiguous, many portions that have been annexed are shaped in such a manner that utility lines could not easily connect if forced to follow routes entirely within city territory. The main sewer-outfall line, for example, extends from the central area of Los Angeles, through Culver City and county territory and into the Westchester portion of the city, to its ultimate destination on Santa Monica Bay. A different but related type of situation is presented by the Los Angeles City aqueduct that brings water from the Owens Valley and by the power lines that bring electrical energy from the Colorado River generating plants. Both municipal utility systems are located on easements that have been granted by other municipalities and counties along their routes. Under existing policies, Los Angeles could not have annexed contiguous territory to provide the necessary routes for these systems.

The doctrine of contiguity does not appear to be supported by requirements of administrative convenience. Police and fire vehicles can operate between two noncontiguous portions of a city, and other municipal employees reach various locations without hindrance. Modern cities are not walled and moated citadels. Los Angeles municipal vehicles move freely over the streets of Beverly Hills when traveling between the Wilshire and West Los Angeles areas. If a noncontiguous portion of a city were sufficiently large and populous to warrant provision of separate police and fire facilities, they could be provided in the same manner that branch stations are established in the larger cities.

Certainty about jurisdiction of a city government would be no less sure without the doctrine of contiguity than under the present rule. Jurisdiction of city police and the enforcement of city ordinances would be no different than at present. Similarly, a city's jurisdiction for assessment and collection of taxes would remain unchanged.

The completely unrealistic quality of each of these supposed justifications for the requirement of contiguity is well illustrated by the annexation completed by the city of San Diego in 1958, when the area annexed was rendered contiguous to the city by a strip of land that lay under the waters of San Diego Bay! By no stretch of the imagination could this be justified on the basis of protecting the free flow of commerce. In this instance the flow of commerce, if any, would have had to be induced where none had ever existed before.

This discussion of the rule of contiguity in the annexation of territory has been raised to illustrate some of the consequences of applying such a doctrine after conditions changed from a relatively simple situation to a highly complex metropolitan one. New policies, as well as new conditions, have invalidated the rigidly held doctrine of contiguity of territory. Yet in California, the Legislature, in specifying that any territory annexed must be contiguous to the city, has adopted the doctrine that was originated by the courts.[10]

One of the more significant consequences of the application of the doctrine of contiguity to annexation proceedings has been the so-called "strip annexation." This type of annexation is the product of maneuvers by cities and by groups of fringe area residents to secure an advantage over their competitors. It arises, in part, from efforts to link a tract or community that is not contiguous to a city by means of a narrow strip of land. Often such linkage is drawn in that fashion because surrounding land owners are opposed to annexation, or the area has not developed a "ripeness" of land utilization that makes it attractive to the city. Therefore, strip annexation is often a symptom of a skimming process that produces a disorderly governmental and economic growth, not to mention fostering inequities in levels of governmental service. Strip annexation is frequently a defensive strategy. By acquiring a strip comprising either inhabited or uninhabited territory, one city may successfully prevent another from annexing intervening territory, inasmuch as the doctrine of contiguity prevents cities from leapfrogging each other's borders. Los Angeles and Long Beach have made especially extensive use of this technique, although numerous cities in California have also used it. One consequence arising from the use of the strip technique is an irregularly shaped municipal boundary, contradicting the concept that municipal growth follows a regular pattern in the form of concentric circles around the original core of the city.

The Legislature has been made aware that strip annexation is troublesome and has attempted to develop a substantive criterion for the dimensions of future annexations. This is limited to a negative

---

[10] *California Government Code*, Secs. 35104, 35302.

definition of the term "contiguity": "Territory shall not be deemed contiguous as the word 'contiguous' is used in this chapter if the only contiguity is based on a strip of land over 300 feet long and less than 200 feet wide, such width to be exclusive of highways. . . ." [11] The new prescription does not eliminate strip annexation, although it does rule out the most extreme possibilities. The basic element of the problem remains untouched.

Uniformity of Procedure. Annexation procedures, like those for incorporation, are uniform in application throughout the state. They apply equally in a county that has one municipality and in one that has sixty or more municipalities. Two broad distinctions are made in procedural requirements, however. One set of provisions applies to inhabited territories, and a different set to uninhabited areas. Annexation of inhabited territory is initiated by petitions circulated within the area that is seeking to join the city. The first step consists of presenting an informal notice to the city council and requesting permission to proceed. In cities having a planning commission, this informal petition must be submitted to the commission for report and recommendation, which must be given within a specified time. Upon receipt of the report, the city council may either consent to or reject the proposal.

In the 1950's, it became clearly evident that in metropolitan areas annexation was a highly competitive process in which there was much manipulation. In view of this, the Legislature changed the procedural rules slightly in an effort to minimize overt conflicts between cities that were ambitious to annex and between rival groups within urban fringe areas. Under the new rule, when a city council approves an application to circulate an annexation petition, a moratorium upon competing activities becomes effective for fifty days. No petitions to incorporate the area may be filed, no notices of intention to circulate annexation petitions may be filed with any other city, and no adjacent city may commence action to annex any portion of the area as uninhabited territory. The annexation proposal and a description of the territory involved must next be submitted to the county government for checking. A county boundary commission is required to verify the described boundaries, the records of ownership, and the assessment of parcels of property located within the proposed area. The county has no authority, however, to pass upon the merits of the proposed annexation.

At the next stage, the proponents are required to publish a notice of intention to circulate a petition, publication to be in accordance

---

[11] *Ibid.,* Sec. 35002.5.

with specifications set forth in the statute. A petition requesting annexation must be signed by at least one-fourth of the registered voters
living within the territory. After the completed petition has been filed
with the clerk of the city council, the council must give a public hearing to those who wish to protest. The city is required to notify all
property owners in the affected area of the hearing, and to publish the
notice in a newspaper of general circulation for two weeks. If written
protests are filed by a majority of the property owners, the proceeding
fails. If there is not a majority protest, the city council may, at its discretion, cancel the annexation or call an election. The city is responsible for conducting the election.

The decision on annexation rests chiefly with the majority of those
voting, although the city council exercises discretion to approve or
reject the proposal. If the council declines to accept the annexation,
after it has been approved by a majority of those voting in the area,
the matter must be submitted to the city's voters at the next general
election.

Annexation of *uninhabited* territory has accounted for much municipal expansion since World War II, because many subdivisions were
offered by the developer for annexation prior to sale of land and the
arrival of home owners. Therefore, this type of annexation often results
from closely-guarded negotiations between land developers and city
councils. It is also used to bring lands owned by a governmental
agency into a city. In some instances, a city annexes its own water-
bearing lands, airport, or other municipally owned property to facilitate control and service. In other instances, annexation has been used
to gain jurisdiction over a county park or a federally owned naval base
or air station. On several occasions, a city has annexed state-owned
tidelands and beaches.

The statute defines an "uninhabited" area, for the purpose of municipal annexation, as an area adjacent to a city and having less than
twelve registered voters residing in it. Action may be initiated either
by the city council or by one-fourth of the owners of the land being
proposed for annexation. Regardless of which party initiates the proceeding, the county boundary commission must be given a formal
notice of intention in order that it may check the accuracy of the
description of the proposed area. If the description is found to be
accurate, the city council may proceed or the property owners may
circulate and present a petition. Notices must be published and must
also be mailed to owners of property in the proposed area. A time
must be set in which to receive written protests. Protests filed by owners representing one-half the value of the privately owned property or

by a governmental agency that represents one-half the total value may quash the proceedings. However, if there are no protests or the number falls short of the required percentage, the city council may decide without further guidance or limitation.

Exclusion of Territory from Cities. In legislative policy, exclusion of territory from an incorporated city is clearly not intended to be merely the reverse of incorporation. Although it has been assumed that there might be some conditions under which property and the residents thereon should be allowed to sever membership in a municipal corporation, procedural restrictions continue to limit the opportunities severely.

In 1889, the Legislature adopted a policy based upon the assumption that any exclusion or withdrawal of territory would be for the purpose of returning it to unincorporated status under county jurisdiction.[12] No thought was given to the possibility that a section of a city might wish to transfer to a neighboring one. The thought that a city might lose "consumers" of its services by their withdrawal from the compact by which the corporation was formed seems to have been completely contrary to the dominant theory regarding the nature of a municipal corporation.

So long as an area is unincorporated, but adjacent to a city, it possesses a considerable negotiating strength and may choose from several courses of action. Once the die is cast for annexation, the situation changes completely, and the decision is well-nigh irrevocable.

The procedure for excluding territory is comparable to that for annexation in that it begins with a petition. The number of signatures required for this petition, however, is such as to guarantee that most such efforts will never achieve their goal. To qualify, the petition must be signed by a majority of the qualified electors of the entire city, measured by the vote cast at the previous general municipal election. If an exclusion petition qualifies, the city council is required to submit the proposition to a special election. A majority vote in the area to be excluded, as well as a majority in the city at large, is required. If an area succeeds in winning exclusion, it is bound to pay its proportionate share of the bonded indebtedness incurred by the city during the time the area was a part of the municipality. After the exclusion is completed, any group of ten taxpayers, who are residents either of the area or the city, may petition the superior court of the county to determine

---

[12] *Ibid.*, Secs. 35500–35600. Sections pertaining to exclusion of inhabited territory are based upon *Cal. Stats.* (1889), chap. 280; those for uninhabited territory are based upon *Cal. Stats.* (1913), chap. 346.

the relative responsibilities of the area and the city for the bonded indebtedness.[13]

The terminology used in the statute is interesting. The term "exclusion" suggests that the larger portion of a city might desire to force out of its corporate borders a troublesome and unwanted portion of its area. Conceivably, there may exist situations in which a majority of the city's electorate may wish to exclude a section that costs more in public works and services than it contributes in property taxes, shunting the responsibility to another tax base. But the requirement of majority approval in both the area and the city prevents any unilateral action. The "exclusion" must be by mutual consent.

It is scarcely conceivable that sufficient signatures could be secured to a petition to exclude either inhabited or uninhabited territory from cities of more than fifty thousand population. The statutes show a tender regard for minorities, particularly minorities of property owners who wish to protect a status quo, yet give no regard to the minority that believes it is not receiving its fair share of the public works and services and wishes to transfer to another jurisdiction or renew its bargaining capacity. The processes of incorporation and annexation become inflexible, by their implications that they cannot be undone once they have been accomplished. The extreme rigidity of this concept inspires many strategies, which will be discussed in later chapters.

A modified exclusion policy, adopted in 1947, allows transfer of territory between cities under rigid safeguards.[14] The process may be initiated by a petition signed by 25 per cent of the registered voters in the area that wishes to transfer. This proposal must be approved by the councils of both cities by a four-fifths majority of the members of each body. After receiving city council approval, the proposition must be submitted to a referendum in the area. If approved by a majority of those voting, the transfer becomes effective. If it fails, the subject may not be brought up again for one year. An area that transfers from one city to another is required to pay a proportionate share of bond

---

[13] *California Government Code*, Sec. 35600. Exclusion of uninhabited territory may be initiated by a petition signed by qualified electors of the city; the number of signers must be one-tenth of the number of voters in the last general election. A notice of intention must be published in a newspaper of general circulation for five days, and persons owning property in the area are permitted to enter protests in writing to the county board of supervisors. The board must hold a hearing if protests are received. The statute specifies several conditions under which protests become controlling and bar further action. If insufficient protests are received, the board of supervisors may exercise its discretion in the matter. If the board approves exclusion, however, the matter must be submitted to the city's voters. Uninhabited territory is also liable to pay its share of bond debts.

[14] *Cal. Stats.* (1947), chap. 832.

debts owned by the city it is leaving and also may become liable for a share of bond debts of the city to which it is transferring. One concludes it is reasonable to expect that there will be a few transfers between cities.

SPECIAL DISTRICTS: A FLEXIBLE DEVICE FOR LOCAL GOVERNMENT

In contrast to the constraints set upon the tactics and strategies of those who would govern metropolitan areas through municipal and county government, the special district offers vast opportunities for maneuver. The limitations upon special districts are few, and the concept of the special district offers so many opportunities for variations that it can be used to fashion almost any institution of local or regional government desired. Here the state has the opportunity to reënter the local government arena by creating new special districts, by abolishing or altering ones that exist, or by declining to act at the request of local groups that seek special treatment.

The complicated array of special districts existing in each of the metropolitan regions in California is the product of local organizational efforts[15] as well as legislative action. The constitution is almost completely silent on the subject of special districts, the one exception being school organization. When the constitution was prepared in 1879, a decision was made that schools were to be financed and administered separately from general city and county governments and governed by boards of trustees elected by district voters. From that basic policy decision, and the assumptions that related to it, the fabric of the publicly supported school system was created by legislation.

Shortly after the constitution was adopted, the Legislature chose also to use the district device to meet requirements in other functions as well as education. Almost from the start, the Legislature distinguished between two broad types of devices, each of which was termed a district. One was the assessment district and the other was the special district.

The assessment district has no corporate being and no group of employees of its own. Its purpose is to apportion the cost of some public improvement among parcels of land that receive benefits directly from the improvement. This type of unit is purely a fiscal device that is based upon a benefit theory of financing and taxation. The special assessment district has been used both for rural and urban

---

[15] See John C. Bollens, *Special District Governments in the United States* (Berkeley and Los Angeles: University of California Press, 1957).

purposes. The earlier uses in California, for reclamation and drainage, were for the benefit of rural lands. Reclamation districts were organized by statute to finance flood control works along the Sacramento River and its tributaries, and to reclaim land for agriculture. Drainage districts were formed to reclaim swamp lands for agriculture. After 1900, the Legislature authorized many types of special assessment districts permitting cities to finance street opening, widening and lighting, and other public works projects. A special assessment district is not considered a unit of government. Although this type of agency is widely employed and may continue for many years, it will not be considered further in this study.

The special district is a unit of local government, albeit one with specifically stated powers and, usually, with limited purpose. It has a governing body that is responsible for making decisions with reference to district affairs. It can own property, and usually it has its own set of employees. Enabling legislation has granted it taxing power to support the function or functions assigned to it.

The "problem" of the special district in the metropolitan area of the state arises partly from the gross number of such units that have been created, and partly from the complexity of the statute law that has been enacted to govern the creation, administration, and dissolution of these units. The Legislature has been so profligate in enacting special district statutes and so inclined to regard each subject as unique that the resulting statutory maze makes classification and systematic analysis difficult. At the same time, this maze offers extensive opportunities for manipulation by well-informed and resourceful groups.

Two sets of broad classifications that are meaningful and useful for analysis of special districts, as they relate to the government of metropolitan areas, can be made initially. One is based upon a distinction between two methods of forming special districts. The other distinguishes between districts that are local in their sphere of activity and those that are regional or metropolitan.

Creation of Districts. The majority of special districts in California are organized under general enabling statutes that pertain to particular subtypes of districts. For example, a municipal water district or a county sanitation district is organized under the enabling statute pertaining to its particular subtype. Districts that come within the broad category of general-law districts are organized upon the initiative of local groups.

A further distinction may be made between types of initiating groups. Each set of initiators is directed to proceed in a particular manner. The majority of districts that are created under general law come into being as the result of initiative taken by private, nonofficial groups who must proceed in much the same manner as those who wish to organize a municipal corporation. A lesser number of districts are organized upon·the motion of local official bodies. A few are created by the board of supervisors after it makes a finding that conditions specified by the Legislature exist and that creation of a local district will realize state policy. A few are initiated by a city council calling an organization election. Each step taken in organizing a district under a general enabling statute is governed by detailed procedural requirements. A particular enabling law will be employed uniformly throughout the state, but the statutes differ widely in their specific procedures.

A small group of special districts have been created by the Legislature by special acts to serve particular purposes and with legislatively-specified boundaries. Although the initiative in such instances undoubtedly comes from local interested groups, the formal process of creating the district is accomplished fully by the Legislature. Usually such action occurs when there is no enabling act available covering precisely the situation identified with the problem. Further, it is usually reasoned that the set of facts involved is unique to the particular area, and hence it is deemed most appropriate for the Legislature to enact a unique statute. Inasmuch as the constitution does not prohibit special acts for districts, except school units, the Legislature has full discretion. In some instances, the Legislature exercises its authority without submitting its decision to a popular referendum in the area affected. In others it proceeds more cautiously and makes the formation of the district contingent upon a referendum. Examples of special districts that are products of special acts are the San Francisco Bay Area Rapid Transit District, the Metropolitan Transit Authority (Los Angeles), and the San Joaquin Valley Air Pollution District.

The Legislature does not follow a completely consistent pattern in dealing with a particular subject. The pattern employed in flood control is one of special acts. The Los Angeles County Flood Control District, created in 1915, and county flood control districts established in several other counties during the 1950's are the products of special acts. On the other hand, the Legislature uses both the special act and the general permissive statute in air pollution control efforts. The Los Angeles County Air Pollution Control District and districts in Riverside, Orange, and San Bernardino counties operate under a general enabling act that permits county boards of supervisors, after making a finding of need for organized air pollution control, to bring a district into being. The Bay Area and the San Joaquin Valley districts, however, are the creatures of special acts. These two districts are distinguishable from the others in that they embrace several counties each. In the transportation field, the Legislature has authorized municipal utility districts to provide transportation as well as several other utility services, but it has also created the San Francisco Bay Area Transit District and the Metropolitan Transit Authority by special acts.

Local and Metropolitan Units. A second broad classification of districts distinguishes between those that are local in their jurisdiction and those that are regional or metropolitan in character. This is a distinction that becomes increasingly important as efforts become more intense to adjust institutions and processes of government to the changing urban environment. Some of both classes of districts are brought into being by local initiative and approved by local referenda. Significantly, the Legislature has been persuaded in several recent instances to create important regional organizations directly by special legislation and without reference to a local vote. Examples are the Metropolitan Transit Authority, the San Francisco Bay Area Transit District, and the Bay Area Pollution Control District.

Most special districts possess an area that is less than that of the county in which they function, hence they are local in character. Many serve only unincorporated territory, therefore they tend to supplement county government, especially that in urban counties. Such districts are best suited to serve communities that are neither strictly rural nor fully urban. They are able to provide a level of service above that provided on a countywide basis. Probably the best example of this is the community services district, although it is unique in that it is a multifunction unit. Its purpose is to permit urban fringe areas to organize a governmental unit capable of providing some of the functions normally furnished by a city. This district is distinguishable from a city in that its powers and responsibilities are fewer and its status in law is less than that of a municipal corporation. Single-purpose special districts located entirely within county unincorporated territory include those providing local library, police protection, park and recreation and garbage collection functions. Many special districts include both incorporated cities and unincorporated territory. Examples of these are county fire protection, county sanitation, and county library districts. A few statutes permit organization of a district that is coterminous with a city or that comprises two or more cities. The chief example is the county sanitation district act, which permits several alternative combinations.[16]

---

[16] *California Health and Safety Code*, Sec. 4711.

Many studies of metropolitan area government lament that municipalities and counties do not possess sufficient flexibility to meet the demands of the expanding metropolis. The special district escapes most of the constraints of the traditional units of local government, and is capable of being adjusted to encompass whatever areas are deemed appropriate.

Some districts overlap the urban county, encompass a territory equivalent to the county's, and have the board of supervisors, serving in an *ex officio* capacity, for their governing boards. Examples in the Los Angeles area are the County Flood Control District and County Air Pollution Control District. This type of organization was sought historically to circumvent several legal limitations upon county governments, including limitations upon tax rates and bond indebtedness.

In a few instances, special districts are employed as devices to combine several counties in a confederation to administer a single function. Examples are the Bay Area Air Pollution District, the San Francisco Bay Area Transit District, and the San Joaquin Valley Air Pollution Control District.

The Metropolitan Water District of Southern California illustrates yet another type of district. It brings together municipalities and local water districts in several counties to form a federated regional organization.

Other generalizations and classifications of special districts tend to require so many qualifications that they become unwieldy. Therefore, our discussion will shift focus to the general attributes or functions of special districts. Many of these attributes cut across the classifications that have been discussed previously. District functions, for example, are subject to the same generalizations, regardless of whether the district was created under general statute or by special act, or whether it is local or metropolitan in character.

Functions. Most special districts are created to perform a single function and their powers are limited to those specified in the governing statute. Because of the limited purpose for which a district is organized, the area of its jurisdiction is determined largely by the location of the property and persons that will draw benefits from the function performed. The area will encompass only those who can be served feasibly. The limited nature of special districts also tends to explain their number and the overlap of their areas. A library district, a county fire-protection district, a water district, and a park and recreation district may be formed in the same approximate area, although usually at different times. Because different combinations of community interests supported the formation of each district, each will have a slightly different area.

Special districts also may add functions by securing an amendment to the basic statute. In most instances, the additional functions are ancillary to the original activity or represent a noncompeting use of public works and facilities created to perform the original function. An example in the Los Angeles area is the group of county sanitation districts that have associated to form a major regional sanitary sewer system. They were organized to construct and maintain trunk sewers, a treatment plant, and an ocean-outfall line. Even before home garbage-disposal units became common appliances, the district management realized the possibility of using this organization to accomplish additional waste-disposal purposes. It obtained legislative authorization to undertake collection and disposal of combustible and noncombustible wastes, to operate refuse-collection vehicles, transfer stations, cut-and-cover fill sites, and other facilities. Another example of a district that has had its functions expanded is the Los Angeles County Flood Control District. Its basic function continues to be construction and maintenance of works to retard and channel the run-off of rain waters in the river systems within the county. Amendments to its governing statute have expanded this to include the design and construction of channels to dispose of run-off from city streets, and the acquisition and use of land for water-spreading basins. Conservation of ground water has become a regular function of the district. Clearly each new function or subfunction was ancillary to the original program.

Examples of true multipurpose special districts are relatively rare. The community services district is in a sense a prototype that operates under a general permissive statute. It represents an effort to unify performance of services to a suburban fringe area that desires to remain associated with the county government. Any area that wishes to achieve a greater array of services or to control land-use must incorporate as a city and become a general-purpose unit. The municipal utility district is a slightly different type of multipurpose district. It may engage in supplying water, transportation, sewage disposal, electricity, telephone service, and a variety of other public utility services. It may undertake such services as it chooses. If it were to perform the maximum number authorized, it would have almost as many service functions as any city.

Powers. A special district is strictly limited in its powers to those specified in its governing statute. By its very nature, the district is a creature of legislative intent, and the doctrines of law governing delegation of legislative authority do not permit broad delegation. Furthermore, the conditions under which districts have been created in California have not induced the sponsors to seek broad powers comparable to those sought by municipal leaders under home rule.

Most district statutes permit the governing body to levy a tax for the support of the function authorized. In almost all cases the tax is levied upon the assessed valuation of property within the district. Occasionally a district relies entirely, or largely, upon charges for the purchase or use of its services. Second, districts are usually authorized to acquire and manage property and to construct and maintain any works and facilities that may be necessary for the performance of their functions. Finally, they may sue in the courts when necessary.

An analysis of special districts' powers, however, reveals a primary emphasis upon those relating to construction, maintenance, and operation of public buildings, plants, and facilities. Included in this array of undertakings are waterworks, sewage systems, libraries, hospitals, parks and playgrounds, flood control channels and drains, and mosquito-abatement works. Missing are such direct person-related services as indigent relief, public health clinic and home or clinic nursing service, and mental-health treatment.

Most special districts are not authorized to make and enforce regulations; they are thus distinguished from cities and counties, which as a group enjoy a general constitutional grant of such authority.

Most districts that have enforcement authority are limited to executing state laws and are not empowered to enact their own rules. An interesting illustration of this is a police-protection district, which may be organized in unincorporated territory to provide protection to persons and property. It has no rule-making authority and exists solely as an administrative agency to assist the district residents achieve a higher standard of law enforcement than can be provided by the county sheriff.

One of the few types of special districts that has been granted rule-making authority is the Air Pollution Control District. The power delegated in this instance is not a general grant; it is one related exclusively to the single function of preventing air pollution. Although the exercise of powers by the district has widely ranging implications, especially for the business community, it still falls short of being an exhibit of the general police power.

It is not entirely certain whether the Legislature would be debarred from creating a multipurpose district and assigning it authority to make and enforce rules with respect to several subjects. If it may grant rule-making authority to an air-pollution district, may it do the same for a water district and a fire-protection district? If it may grant such power to a series of single-purpose districts, may it do the same for a multipurpose district that is authorized to perform the same functions as several unifunctional ones? Thus far, the California Legislature has not undertaken to do this, and hence the judiciary has not expressed an opinion on the matter. Political pressures opposed to extending rule-making powers to special districts have been sufficient to limit the question.

Finance. Special districts are supported in most instances by *ad valorem* property taxes. Districts that operate a utility enterprise, such as water distribution or sale of electric power, use their revenues to support operations and amortize indebtedness, but they have authority also to levy a general property tax if necessary to guarantee repayment of district indebtedness.

A recent legislative enactment permits cities that are members of a county fire-protection district to contribute revenues from the city sales tax to pay the share of the district tax that normally would be paid by a district property tax. Although the cities now rely upon a sales tax to supplement their revenue, the property tax and income from sales of services seem likely to remain the chief sources of district revenues. District areas are too limited to make other sources feasible for the types of districts that now exist. A regional or metropolitan district, possessing a larger area, could possibly develop newer revenues, if authorized to do so.

One of the most important consequences of the use of the special-purpose district has been the pyramiding of taxes upon property. Furthermore, the number of special districts complicates the property owner's task of presenting his views to tax-setting authorities. When he must seek access to numerous bodies that are located at various places and make decisions at different times, his task becomes doubly difficult. When he seeks to enlist the support of other like-minded citizens, he must look for several sets of associates because the districts taxing his property may not all have the same set of constituents. It is not surprising, then, that special districts are regarded as mysterious, unresponsive units of local government, the domains of special influence groups that can successfully defy the less organized body of property owners and voters.

Governing Body. Special districts are as varied in the mode of selecting their governing bodies as they are in other characteristics. Some are governed by boards whose members are elected directly by the voters of the district. Examples of this, drawn from among those operating under general statutes, are sanitary, hospital, park and recreation, municipal utility, and community services districts.

Several others have governing boards composed of elective officials who serve *ex officio* by reason of their position on the governing body of a city or a county. For example, in the Los Angeles area, the five members of the county Board of Supervisors serve *ex officio* as the governing body of the flood control, the air-pollution control, the county fire-protection, and the county library districts. Governing boards of county sanitation districts are also made up of *ex officio* officers. If a district comprises city territory only, members of the City Council serve on the board. If the district comprises unincorporated territory only, the Board of Supervisors serves as the district board. If it comprises both city and unincorporated territory, its board is made up of a member of the city council of each city involved and of the chairman of the Board of Supervisors.

The Metropolitan Water District of Southern California illustrates yet another type of indirect selection. Its board members are selected by the governing bodies of the cities and local water districts comprising its constituency from among citizens of the communities.

A few districts, including the MWD, the county sanitation districts, and the San Joaquin Valley Air Pollution Control District, represent interesting examples of efforts to coördinate several entities in a particular functional field by federation. The water district is made up of cities and local water districts and each constituent unit is guaranteed at least one representative on the district's board. The number of members is weighted in proportion to the assessed valuation of property; and voting in the transactions of the board is conducted by a system of weighted votes, in which representatives of the larger units have plural votes based on their share of the assessed value of land. Although the city of Los Angeles is the largest single constituent unit in the district, its representatives cannot cast more than a simple majority of the board's votes. The sanitation district represents a somewhat more complicated arrangement. Each district in Los Angeles County has its own governing board, made up in the manner described previously, although all have contracted with one of their number, District Two, to provide the central management staff for the entire system. Periodically, the boards of the several districts convene in joint session to consider policies and to be briefed by the general manager. The San Joaquin Valley Air Pollution Control District is governed by a board that comprises representatives of counties and cities. Each county in the district is entitled to one representative from its board of

supervisors. The cities within each county are allocated one representative for the group, chosen by a city election committee that is composed of delegates from each city in the county.

Dissolution and Consolidation. As in the case of other features, there
is no single statutory formula for dissolution or consolidation of special
districts. Some special district laws contain no provision for dissolution,
hence when a group wishes to abolish this type of district it must induce the Legislature to amend the statute. Most of the types of districts with which we have been concerned, however, may be dissolved
by the unit's governing board and voters. Inasmuch as a district exists
to provide a service and was brought into existence at the request of
local persons, there is little likelihood that a district will simply dissolve and its functions cease to exist. If change is required, a merger of
jurisdictions is more likely to occur.

Few districts are dissolved automatically when the territory is incorporated as a municipality, the community service district being the
principal exception. Some single-purpose districts, such as local library
and garbage-disposal units, are also dissolved automatically. A few
districts, such as those for county library and county fire protection,
would be affected but not stricken by incorporation. The city council
may decide to withdraw the municipality from such districts and
establish municipal departments. Portions of such districts remaining
outside the city would not have their status changed, however, by any
city action.

Other districts, such as county sanitation, flood control, air pollution,
and the MWD, are affected only slightly by incorporation or annexation activities, and the flood-control and air-pollution-control units
have no relationship with municipal boundaries, as these districts
relate to areas of service.

Consolidation of districts by local action was not contemplated when
the Legislature enacted the basic statutes, therefore, whenever consensus develops to consolidate special districts of one functional type,
legislative authorization must be sought. County fire-protection districts in one area of Los Angeles County were merged some years ago
to improve administrative control.

A consolidation of districts performing unrelated functions would
alter the basic concept of districts, hence the Legislature has not
authorized it. If events were to produce a need for this type of action,
incorporation as a city would be more meaningful. If, however, the
demand were to consolidate several single-purpose districts to produce
a multipurpose special one with metropolitan status, the matter would

clearly call for legislative action, because it would produce a fundamental change in the relationships between local governments.

BASES FOR INTERGOVERNMENTAL COÖPERATION AND JOINT ACTION

California local government has been characterized by an unusually large amount of intergovernmental coöperation and joint action. Much of this activity is the product of informal coöperation by career administrators and by political leaders of different jurisdictions to achieve common goals and does not require legal authorization. Some intergovernmental action, however, depends upon a legal basis, because the basic assumption is that each local unit is created to serve its constituents and is primarily confined to its own territorial jurisdiction in doing so. Inasmuch as the state constitution is silent on the subject, positive developments that have occurred depended upon legislative policy to legitimize local efforts.

Local governing bodies and key local administrative officers undoubtedly may enter voluntarily into informal understandings with their opposites in other local governments to act in concert. If two city health officers, for example, wish to exchange information regarding communicable disease conditions or to coördinate their efforts, they would not have to look to written law. However, if two local health officers wish to spend public money for facilities that are to be operated jointly or to reorganize their respective programs by transferring functions to the other jurisdiction, and thereby develop some functional specialization, they must find appropriate legal support.

As early as 1895, the state of California recognized a need for some intergovernmental action at the local level. The first two functions in which this was encouraged were those in which an obvious duplication existed. Cities were permitted to transfer the assessment of property for tax purposes and the collection of the property taxes to the county government by enacting a municipal ordinance. The rate of compensation that the city was to pay for the services was to be worked out by agreement between the two governing bodies.[17] Inasmuch as the county had been assigned the duty of assessing property for tax purposes and of collecting taxes for school districts as well as for its own purposes, it was already the basic unit for performing those functions.[18] Municipal activities were clearly redundant.

[17] *California Government Code*, Sec. 51501; based upon *Cal. Stats.* (1895), chap. 182, amended by *Cal. Stats.* (1913), chap. 254.
[18] During the period 1879–1907, in which the state levied a general property tax, counties performed the same services for it as the districts.

A second development visualized joint action between cities. By 1903, many cities in California were concerned with securing water rights and constructing works for the capture, storage, and distribution of water for the use of their inhabitants and such municipal purposes as, for example, fire-fighting, street cleaning, and park irrigation. Although most cities preferred to obtain and develop their own water resources, in some instances joint action was agreeable. The Legislature authorized any group of two or more cities to acquire and develop water sources and to construct and operate jointly the necessary public works. The relationship involved in financing, constructing, and operating public works was recognized to be a more complex one than assessing property or collecting taxes. A city might choose to reëstablish its own tax collection office with relative ease after withdrawing its previous assignment to the county, but it could not dissolve or divide a public-works system so easily. Consequently, cities were directed to secure the consent of their respective electorates before they entered into a joint water program. Inasmuch as the only means contemplated for financing public waterworks was a bond issue guaranteed by the general revenues of the coöperating cities, the electorates were given a second veto through the requirement of a bond election.[19]

More extensive functional consolidation among local governments was looked to in 1913 when cities were authorized to transfer other functions, as well as tax assessment and collection, to counties. Nevertheless, this authority was severely restricted. A county was permitted to accept additional municipal functions only if it had a county charter that approved. A similar restriction controlled the city actions. The limitations were eased somewhat in 1915 by eliminating the requirement for county charter authorization and by allowing either party to rescind the agreement at any time by mutual agreement. Unilateral rescinding necessitated a year's notice to the reluctant party.[20] Both statutes were essentially conservative in their procedural requirements. Although the 1915 act contemplated that the city would pay the county for performing the transferred functions and that the rate of compensation would be determined by agreement, the emphasis was on the transfer of the function rather than on the compensation aspect. The authorized process was similar to that involved in negotiating a contract, but it was also more cumbersome.

In 1935, the state sanctioned the concept of a negotiated intergov-

---

[19] *California Government Code,* Secs. 38731–38742; based upon *Cal. Stats.* (1903), chap. 279.

[20] *California Government Code,* Secs. 51330–51335; based upon *Cal. Stats.* (1915), chap. 161.

ernmental contract. County boards of supervisors and city councils were authorized to enter into contracts wherein the county would perform one or more functions for the city. A contract was to have a maximum term of five years, subject to renewal for a similar period. Both the explicit and implicit terms of the statute opened up a new relationship between the local governments. County officers and employees named in the contract were authorized to exercise all the powers conferred upon the city officers whose duties they were to perform. This relationship and status enabled county officers and employees to work within the city and act in the capacity of city personnel—not solely to perform their functions from their offices in county establishments. A county tax-collector was able to collect city taxes at his county office, but a county building-inspector who performed duties under contract for a city would necessarily have to perform his duties in the city. Furthermore, the contract concept implied negotiation, not only with respect to compensation for services performed, but also with regard to service levels. When a city had transferred a function to the county previously, it had tacitly accepted the county's service level. When negotiating a contract, however, the city could more easily influence the level of service to be obtained, if it chose to do so.

The 1935 act contained some politically realistic guarantees intended to encourage cities with established bureaucracies to contract with the county. City employees who might be transferred to the county had their pension rights guaranteed. City pension money or property accumulated by the transferred employees were to be held in trust by the county. Furthermore, the act sought to protect employees' seniority rights when departments were consolidated by city-county negotiations. Although these guarantees did not solve all the personnel problems that might conceivably arise, they did recognize that career employees constitute an important and vocal group that would be concerned about any proposed consolidations of functions.

Joint exercise of powers is another form of intergovernmental coöperation. The concept involved is basically a simple one. Two or more agencies may agree formally to exercise jointly a power that each possesses. The analogue in the business world is the partnership. Just as in a partnership, the relationship contemplated is subject to many variations. Two or more agencies may agree to perform a task in concert, with each performing its share. For some functions (tasks) a more effective arrangement may prove to be one in which the partners assign administrative responsibility to one partner. A variation places the responsibility upon someone outside the partnership. Requirements of partnership operation may vary in certain other respects as well. It may involve conduct of functions that require the use of personnel and equipment but not public works, or, again, it may involve the construction and maintenance of works.

In 1921, the California Legislature adopted a Joint Powers Act, couched in broad terms. It permitted a county, city, public district, public corporation, the state itself, or any federal agency operating in California, to enter into an intergovernmental agreement for the joint exercise of powers. The parties who enter the agreement are ostensible equals who arrive at an understanding concerning what each partner shall do, what the respective financial contribution shall be, and what responsibilities each agency entering the agreement shall bear.

Initially the Joint Powers Act made it possible for local government agencies to develop a suitable means for coping with unusual problems. County sanitation districts, such as those organized in Los Angeles County, were able to select one district to administer a joint-district metropolitan sewage-disposal system. The city of Los Angeles was able to join with seven other municipalities to organize and administer a joint municipal sewage-disposal system. The city and the county of Los Angeles were able to join with the Sixth District Agricultural Association, which was established for the purpose of providing fairs and expositions, and operate a coliseum and sports stadium. Under this act, the cities and counties in the San Francisco area have developed an association to study problems of metropolitan-wide concern.

THE FINANCIAL BASE FOR LOCAL GOVERNMENTS

State fiscal laws have influenced the interlocal as well as the state-local relationships and therefore have influenced the tactics and strategies employed by local leaders in their struggle to govern metropolitan areas. The consequences of changes in state fiscal policy were not always anticipated, but the side effects of state fiscal policies have been important.

Counties, cities, and special districts, being creatures of the state, can have only those sources of revenue that are permitted by state law. Counties and special districts are even more limited in this respect than cities. Any modifications of their revenue programs can be made only with the express authorization of the Legislature. Cities have a limited amount of freedom to develop new revenues when they elect to operate under municipal home-rule charters.

All local units are restricted in their financial activities by the fact that they have limited territory as well as powers. Many objects of taxation that produce large revenues can evade local taxation more successfully than they can state or national, by moving out of the jurisdiction of a local government that attempts to tax them heavily.

Two elements of state fiscal policy are especially important because of their effect upon local governments, particularly those within metropolitan areas. The first consists of the role given to local governments in determining taxation policy. The other relates to the allocation of sources of revenue between the state and the several types of local government. These two elements often interrelate. An example of this arises from the combination of policies that assign the general property tax as the principal local tax base with the policy that limits the power of the local governments to tax that base. Assignment of the general property tax as the chief source of local revenue causes property owners to be deeply preoccupied with local governmental affairs, and gives this group (or series of groups) a proprietary attitude towards the local units of government. In consequence, property-taxpayer groups have successfully demanded certain limitations be placed upon the taxing powers of cities and counties. General-law cities are restricted to a maximum property tax rate of $1 per $100 assessed value of property. Furthermore, because property taxes have been obligated to repay bond indebtedness, cities and counties have been limited in their legal capacity to borrow by bond issues. Cities are restricted to a sum equal to 15 per cent of the total assessed valuation and counties are kept to 5 per cent. Local representative bodies are restricted by pressures from economy-minded groups in their own constituencies as well as state legal limitations. State law makes one concession to local political processes by permitting cities to exceed the tax-rate limitation when approved by a majority of the electors voting at an election called for that purpose.

Plans in Effect, 1879–1907

California has worked under three major tax plans since 1879, each plan having been approved by the state's electorate and made a part of the state constitution. Legislation developed details and implemented the basic decisions. Each plan had a significant impact upon local governments because it determined the effectiveness of local units in fulfilling their respective roles.

During the period between 1879 and 1907, taxes upon property formed the chief sources of revenue both for the state and for its local governments. Functions performed by all governments during that period were relatively few in number, however. The state did not make excessive demands upon the tax base for its purposes because it had assigned most administrative responsibilities to the counties, cities, and districts. When the state began to assume responsibility for new and expanded functions, revision of the state's total tax structure became essential.

PLEHN PLAN

A tax plan devised by Professor Carl C. Plehn, of the University of California, adopted by the Legislature in 1907 and approved by the voters in 1909, set up a new, specialized source of taxation for the state and assigned the traditional property tax to cities, counties, and districts. The state was to draw its revenue from taxes upon the gross earnings of privately owned utilities and certain businesses that operated on a statewide basis. Supporters of the plan contemplated that, by the division of the sources of revenue, property would be relieved of a portion of its tax load and the state and its local governments would be able to develop their respective roles without competing for shares of the same revenue base.

Political consequences of the Plehn Plan were somewhat different than anticipated. Firms that were subject to state taxation tended to draw together in one group and to express an interest chiefly in state government, favoring those functions that contributed to their satisfactions and opposing those that did not. They opposed rises in state-tax levels and insisted that a larger share of the cost of some functions be transferred to local governments and therefore shifted to the property-tax base. Property taxpayer groups, in turn, became alarmed over increases in local taxes and urged that larger portions of the cost of new or improved functions be transferred to the state.

The struggle between state and local taxpayer groups was most notable in the education field. At the time the Plehn Plan went into effect, counties and school districts provided the major share of the financial support for elementary and secondary schools. Efforts to get the state to increase its share of the costs met heavy resistance in the Legislature, which was under pressure from the state taxpaying groups. In 1920, the school groups accomplished a major breakthrough when they amended the state constitution by initiative petition to set a formula for state support.

The period in which the Plehn Plan was in operation was one in which policies favoring separation of state and local spheres of activity received strong support from the municipal and county home-rule movements. Even though the state developed a number of administrative programs, staffed by state personnel and financed from state funds, little effort was made to use them to encroach upon activities of cities or counties.

The Great Depression of the 1930's brought to light still other consequences of the Plehn Plan. During the previous decade, the cities had made lavish use of special assessment districts to finance public improvements such as street opening, widening, and lighting, and drains. The districts had proved to be attractive methods to escape from the tax limit set upon municipalities. Likewise, counties had made considerable use of special districts to finance projects in suburban fringe areas. When the Depression began to be felt, in the early 1930's, cities and counties looked for ways to shift costs of some functions from property to other tax bases. For example, a group of municipal leaders in Los Angeles County persuaded the Legislature to permit cities to transfer their public health services to the county. City-county contracts for assessment of property and municipal property-tax collection assumed new significance also as means by which cities could reduce the strain upon their financial base.

RILEY-STEWART PLAN

The present tax plan was fashioned in 1933, based on suggestions made by State Controller Riley and a member of the board of equalization, Stewart. Public-utility property was returned to local tax rolls, and property generally was continued as the basic source of revenue for county, city, and special district governments. State-tax sources were shifted to sales and use, personal income, and a variety of taxes upon statewide business. In the same year that the Riley-Stewart Plan was adopted, the nation repealed prohibition and California decided to permit private production and sale of liquor, subject to state licensing and taxing. The principal state taxes have proven to be large producers of revenue, although they are closely related to business conditions and hence fluctuate in yield with fluctuations in the flow of money. Local taxes have risen in yield as land values increased and have been less subject to short-term fluctuations.

Two subsidiary fiscal policies must also be considered when analyzing the impact of the Riley-Stewart Plan upon local governments. One is the program of sharing certain state-collected taxes with the local governments; the other is the Bradley-Burns sales-tax law, which permits cities and counties to levy local sales taxes.

California began administering a program of state-collected locally shared taxes twelve years before it adopted the Riley-Stewart Plan, sharing a portion of its income from taxes upon gasoline used in motor vehicles and vehicle license fees. Both revenues were earmarked to finance construction and maintenance of streets and roads. A later statute, the Collier-Burns Act of 1947, set a formula for the distribution of these revenues among the cities, counties, and the state Division of Highways that has prevailed for several years. The local shares are distributed on the basis of population. A third tax on motor vehicles that is shared with local governments is the so-called in-lieu tax. This is a state-levied tax upon the value of vehicles, collected at the same time as license fees and is in lieu of local property taxes. In exchange for the transfer of taxing jurisdiction to the state, cities and counties receive revenues proportionate to their share of registered vehicles.

When the state took exclusive jurisdiction to tax production of liquor and to license liquor retailing, it agreed to share the proceeds of these taxes and licenses with the cities. The local shares are earmarked by state policy for the support of police services.

Policies governing the sharing of state taxes with local governments, subject to earmarking conditions, have produced several consequences. They have offered a very large incentive to the cities and counties to organize themselves in statewide bodies to bring pressure to bear upon the Legislature for the purpose of increasing the local shares. Secondly, they have brought into local treasuries considerable sums for which city councils and boards of supervisors are not directly responsible to a taxpaying group. These bodies are freer from taxpayer pressure in spending state-shared funds than in appropriating local property-tax money. The only incentive for economy in the use of the state-shared funds is the desire to respond to as many demands for streets and roads as possible. This incentive is blunted, however, by the thought that the funds will continue to flow steadily from the state. The earmarking of revenues complicates local budgeting and fiscal planning, although it tends to relieve some of the demands that might otherwise be made upon the property-tax base. At the same time, however, earmarking tends to discriminate between functions. Budgets for street and road work are better financed and more constant than those for other functions. At the same time, the allocation between the cities and counties does not end the bickering between cities and counties over financing particular projects. Cities insist that counties should pay for county roads within cities as well as roads and streets in unincorporated areas. Furthermore, because the gasoline tax is allocated on the basis of population, cities are induced to seek population growth, from annexation as well as migration.

Local governments' need for new sources of revenue to supplement taxes on property led to the Bradley-Burns sales-tax law, particularly because of evidence that the state sales-tax was a good revenue-producer. A few chartered cities, such as Los Angeles, first adopted a local tax, but a sales tax imposed by an individual city could often be evaded. There was much complaint also from merchants that the tax tended to drive customers to nontax cities. When the state authorized general-law cities to levy a sales tax more cities were induced to experiment, but this did not eliminate the tendency of shoppers to seek nontax areas. The counties were also anxious for an opportunity to tax sales in order to augment their tightly limited tax bases. The Bradley-Burns Act mediated the city and county demands by permitting both to join in a uniform program with a fixed tax rate of 1 per cent. State sales-tax administrative facilities were made available to collect the local taxes.

Adoption of the local sales-tax program, on top of the sharing of state-collected taxes, removed one of the principal barriers to the incorporation of fringe areas: the opposition of tax-conscious property owners. Fringe areas that possess a moderately large population and one or more active shopping-centers are often in a position to inaugurate city government without resorting to a property tax. Property-owning groups, previously the most vigorous opponents of incorporations, now have less reason to oppose. Inasmuch as a uniform sales-tax rate applies throughout an entire county, merchants have little reason to object to the tax or to incorporation. The sales-tax policy has made communities take an interest in developing commercial centers, a phenomenon that has strengthened the suburban cities.

SUMMARY

Legal constraints developed by the state have thoroughly affected the status and conduct of local governments. These constraints have determined the "rules of the game" by which those who sought to influence the governments of a metropolitan area could operate. Although the state remains the "fountainhead of legal authority" with respect to local governments, California has delegated much of the real determination to the local level where groups, both official and unofficial, vie to determine the decisions. The state's influence upon local governmental decisions is chiefly indirect, but the consequences of state policies are important.

An analysis of the constraints upon local government structure in a metropolitan area indicates that they encourage the proliferation of local units. It is easier to create new organizations and set up overlays over old organizations than to make such drastic changes in local government as consolidation or dissolution. The latter are made exceedingly difficult by requirement of local referenda. Groups with locally oriented interests and objectives find in the legal constraints a variety of choices by which they may protect their interests and fend off the challenges of groups that have interests extending over wider areas.

FIVE

Strategies in Change of
Legal Constraints

THE CALIFORNIA LEGAL SYSTEM that determines the constraints upon those groups and leaders seeking to influence local governments is built upon an assumption that changes should be made in the system from time to time. Explicit methods of amendment or modification are provided. The very nature of the available procedures, however, tends to produce modifications rather than abrupt or large-scale change in the general operating rules. The legal system, which includes the legislative and judicial processes and the methods for constitutional change, has built-in elements that make abrupt or large-scale change difficult to produce. Checks, balances, and countervailing forces operate at every turn.

Groups motivated by the belief that a change in the legal constraints is likely to yield an advantage to them have a relatively free choice of methods to employ in achieving their goal. Varying degrees of changes in the basic rules of local government, which were discussed in Chapter Three, may be accomplished either by amending state legislation or the state constitution, or by obtaining a judicial interpretation that will favor a particular course of action. The extent of change desired will partly determine the choice of method. The selection may also be determined either by the financial ability of the group to promote its desire for change, or by an estimate of its ability to persuade incumbents of key positions in the appropriate institutions of government.

GAINING ACCESS TO THE LEGISLATURE

Those seeking to amend state legislation must, of course, gain access to the Legislature. So may those who propose to amend the state constitution, although for this purpose, they may choose the alternative of gaining direct access to the voters by means of an initiative petition. The California Legislature is reasonably accessible to all groups that seek to present a proposal, particularly on matters of local government. There is no requirement, implied or otherwise, that groups must approach the Legislature through an unofficial leader or association. The only state political machine that existed in California had its monopolistic control of the Legislature broken in 1910. Nor are groups that seek legislative change required to approach the legislature through the executive branch or some bureaucratic intermediary. American states, including California, avoid the parliamentary arrangement wherein legislation relating to local government is prepared in a ministry of local government or a home office, and is introduced by the administration as a government bill. Legislative proposals in the California Legislature are introduced solely by members of either house. They may originate entirely with the legislator, may be suggested to him by groups or influential individuals, or may be introduced at the request of the Governor, a state administrative department, a city council, or a board of supervisors.

Thus far, political parties have not controlled or channeled legislation that is primarily concerned with local government or metropolitan areas. Although party organization has returned to the Legislature and legislative programs often produce partisan divisions, this element has not affected local governmental matters to any large degree, nor has it limited access by interested groups to the Legislature.

GROUP ACTION

Access to the Legislature on matters relating to local government is sought by a large array of groups. Some of these are composed of public officials; many are made up of private individuals. In matters relating to local and metropolitan affairs, California has an extensive number of official groups that seek to influence state policy-making through legislation.

Prominent in this official group is the League of California Cities, which was organized in 1898. During its first thirty-five years, it was led by elected officers of some of the larger cities. It focused its members' attention on state legislation, but it also promoted exchange of information for improvement of municipal administration. It was a constant champion of municipal home rule. Reorganized and given new, aggressive leadership in the 1930's, the League has become a powerful statewide force in all matters relating to cities and urban affairs. Membership is composed of all types of cities, including free-holder-charter and general-law cities, the largest in the state as well as the smallest. Because memberships are subscribed in the name of the municipal corporations, the elected officials who vote the funds for membership fees tend to take the leading roles in determining the League's policies. The mayors' and councilmen's section draws enormous attendance at the League's annual sessions, at which it considers matters involving the organization's stand on legislative matters. Other sections, such as the city managers', city attorneys', and planners', bring administrative officers of the cities together to study matters of mutual interest.

The League of California Cities is elaborately structured to combine a maximum of official participation with a core of leaders who plan, channel, and push the development of policies. Each section has its own organization to deal with matters of specialized interest. Through section representatives that comprise the board of directors, the league achieves leadership for the organization as a whole. A series of regional groups also operate within the league framework, meeting periodically to discuss matters of area interest and to exchange information. One of the most active regional groups is the Los Angeles County division, which serves partly as a rallying point for the cities in their relations with the county government and partly as a vehicle in which to discuss problems that are unique to the area. Although the league tends to work as a statewide organization, particularly when it formulates programs for legislative action, regional groups often compete with the statewide organization when matters at their level become highly controversial.

The board of directors and central staff channel the work of the league, presenting the demands made by municipal officials of the state Legislature and administration. The executive director is not only the chief staff officer but also the principal legislative advocate. Committees appointed by the president participate extensively in policy development, a continuous activity in the league. The board of directors and the annual conference are the chief policy-determining bodies of the league.

By reason of the nature of the league's membership, its official stand on state legislation must interest broadly all municipalities in the state. Matters that are local to one city or to a group of cities with a special problem must be dealt with by some other grouping than the league.

Prominent in the league's interest are such matters as powers of cities, liabilities for damages and claims, and employer-employee relations in the public service. State-collected locally shared taxes constitute a subject that draws all cities of the state into accord. Similarly, a common bond is found in policies relating to incorporation, annexation, and relationship with county governments and county-influenced special districts. Although many individual cities throughout the state demonstrate a lively interest in enlarging by annexation, the league tends to encourage increases in the number of incorporated cities. Because the single-purpose special districts tend to interfere with incorporation desires, league leadership usually looks with considerable disfavor upon that type of local unit. Historically, the league has been a successful advocate of increased municipal home rule; hence, it is enormously sensitive to any efforts to assign greater responsibility to state agencies for programs in which the cities are interested.

The league is far from being solely negative in its legislative program, however. Under an aggressive and usually well-informed leadership, it often seeks legislative changes. Its interest in change is notable in the tax field, where it constantly seeks new authority for cities to develop their financial resources. It has been very active in seeking adjustments in intergovernmental relations in such fields as water pollution, air pollution, civil defense, water supply, and law enforcement. League legislative advocates have been active in devising new institutional arrangements to conduct intergovernmental relations. Examples are: regional boards to determine standards for water pollution control, and several types of intergovernmental boards to perform regional planning and air pollution control.

Because the league has been highly successful in its legislative programs for nearly thirty years, it prefers the legislative process as a means to determine state policy. It tends to disfavor delegation of rule-making authority to state administrative bodies. It prefers instead to see the Legislature spell out its intent with a new program, but leave itself free to alter policy and to reinstruct administrators after it observes experience. It tends to look askance upon the constitutional amending process because it limits the Legislature. Furthermore, if a constitutional amendment proves to be unsatisfactory, further amendment requires a greater expenditure of time and effort than is required to amend statutes.

A second powerful statewide body of officials is the County Supervisors Association, a more recent entrant into the legislative arena. The county elective officials were slower to accept the idea that they had sufficient interests in common to warrant joint action. Historically, the county boards sought access to the Legislature individually to obtain changes in the governing acts and salary changes for each county. The county home-rule movement, plus the development of urban counties, tended to emphasize differences among the counties rather than common interests. Development of state and federal grant-in-aid programs in social welfare and health, and the enhancement of state-collected locally-shared taxes upon gasoline and motor vehicles, produced sets of common interests. Several counties, rural as well as urban, became concerned with air pollution control and land-use planning. More recently, county political leaders have been deeply involved with water supply and apportionment of legislative districts.

The internal organization of the Supervisors Association, by which it determines its policies, is less complex than that of the League of California Cities. In the first place, it does not include administrative officials, either elected or appointed. Therefore, its membership is smaller and has a relatively narrower range of interests in legislation. Association policies are developed through committees that bring their proposals to the annual conferences for adoption. The board of directors, which is organized in a manner calculated to achieve balance among different regional group interests, has responsibility for association affairs between the annual conferences. A headquarters staff, located in Sacramento, provides information, planning, and assistance for committees. The general manager serves as head of the staff and as principal legislative advocate.

The reasons that delayed the Supervisors Association in becoming a truly statewide spokesman for county government have also caused it to be somewhat slow in articulating policies relevant to the counties' role in metropolitan government. Relatively few county boards of supervisors were willing to accept the role of provider of services for the suburban fringe around the central cities. Most preferred to continue the traditional services on a countywide basis and to leave to the individual community the initiative to seek additional services by means of special districts. Los Angeles County was the notable exception in this matter, although recently several counties have reassessed their policies and responded to the pressures of suburban populations.

The association usually proposes a number of changes to statute law at every session of the Legislature. Most such changes seek to give county officers greater discretion in handling local matters. It may be observed, however, that the county group is less often concerned with achieving changes in the basic system of county government than in protecting the status of the county. Examples of significant developments in which the association has participated included the community services district, the Bradley-Burns Sales Tax, and the air pollution control district acts.

Both organizations of local government officials employ most of the usual tactics of legislative lobbying. Both seek to ensure that legislators favorable to their views are appointed to those legislative committees that handle key subjects. Both have staffs of advocates to appear before committees and to keep close contact with legislators who are handling bills in which the organization is interested. Both serve to channel information to the organization's members regarding legislative business, and to mobilize local influences that will be persuasive when bills come to a vote in committee rooms and the legislative chambers. Both organizations are formidable networks of political influence that stretch from all parts of the state into the legislative halls. Like most such networks, they are brought into play to intervene in a relatively limited number of contests that are of highest interest to the organization.

Larger cities and counties tend to play lone roles in the legislative area because the associations do not meet their special needs. The Los Angeles County Board of Supervisors, for example, approves a lengthy list of items to be advocated before the Legislature at each session. Examples include taxation of the possessory interest in inventories held by aircraft firms doing work for the federal government, changes in the municipal court district law, and changes in eligibility requirements for poor relief. Administrative employees are assigned to work as legislative advocates in Sacramento during the legislative session. Individual members of the Board of Supervisors, and administrative officials, are dispatched to the state capital for hearings and conferences as need arises. The mayor and top administrative officers of Los Angeles City visit the capitol periodically to support city proposals; and a member of the City Attorney's staff is in regular attendance.

Statewide associations of administrative department heads concern themselves with legislation that affects their program interests. Most such associations are found among elective county officials, such as assessors, district attorneys and sheriffs. City officials have their associations within the framework of the League of California Cities. Appointive county administrators do not, as a general rule, engage in legislative action, except where directed to so do by their board of supervisors in behalf of programs advocated by the supervisors. The elected administrators are not under the same restrictions and, therefore, take an active role in legislation relating to their programs.

Statewide organizations of governmental employees have appeared on the legislative scene in recent years. The California Teachers Association is one of the oldest organizations, having exercised a very powerful influence for many years in matters relating to state and district school support, certification of teachers, curriculum, and other public school matters. This group has not concerned itself with affairs relating to metropolitan area problems, other than to support the continuance of school administration separate from general city and county government. Loosely organized federations of city and county employee groups advocate legislation relating to retirement benefits, working conditions, and similar employment matters. More recently they have advocated that the employing governments be required to recognize employee groups for purposes of negotiating wage scales and employment policies. Locals of the International Firefighters Union have been active in metropolitan organization problems as well as in employment matters. Some have sponsored legislation relating to county fire districts and metropolitan fire protection.

Another set of legislative advocates that has made an impact occasionally on the structure of local government is composed of attachés of the court system. These include the clerks of superior court and the municipal court districts, marshalls, and representatives of the township justice courts. Although their primary interests are salary and working conditions, they have been very active in court reorganization plans because their employment has been involved.

No statewide organization comparable to the League of California Cities or the Supervisors Association serves the entire group of special districts. Units of this class of local government do not possess sufficient interests in common to motivate organization for legislative purposes. Certain subtypes of special districts do have statewide organizations, however. The Association of School Trustees and the Irrigation Districts Association are thoroughly organized bodies of local officials that work to influence the Legislature on matters relating to their particular group interest. The former has been influential, for example, in the school district consolidation and reorganization program.

The array of associations of public officials and employees is extensive and complex. Combinations of these groups to take legislative action change with the subject. There are numerous recurrent rivalries, but there are also numerous alliances and temporary combinations.

A different situation exists among private groups involved in the legislative process. No set of private organizations is interested exclusively in local governmental matters. Most private organizations that intervene in the legislative process in regard to local government matters do so when a particular subject impinges upon their special group interest. Consider an example relating to taxes. Firms involved in developing utilities or petroleum, and those with large investments in property that may be taxed by local governments, understandably are interested in learning about proposed changes in legislation relating to taxation. Legislative advocates for associations of firms, as well as the staffs of individual firms, follow closely in the Legislature and among local governments that might have an impact upon the tax structure. For example, proposals by local government associations to increase the tax upon gasoline and to share it with local governments bring an immediate reaction from the major oil companies and the automobile owners associations (Southern California Automobile Club and California Automobile Association).

Private firms doing business in various phases of urban development have become actively interested in problems arising from the increase in number of local governments. Individual entrepreneurs and firms engaged in land management and development, in mortgage and construction financing, and in construction have taken an active part in specific matters. They are particularly concerned with questions regarding the jurisdiction of local government in matters of planning, zoning, building standards enforcement, and street and road construction, and they are alert about legislative proposals that relate to those matters. Leaders of such firms have not crystallized an industry policy or attitude, however, that is reflected by association action in the legislative field. Generally speaking, associations and private groups do not initiate proposals for changes in the legal system as it relates to local government. They are chiefly preoccupied with defending their established interests against anticipated encroachments.

One type of group in the private sector that does interest itself in changes in the local government pattern is the general business association or chamber of commerce. In the Los Angeles area, the Los Angeles Chamber of Commerce has been an important influence for a long period of time, overshadowing a number of other local organizations. It is concerned primarily with matters that it identifies as stimulants to capital formation, investment, and development of manufacturing and trade in the Los Angeles metropolitan area. Prominent among its continuing subjects of interest are local finance, transportation, water supply, air pollution control, and, in a less prominent sense, law enforcement. Its state and local government section formulates the basic attitudes of the organization on legislative subjects and mobilizes support among the membership for specific items.

Two quite different organizations that have a continuing interest in local government, both on a local and a statewide basis, are the California Taxpayers Association and the League of Women Voters. The association is a statewide organization working for expenditure control in state and local governments. It often coöperates with local taxpayers associations that are financed by local business and land-owning interests. The league is organized at the state level and at the local community level. It relies chiefly upon volunteer workers who support its programs.

The association's interest, as its name implies, is primarily in taxation and costs of government, although, in pursuing these interests, the organization has devoted much staff time to studies of local government structure, powers and duties, and methods of measuring governmental performance. It rarely sponsors legislation, but is active in providing information to legislators and in opposing legislation relating to public expenditures.[1] Likewise, the association works with local governing bodies on matters relating to taxation and expenditures; its advocates appear regularly at local budget hearings.

The League of Women Voters is a nonpartisan organization with considerable influence on matters relating to governmental structure, personnel policies, and some substantive matters. At the state level, it has concerned itself more with administrative organization and constitutional revision, joining with other statewide groups in sponsoring legislation and constitutional amendments. It has also studied the metropolitan organization problem. Its officers and advocates present the league's policies on specific measures, which are determined at an annual convention after the local units have studied a general subject and crystallized group viewpoints.

GROUP MOTIVES

The reasons that compel groups, both those comprising public officials and those made up of private parties or firms, to seek access to the Legislature to change the system of local government in a metropolitan area will vary with the group interest and with political circumstances. However, a few generalizations can be postulated. The first is that these groups seek to gain extension of local governmental powers or to provide a new institution of local government when a crisis presents a new situation or set of demands. This is illustrated in the events that led to the organization of an air pollution control district in Los Angeles County. The cities had treated the problem as one related to public health and had used techniques that had long been associated with nuisance abatement. When it became apparent that a governmental unit with a larger jurisdiction than a single city

---

[1] S. J. Arnold, "General Managers' Report," *Tax Digest* (March, 1960), pp. 57–63.

would be required, and that new methods and powers would have to be developed, several groups, official and private, sought access to the Legislature and advanced proposals for solving the crisis that favored their group interests.

A second motive is the desire to obtain state assistance for local activities. Periodically the organized municipalities and counties have gone to the Legislature for increased portions of the state-collected gasoline tax. Individual cities have sought grants of state-owned tidelands for municipal harbor and recreation uses. In support of the same interest, some cities have sought to have state-owned beaches assigned to them.

Within a metropolitan area, numerous rivalries and conflicts arise periodically between units of government, and groups often turn to the Legislature for restraints that will modify or eliminate the contention. This may be illustrated by the efforts to modify the disputes that have arisen over attempts by some groups to outplay their rivals by circulating an annexation petition before an incorporation proposal can be completed and filed. After this type of dispute had disturbed several communities, official groups, such as the League of California Cities, urged a change in legislation.

Desire by a set of officials to gain advantage over another at a different level of government is yet another motive to persuade the Legislature to change the rules. The moves that culminated in the authorization of community services districts illustrate this type of situation. Municipal officials sought to establish a type of local unit that would induce urban fringe areas to incorporate or to annex to municipalities. They sought to compel the fringe areas to finance the cost of services they received that exceeded the level provided by the county on a countywide basis. County officials sought to retain the fringe areas under county influence. The district plan met the objectives of both groups. A somewhat similar situation produced the county sanitation district law. Groups that sponsored this enabling legislation hoped to provide rapidly developing suburban cities a mechanism to improve sanitation. They feared that the suburbs would be forced to join the central core city that had a well-developed sewage disposal system, unless a new type of unit were created.

Occasionally groups seek access to the Legislature to overcome an adverse decision by the courts interpreting statute law. One example of this was the successful effort to change the criterion for incorporation action from "inhabitants" to "registered voters" after the Superior Court had interpreted the term "inhabitants" to include residents of a nursing home. Another was the unsuccessful attempt made by Los

Angeles County in 1959 to overcome the adverse decision of the state Supreme Court denying a county government power to tax the possessory interest in materials used by airframe companies in fabricating craft for the federal government. The decision seriously upset the county's financial plans at a time when it was involved in a vigorous competition for metropolitan leadership.

Each motive for group action to seek change in the legal constraints upon local government in a metropolitan area has a fairly limited scope. Some groups seek to create a new class of limited local governmental institution; others strive for a change in powers or processes of existing institutions. Each effort is designed to meet an identifiable "problem" or to gain advantage over a specific adversary. One is reminded of the oft-remarked generalization that "politics is the art of achieving the possible." The strategy of change is to produce a sufficiently limited proposal that can be accomplished in a single legislative effort. A more elaborate plan that depends upon changes to be made in two or three successive legislative sessions faces the danger that the pattern of influence may be different in the later meetings.

CONDITIONS CONTROLLING ACCESS

Groups seeking to change the legal constraints obviously must find an official legislative author for their proposal. Bills must bear the name of at least one sponsoring legislator, although he may be a member of either house. Almost no group is barred from gaining access for want of a legislative author. A reputable group can find a sponsor to introduce almost any bill, although some legislators protect themselves by causing the phrase "introduced by request" to be printed at the top of the bill if they are not fully conversant with it.

Strategies of bill introduction are no different in local government legislation than those involving any other subject. Certain legislators carry greater influence with their colleagues on particular subjects than do others. A bill introduced by the chairman of the Committee on Municipal and County Government would undoubtedly be recognized as one that was more nearly acceptable to the major groups involved than would one introduced by a member not normally active with the subject. For a number of years, the League of California Cities relied upon the senator from Imperial County to sponsor major legislation although he represented a rural county. An alternative to having an influential legislator introduce a proposal is to have multiple authorship. Numerous bills carry the signatures of several sponsors, and thereby gain additional strength and prestige.

The interim legislative committee has been a significant device to introduce legislation on metropolitan affairs, much as it has been for other subjects. This type of committee is appointed to serve between the time of adjournment of one and the beginning of the next regular session. It may be created either by one house or by the two houses jointly. Often the membership of certain regular standing committees of the session is appointed to an interim body, becoming a continuing forum and an incubator of new legislation. The ostensible purpose of an interim committee is to study a problem, which has been defined in the resolution creating it, to report information, and to propose legislation. Committees on municipal and county affairs, public works, planning and resources, and revenue and taxation have functioned extensively in matters relating to metropolitan affairs.

Most interim committees employ staffs to prepare research studies and arrange public hearings, although some have employed outside consultants to prepare reports for committee study. The outcome of most interim committee work is a sheaf of proposals to change existing policies and rules. Hence, it may be generalized that an interim committee has a built-in incentive to propose change, because such action tends to justify the labor put forth by the committee members and staff.

Development of the interim legislative committee system has brought a method of access to legislative deliberations that did not exist previously. Most interim committees hold public hearings in various places throughout the state. Groups and individuals are afforded an opportunity to make oral and written presentations and to talk informally with committee members. Therefore, the committee's report and the legislation it sponsors contain many ideas for change that were negotiated by individuals and groups at various times during the activities of the committee.

Standing committees of both houses of the California Legislature are reconstituted at each biennial session. Their number and size are determined by each house. Assembly committee assignments are made by the Speaker; those in the Senate are determind by the Rules Committee. In the 1959 and 1961 sessions, party organization figured more prominently in committee assignments than it had previously. In every session, however, interested groups play an important role in the strategies of determining committee assignments. The legislators' interests and previous experience are also influencing factors. For example, the committees that handle local government legislation draw many legislators who have had experience in local government. Usually the Assembly Municipal and County Government Committee has a majority of former mayors and council members. Relatively few members of the lower house have been county supervisors or held county offices. The Senate shows more experience with county government; relatively few senators have held municipal offices. The Senate Committee on Local Government usually contains a majority of former supervisors or other elective county officers. Bills pertaining to the powers, structure, and interrelations of local governments are normally referred to these two committees.

Committees of the California Legislature do not have the degree of control over legislation comparable to those of Congress; nevertheless, the choice of the committee to which a bill is referred is a very important element in the legislative process. Attitudes and interests of the committee members have much to do with the treatment given a bill at that stage. A committee whose majority is adverse to a bill may prevent a report being made or may amend the bill in ways that tend to ensure its defeat if it is reported out. Favorable committee majorities are essential, not only to the passage of bills, but also to the strategy of timing a bill's progress through the Legislature. Committee chairmen are also very influential in this respect.

In addition to legislative organization and procedures, constitutional prescriptions are important factors influencing the strategy of change in legal constraints. As shown in Chapter Three, the California constitution prohibits special legislation regarding municipalities and counties and insists that statutes shall be general in scope and application. On the other hand, it permits classification of local governments for purposes of legislation, although in practice this method is no longer used extensively. Occasionally a legislator drafts a bill in such a way as to limit its application to one large city. Such special-purpose legislation is almost invariably introduced at the request of local groups; seldom in the last fifty years have legislative majorities supported the use of classification to harass a local government. Similarly, an increasing percentage of legislation pertaining to counties is general in application.

The nature of the state legislative process is such that group action becomes essential for the exercise of influence. Although access to the Legislature is relatively open and unrestricted, it alone does not guarantee success for proposals. The volume of subjects that must be considered by members of the state Legislature at any one session is so enormous that competition is keen to persuade legislators to focus upon selected items. In this competition, there are two sets of interests. One involves the groups whose concerns are with the individual legislator's constituency. The other is composed of interests that have a much wider range. The session statutes are filled with items promoted by small, parochial interests and approved by the majority of legislators at the request of one or two colleagues. At the same time, much legislation receives attention only because a broadly based, influential group supports it and organizes the pressure to secure its adoption. Lacking that organized group pressure and support, many bills never move through the committee stage and receive legislative consideration.

Much has been written in studies of the legislative process concerning the function of pressure groups in making technical information about specialized subjects available to legislators. This informational function is especially important when the subject is local governmental structure or powers and activities, particularly those relating to government in the metropolitan areas. Problems relating to the incidence of taxation or the institutional organization of special districts require much specialized technical knowledge if workable legislation is to be adopted. If pressure groups did not exist or if they did not maintain staffs to provide information, the legislature would have to create its own organization to provide this, or turn to sources that might not be as well informed. Pressure groups representing public officials play an especially important role in providing technical information. Indeed, the problem is one of counterbalancing the information provided by pressure groups, to ensure that legislators have access to competing ideas and may evaluate alternative approaches to proposed legislation.

There is considerable evidence to indicate that pressure groups often provide still another function, which might be termed "the mediation of group demands." Certain types of legislation, for example, interest a rather small number of highly organized and influential groups. Legislative leaders invite spokesmen for the interested groups to argue their respective points of view openly before legislative committees. In the process that follows, committee leaders modify or amend the legislation to give each major group a sufficiently high percentage of its demand to induce the group to forego opposition and give support. Frequently, the Legislature declines to consider specific legislation until the contending pressure groups have "ironed out" their differences and have agreed to support a bill that reflects the intergroup adjustment. The Collier-Burns gasoline-tax legislation of 1947 is an illustration. Conferences between legislators interested in highway legislation and representatives of the organized cities, counties, automobile clubs, and the petroleum industry, held prior to the legislative session, failed to produce an acceptable bill. Skeletal legislation remained in committee until the differences between the contending interest groups were resolved at a series of conferences held outside the legislative halls. The legislative authors of the proposed bill were active participants in these conferences, attempting to bring about a reconciliation of the numerous interests that were involved. When a "formula" for the allocation of tax revenues between the state, the cities, and the counties was worked out, and an acceptable policy governing limitations upon expenditure of the funds was agreed upon, the matter was brought back into the Legislature and the bill was amended in committee to conform to the agreements reached outside. Although there was further discussion at each stage during the passage of the bill, the most substantial contentions had been resolved outside.

Products of Access by Official Groups

The end or product that official groups seek to obtain by going to the Legislature will vary according to the nature of the problem involved. One type of product will be a special act that creates a unique special district. This is less often sought by official groups than is general legislation. Demand for this type of legislative product usually arises where there is a reasonably plausible basis for a finding that unique conditions exist and that general legislation will not provide the necessary authority. For example, a special district may be created by a special act to provide a metropolitan-wide service when the regular general-purpose governments, the cities and counties, were unable to provide it.

A type of product that is more frequently sought by official groups is a general statute that authorizes the creation of a special district in accordance with procedures set down in the legislation. The initial urging may spring from one community and from one set of leaders. However, the factors involved in the situation are not so unique that they may not be anticipated in other areas of the state. General legislation, of course, also pertains to municipal or county government. By its very nature, the general statute affects a wide range of interests.

Another type is the city or county charter, and amendments thereto, that pertains to a specific local government. Under California law, all such charters and amendments must be approved by the Legislature. These subjects are introduced as concurrent resolutions, normally by a legislator from the area in which the charter applies. Actually, approval of a charter or an amendment by the Legislature makes that instrument state law rather than local law.[2] As the result of this procedure, charters and their amendments might, theoretically, be given the same scrutiny as legislation drafted and adopted entirely by the

---

[2] *Kubach v. McQuire*, 199 Cal. 215, 248 P. 676 (1926).

Legislature.[3] In practice, however, this is not done. Although opposition to a specific charter or specific amendments has arisen on some occasions, the California Legislature has never rejected any local charter or amendment thereto. In most instances, the ratification of charters and amendments is routine and is given little attention by groups that would otherwise be alert to scrutinize legislation.

A fifth type of product of legislative action is the constitutional amendment. In California the process used by the Legislature to propose constitutional amendments differs relatively little from that used in considering statutes, except that an extraordinary majority of two-thirds of the voting members of each house is required instead of a simple majority. The Legislature acts as a screening device to sift the various proposals for constitutional amendments; not all amendments submitted to it ultimately gain the necessary support to achieve a place on the ballot for a popular referendum. Proponents of constitutional amendments, however, often plead successfully that their proposition should be supported by the legislators to the extent necessary to place it upon the ballot. Some legislators who profess to be personally skeptical or opposed to certain features of a proposed amendment justify their vote on the ground that the electorate should be given the opportunity to decide.

ACCESS TO THE PEOPLE THROUGH
A CONSTITUTIONAL AMENDMENT REFERENDUM

The California constitution may be amended only with the consent of the electorate; that is, a majority of those voting at an election. Access to the people to secure this type of change in the basic rules may be secured via the Legislature or by a petition. In order to qualify a petition for the ballot, it must be signed by a number of registered voters equal to eight per cent of the total that voted for the office of governor at the previous general election.

REASONS FOR SEEKING ACCESS

Inasmuch as the Legislature is open to access by numerous interested parties, and has extensive authority to legislate for local government, why should interested groups seek access through the people to obtain a constitutional amendment? What can be secured via this more cumbersome route that may not be obtained through the legis-

---

[3] The Legislature has no authority to make any alterations or amendments to a city charter. Its sole power is to ratify or reject. *Williams* v. *City of Vallejo*, 36 Cal. App. 133, 171 P. 834 (1918).

lative process alone? Basically a constitutional amendment is designed to limit the powers of the Legislature, specify the manner in which the Legislature shall act, or express directly the approval of the electorate for an exception to general policy. The Constitution of 1879 contained so many constraints upon the Legislature that doubts are sometimes raised regarding the power of that body to adopt certain specific proposals. In these instances, proponents tend to seek constitutional amendments to clarify the legislative power or to have the proposal written into the constitution in full.

Those who seek to change local government in a metropolitan setting will undoubtedly seek to specify how the Legislature shall act, rather than to place further limits upon that body. In numerous instances, however, the purpose may be to legitimize a plan of government that the Legislature may not be willing to adopt or one that constitutes an exception to general policy. Efforts to legitimize local plans that are at variance with general policies are illustrated by two initiative constitutional amendments proposed in 1914, relating to city-county consolidation and annexation. One was adopted, and one rejected. The proposals developed after representatives from Oakland, Los Angeles, and San Francisco failed to agree on a draft amendment to facilitate the establishment and extention of consolidated city and county governments. The San Francisco and Los Angeles representatives agreed to support one proposal: to permit consolidated city-counties to extend across county lines. This would have made it possible for San Francisco to annex Oakland and Alameda County areas. Oakland representatives initiated an alternative proposal that would limit San Francisco to annexing areas in San Mateo County, which had been part of San Francisco at one time, and would prevent it from annexing Oakland. Although both amendments qualified for places on the state ballot, advocates of moderation prevailed before the election. The proposal to permit city-county consolidation and annexation of territory was bitterly opposed by suburban groups, who denounced it as a "cunningly devised scheme to dismember and weaken the counties and to withhold contribution by the cities to the development of the back country from which they draw their patronage and sustenance." [4] The chambers of commerce and the governing bodies of San Francisco and Los Angeles withdrew their support from their original plan and supported the more limited "Oakland plan," which was adopted by the state-wide electorate.

Two legislatively proposed constitutional amendments, one success-

---

[4] See V. O. Key, Jr., and Winston W. Crouch, *The Initiative and the Referendum in California* (Berkeley: University of California Press, 1939), pp. 461–462.

ful and one unsuccessful, illustrate efforts to legitimize a plan for structural reorganization of government in the metropolitan area. Both were drafted in such a manner as to apply in any part of the state, although they grew out of events in the Los Angeles metropolitan area. One plan was proposed by Assemblyman Vincent Thomas of San Pedro. It permitted any chartered city to organize one or more boroughs within the city and to delegate powers to a borough government. There was no organized opposition to this amendment, which was adopted in 1952.[5] The second amendment, introduced by Assemblyman Frank Lanterman of La Canada, sought to permit chartered counties to organize boroughs within the unincorporated territory and to establish methods for assessing the cost of local functions within them.[6] The organized cities, which feared that the suburban areas might choose to organize as boroughs rather than incorporate as new cities or annex to existing cities, opposed it. Although both houses of the Legislature approved it, the electorate rejected the amendment at the 1956 general election.

An illustration of an effort to amend the constitution to achieve approval for an exception to general policy was illustrated when the city of Vernon sought to obtain a home-rule charter. Vernon is not eligible for a charter, because it has less than the required amount of population. The amendment proposed not only to grant a charter but to empower the city to determine for itself the manner in which it would depart from state policy to annex uninhabited territory.[7]

Some students of local government law contend that the Legislature has authority to enact any statute necessary for metropolitan organization, on the premise that it has full power with respect to local government, except where limited by the constitution. As indicated in Chapter Three, the constitution merely directs the Legislature to provide, by general statute, for a system of county government and for the government of cities. A possible barrier to metropolitan reorganization is the constitutional prohibition upon legislation by special act, inasmuch as each metropolitan area is likely to differ from the others in organizational details. The Legislature, of course, may draft a statute that is general in language and that applies to any community that possesses the criteria set forth in the law. This type of classification has been approved by the courts when criteria were based upon such characteristics as population. A political objection to the classification

---

[5] *California Constitution*, Art. XI, sec. 8½.

[6] *Cal. Stats.* (1955), res. chap. 129.

[7] *Ibid.* (1953), res. chap. 99, p. 3970. The proposed amendment was defeated at the general election in 1954.

method is that a statute may affect other areas than the one it was intended to help. Because of this difficulty, some groups, having drafted a plan that was calculated to meet the needs of a specific area, have sought a constitutional amendment instead.

The present constitution has some lengthy passages that were designed to legitimize a metropolitan organization plan applicable in one area, but that do not meet others' needs. For example, a chartered city having fifty thousand or more population may form a consolidated city and county government by the process of drafting and adopting a municipal home-rule charter. The implication is that the city must secede from the county and form a consolidated city-county with a smaller territory than the original county. When the Sacramento Metropolitan Area Advisory Committee contemplated consolidating several cities and Sacramento County to form one unit, the constitutional provision did not supply the authority they desired. Furthermore, the existing constitutional language requires a referendum in each of the incorporated cities involved in a proposed city-county consolidation. No adequate recognition is given to the possibility that referenda might carry in some cities but not in all units. A proposal, such as the Sacramento one, based upon the premise that a complete consolidation of the county and the cities is essential, can be defeated by one recalcitrant city. The constitution does not provide realistic procedures or offer an alternative for the government of the area that chooses not to join a consolidation,[8] but permits it only to block its neighbors' plan.

When there is uncertainty in law, as in the Sacramento situation, the view that usually prevails is that a constitutional amendment must be sought to clarify authority and legitimize a specific plan, rather than risk extensive litigation on a procedure that has doubtful validity. Metropolitan reorganization plans often are forced to surmount two hurdles: a statewide referendum or a constitutional amendment and local referenda on the detailed plan. The San Francisco and Oakland proposals faced this situation in 1914. Promoters of a plan for metropolitan reorganization might prefer to seek the consent of the majority of the state electorate rather than face several separate local electorates, yet because local referenda have been required for several years, such a tactic is likely to raise strong opposition from home rule supporters. Experience with local referenda in various parts of the nation have generally been disappointing, however. Local electorates in Cleveland and St. Louis defeated metropolitan proposals in 1960. The latter rejected another plan in 1962. Miami and Dade County, Florida,

---

[8] Statute law at present provides only for creation of new counties (*California Government Code*, Secs. 23300–23492).

approved a metropolitan reorganization after the statewide electorate had adopted a constitutional amendment. In a series of local elections held after the original adoption, opponents jeopardized the plan. In 1962, Nashville, Tennessee, adopted city-county consolidation, after having once rejected a similar proposal.

CONSTITUTIONAL AMENDMENT PROCESSES COMPARED

Groups motivated to amend the state constitution in order to change the government of a metropolitan area would probably have one of two purposes in view. One would centralize the control of the formal governmental structure by some type of reorganization. The second would enable the leadership in one of the existing governments, such as a central city or a county, to achieve an influential position in the affairs of the metropolitan area.

If a constitutional amendment is necessary to achieve either objective, the legislatively proposed amendment is likely to be more easily obtained than one proposed by petition. Approval by a two-thirds majority of both houses is not a serious barrier. A constitutional amendment goes on the ballot automatically at the next general election held after the legislative session ends, and the proponents usually strive to have their measure given a prominent place on the ballot, with the intent of fixing the ballot number favorably in the voters' minds. The Secretary of State no longer exercises much discretion in assigning the propositions places on the ballot.[9] California state ballots have been relatively long since 1912, and many observers believe that ballot position has much to do with the success of propositions. Proponents of a constitutional amendment hoping that the electorate will be favorably impressed by the fact that the Legislature has already approved the proposal, usually keep their electioneering to a minimum, unless serious organized opposition threatens to campaign. Minimum information is given by means of a booklet published by the Secretary of State and distributed to all voters at government expense. Proponents and opponents are provided an opportunity to present their statement, and the Attorney General's office prepares an analysis of the contents of the proposed amendment.

Groups proposing or opposing a constitutional amendment must decide how extensively to wage a publicity campaign to achieve their objectives. If a vigorous campaign appears to be necessary, and if they have sufficient funds available, they will probably decide to employ a public relations firm to plan and conduct an advertising campaign.

---

[9] *Ibid.*, Sec. 3812.

This is likely to be done if there is organized opposition, widespread misunderstanding, or apathy toward the proposed constitutional amendment. Public officials are precluded from this type of campaigning; and public funds may not be spent to advocate adoption or rejection of policies.

Success in the use of the initiative petition method of amending the state constitution depends heavily upon some type of organized political effort. Obtaining the necessary number of signatures of qualified voters on the petition requires organization, skill, and considerable funds. Petition proponents are required to complete the gathering of signatures to the petition within ninety days. Currently, initiative petitions must receive more than four hundred thousand signatures, and to secure this number of valid signatures in ninety days obviously requires careful planning and organization of efforts. A group with an extensive membership, or with access to groups of people who are sympathetic to the proposed view, may be able to obtain the necessary signatures with a minimum expenditure of funds. Proponents usually find it necessary to secure the services of a firm that makes a business of obtaining signatures. Two or three firms have dominated this particular activity for several years, although several are available. The cost of circulating petitions for a statewide initiative proposition ranges from fifteen to fifty cents for each valid signature.

The most expensive portion of an initiative campaign, however, involves the appeal to the electorate. Although sponsors of initiative propositions are accorded the same access to the official information pamphlet as others, they cannot afford to rely solely upon this medium. In the period since 1945, most groups that have submitted measures to the ballot by initiative petition have employed the services of one of the several public relations firms in Los Angeles and San Francisco specializing in this type of political activity. To create a favorable majority, proponents must appeal to a wide audience. This involves use of radio and television as media to present paid speakers and discussion programs, spot announcements, and repetition of attention-catching slogans. Newspaper advertising is often utilized to spell out the proposition's strongest points and to rebut the arguments made by opponents. Billboard advertising takes a large share of the cost of this type of campaign. Most advertising displays are concentrated in major urban areas, at principal traffic intersections, or on main roads and highways, to appeal to the maximum number of observers. A successful initiative campaign usually costs at least three-fourths of a million dollars, according to information filed with the Secretary of State by proponents of initiative measures in recent years. The extent and

effectiveness of the campaign seems to depend upon the availability
of funds, and large amounts of funds are forthcoming only if the
donors' interests in the success of the campaign are proportionately
great. It seems unlikely that a metropolitan reorganization plan would
offer sufficient inducements to cause groups to contribute adequate
funds for a successful statewide initiative campaign.

In almost fifty years of experience with the initiative process in
California, only three measures relating to metropolitan organization
have been proposed. Each appeared shortly after the initiative method
was adopted, when interest in the process was keen, and when the
organized pressure groups representing local government officials were
relatively weak.

In the fifty-year period between 1911 and 1961, the Legislature proposed approximately sixty amendments to the local government article
of the constitution, and won approval for two-thirds. Although only a
small number related to metropolitan-area government, it is clear that
when a constitutional amendment is needed to bring about a change
in local government, proponents will more likely select the legislative
method than the initiative petition.

Seeking access to the people of the state in order to amend the constitution is a cumbersome and expensive process in any event. It is
sufficiently complex that groups will seek all other channels of decision-
making before turning to it.

GAINING ACCESS TO THE COURTS

Access to the courts is sought less often by those who seek to control
the course of government in a metropolitan area than access to the
Legislature or the people. The role of the courts in shaping institutions
and events in metropolitan area government is less direct, and certainly
more restricted, than that of the Legislature. In American local government law, the judiciary is more often invited to intervene in disputes
relating to the powers of local governments. In this intervention, the
courts have the choice of denying or approving the specific manner in
which the local government proposes to exercise the power in question.
Approval may either be limited or couched in language sufficiently
broad that it allows local political and administrative ingenuity considerable leeway. Proponents of a liberal interpretation of the powers
of local government, however, have not considered turning to the
courts until they had an expression of the state's intent in a statute or
constitutional amendment.

In matters concerning intergovernmental relations or relations be-

tween the public and private sectors of the economy, the courts may
be asked to consider questions involving property rights or the right
to use such natural resources as water or land. If the Legislature has
acted, the courts concern themselves with interpreting the statutes and
the constitution, but if the Legislature has been relatively silent on the
particular subject, the courts may be induced to develop a body of
law, as they have done with respect to water rights.

The judicial concept of American government is such that the courts
seldom permit themselves to be involved in situations in which they
may be called upon to direct local governments to perform a positive
act. Although the courts regard local governments as being subordinate
to the state, and therefore bodies that may be directed to conform to
a clearly expressed state mandate, they usually prefer to direct local
officials to accomplish a given result, rather than specify how they
should proceed.

In the majority of instances in which court action is sought with
respect to local government, the intent of the parties seeking it is
negative: to prevent action, or to deny recognition of governmental
power. In some instances, as when one city brings suit against another
regarding an annexation or exercise of extraterritorial power, the intent
of the complainant may be to block an opponent's action and gain
freedom to proceed by political means. Complainants seldom have
brought suit deliberately to change the system of local government.

In spite of the negative aspects that have been analyzed, court action
has played a significant role in helping to shape the pattern of local
government in the Los Angeles metropolitan area. In no instance can
it be said, however, that the judiciary was the sole determinant, although it contributed materially to shaping the ultimate results. A few
examples will illustrate.

Water has been so significant for the development of the economy
of this area that court decisions with respect to water rights have been
crucial. As a consequence of decisions regarding the control and use
of water in this metropolitan area, the city of Los Angeles became the
core city of the metropolis, and achieved control over a vast land area.
Decisions protecting Los Angeles' pueblo water rights and giving it
priority over the riparian claims of the cities and private owners located higher in the river basin gave the city a peculiar advantage over
its rivals. Court interpretations of the concept relating to surplus water
supplies strongly influenced political decisions on the sale of water and
annexations. Other rulings prevented the municipalities from becoming
general-enterprise corporations marketing water to the highest bidder.

In *Pasadena* versus *Alhambra*, the court determined the apportionment of ground-water rights among a number of municipalities, mutual water companies, special districts, and private parties within a water basin that was also a substantial portion of the metropolitan area.[10] It legitimized an elaborate arrangement that was worked out by the state water resource agency, a referee, and the interested parties. The result of the entire transaction was to stabilize the ground water situation and settle in systematic fashion a troublesome set of problems that affected an entire basin area.

The courts have acted in a markedly different manner when confronted with annexation disputes. They have influenced the pattern of annexation activities in the Los Angeles area by declining to adjudicate the substantive issues. Generally, they have followed the rules enunciated in 1908 in *People ex rel Peck* versus *City of Los Angeles*.[11] Opponents of the Los Angeles effort to annex a shoestring-strip of land connecting the city with the harbor area challenged it as being contrary to the spirit of the statutes and as an unreasonable effort to block the growth of other incorporated cities. The state Supreme Court held that the judiciary was able to act in such matters only if there were a substantial violation of a statute or if there were evidence of fraud. Short of those two conditions, the matter was not deemed to be justiciable. The size and shape of annexations, and the consequences of actions for neighboring municipalities, were deemed to be political matters that were to be resolved by the electorate and city councils in the areas involved. If the results of political action were objectionable, or if they produced inconsistencies in public policy, the Legislature, rather than the judiciary, was responsible. The political events that resulted from adherence to that doctrine came to be characterized by opportunism and sharp maneuvers. Although the Legislature was prevailed upon from time to time to correct abuses in annexation practices, action was confined chiefly to making limited changes.

People versus *City of Los Angeles et al.* illustrates an action in which the Superior Court, at the request of a state agency, directed a group of cities to act and also supervised the selection of method for accomplishing the task.[12] All the parties directly involved were public agencies: the State Department of Health, the cities of Los Angeles, Glendale, Burbank, Vernon, Culver City, Santa Monica, and Beverly Hills,

---

[10] *City of Pasadena* v. *City of Alhambra et al.*, 33 Cal. 2d, 908, 207 P. 2d 17 (1949).

[11] 154 Cal. 220, 97 P. 311 (1908).

[12] The litigation produced several appeals, but the central case is to be found in *People* v. *City of Los Angeles et al.*, 83 Cal. App. 2d 627, 189 P. 2d 489 (1948). The State Supreme Court declined to review the decision, and the United States Supreme Court rejected an effort to appeal one point to that body.

and the South Bay Cities Sanitation District. One basic issue in the case hinged on determining whether the city of Los Angeles, as the owner of the main trunk sewer, treatment plant, and ocean-outfall line, was responsible for bearing the full cost of rebuilding and expanding those facilities. Was Los Angeles solely responsible also for the pollution of the beaches because it was the owner of the facilities that discharged inadequately treated sewage into Santa Monica Bay, even though the sewage was drawn from all of the cities that were parties to the intercity contract? The court concluded that each city in the system was equally responsible for causing the pollution and directed each to contribute to the cost of correcting the deficiencies in the facilities. Although the court granted that each city might seek an alternate means to solve the waste-disposal problem, it ultimately rejected all alternatives and ordered each municipality to pay a share of the cost of reconstructing the system. It rejected a merger of this system with the County Sanitation Districts and supported the retention of two metropolitan sewer organizations.

By acting as it did, the court produced a solution to the immediate problem, but it did not alter the administrative machinery. Within two years, the pollution problem reappeared, and again the courts were asked to intervene to force the cities to correct the physical plant.[13] The ruling on the second occasion was similar to the previous one: the cities were directed to correct the facilities and to share the cost, but the long-range problem of administrative organization was left untouched.

A different type of judicial action, one affecting the pattern of intergovernmental relations in the metropolitan area, is illustrated in *Los Angeles* versus *Huntington Park*.[14] In this situation the city of Los Angeles sought to obtain a right of way through two suburban cities for its municipal hydroelectric power line and was blocked by the councils of those cities. Los Angeles had determined that its interests demanded additional electric power and that the power could be obtained advantageously from plants at the Boulder Canyon site on the Colorado River. To bring the power to Los Angeles by the easiest route meant crossing the borders of suburban cities. Two suburbs, Huntington Park and Southgate, argued that their interests would be damaged by a line of giant power towers, and, operating under their

---

[13] *People v. City of Los Angeles*, 160 Cal. App. 2d, 494, 325 P. 2d 639 (1958).

[14] *City of Los Angeles* v. *City of Huntington Park; City of Los Angeles* v. *City of Southgate*, 32 Cal. App. 2d 253, 89 P. 2d 702 (1938). The Legislature had authorized the courts to determine the conditions under which one city could construct utility facilities in or through another city, if the cities failed to agree on terms (*Cal. Stats.*, chap. 4923, p. 147).

concept of home rule, they rejected Los Angeles' request for a right of way. Had the suburbs' viewpoint prevailed, Los Angeles would have been denied the power resources it sought, or forced to choose a more expensive route. The state had provided a means to resolve this type of quarrel between cities. General legislation authorized any city whose application for a right of way had been denied to sue in Superior Court for relief. After reviewing the evidence and arguments submitted by Los Angeles and its suburban opponents, the court declared itself satisfied that the Los Angeles proposal protected adequately the rights of each party and was the only practicable plan.

Access to the courts is restricted basically by judge-made and statutory rules determining who may sue. The California courts do not give advisory opinions to interpret the state constitution or to spell out a theory of law. Each case considered by the state Supreme Court and the district courts of appeal, as well as by the county trial courts, must be initiated by litigants who can satisfy the court in the original instance of their interest in the matter and their right to sue. There can be no case unless there is a contest between parties who have a substantial interest to be served. In some instances, for example, in suits to test the interpretation of a city charter or a state statute or to determine the rights of various property owners to withdraw water from underground pools, the "contest" may be contrived by the interested parties in order to secure a judicial determination. Yet in these instances, the complainant and the respondent respect the procedures of the judicial process by playing their respective, traditional roles in shaping the issues of the suit, presenting evidence, and arguing the points of law. The judicial process does not require that contestants be mortal antagonists, but only that they play their prescribed roles in assisting the courts to reach a decision.

Parties to court actions relative to metropolitan governmental matters may be taxpayers, private owners of property alleged to be damaged by an action of government, a governmental unit threatened with adverse action by another local governing unit, or the state Attorney General acting on behalf of a state agency that seeks to enforce a particular program. In each instance, the party to the suit must convince the court that it has a direct interest in the matter and that adverse legal effects would result if the court were not to act.

In most instances, the party initiating a suit has had a choice of several alternative lines of action and has selected access to the judiciary because he regarded this alternative as the most effective means to accomplish his goals. Court actions do not follow automatically as the result of any legal requirement. The complainant has the choice of suing or of absorbing his claimed losses. He may seek access to the Legislature to obtain a change in statutory powers or responsibilities of the local government that is involved. He may choose to gain favorable action first, by attempting to influence administrative or political decisions, and, failing in that, may seek to persuade the judiciary to intervene.

Timing in filing a suit against a local government is an element in the strategy of using the judicial process to achieve a favorable result. No clear rule of logic or of law governs in such considerations. The timing of pressing for judicial action depends upon the exercise of judgment, weighing the relevant sets of facts in any individual situation. It may be hypothesized that a great many disputes between local units and between citizens and local governments never materialize as litigated cases, because all parties involved in the particular matter ultimately choose to avoid the expense and delay, and even the uncertainties, involved in such action.

Although the timing of judicial action is significant, it should also be pointed out that the law throws certain limitations around this element of strategy. Time periods for filing suit in many types of matter are limited by statute, in order to bring a degree of certainty and stability to the judicial process. In matters where the statutes are silent, the courts recognize a limitation. If a party has been negligent and has slumbered on his rights for an unduly long period or has taken no positive steps to exercise his rights, the courts are prone to take the view that he has waived whatever rights he may have had in the first place. The law is less consistent in this matter when it is a local government, rather than a private party, that is alleged to have slept on its rights. Because the local government exists to serve a public interest, and its citizens might be deprived of their rightful interests by negligent or venal officials, the courts have taken a more lenient view of efforts by governments to establish a claim to take court action, even though a long delay may have occurred.

In one type of action, the determination to file a suit is vested in someone other than the parties that have the most direct interest. The California Legislature has authorized the state Attorney General to challenge the validity of incorporation and annexation actions. In these types of matters, the Attorney General may not initiate action, unless the state government has a direct interest by reason of state property or resources being involved. The initiative lies with taxpayers located in the area in which the incident occurred, who may appeal to the Attorney General, requesting the state to commence a type of action known as *quo warranto*. After completing an investigation the

Attorney General may decide to file a suit, his determination being final.

In conclusion, it is evident that the judiciary is not prepared to alter radically the local governmental system within a metropolitan area. If the objective of any action group is to accomplish such a radical alteration, it must appeal to the Legislature or to the people. The courts seek to devise formulas by which to adjust the institutions of local government within a relatively strictly constructed legal framework.

SUMMARY

The legal system that provides the institutional framework for local governments in California contains a basic assumption that change is desirable, and it makes several alternatives available to those who seek to implement change. The state constitution, which is the basic set of constraints, provides more than a few access routes to accomplish change.

If the voters of the state approve, a group that desires to secure drastic change in the governmental pattern of a metropolitan area may accomplish its aim. Nevertheless the strategies that are necessary to win the voters' approval are complex and are fraught with many counteractive tendencies.

Those who seek to change the system may seek to influence the Legislature, a pivotal institution in California government. Access to the Legislature is relatively easy; nevertheless, the legislative process has developed many elements that militate against taking radical action with respect to local governments. A number of groups have become institutions to channel powerful influence and they demand a voice in any action that promises substantial change.

The judiciary is available to produce certain types of change in the system of local government; it too, however, is geared to modification rather than drastic change. The judiciary is sought by those who challenge the effort of a local government to perform a function or exercise a power. In matters relating to intergovernmental operations and to certain subjects, such as water rights, the courts have had a significant impact upon the local governmental pattern of the Los Angeles area. The secondary effects of judge-made law have been significant, both when the courts acted and when they declined to accept jurisdiction.

Within the institutional framework of the state's government, there are many possible strategies for action. Success of any one set of strategies appears to depend upon numerous factors in addition to the strength of the groups that seek to block change.

PART II
CONTENDERS FOR LEADERSHIP

SIX

The Central City:
Integration by Annexation

INTEGRATION of the local governments within a metropolitan area by annexation to the central city has long been advocated.[1] This method has been cited by numerous studies as the major solution to the organizational problems posed when a large number of relatively small local governments exist within a densely populated area.[2] Mayors and political leaders of the central cities in almost every major metropolitan area in North America have vigorously advocated this alternative to fragmented power, and those in Los Angeles have not been exceptions.[3]

During the period comprising the years 1906 to 1927, this city sought vigorously, and with remarkable success, to integrate the metropolitan area by annexation. The official municipal policy concentrated on annexation and the efforts of many city agencies were directed toward

---

[1] Among the first to emphasize this view was Paul Studenski, *The Government of Metropolitan Areas in the United States* (New York: National League, 1930), pp. 29–42.

[2] Edwin A. Cottrell and Helen L. Jones, *Characteristics of the Metropolis* (Los Angeles: Haynes Foundation, 1952), pp. vi–vii; Public Administration Service, *The Government of Metropolitan Miami* (Chicago: Public Administration Service, 1954), pp. 70–72; John C. Bollens, *The States and the Metropolitan Problem* (Chicago: Council of State Governments, 1956), pp. 25–52; Harris County Home Rule Commission, *Metropolitan Harris County* (Houston: Harris County Home Rule Commission, 1957), pp. 11–13.

[3] The report of the Annexation Commission, appointed by the City Council at the suggestion of the mayor in 1913, and statements by Mayors George Alexander and Henry Rose, are examples.

maximizing its central objective. The business community of the central area also gave the program its hearty backing. This chapter will analyze the principal annexation methods that are commonly employed and the factors that produced the Los Angeles policy, and consider the consequences of the efforts to integrate the region.

STANDARD ANNEXATION METHODS

Integration of a metropolitan area by annexation to the central city may be accomplished in a variety of ways, depending chiefly upon the legal constraints of the particular system and the political attitudes prevailing at the time in the individual metropolitan area. Several alternative concepts are featured in those countries whose institutions stem from the Anglo-Saxon system of local government. One set involves a choice between decisions made at the central government level and those at the local level. Another set involves decisions produced by a political process, in contrast to those arrived at by the more formal methods employed by the judiciary or by administrative agencies. Yet another lies between political decisions that are made by representative bodies, such as a central legislature or a local council, and those made by voters in the areas involved in the transaction.

Annexation may be accomplished by the action of a central legislature. Metropolitan London, for example, was integrated by a series of parliamentary acts which were sponsored by the national government upon the recommendation of royal commissions appointed to study the problems of governing the capital city.[4] Greater New York, another example, was created in 1898 by action of the state legislature, although the consolidation had been approved by advisory referenda in the five areas brought together by the legislative action. Several of the large central cities of American metropolitan areas have had their boundaries expanded extensively by legislative action; in most instances, however, this type of integration took place in the nineteenth century.

Integration may be accomplished by a central administrative body, exercising authority delegated it by a central legislature or by the people. In such instances, the legislature usually establishes criteria to guide the judgment of the administrative body and prescribes specific procedures to be followed. In Canada, several provincial legislatures have delegated authority with respect to certain aspects of local government to a provincial administrative board. An example is the Ontario Municipal Board, the initiator of the Toronto Metropolitan

---

[4] The Local Government Act, 1888, created the London County Council, and the London Government Act, 1899, created the metropolitan borough councils.

Plan. The city of Toronto proposed, in 1950, to amalgamate the suburban communities and form a unified metropolitan government. The Municipal Board rejected the city proposal and recommended to the provincial government a plan that was used as the basis for the organization ultimately adopted. The Provincial Administrative Board, in this instance, was a disinterested body not politically involved in the affairs of any one metropolitan area. Therefore, it could take a broader view of the matter than could Toronto or suburban officials.

The judiciary is another type of disinterested agency that has been authorized to pass upon annexations to a central city. The Virginia plan is based upon this method of determining boundary adjustments. It is complicated somewhat by the fact that incorporated cities are normally detached from the county; hence, any annexation to a city involves transfer of jurisdiction from the county to the city. Virginia has chosen to produce its readjustments of local government by means of judicial process, in which the interested parties present their arguments and briefs of fact and law to assist the disinterested court make its decision. Voters and elected officials are kept outside the decision-making process.

In other American states, the legislature has the basic jurisdiction to determine how the boundaries of municipalities may be altered, subject to any limitations placed upon it by the state constitution. In most of the states, the concept of local home rule has led the legislature to authorize the voters, in the areas involved, to approve or disapprove proposals to annex territory to the central city. Chicago is an important illustration of integration by voluntary annexation. Although the Illinois legislature assigned much territory to Chicago between 1850 and 1870 without local referendum, the city annexed a greater total of suburban territory, 157.5 square miles, during the period of 1887 to 1924, with the approval of voters in the areas affected.[5] Atlanta, Georgia, also acquired a vast acreage in suburban areas in 1952 by vote of the people affected.

When a state legislature delegates authority to local bodies or groups to determine annexation actions, one of two alternative concepts is likely to prevail. According to one, annexation is an action by which unincorporated territory requests to join a municipality in order to obtain the benefits which urban government can provide. Under the other, a municipality reaches out on its own initiative to acquire territory because the city expects to benefit in some manner from the action. We need not delve, at this point, into the various political motivations that figure in annexation movements. Nevertheless, the

---

[5] Studenski, op. cit., p. 74.

controlling concept of the nature of annexation determines the type of legal action that will be permitted or required.

The state of Texas is one that regards annexation as a process primarily of interest to and for the benefit of the existing cities. The Legislature there has delegated to city councils authority to annex adjacent territory solely by action of the local body and without reference to the voters residing in the area to be annexed. By employing this procedure, the city of Houston, for example, has extended its boundaries enormously and has largely integrated the metropolitan area in which it is located. Only a few enclaves, comprising previously incorporated municipalities that could not be absorbed by the core city by the prescribed process, have been omitted.

The California system of annexation, as analyzed in Chapter Four, is based upon two considerations. First, annexation is considered to be a joining of territory outside a city with the municipality by mutual consent. Second, if the area to be annexed is inhabited, the action must be approved by a popular referendum in the area to be received.[6] It is within this context that the city of Los Angeles operated in trying to integrate the metropolitan area by annexation.

LOS ANGELES EXPANSION POLITICS

The major integration era in Los Angeles can be divided into two periods for purposes of analysis. The period of 1906 to 1913 was characterized by considerable annexation activity. During that time, the city of Los Angeles reached out to the far corners of the adjacent area to induce voters resident in territories that were strategically important for the city's own interests to join it. Harbor development and water supply shared distinctions as motivations for annexing activities. The second period, 1913 to 1927, saw the greatest expansion of the central city's borders. During that period almost every move for annexation had water politics in its background. The official city position was to encourage communities to join, in order to integrate the metropolitan area under control of the central city; numerous areas showed a frantic desire to enter the city.

In discussing the integration era, it is necessary to use the term "annexation" in its general sense. Technically, both annexation and

---

[6] Prior to 1923 annexations had to be approved by the voters in the city as well as in the territory to be annexed. After that date the City Council was authorized to act for the city. Some annexations voted in the 1920's depended upon approval by a two-thirds majority of those voting because annexed territory was required to assume a portion of the city's bonded indebtedness for the water system.

consolidation were involved. Not only were 230,422.98 acres[7] of unincorporated territory added to the city, but such incorporated municipalities as San Pedro, Wilmington, Hollywood, Eagle Rock, Sawtelle, Barnes City, Watts, Hyde Park, and Venice agreed to consolidate with Los Angeles.

The original city had a territory that was laid out in a square pattern, four miles per side, conforming to the Spanish pueblo grant. Its geographic location was related to the passes through which overland trails and roads brought commerce from northern California, Arizona, and areas eastward. Its location was also related to the Los Angeles river, whose resources the pueblo grant reserved for the use of those who colonized and developed the community. It was at that junction that the center of the city's commerce, administration, and residential life was located.

The first annexations of territory to the city of Los Angeles were made chiefly to ensure continuance of the water supply that land owners in suburban areas had been accustomed to draw from the Los Angeles source. Court decisions had ruled that the city could not dispose of its surplus pueblo-water to buyers located beyond the city limits.[8] The immediate consequence of these rulings was that land owners applied to have their lands annexed to the city, and the municipality acquiesced.

The next set of annexations was for the purpose of bringing the harbor at San Pedro–Wilmington within the boundaries of Los Angeles and thereby linking the political and economic fortunes of the two areas. The first action involved annexation of a "shoe-string strip" that was approximately one-half mile in width and sixteen miles in length and that extended from the southern boundary of Los Angeles to the northern boundary of Wilmington. The strip jogged at one point to avoid splitting the community of Gardena. This annexation was completed in November, 1906. The final step that was required to bring the harbor within Los Angeles was delayed until new legislation could be obtained from the state to permit two or more contiguous cities to consolidate. The new consolidation legislation became effective in March, 1909. In June, the Los Angeles City Council sought to assure the San Pedro and Wilmington residents that they would receive adequate municipal services and public works if consolidation took place. On August 4, Wilmington voters approved consolidation and on August 11, San Pedro voters did similarly. Los Angeles City voters,

---

[7] 359.99 square miles.

[8] See Chapter Two, p. 56.

acting on the same days as those of the other municipalities, approved the two actions.

Water supply became a major factor again in annexation activities during the first period. The communities of Hyde Park, Green Meadows, Gardena, Shorb, Hermon, Eagle Rock, Tropico, Ivanhoe, Cahuenga, Colegrove, and Ballona requested admission to Los Angeles, in 1907, in order to assure themselves of an adequate supply of water, but the voters of Los Angeles defeated the proposal. The opposition within the city expressed the view that the areas that proposed annexation lacked sufficient taxable wealth to offset the demands they would make for city water. In 1910, however, Los Angeles eagerly accepted the requests made by the town of Hollywood, and added the community's 11.1 square miles to the city's territory. Unincorporated East Hollywood was deemed by the City Water Department to be in a strategic position to aid the city's interests because a portion of it was located on the Los Angeles river.[9] In 1912, the city admitted several communities in the Arroyo Seco district, which was north and east of the original city. In this instance, the city made acceptance of responsibility for a portion of the city's bonded indebtedness a condition of admission.

The second period in the great era of Los Angeles expansion came after the city government had decided a policy for the disposal of surplus water. With the arrival of the Owens Valley water in 1913, via the city aqueduct, a spectacular expansion set in.

Prior to the arrival of the new supply, however, the City Council adopted the policy, proposed by Mayor Rose and the Public Service Commission, that the city's surplus water be made available only to areas that would become part of the city, agree to support the cost of local distribution systems, and assume a share of the aqueduct cost. The objectives of the proponents of this policy were further stated in the report of the specially appointed Annexation Commission to the council:

> Annexation and consolidation will give Los Angeles official standing as the metropolis of the Pacific Coast. Greater Los Angeles, coextensive with the territory receiving aqueduct water, will have a population, assessed valuation, bank clearings, building permits, and so forth in excess of any other city on the Pacific Coast. All this has an economic value to which Los Angeles is entitled by reason of the great investment it has made and the risk it has incurred in the Owens River Aqueduct enterprise. Where

⁹ Richard Bigger and James Kitchen, *How the Cities Grew* (Los Angeles: Bureau of Governmental Research, University of California, 1952), pp. 164–165.

the aqueduct water is placed—be it north, south, east, or west—there will the greatest development of the future be found. And that development should be a part of and help constitute the Greater Los Angeles that is to be.[10]

Immediately following the adoption of the city's water policy, two sections, Bairdstown and Palms, requested admission. Decision on both applications was withheld until the city could decide upon the much more dramatic proposal that the San Fernando Valley be annexed as one large parcel. After a spirited election campaign within the city, approximately sixty thousand Los Angeles voters turned out to approve two annexations (Palms and San Fernando Valley) that more than doubled the territory of the city, expanding it from 107.6 square miles to 284.8 square miles. Bairdstown and two other small additions were approved within the year following.

Much of the San Fernando Valley land was devoted to agriculture, including tree crops, vegetables, and dairy farming, as well as grain raising. Inclusion of this large agricultural section in the city made this municipality one of the major centers of agricultural wealth in the state. In recognition of the point that agricultural needs for water differed from those of urban users, the Public Service Commission established two sets of water rates, one for agriculture and one for domestic users.

In 1916, the question of sale of water to areas outside the city arose again when a proposal to sell water to the cities of Santa Monica and Sawtelle was placed on the municipal ballot. Those favoring the proposition again argued that selling surplus water would bring in needed revenue and avoid the demand for municipal services that annexation produced. Opponents countered that it was unfair to expect outside landowners to invest large sums for improvements when the water supply could not be guaranteed, and that it was unfair for the city taxpayers to furnish the water without compelling the recipients to pay a portion of the cost of the aqueduct. It was also feared that if the city engaged in the sale of surplus water to areas of its choosing, the state might force it to sell water, under state regulation, to communities between Owens Valley and Los Angeles. The vote in the 1916 election seems to have finally settled the issue; the subject did not recur after its second defeat by the municipal voters.

At the same election at which water sale was rejected, the Los Angeles voters approved another large annexation and one small one.

---

[10] Los Angeles City, *Council Records*, XCIV, 141, quoted by Vincent Ostrom, *Water and Politics* (Los Angeles: Haynes Foundation, 1953), p. 155.

The Westgate addition lay in the western section, terminating at the
ocean, portions of it lying between the cities of Beverly Hills and
Santa Monica. The entire addition comprised a total of 48.67 square
miles. Upon completion of that annexation, the city began an extensive
development of a water-distribution system within it. In order that
water mains might reach this section, lines had to be extended over
the Santa Monica hills, which were outside the city limits. Storage
reservoirs were constructed in several of the canyons. In time, most
of the hill areas were annexed to the city, although there were relatively few residences and little development. As a consquence of these
moves, the city found itself confronted with a mountain fire-patrol
problem and rural road-construction problems that were not common
to cities.[11]

In the six year period extending from 1915 to 1920, Los Angeles
more than tripled its land area, raising it from 107.62 square miles to
364.4 square miles. In 1921, the post-war economic depression halted
annexation activity, but the earlier trend was resumed in 1922. During
the next six year period, thirty-four unincorporated areas and five municipalities joined Los Angeles. Some 76.74 square miles were added to
bring the city's total area to 441.10 square miles.

An important addition during that period (1922–1927) was the West
Coast annexation, which at the time of joining was held chiefly in
large parcels by owners who were engaged in farming but were de-
sirous of securing a firm water supply. The city benefited from the
addition because it acquired full control over the site surrounding the
city's ocean-outfall sewer at Hyperion. Two decades later, the addition
also became the site of the city's International Airport and of major
developments of housing and aircraft industries.

Large annexations virtually ceased as the year 1927 came to a close,
the consolidation of Barnes City being the final one in that period.
One partial exception was the consolidation of the city of Tujunga
with Los Angeles, which was not consummated until eight years later.
Proponents of the Tujunga consolidation first submitted the matter to
a ballot in 1927, but it took three unsuccessful efforts before they were
able to muster a favorable majority. Court tests of the procedure delayed the final step in the consolidation until 1935, when Tujunga's
8.70 square miles were added to Los Angeles.

Los Angeles has made eighty-five annexations since 1927, but almost

---

[11] A large part of the hilly area that lies between the San Fernando Valley and
Beverly Hills was annexed as part of the Laurel Canyon addition in 1923. In the
period after 1945 these areas in the Santa Monica hills became the sites of de luxe
subdivisions offering high-priced "view sites" for upper-income families.

all have been relatively small parcels, ranging from less than one acre to one hundred acres. Many of these additions have rounded out city boundaries or have added an enclave or "island" that had been missed earlier, because of the owner's desire to have his property exempt from municipal responsibilities and benefits so long as it remained undeveloped property. The largest annexation after Tujunga was an addition of 1.74 square miles in the Calabasas area, located on the western edge of the San Fernando Valley.[12] Although Los Angeles has continued to annex acreage steadily, year after year, the great expansion came to an end in 1927. Between 1906 and 1927 the central city had more than quadrupled its land area.

The configuration of the city that resulted from the annexation movements was a curious one that exhibited little compactness. The central area was the only portion that was reasonably compact. The main body of the city consisted of the old central section, plus the San Fernando Valley, the Hollywood–Santa Monica hills, and the West Los Angeles section. Within this great area there are numerous "islands" or enclaves, such as the incorporated cities of San Fernando, Beverly Hills, Culver City, and Santa Monica, and several unincorporated areas. The largest among the latter are the West Hollywood–Sherman and the Baldwin Hills–LaBallona areas.

The Shoestring Strip–Wilmington–San Pedro part of the city lies appended to the municipality like a pendulum on a huge clock. In several areas, the irregular shape of the city's boundaries, with the consequent lack of compactness, has produced problems for those administering water and sewage service and police and fire protection. In numerous instances it was necessary to cross other cities or county territory.

By 1927, Los Angeles had access to relatively few remaining unincorporated areas, had it desired to continue annexing. The East Los Angeles section remained an unincorporated corridor through which Los Angeles might have spread to the eastern portions of the county. In the southern portion of the county, an area remained on the east side of the Shoestring Strip annexation; and the Palos Verdes hills, on the western edge of San Pedro, also remained unincorporated. Nevertheless, it was evident that a ring of incorporated suburbs had closed around Los Angeles and limited the city's opportunity to claim new territory.

Although eight cities consolidated with Los Angeles during the big expansion period, others demonstrated by vote of their electorates that

---

[12] City of Los Angeles, Controller, *Annual Report, 1959–60* (Los Angeles, 1960), pp. 134–136.

they were prepared to resist integration into the central city and to retain municipal independence. Tropico twice defeated proposals to consolidate with Los Angeles, and then decided to join Glendale. Santa Monica voters twice rejected consolidation with Los Angeles, as did those in Burbank. Beverly Hills and Alhamba voters each rejected a similar proposition. Consolidation petitions were circulated in Inglewood, Hawthorne, Culver City, and Pasadena during the 1920's and early 1930's, but in no instance did they acquire sufficient support to achieve a place on the municipal ballots.

INTEGRATION HALTED

Why did the move to integrate the metropolitan area by annexation to the core city slow its pace and come to a virtual stop before achieving the objectives so glowingly announced in 1913? Two sets of factors are evident. One that was in operation in the late 1920's helps to explain the slowing of the annexation pace in 1927. The second relates to later time periods and helps to explain why the integration drive was not renewed after World War II, when suburban areas began to hum with subdivision activities and to fill with population.

The first set of factors include: The decision by the city government to discourage further annexation overtures in order to preserve the existing water supply; recognition by city water officials that water importation was a high cost operation; and development of a suburban ring around the core city. The second set include: The economic depression of the 1930's; the recall of Mayor Shaw; lack of coördination in city administration; pressures to decentralize municipal operations and to fragment the city; preoccupation of the city administration with meeting demands for increased service; and inducements for newly developed areas, located on the perimeter of the central city, to incorporate rather than seek annexation.

WATER SUPPLY LIMITED

In a real sense, the annexation "boom" was halted by official city action, based upon the advice of Water Bureau officials that accepting additional land that could claim water from the city's supply would place an unreasonable strain upon the system. Although additional water was anticipated from the Metropolitan Water District, that supply could not become available for several years. In the meantime the city was facing a serious situation, aggravated by fluctuations in annual rainfall that threatened to produce droughts.

William Mulholland, the Chief Engineer of the Water Bureau,

warned the city administration, in 1922, that when the existing irregularities in the profile of the city's boundaries were made symmetrical ". . . it will be found that there is quite sufficient area within the city to absorb, when fully developed, the present water supply."[13] Three years later the Public Service Commission stated to the City Council that it was not possible to provide adequate water supply to the numerous areas that were applying for annexation.[14] Every year the Water Engineer and the commission called attention to two facts: that the area was experiencing a drought, and that the supply of water available to the city was limited. Mulholland reported in 1927:

> Considerable attention has been given to a study of the available water supply for this city. The supply of adjacent local sources available for Los Angeles has been developed to practically its limit. . . . This condition of our water resources, coupled with the expected growth of the city, emphasizes our obligation to seek an additional supply which will be adequate to meet these demands.[15]

The commission pointed out on several occasions that "the present sources of supply . . . have their limitations, and in fact the population now served from the Los Angeles aqueduct source is in excess of the original number contemplated to be served." [16]

At the same time, the city was finding it increasingly difficult to finance the expansion of the water system that was constantly being demanded. In 1925, the Board of Water and Power Commissioners, at the recommendation of Chief Engineer Mulholland, requested the City Council to permit it to raise the water rates substantially, but although the council approved the raise, the mayor vetoed it. On several occasions, the water administration pointed out that the city faced a number of unusual factors that added to the cost of water. Mulholland explained the situation as follows:

> There is no earthly reason for the persistent low rate charged for water supply in this city. The city in every way being a difficult one to supply and the fact that our rates compare with those of most easily supplied cities in the United States give us emphatic reasons for demanding higher rates. In the first place our water is brought from greater distances, with greater difficulty and initial cost than any city in the world and is supplied to a region of rougher topography, requiring greater lifts and more diversified

[13] Los Angeles *Herald*, Dec. 18, 1922.
[14] Los Angeles *Record*, Nov. 21, 1925.
[15] Board of Water and Power Commissioners, *Annual Report, 1927*, p. 7.
[16] Board of Water and Power Commissioners, *Annual Report, 1926*, p. 5.

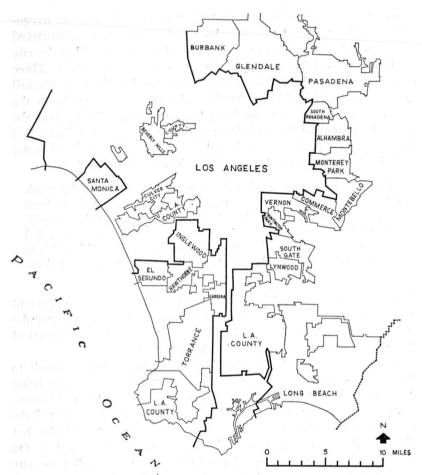

Fig. 5. Municipalities surrounding the city of Los Angeles.

and expensive conditions than any existing city in the United
States. We earnestly call attention to this fact and to the impend-
ing, increasing cost of our future supply.[17]

The Suburban Ring Develops

By the time Los Angeles relaxed its expansion activities in 1927, a
ring of suburban municipalities had almost closed the gaps in the
blockade around the core city. Incorporations, annexations to the suburban cities, and defeats of Los Angeles' consolidation proposals had
combined to tighten this ring. The concept that all territory of a mu-

---

[17] Department of Water and Power, *Annual Report, 1928*, p. 8.

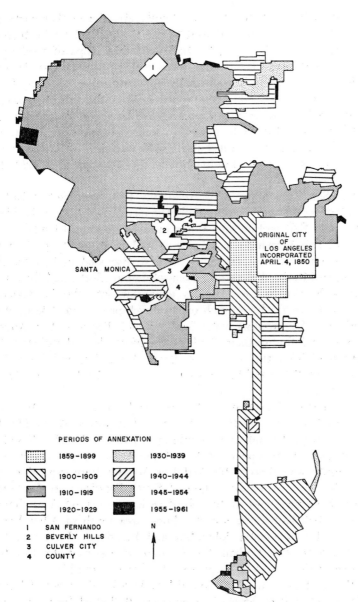

FIG. 6. Annexations to the city of Los Angeles.

nicipality must be joined in a contiguous parcel prevented Los Angeles from expanding in certain areas, unless it could draw an annexation boundary with a long "shoestring" connecting link to reach around the blockading cities. This strip annexation technique was tried in the

Bell-addition incident, but the city finally abandoned that particular effort in 1927 and did not attempt to use the method again. In some earlier annexations, Los Angeles had used thin strips of territory to connect it with large tracts that were seeking annexations. In each case, however, it had followed up by annexing other adjoining lands, to gain control over sizable communities. After the suburban ring of cities began to close around Los Angeles, however, the central city would have been forced to resort, in many instances, to the use of strips and corridors to connect itself with any new areas that might seek annexation. Let us examine briefly the situation as it existed in the later 1920's.

In the San Fernando Valley, relatively few communities had incorporated as cities and consequently the city of Los Angeles had been able to enter that section and annex on a large scale. Glendale, Burbank, and San Fernando had incorporated in the early part of the century when water importation was first discussed in Los Angeles. Glendale and Burbank resisted all consolidation efforts, and their areas formed a barrier to Los Angeles expansion into the La Canada–La Crescenta area, where much urban development was taking place. Nevertheless, by merging with Sunland and Tujunga, Los Angeles slipped around the northern flank of the blockade and threatened to cut off Glendale's future expansion. Burbank was left with limited expansion possibilities; and San Fernando was completely surrounded by Los Angeles.

In the northeast section of the metropolitan area, Pasadena and South Pasadena were relatively old cities that possessed considerable wealth and strength and were unwilling to join Los Angeles. Pasadena annexed most of the upper reaches of the Arroyo Seco to protect its water supply, and thereby blocked Los Angeles from expanding further in that area. Alhambra adjoined South Pasadena on the latter's southern boundary; and so the suburban barrier extended southward. Monterey Park had incorporated a huge area south of Alhambra, in 1916, in order to counter Alhambra and Pasadena efforts to extend their sewage treatment plant. The incorporation served also to extend the barrier to Los Angeles' expansion further eastward.[18]

Southeast of the central portion of Los Angeles, the cities of Vernon and Huntington Park blocked annexation. Both had been organized prior to 1910, and Huntington Park had expanded slightly. Considerable suburban development took place in the southeast section in the 1920's, a part of the general post-war growth. New cities were formed:

---

[18] The city of Montebello was carved out of Monterey Park in 1922, and expanded its boundaries.

Lynwood, in 1921; South Gate, in 1923; and Maywood, in 1924. In 1926, Los Angeles attempted to annex the area known as Bell, between Maywood and South Gate, but Huntington Park succeeded in annexing a part of it and after an extended struggle, Los Angeles abandoned its efforts. Shortly thereafter, Bell incorporated. The result of the sequence of actions was the completion of a solid line of suburban cities that bounded Los Angeles on the southeast: Vernon, Huntington Park, Maywood, Bell, South Gate, Lynwood, Compton, and Long Beach. During the period when the incorporations were negotiated along Los Angeles' southeastern border, Long Beach was engaged in a vigorous expansion program of its own. By 1927, the Long Beach northern expansion had reached the southern limits of Compton, pre-

TABLE 3

INCORPORATING IN THE SUBURBS

City	Date of incorporation
Bell	1927
Beverly Hills	1914
Burbank	1911
Culver City	1917
El Segundo	1917
Gardena	1930
Glendale	1906
Hawthorne	1922
Hermosa Beach	1907
Huntington Park	1906
Inglewood	1908
Lynwood	1921
Manhattan Beach	1912
Maywood	1924
Montebello	1920
Monterey Park	1916
Palos Verdes	1939
Pasadena	1886
Redondo Beach	1892
San Fernando	1911
San Gabriel	1913
San Marino	1913
Santa Monica	1886
South Gate	1923
South Pasadena	1888
Torrance	1921
Vernon	1905

venting Los Angeles from expanding eastward from its Shoestring
Strip.

In the South Bay–Centinella Valley area, Los Angeles was not fully
contained, but a substantial blockade had developed. Redondo Beach
was the oldest city in that area, dating from 1892. Hermosa Beach
had been organized on Redondo's northern border in 1907, and Manhattan Beach had incorporated on the north side of Hermosa in 1912.
El Segundo, adjacent to Manhattan, had been organized by the Standard Oil Company as a site for refineries and oil storage. Los Angeles
had succeeded in reaching the ocean at Hyperion and had consolidated
with the city of Venice, but its further expansion was stopped.

In the Centinella Valley section, Inglewood was the oldest city, having been incorporated in 1908. It was joined on its southern border
by Hawthorne in 1922. In the lower reaches of that valley, Torrance
was incorporated in 1921, and set out to annex large portions of the
surrounding area. Gardena incorporated in 1930 after several previous
efforts, to incorporate and to join Los Angeles, had failed.

Although there were unincorporated territories, west of the South
Bay and south of Centinella Valley, available for development in 1927,
they were diminishing. Torrance annexed large tracts and thereby expanded its borders in such a manner that it produced a solid block of
suburban territory that extended from the western edge of Los Angeles' Shoestring Strip to the Santa Monica Bay.

When the Los Angeles expansion drive came to a halt, the core
city was almost solidly enclosed by suburban cities, mountains, and
the Pacific Ocean. Although the ring was not quite complete, the
countervailing force of suburban independence had made its impact
felt.

DEPRESSION AND SCANDALS STRIKE

Economic depression, which began in 1929 and extended far into
the decade of the 1930's, quieted most of the forces that had been demanding urban development and expansion in the previous decades.
Enthusiasm for undertaking new municipal services was dampened;
only the Metropolitan Water District aqueduct was pushed, to relieve
unemployment. Neither Los Angeles nor its neighbors were capable of
servicing new areas.

The city had scarcely recovered from the enervating effects of the
depression when public attitude toward its government was jarred into
critical or negative positions by new developments. Rumors flew that
city jobs were being purchased and that there was graft in the police
and planning departments, and were denied. The mayoralty election

of 1937 was marked with an undertone of suspicion and charges, although Mayor Frank Shaw was reëlected with a comfortable margin of votes. The situation culminated in 1938, however, with the bombing of a private investigator's automobile by persons who were soon identified as members of the police intelligence squad. Evidence made public by the resulting investigations shook public confidence in the city police, fire, civil service, and public-works departments, and raised strong antagonism to the mayor and his close associates. A recall petition qualified against the mayor, and its proponents persuaded Superior Court Judge Fletcher Bowron to stand for election against Shaw. At the special election, Shaw was removed and Bowron was designated to replace him. The new mayor promptly set about restoring confidence in the city government by appointing new persons to key positions and reorganizing municipal administrative machinery. Nevertheless, Los Angeles was scarcely in a position to persuade other communities to come under its jurisdiction. Leaders of the suburbs were occupied with strengthening their respective jurisdictions. In large part, though, the city officialdom was preoccupied with the rebuilding job, with meeting the problems that arose in serving a city recovering from the effects of the depression, and with developing many sections that had been annexed twenty years earlier.

When the Colorado River water reached the metropolitan area in 1941, Los Angeles ceased to be the dominant possessor of the prize for which so many had contended. Membership in the Metropolitan Water District of Southern California and access to the new supply were open to any city, and any group of cities that might choose to band together in a water district, that would accept the terms for admission to the MWD.

The period in which the United States was involved in World War II, 1941 to 1945, was one in which municipal expenditures were kept down. Manpower and materials were shifted to activities more directly involved in the war efforts.

INTERNAL PRESSURES AND CONFLICTS

When the postwar migration swelled the population of all communities in southern California, the core city, as well as the suburbs, experienced enormous pressures to meet internal problems. Areas that Los Angeles had annexed between 1913 and 1927 that were either partially developed or in agricultural use were subdivided by developers and filled with population. The Westchester [Westgate] area, estimated to have had 946 population and 394 dwelling units in 1940, grew to 21,668 persons and 5,979 dwelling units by July, 1947. The Encino

Statistical Area, in the San Fernando Valley, had 37,312 population and 11,916 dwelling units in 1940 and comprised 69,055 persons and 20,446 dwelling units in July, 1947. The San Vicente Statistical Area, in West Los Angeles, had grown somewhat less spectacularly, but it had moved from 7,737 persons and 2,478 dwelling units in 1940, to 12,438 persons and 3,444 units in 1947.[19]

This kind of development continued steadily in much of the San Fernando Valley, Westchester, and West Los Angeles areas. Each of the areas in which extensive development took place demanded improved streets, storm drains, and sewer connections; increased street lighting; expanded water and power facilities; enhanced police and fire protection, new recreation centers, and many other municipal services. The city government was too occupied with meeting the challenges of population growth and physical developments within the city's existing boundaries to be able to plan successfully for adding new areas.

A new kind of political tension developed as subdividers turned agricultural acres into housing tracts, shopping centers developed, and new industrial and manufacturing areas took shape in the outlying sections of the city. For the first time in its history, the city of Los Angeles was faced with the problem of holding in the municipal family the areas it had jubilantly drawn to itself two decades previously. Demands for increased public works and improved levels of service in several sections of the city were followed by agitation for a degree of community governmental autonomy. Discontent, arising from failures to receive prompt action on numerous matters, such as zoning, parking and traffic problems in shopping and residential areas, and construction of new fire stations, libraries, and police facilities, caused leaders in several areas to push for "secession" from the city. Old discontents, as well as new frustrations, led to innumerable tensions within the city's politics. For the most part, these tensions were most serious in those sections that were farthest from the city center and were also experiencing the greatest rate of population growth.

A variety of community groups actively discussed "secession" from the central city. In part they were discontented with the councilmanic form of government,[20] because the rapidly growing districts had insufficient representation to voice their demands successfully. In every instance their frustration arose from failure to achieve local community

[19] Los Angeles County Regional Planning Commission, *Dwellings and Population*, Bull. 23 (July, 1947).

[20] Los Angeles *Daily News*, Nov. 12, 1947.

demands. Secession was advocated most vigorously in the San Fernando Valley and the harbor areas.[21]

Mayor Bowron moved to counter the secession proposals and to alleviate the political pressure by reviving the borough concept, which had been suggested in 1909. His plan would have divided the city into five boroughs: Central, Harbor, West Los Angeles, Hollywood, and San Fernando. Each was to have a policy-making board, elected by the voters of the area, and the chairman of each board was to sit with the central-city governing body. Borough boards were to have authority to determine location and improvement of secondary streets, garbage-collection routes and procedures, location of bus and street car stops, and local zoning.[22] It was further suggested that the boards should have authority to set borough tax rates and to spend the revenue within the borough. The central city was expected to retain responsibility for such matters as police administration, fire protection, public-health programs, and over-all city planning.

Although the mayor presented his plan in several radio broadcasts, and most of the central area daily newspapers carried feature stories and news about the proposal, no specific action resulted. Individual city council members were quoted in the press as being favorable to "some type of borough plan," but no charter amendment was presented to the electorate.

In the San Pedro area, old political discontents were revived. It was recalled that when the city of San Pedro had been persuaded to consolidate with Los Angeles in 1909, representatives of the central city had agreed to amend the charter to provide for a borough form of government. Although an amendment had been enacted, the state courts had invalidated it. The entire subject had been permitted to languish, and no effort had been made to correct the features to which the court had objected. When interest in the concept of borough government was revived in 1947, no legal basis for such a plan existed. Assemblyman Vincent Thomas of San Pedro responded to this situation and persuaded an interim legislative committee to study the borough plan, as it applied to large cities. Upon completion of the inquiry, Thomas introduced a constitutional amendment authorizing a city to amend its charter to permit division of the city into one or more boroughs and to provide for local government within them. The Thomas amendment was approved by the Legislature and was adopted by the voters in 1952. Although no specific action was taken to amend

---

[21] *Ibid.*

[22] Los Angeles *Examiner*, March 7, 1948.

the Los Angeles charter in conformity with the amendment, it was generally believed that the San Pedro area had improved its bargaining position with the city hall officialdom.

Community organizations in the San Fernando Valley and Westchester areas kept interest in a borough plan of decentralized city government astir between 1947 and 1953. Community chambers of commerce and weekly newspapers, in company with other similar local groups, publicized the general concept in group meetings, feature stories, and editorials. In many instances, it seemed that agitation for this plan was used as a means for bargaining with council members and city administrative departments on city services and policy decisions. Most of the discussion of proposed legal powers for boroughs and boundary limits remained nebulous.

Mayor Bowron renewed his backing of the plan in 1952 and offered a more detailed proposal. He advocated that the charter be amended to permit any area within the city to organize a borough government with an elective board to levy taxes for support of local or community functions. Some of the functions would serve to supplement the levels of performance offered by the citywide government; some would provide services that were unique to the borough. The mayor's second plan went further, specifying that city administrative departments, such as police and fire, could be decentralized, with borough officials directing the units stationed in their locality, subject to over-all supervision and coördination by city department heads.

While the mayor was developing his design of decentralized city government, other issues absorbed attention. Chief among these was the question of extending the city's public-housing program. Acquisition of land for a large public-housing project in Chavez Ravine became a major issue in the mayoral election of 1953, in which Mayor Bowron was defeated for reëlection by Congressman Norris Poulson. During the campaign, community leaders in the San Fernando Valley reiterated their complaints that the city administration had not been sufficiently attentive to their demands for improved streets, traffic control, and a host of other items.

Discussion of the borough plan was suspended with the advent of the new administration. The mayor made a special point to select persons from the dissident areas for city commissions and to direct city departments to make a special effort to develop programs that would assist those communities in which the greatest growth was taking place. The mayor and his staff were careful to develop the public image of central-office concern with community as well as city-wide problems. Revision of council district boundaries to give the San

Fernando Valley greater representation also assisted in quieting discontent. Three of the fifteen councilmen were allocated districts wholly within the Valley, and local interests were given greater recognition.

The secession issue reappeared in 1961, arising from disputes between community groups and city departments. Home owners in Westwood were disturbed over zoning changes that permitted construction of high-rise apartment and office buildings, as well as proposed street changes. Groups in the San Fernando Valley demanded new changes in city council districts to increase the section's representation. Rises in valuation of property for tax purposes caused considerable disgruntlement. Several groups discussed ways of withdrawing from the city.

FORMAL STRUCTURE LIMITS LEADERSHIP

The structure of city government in Los Angeles has produced several results that affect the city's role as a contender for metropolitan leadership. The first effort to modernize and strengthen the formal government was made in 1903. From then until 1924 the city charter was amended numerous times to permit new departments to be added and to set policies. In the midst of the city's great expansion period a board of freeholders was selected to write a new charter, because it was believed that the growing city needed a more carefully designed governmental structure.

Under the previous charter, the mayor was elected for the relatively short period of two years. There was no formal limitation upon eligibility for reëlection, however. The mayor appointed the Chief of Police, Fire Chief, Health Commissioner, and members of several commissions, the latter with the approval of the City Council. Commission members held office for four year terms, staggered in such a manner that no two positions on a commission became vacant normally in the same year. The mayor was given unusual responsibility with respect to police and fire administration, being designated chairman of the commissions heading those departments. The balance of membership of both commissions consisted of two citizens appointed by the mayor, with the approval of the Council. Most other commissions, including those for harbor, public service, and public works, had authority to appoint their chief administrators. The mayor's formal powers with respect to the city administration were limited, both by reason of the restraints upon his power of appointment and his relatively short term of office.

The City Council was elected at-large. All nine members were elected at the same time and for the same length of term as the mayor. Being elected on an at-large basis, each council member could take a citywide view in considering policy problems. None was obligated to obtain public works or factors for any particular area or to please a place-oriented constituency. They were concerned, however, with publicity media that were citywide in coverage and influence, and were respectful of those sources of campaign funds having a major interest in municipal affairs. Generally, the successful candidates for council offices were residents of the older portions of the city.

The changes produced in city government structure by the new charter emphasized checks upon the executive power. Although the mayor's term was doubled, from two to four years, the chief executive was expected to coördinate the various administrative departments by indirect rather than direct means. Additional commissions were created, and older commissions were increased in membership, to give the mayor more opportunities to appoint citizens whom he wished to associate with the city's administration. All these appointments were subject to council approval, however. Each commission was authorized to appoint the administrative head of the department and to supervise departmental operations. Because commissioners' terms were staggered, a newly elected mayor could not obtain control of any commission until the third year of his term, or normally appoint a complete commission unless he were reëlected for a second term. In substance, the charter placed the supervision and direction of the city's administration upon the part-time lay commissioners, who were relatively independent of the mayor and inclined to be preoccupied with a single program.

An elective city controller was to have responsibilities for post-auditing city expenditures. The city attorney, also an elected officer, advised the mayor, council, and other municipal officers on legal matters.

A new concept of budget preparation and control was introduced by the 1924 charter. A central administrative unit, the Bureau of Budget and Efficiency, was created to provide staff assistance to the mayor and council. However, it was placed in a position of dual responsibility that compelled it to be moderate and cautious. The director was to be chosen by the mayor, with the approval of the council, and the council was given equal authority with the mayor to direct the bureau to provide information and make studies.

Council membership was increased from nine to fifteen, and the at-large method of election was replaced by a single-member district plan. Each council member became the spokesman for a geographic district and a set of local constituents. Each proved to be greatly concerned with public works construction and maintenance in his district and with the activities of the service departments. The charter required the council to meet in session five days per week and gave it authority to pass upon many routine administrative matters. The post of council member thereby became a full-time responsibility. Initially, the council majority came from districts located in the older sections of the city, because the bulk of population was concentrated there. Council members elected from districts that included the harbor, West Los Angeles, Hollywood, and the San Fernando Valley represented constituencies that required street improvements and public works to meet the needs of developing areas. As population increased more rapidly in the outlying districts than in the older central sections, the struggle to realign district boundaries became intense.

The mayor, as the city's chief executive with a citywide constituency, had to reckon constantly with the council's interest in local parts of the city. Furthermore, as indicated previously, the mayor had limited power to impose his program views upon the departments. His efforts to initiate, to coördinate, and to plan were subject to checks at every turn by powerful forces.

The first really significant effort to coördinate the city administration was begun in 1951, when the charter was amended to create the position of City Administrative Officer. This position was superimposed upon the Bureau of Budget and Efficiency, which became the nucleus of the Administrative Officer's staff. The CAO, appointed by the mayor with the approval of the City Council, became a pillar of strength for the mayor in regard to administrative matters, but he was not exclusively the mayor's aide. He was assigned extensive responsibilities for budget preparation and budget execution and for studies relating to improvement of organization and procedures. Within the framework defined for him, the City Administrative Officer was able to establish a role displaying some strength. In the area of administrative management, the CAO established a niche in which he and his staff were respected and given considerable influence. Among the accomplishments was a performance budget method by which the process of central review and evaluation of departmental spending was strengthened.

The impact made upon the city government by the City Administrative Officer was due to several factors, including the management skill of the first incumbent, an uninterrupted tenure of ten years in service, and an experienced technical staff of civil servants available upon taking office. Mr. Samuel Leask was first appointed by Mayor Bowron in 1951 and remained to serve for the eight years of Mayor Poulson's administration. Throughout this ten-year period, the City Administrative Officer held the confidence of the mayors and the City Council alike, but also possessed strength independent of both sets of officers. Upon Leask's resignation in 1961, to join the state administration, the incoming mayor (Yorty) appointed Mr. George Terhune, who had been Chief Assistant CAO and a career man in the city's budget office. In January, 1962, Terhune gave way to Mr. Erwin Piper, a former career administrator in the federal government.

Amendments to the 1924 charter have changed the status of departmental general managers and strengthened departmental management. Department heads have been given greater security of tenure by placing them in the classified civil service, and their powers, with respect to the management of departmental operations, have been clarified. They continue to be appointed by the commissions, but their removal is limited by civil service procedures. Commission responsibilities are less administrative than formerly and relate more to policy making. The managers are responsible for directing the work of the departments, within the framework of commission policy. Changes in the position of the departmental managers tended to produce greater continuity in the city's management and resulted in developing a group of professional administrators. This result greatly strengthened city program administration, although it did little to improve coördination between departments.

Civil service control over selection, classification, and promotion of a large percentage of city employees provided a permanent corps of administrative personnel. By charter amendment, adopted in 1903, Los Angeles became one of the first cities in the country to have a formal civil service program (see table 4). A considerable number of positions are exempt, although, except for a relatively small number allocated to the mayor's staff, most of the exempt positions are not subject to direct appointment by the mayor. Departments such as water and power, library, parks and recreation, airport, and harbor have substantial control over their personnel programs, other than for examinations and promotions.

The mayor has relatively little formal responsibility for personnel policies. Similarly, mayoral control of departmental programs and policies, to the extent it exists, has been accomplished by informal methods, outside the limits of the 1924 charter. For example, when Mayor Bowron took office, following the recall of Mayor Shaw in 1938, he took advantage of the situation to demand the resignation of all commissioners. Ultimately, he reappointed a considerable number, but he also reconstituted the police, fire, and civil service commissions. From that point, all commissioners were Bowron appointees. Although this action did not result in a continual involvement of the office of

TABLE 4

EMPLOYEES IN CLASSIFIED AND EXEMPT SERVICES
CITY OF LOS ANGELES

Services	1903	1907	1912	1916	1920	1924	1928	1932	1936
Classified	563	2,017	9,589	4,234	4,566	9,705	13,872	13,464	15,803
Exempt	560	87	8,057	1,936	2,123	3,828	3,627	3,793	3,962
Total	1,123	2,104	17,646	6,170	6,689	13,533	17,499	17,257	19,765

Services	1940	1944	1948	1952	1956	1961
Classified	a	15,565	25,547	28,063	30,918	34,027
Exempt	a	515	1,167	1,919	2,462	3,000
Total	20,761	16,080	26,714	29,982	33,380	37,027

SOURCE: Unpublished data supplied by Los Angeles City Civil Service Department.
a Figures not available.

Mayor in departmental affairs, it did strengthen the idea that the mayor should have cognizance over departmental policies. This was continued, when Congressman Poulson defeated Mayor Bowron, by the incoming executive again requesting the resignation of all commissioners. Poulson, too, reappinted many who had served previously, but his action emphasized the prerogatives of the mayor. When Mayor Poulson, in turn, was defeated by former Congressman Samuel Yorty in 1961, the new mayor followed the precedents set by his two predecessors. Mayor Yorty, however, reappointed relatively few commissioners; instead, he reconstituted most commissions and espoused a policy of strong executive participation in public works, police, health, planning, harbor, and airport programs. The mayor's prerogatives were further strengthened when two commissioners who refused to resign because they clung to the view that commissions were responsible for their department's programs were superseded by City Council action approving the mayor's nominations of replacements.

The 1924 charter undoubtedly produced a system of city government that depends upon maintaining a delicate balance between the mayor, the council, and the commissions. The mayor appoints commissioners, proposes a budget that includes support for most departments other than the so-called proprietary departments of harbor, water and power, and airport, and may veto appropriations and ordinances approved by the council. The council adopts, modifies, or rejects the mayor's proposals for ordinances and appropriations, and exercises a check upon his appointing powers. The commissions have responsibilities specifically assigned them by the charter, and in performing those responsibilities, they find it necessary to have continuing relations with both the mayor and the council. After the City Administrative Officer was injected into the structure, a fourth force was involved in the bargaining process that produces the city's policies and programs. Largely through his influence on the budgetary process, the CAO makes a considerable impact upon the whole system. Yet, it cannot be said that the system of city government created by the charter provides strong executive leadership, in the sense that the term has generally been used in American government and administration.

RESISTANCE TO CHANGE

Proposals to further rewrite the Los Angeles city charter in order to strengthen the mayor's position, or to make the city a stronger contender for metropolitan leadership, have often stirred the opposition of groups that were loath to see changes made that might attract suburban areas to seek annexation, expanding the city's boundaries still farther. It was reasoned that a city preëminently successful in managing its affairs might well attract suburban communities to join it, as many had done in the 1920's.

Charter changes that would permit decentralization, by means of a borough plan, were regarded by these groups as devices to make the city more attractive to suburban communities. A number of those who spoke glowingly of the general concept of the borough plan felt that if the plan worked successfully, suburban communities would undoubtedly be attracted to apply for annexation, and would seek to protect their community status by organizing as boroughs.[23] Others, such as Councilman Ernest E. Debs, advocated that "The only possible answer to the problem [metropolitan government] is the consolidation of all cities and areas into one county government under a borough system."[24] Either use of the borough plan, if it produced expansion of the Los Angeles City area in any appreciable degree, would have upset the modus vivendi with respect to service territories that had been established between the city Water and Power Department and the privately owned utility. Upsetting that balance would have meant reopening the political struggles of the 1920's among the utility groups, and a number of influential leaders at city hall were loath to see that occur.

A more remote and less specifically stated fear was expressed against altering the balance of power in the city's formal governmental structure. It was concerned less with the potentialities of a strong mayor

---

[23] Ibid.
[24] Los Angeles Daily News, Nov. 12, 1947.

than with the unpredictable consequences that might arise from a complete rewriting of the city charter. Groups that were accustomed to working with the various units of city government had adjusted themselves to its manner of doing business and to the key persons who were involved in making decisions. These groups felt that if a complete rewriting of the charter were to be undertaken in order to clarify the role of the mayor, there would be no opportunity to prevent other changes from taking place. The status quo appeared to be much more satisfactory than an unpredictable future of continuing change.

INTERGOVERNMENTAL COÖPERATION EMERGES SLOWLY

As the city of Los Angeles strengthened its internal administration, it was reasonable to expect that some of the neighboring suburban cities might seek coöperative arrangements with the central giant, if the latter were willing to negotiate. On the other hand, recalling the inter-municipal battles of the 1920's, in which many suburbs feared over-tures by the big city were Trojan-horse moves, it was reasonable to expect that the suburbs would be wary. It was equally predictable that Los Angeles would be slow to offer contracts or other coöperative ar-rangements, for fear that the motivations would be misunderstood or the overtures rejected, regardless of their merits.

Intergovernmental contracts were worked out in two functions re-lating to public works and utilities, with significant results. In each case, the suburban cities received considerable benefits from the con-tracts; and considerable savings resulted from reducing duplication of work. In each instance, Los Angeles was the entrepreneur and the suburban cities were beneficiaries.

The oldest and most extensive system of intercity coöperation was in sewer utilization. Los Angeles and Vernon concluded a contract in 1909, whereby Los Angeles was permitted to extend one of its sewer mains across Vernon territory and, in exchange, allowed Vernon to discharge a specified amount of sewage into the Los Angeles system. The irregularly shaped boundaries of Los Angeles, and the terrain of the metropolitan area, caused Los Angeles to seek similar arrange-ments with other cities. Burbank, Glendale, San Fernando, Culver City, Beverly Hills, and Santa Monica entered into contracts with Los Angeles because of mutual benefits. When negotiating contracts, ex-cept with Vernon, Los Angeles required each suburban city to pay a share of the cost of operating the treatment plant and outfall system, measured in proportion to the amount of waste the city discharged.

Los Angeles maintained full control over the mains within its territory and over the treatment and outfall systems.

Several elements benefited from this contractual relationship. The suburban cities were relieved of the expense of building their own treatment and disposal systems. The metropolitan area, as a whole, escaped the nuisances and threats to public health that would have arisen if each city had attempted to operate a complete, separate sewage-disposal system.

The coöperative system was subjected to severe stress, in the postwar era, when the state Department of Health complained that the outfall sewer at Hyperion was inadequate and caused pollution of the bathing beaches on Santa Monica Bay. The city and the state agency fought a series of administrative battles, between 1944 and 1947, culminating in the state seeking a court order to restrain the city from further polluting the beaches and to compel it to construct new and improved works. The state was joined in the action by cities whose beach fronts were on the Santa Monica Bay.

One basic issue in the dispute was whether Los Angeles alone was responsible for reconstructing the treatment plant and the outfall sewer, or whether each city in the system should be required to pay a share of the cost. The contracts were specific only on maintenance costs and the conditions governing use of the system. Culver City and Vernon took the view that the coöperating cities were not obligated to contribute to the rebuilding and expansion and that Los Angeles alone was required to do this, because the works belonged to Los Angeles and existing contracts were silent on construction costs. The Superior Court took the view that each city was committing an offense by contributing to beach pollution and that each would be directed to establish a satisfactory system of sewage disposal. In its final ruling, the court found that the suburban cities were unable to establish independent disposal systems because they lacked financial resources and because the built-up condition of adjacent areas prohibited construction of new disposal facilities. Proceeding from this reasoning, the court accepted the plan proposed by Los Angeles for reconstructing and expanding the Hyperion system and directed each of the cities in the contract system to contribute to the cost of the work in proportion to the amount of sewage contributed by each. No change was made in the administrative arrangements for control and maintenance of the facilities. The contracting cities were given no voice in policy-making or in determining when enlargement or reconstruction of the plant would be desirable.

The problem was repeated in 1960, when two cities that front on the Santa Monica Bay, Hermosa Beach and Manhattan Beach, brought suit against Los Angeles in Superior Court alleging that the Hyperion plant was polluting their beaches. When the court directed Los Angeles to correct the situation, the city proceeded unilaterally to construct extensive outfall-works, financing the project from bond funds voted by its electorate. After the work was undertaken, the city set out to negotiate with the contracting cities for reimbursement. In neither episode were the contracting cities given a voice in determining the method to be used or the type of works selected.

The second function in which the city of Los Angeles entered into coöperative relationships with neighboring cities was electricity supply. When the city contracted with the federal government to take a portion of the power generated at federal plants on the Colorado River, it also agreed to supply Pasadena, Glendale, and Burbank with specific amounts of power. By selling power to its neighbors, Los Angeles not only assisted public-ownership cities, but it also obtained stand-by–service commitments from the cities so aided. Furthermore, duplication of transmission lines would have been contrary to public interest.

Other coöperative relationships between Los Angeles and its neighboring cities are less formal. The central city participates in mutual aid agreements for fire suppression and disaster relief, maintaining smooth relations generally with neighboring departments at the administrative level. It also maintains a number of coöperative arrangements in police administration, including training of suburban city police recruits in its police academy.

In general, however, the city of Los Angeles has remained aloof from its neighbors and has concentrated upon its internal affairs. The attitude held by suburban groups is that Los Angeles administrative departments perform their work in a different manner than those in the smaller cities because of the city's size and the peculiarity of its problems. Many suburban officials express the belief that because Los Angeles pays higher salaries for many classes of positions, it "skims off the cream" of those who desire to work for municipalities, especially in police and fire work. City councils regularly complain that each time Los Angeles grants a wage increase to its employees, employee groups in the suburban cities demand comparable increases. The complex of relationships and attitudes that has developed between Los Angeles and its suburban neighbors often results in expressions of respect for the big city's bureaucracy, but equally in expressions of feeling that a gulf exists between them.

A major effort was made to bridge that gap in 1961, when Samuel

Leask, Jr., and George Terhune, the City Administrator and Assistant Administrator, respectively, published a proposed "Metropolitan Government for Los Angeles: A Workable Solution." The plan called upon the Legislature to create a Los Angeles Metropolitan Municipal Service District, which would be governed by a board whose membership would be apportioned among the cities and the county government on the basis of comparative assessed valuation. Board members would cast multiple votes in proportion to the taxable resources of the city they represented. Smaller cities within the county would be grouped in four areas for the purpose of selecting representatives to the Metropolitan Municipal Board. Under this plan, functional responsibilities were to be divided between the district, cities, and the county. The former would concern itself with metropolitan aspects of functions; the cities would be responsible for local affairs; and the county government would administer local affairs in unincorporated areas.

The Leask-Terhune Plan was widely discussed but was received coolly by the suburban cities and the county. A legislative interim committee on municipal affairs expressed little interest. Shortly after publishing the plan, Leask accepted appointment in the state administration.

A further effort to improve relations with suburban cities was made by the Yorty administration in 1962, by undertaking studies of costs of administering selected municipal services, for the purpose of developing a contract-services policy. Administrative spokesmen pictured this activity as preparation to respond to anticipated requests. The central city did not propose to actively seek contracts with neighboring cities, although it planned to modify the prevailing attitudes on city-suburban relations.

SUMMARY

Integration of the Los Angeles metropolitan area by annexation to the central city was attempted vigorously and with considerable success in the period between 1906 and 1927. Much of the annexation was without plan for rational boundaries and shape of the city, as they related to administration of city functions. Large areas were annexed at the request of groups of property owners seeking the assurance of the city's water resources. Although some areas that proposed annexation were rejected by the city, particularly in the earlier part of the period, most were accepted. The city administration carried on an active campaign to persuade voters in several areas to request annexation, however, using water supply and other municipal services as inducements. The city was particularly anxious to annex the harbor area at San Pedro–Wilmington and promised special attention to local demands in order to obtain it.

The central city's great expansion program closed in 1927 and has never been reinstituted, although relatively small additions continue to be made at frequent intervals. This change resulted partly from decisions made within the city government and partly from the impact of forces and groups that opposed the city and sought to erect barriers to further city expansion.

Because of its size and location, the city of Los Angeles is a significant factor in any effort to determine policies for the metropolitan area. Equally, it is a major factor to be reckoned with if the area's governmental system is to be altered. For the past twenty years the government of this city has been preoccupied with stresses and demands produced by population growth, shifts in densities, and changes in the population mix in many areas. Consequently, city leaders in recent decades, unlike their predecessors, have had neither opportunity nor incentive to consider matters of regional scope.

Several developments have strengthened the administrative system of the big city and have enabled it to perform its functions in a more effective fashion. As the strength increases, the city may become an even greater factor in the contest for power and influence in determining issues that have metropolitan-wide significance. The influence that the city exercises at the present time, however, does not depend upon continued increase in its territorial size. The original objective, to integrate the metropolitan area by annexation to the central city, appears not to be feasible. The efforts made in the 1920's to accomplish this produced their own counteractives. The city now employs other strategies to maintain its place as one of the principal contenders for metropolitan leadership.

SEVEN

The Urban County

LOS ANGELES COUNTY government has been a major contender for metropolitan area leadership for approximately fifty years, because it possesses the institutional strength required to provide governmental functions for a vast population. Starting from a position of extreme weakness, the county government steadily exploited a number of opportunities to pull itself into a lead in the competition among the local governments in the region. In the present decade, Los Angeles County is facing several serious challenges, however, from combinations of competitors. It appears now to be undergoing a reorientation that is likely to give it a different but still strong position.

The county is the one unit of local government in the metropolitan area that has jurisdiction over a sufficiently large portion of the territory to make it a potential metropolitan unit. Although the federal Census Bureau combines Los Angeles and Orange counties to comprise the Los Angeles–Long Beach Standard Metropolitan Area (SMA), the Los Angeles County portion is sufficiently large to warrant considering it alone. Obviously, all cities fall short of the county's land area. The only special districts that rival it in extent of territory are those governed by the County Board of Supervisors as the *ex officio* district board.[1] Examples are the flood control and air pollution control districts.

In another respect, however, the county is poorly shaped for the purpose of providing a base for metropolitan government. In its north-

---

[1] The Metropolitan Water District of Southern California extends so far beyond the Los Angeles Standard Metropolitan Area that it is not considered for comparison here.

ern reaches it contains much mountainous and desert land that is not
related directly to those urbanized portions considered to be the metropolitan area. The San Gabriel mountain range divides the Antelope
Valley portion of the county from the densely populated coastal plain.
Development of the northern part of the county, up to the present
time, has been restricted, in large part, by a limited local water supply. Inasmuch as the state water plan proposes to route an aqueduct,
which will bear Feather River water to southern California through
the Antelope Valley, the picture will probably change when the project
is completed.

In spite of the fact that the county possesses an advantage over
local units in territory, it would not have been a contender for metropolitan leadership if it had continued to employ the traditional form
of county government it had prior to 1912. The basic pattern of county
government in California is not much different from that in many other
states; it is one that is both uncoördinated in its functioning and lacking in authority to perform many of the functions that urban residents
regularly expect to receive. Traditional county government is conducted by innumerable independently elected officers, whose tenure
may be short and whose training for their jobs is often meager. County
government, in the stereotype sense, is government by influence, rather
than by systematic policy and professionalized administration.

Los Angeles County took itself out of the traditional category in
1912 by adopting a county home-rule charter in which it overhauled
its governmental mechanism and produced a more integrated instrument. Since that time, the county has further strengthened its government periodically to enable it to survive a series of challenges from
other governments.

Inasmuch as county government derives its basic authority from
the state, much of the strengthening that took place in Los Angeles
County was made possible by state legislation that offered options to
all counties. Los Angeles was unusually active, however, in availing
itself of opportunities offered by changes in state law that permitted
new functions as well as improvements in governmental machinery.
Such diligence enabled this county to meet most demands made upon
it by urbanization.

Counties generally have dual roles: some of their functions are
performed countywide and serve residents of cities as well as those
in unincorporated territory; other functions are solely for the unincorporated territory. From this dual situation, Los Angeles derived much
of its strength as a metropolitan leader. Its relatively strong tax base,
drawn from a large jurisdiction, and its expansive array of services,

performed on a countywide basis, make the county an influential unit of government.

California state law assigns to counties certain functions that, when operated in an urban setting, give those units a very prominent role. Among these are: poor relief, public-hospital care, assessment of property for tax purposes, support of the trial courts (including providing jails, prosecution and probation administration, in addition to providing courtroom facilities and staffs), registration of voters, and administration of the general elections. Other functions that are optional under state law may further enhance the significance of a county as a metropolitan administrative unit.

The dual nature of the county's role has also produced some of the greatest dilemmas for this unit and has given its opponents a base from which to challenge the expansion of its influence. Fundamentally the dilemma arises from the problem of financing services for the unincorporated areas. Services provided from the county general fund are likely to partially subsidize the unincorporated "fringe area," in which there is an uneven ability to finance local services. It is difficult to achieve equitable administrative standards throughout the county, however, unless the general fund is used to equalize the ability of local areas to support basic levels of performance.

By means of special districts that are closely interrelated with the county government, unincorporated areas that have the financial ability to support services above the basic level are served a richer administrative fare. In general, the use of special districts has considerably enhanced the role of the county as a metropolitan leader.

In another dimension, the county has become a major force among the local governments by contracting with the municipalities within its borders to provide them a large variety of services. Although city-county contracts are not unique to Los Angeles, they have been used more extensively in this county than in any other place in the state or nation.

THE EMERGING URBAN COUNTY

Adoption of the county charter in 1912 marked the beginning of Los Angeles County as a major force in the metropolitan area. In part, this move was a protective one, and also it was the product of group efforts to improve and strengthen local governments in the area generally. The county first came under serious attack from its rivals in 1891, when Mayor Henry Hazard of the city of Los Angeles advocated the consolidation of the city and the county. The Hazard proposal sought to bring all settled areas in the county under a city-county form of government, which would operate under a municipal home-rule charter. The rural areas were to be trimmed away and reassigned to some other rural unit by the state legislature. The mayor's proposal grew out of the exuberance prompted by the city's adoption of a home rule charter two years previously, the first charter in southern California, and the second in the state. The mayor contended that the home-rule charter made the city the most effective local unit in the area.

Although the City Council took no formal action on the Hazard Plan, the Los Angeles Consolidation Commission, a body that was formed in 1906 to work out policies relating to consolidating Wilmington, San Pedro, and Los Angeles, came forth with a similar recommendation. It outlined a long-range plan of city-county consolidation that was intended to bring together the portions of the county located on the coastal plain, south of the San Gabriel Mountains. Within this proposed city-county, communities were to retain their identity and local powers by means of a borough form government.[2]

During this period in which central city leaders were advancing schemes to expand the city's influence, several proposals that Los Angeles county be divided into several units were aired in local papers. They were based upon the desire of groups situated in suburban centers, such as Long Beach and Pomona, to have their city designated as the seat of government for a new county.

Countering the proposals to divide the county, other plans sought to bring about functional consolidation by authorizing the transfer of certain activities from the cities to the county. A commission appointed by the Los Angeles City Council and the County Board of Supervisors, in 1903, drafted a proposed statute to permit this type of consolidation. In 1905, the Los Angeles City charter was amended to authorize limited consolidation, contingent upon passage of enabling legislation.

FORMAL GOVERNMENT MODIFIED

The Los Angeles County charter was the first in the United States to be written for a county by the home-rule method. One notable characteristic of the document was its brevity and simplicity. In general, the charter dealt broadly with matters and avoided the plethora of specific details that characterized many municipal home rule charters of that era.

Another significant feature of the charter was the application of the short-ballot principle. Numerous county officers that had been elective

---

[2] The various proposals for local governmental reorganization in Los Angeles have been discussed systematically in Edwin A. Cottrell and Helen L. Jones, *Characteristics of the Metropolis* (Los Angeles: Haynes Foundation, 1952), pp. 71 *et seq.*

were made appointive; only the five members of the Board of Supervisors, the District Attorney, Sheriff, and Tax Assessor were left in the
elective list. Some offices that had been separate, but that were related
by function, were combined, and the Board of Supervisors was empowered to consolidate others when need arose.

By bringing all but a very small number of county employees under
civil service, an effort was made to lay the foundation for a permanent
staff that would be insulated from elective politics. Patronage was
limited, and emphasis was placed upon competence for employment.
Supervision of employment practices was placed in the hands of a
Civil Service Commission, whose members were to be appointed by
the Board of Supervisors for six-year terms. Based on a theory of
countervailing political forces, the charter prohibited appointment of
any two persons who were members of the same political party to the
commission.[3] After the first two years of the commission's activity,
political partisanship ceased to be a serious matter in commission
affairs.

A rudimentary effort to improve county management was also made
by creating a Bureau of Efficiency within the Civil Service Commission
organization. Those who wrote the 1912 charter conceived of civil
service administration as being more than recruitment, examination,
and classification of employees, and therefore they added the promotion of efficiency of individual performance and effectiveness of administrative organization. It was these latter responsibilities that were
assigned to the Bureau of Efficiency, established as a separate unit
within the commission's staff. A Board of Efficiency, composed of the
County Auditor, the three members of the commission, and the Chief
Examiner of civil service, determined standards and ascertained that
salary rates were commensurate with the classification schedules.[4]

A further significant change in county administration, produced by
the 1912 charter, was the unification of county road administration
under a single Road Commissioner, appointed by, and responsible to,
the Board of Supervisors. Prior to this, Los Angeles, like other California counties, had had five Road Districts, each coterminous with a
supervisoral district in which each supervisor exercised oversight. This
change made it possible for the county to consider its road needs more
systematically when determining routes and allocating funds.[5]

---

[3] The charter was amended in 1948 to remove party membership specifications.
[4] The Board of Efficiency was abolished in 1948, after its duties had been taken
over by a chief administrative office created by the Board of Supervisors.
[5] A similar unification of county administration was required of all counties in
California by the Collier-Burns Act in 1947.

Adoption of the county charter did not give Los Angeles County new powers, nor did it alter the basic form of county government. It did permit the county to experiment with some structural changes to meet conditions that were emerging in this locality. The very fact that a charter was prepared and adopted gave public support to the attitude that county officers should endeavor to develop new methods to meet the new demands confronting county government.

STRENGTHENING THE MACHINERY

The number of administrative personnel employed by Los Angeles County has increased steadily throughout the years since 1913, reaching the figure of forty thousand in 1961 (see table 5). This county has become one of the largest local governments in the United States.

TABLE 5

EMPLOYEES IN THE CLASSIFIED SERVICE
LOS ANGELES COUNTY

Year	Number of employees	Year	Number of employees
1914	3,324	1938	16,207
1915	4,311	1939	15,818
1916	4,073	1940	16,409
1917	2,819	1941	16,848
1918	2,939	1942	16,987
1919	2,744	1943	15,353
1920	3,266	1944	16,917
1921	3,901	1945	16,196
1922	4,464	1946	17,872
1923	4,999	1947	19,028
1924	6,299	1948	20,760
1925	6,907	1949	22,751
1926	7,909	1950	24,295
1927	9,409	1951	24,742
1928	10,300	1952	26,154
1929	11,251	1953	27,707
1930	12,369	1954	30,219
1931	13,373	1955	29,947
1932	13,264	1956	32,651
1933	13,838	1957	34,303
1934	13,916	1958	36,687
1935	14,238	1959	37,605
1936	15,014	1960	39,081
1937	15,435	1961	40,105

SOURCE: Unpublished data supplied by Los Angeles County Civil Service Commission.

Budgeted expenditures, voted annually by the Board of Supervisors, have risen in similar fashion. Causes of this expansion will be considered at greater length later in this chapter.

As the county government transformed from the traditional type to a major unit of metropolitan government, the County Board of Supervisors required more effective assistance to perform as an executive body. The situation revolved around two major problems. One required the development of staff and central supervisory assistance through which the board could direct the management of county affairs. The other involved adaptation or revision of the board's own organization for gathering information and for servicing constituent interests.

The Board of Supervisors had very little staff assistance between 1913 and 1938. Ostensibly, it could call upon all departments of the county government to provide information and advice. Actually, the board had little more than a clerical staff to communicate board policies to operating departments and transmit information to the board in return. It attempted to deal with the expanding administrative structure by giving each of its members cognizance over the affairs of a group of departments. When the board prepared the annual expenditure ordinance, the County Auditor played an influential and useful staff role. Herbert Payne, Auditor between 1918 and 1938, often performed informally the functions of a chief administrative officer for the board. During the 1930's, a Bureau of Administrative Research was set up, and reported directly to the Board of Supervisors. This organization performed budget investigations and did management analysis studies. Under the direction of Harry F. Scoville, this bureau supplied a much needed central staff service. It also made two contributions that had long-range significance for the county government. It demonstrated the necessity for central staff and for central administrative direction, if the county government were to perform the functions that were being demanded and that the elected Board wished to provide. It also provided a pool of administrative talent that was drawn upon during the following thirty years to supply top-level administrators for the county.

Upon the insistence of the Committee on Governmental Simplification, and other citizen groups, the Board of Supervisors decided, in 1938, to establish an office of Chief Administrative Officer (CAO).[6] They assigned to the position the duties of supervising administration and assisting the board to obtain information upon which it could de-

[6] Los Angeles County, Committee on Governmental Simplification, *Final Report* (Los Angeles, 1935).

termine policy. The first incumbent, Wayne Allen, was recruited from private business to hold the position of County Purchasing Agent as well as CAO. Allen held the appointment for approximately ten years, with two leaves of absence for military duty. Alfred Campion, who acted as CAO during the war years; Arthur J. Will, who succeeded Allen in 1953; and Lindon S. Hollinger, appointed in 1955, were all career government administrators and were promoted from within county service. Although citizens' groups made numerous recommendations that the charter be amended to give the Chief Administrative Officer more specific powers and greater formal strength, the Board of Supervisors consistently declined to do so.[7] Gradually the office achieved a status of prestige and power in the county administrative hierarchy, although the board remains legally the administrative head of the county service. Due to the close relationship that developed between the CAO and the board, however, the former has come to have extensive authority in administrative matters.

The county Chief Administrative Officer has consistently drawn into his office a sizable staff of career specialists in budget and management analysis, salary studies, and legislative analysis. To a large degree, these specialists have been recruited at junior grades, trained in the central staff or secured from the departments, and promoted within the group to form a strong corps. From time to time, members of this staff are encouraged to accept appointment to key line administrative positions. In this manner, the county's needs for experienced administrators are supplied, and the CAO's central staff extends its influence and its points of view into line departments. Although department heads are appointed by the Board of Supervisors under civil service procedures, the CAO frequently exercises a strong influence over the ultimate choice. This program of management development within the county career service is one of the significant features that explains the county government's comparative strength.

The Chief Administrative Officer has also had a strong influence upon county administration through budget control, coupled with pressure and advice concerning departmental procedures and organization. Although the county Chief Administrative Officer does not have the formal powers that are normally associated with a county manager, in reality the office performs in a manner comparable to that of a manager. The CAO achieves results by persuasion, astute advice, and by

---

[7] Cottrell and Jones, op. cit., pp. 102–104, discuss the recommendation of Town Hall's Municipal and County Government Section. See also Los Angeles County Charter Study Committee, Recommendations of the Charter Study Committee Presented to the Board of Supervisors (Los Angeles, 1958).

weight of professional competence. The strength of this office has done much to strengthen the county government.

The five-member, elected Board of Supervisors remains the executive and legislative head of Los Angeles County government. The post of supervisor is a full-time one, and is compensated at a rate equivalent to that of a Superior Court judge.[8] In 1961, this rate was $21,000 per year. Each supervisor represents approximately one and a half million persons, a constituency larger than that of almost any legislator except the state senator from Los Angeles County or the United States senators. The size of the constituency and the complex composition of the supervisoral districts have often been used as bases for urging a complete reorganization of the board. Most proposals have stemmed from a theory that the body can represent constituency interests better if each supervisor were to be given a smaller, more compact district. This would increase the size of the board. The plans have usually been based also upon a second theory, that the board should be divested of its administrative responsibilities.

The supervisors have shown themselves strongly opposed to efforts to enlarge their number and to alter their powers and responsibilities.[9] They have chosen instead to strengthen their own staff services, in order to assist each supervisor in servicing his district. Each board member has been provided a crew of field deputies, whom he may use in his headquarters at the county administrative center or in field offices located in various parts of his district. Assignments vary, but they often include interviewing constituents, gathering information, making speeches, representing the supervisor at meetings, and doing all types of staff work. By team organization, the individual supervisors attempt to keep in close touch with their districts. Doubtless, this approach has done much to strengthen the political effectiveness of board members. A measure of their effectiveness is shown by the relatively low turnover in board membership. In twenty-eight years, only two incumbent supervisors have been defeated for reëlection. Some have retired or have sought other, higher elective offices. Nevertheless, the board membership has been unusually stable since 1934.

The Board of Supervisors transacts its formal business normally in

---

[8] The compensation of county boards of supervisors has been subject to study throughout the state from time to time. As administrative salaries rose, the problem of setting supervisoral salaries in proper relation to those of key administrators became difficult. The method of equating the salary with that of a Superior Court judge has been reasonably satisfactory.

[9] In 1962 a charter revision committee recommended increasing the board membership from 5 to 7, and giving the CAO power to appoint department heads. The board refused to change the status of the CAO, and the electorate rejected the proposed increase in board membership.

one session per week, although for a number of years a second session has been scheduled at certain periods of the year when agendas become heavier. Much of the work of the board, however, is accomplished by intrastaff study and conference prior to public hearings and formal sessions.

Changes in the governmental pattern in Los Angeles County have had important impacts upon the role and functioning of the Board of Supervisors. As will be discussed later in this chapter, the amount of unincorporated territory has shrunk as cities have been created. The county has not been displaced in all governmental matters as this has occurred, although each supervisor has been left with a lesser number of constituents for whom he is the sole representative in local government. Each of the five supervisors has several cities within his district, and he is advised concerning matters of local interest through the elective municipal officials. This situation has caused the supervisors to change their methods for servicing their district constituencies and campaigning for office. Significant of the change is the point that each supervisor who held office in 1962 is a former city council member or mayor. The salaries and political prestige of county supervisors are greater than those of council members of any of the seventy-two cities. Only the position of mayor of the city of Los Angeles equals or exceeds the status of county supervisor.

FUNCTIONAL CONSOLIDATION

Functional consolidation is a less drastic means of simplifying the pattern of local government than is territorial consolidation. Usually it is accomplished when both governments involved believe that they will receive benefits that substantially outweigh disadvantages. At the same time, functional consolidation aids, rather than lessens, the possibility of each local unit of government continuing in existence.

Within two years after the Los Angeles County voters adopted the charter, the state boosted the county's role in the metropolitan area government by authorizing functional consolidation. A constitutional amendment permitted a county to perform certain functions for municipalities within its borders.

Soon afterward, the city of Los Angeles moved to transfer the administration of charities and inspection of weights and measures.[10] Both functions came to be exclusive responsibilities of the county to perform within all its municipalities and also in unincorporated areas.

---

[10] Although charities had been the responsibility of county government for many years, the city had developed some activity in that field prior to the transfer.

Thereupon, the county assumed the financial support of the functions without assistance from city sources; complete functional consolidation was effected.

A second type of functional consolidation was developed by means of city-county contracts, which permitted a city to transfer certain functions to county administration but required the city to pay a portion of the administrative costs. This type of consolidation was not true functional consolidation, inasmuch as the arrangement depended upon a contract that could be abrogated or renegotiated by either party. This type will be discussed more in detail later in this chapter.

CONFLICTING CONSOLIDATION PROPOSALS

Concurrently with the development of functional consolidation between the county and certain cities, discussion continued on various types of territorial consolidation. One of the most concisely eloquent proponents of county leadership in governmental reorganization was Supervisor John J. Hamilton of Pasadena. He argued:

> The essential fact is that all the cities and rural districts in the county, connected as they are by the boulevard and interurban systems, are one community with identical interests. The chartered County of Los Angeles is the sufficient and necessary bond holding them together. It is the future city, and the various municipalities, handling their local affairs, are the future boroughs of that city. The true line of development is by transferring city functions, one by one, from all cities to the county, until all duplications are wiped out and city and county consolidation is accomplished on a sound basis.[11]

In the same year that Hamilton made this argument, the Los Angeles City Council concurred with the specially appointed City and County Consolidation Commission's recommendation that the city refrain from separating from the county and becoming a consolidated city-county. The Los Angeles Realty Board and the Taxpayers' Association of California urged consideration be given to consolidation of local governments and opposed separation.

A further effort to consider consolidation, either functional or territorial, was undertaken in 1930 by a semiofficial group known as the Los Angeles Citizens Committee on County Government and Local Autonomy. It presented no actual plans for consolidation, however. Two years later, Mayor John C. Porter, of Los Angeles, and the City

---

[11] John J. Hamilton, *The Community Program of Greater Los Angeles* (Los Angeles: John J. Hamilton, 1916), p. 13.

Bureau of Budget and Efficiency reopened the question of separation of governments. They urged the city to separate from the county and form a consolidated city-county. The bureau estimated that city tax-payers would save over $9 million per year by making the move. According to the analysis, the chief disadvantage for the city would be the inability to annex territory. The part of the county that would be left remnant following the city's secession was thought to be sufficiently strong to guarantee a viable government. The county responded very critically to this city proposal. The County Counsel pointed out numerous legal obstacles, and the Bureau of Efficiency disputed the estimate of alleged savings. The latter also emphasized that the growth and development of the central city depended upon the continued economic growth of the entire county. This dispute between the officialdoms of the city and the county continued for several years. Both sides continued to study the costs of local government and to search for a type of consolidation that would be advantageous to their respective interests.

The county's studies culminated three years later in the Report of the Committee on Governmental Simplification, a project whose competence has been widely acclaimed. This committee found a great need for centralization of those functions that had metropolitan-wide importance, and suggested that the county was best suited to perform such functions. It also made several specific suggestions for improving the administrative organization of the county government, in order to prepare that unit for a more significant role in metropolitan affairs.

CONSOLIDATION OF HEALTH SERVICES

Further functional consolidation was accomplished when the smaller cities in Los Angeles County sought to relieve themselves of the costs of public health services. In 1932, representatives of sixteen municipalities petitioned the board of supervisors, through the County League of Municipalities, to authorize the County Health Department to enforce state health laws within municipalities. When the County Counsel advised that the county lacked authority to comply with the request, the county and the cities joined to request the Legislature to provide enabling legislation. The city of Pasadena opposed this plan at first but withdrew its objections when the proposed draft was reworded to make the transfer of the function dependent upon the initiative of individual cities. The Legislature adopted a statute in its 1935 session permitting any city to transfer responsibility for the basic public health program to the county, and authorizing the county to perform the work at its expense.

Shortly after this statute was adopted, the majority of the cities in Los Angeles County transferred their health programs to the county. Only Los Angeles, Pasadena, Long Beach, Vernon, and Beverly Hills retained their own departments. As other municipalities incorporated, at later dates, they authorized the county Health Department, which had provided health services in the area prior to the incorporation, to continue work. Four of the five cities that did not join the functional consolidation in the 1930's have continued their independent programs. Beverly Hills, however, chose to transfer its health service to the county in 1960, after its Municipal Health Officer retired.

Consolidation of the Los Angeles City Health Department with that of the county has been one of the hardy perennials of intergovernmental relations discussions.[12] On some occasions, the county has taken the initiative to propose consolidation; on other occasions, city officials have raised the matter. Numerous surveys have been made by budget analysts and by citizens' commissions. City officers have shown more interest in consolidation when finances were scarce and budget-balancing was difficult. Inasmuch as the county Health Department is financed from the county general-tax rate, which is paid by all property owners in the county, the point is often made that Los Angeles City residents support both health departments, although the county agency does not act within the city. Duplication of organization and the city's desire to transfer its financial responsibilities for the health function to the county tax base are the main points to be considered. No specific action has resulted, however.

OTHER FUNCTIONS PROPOSED

Countywide consolidation of fire suppression services, of building permit and inspection administration, and merger of the Los Angeles

---

[12] Consolidation was first proposed by Dr. Pomeroy, county health officer, in 1924. In 1931 Mayor John C. Porter proposed consolidating the two departments, but the city health officer opposed the idea. In 1932 the Taxpayers' Association of California, after making a survey, recommended that the county be permitted to undertake the work for all units under a contract. In 1933 Mayor Frank Shaw proposed consolidation, and the city and county budget bureaus were thereafter instructed to make a study. The Governmental Simplification Commission appointed by the Board of Supervisors made this subject a part of its study, and it recommended that the county become the metropolitan health administration agency. In 1945, upon resigning as county health officer, Dr. Swarthout recommended that the city health officer be appointed to his post and that the two departments be merged. Mayor Bowron opposed the proposal and the matter came to nought. In 1952 a citizens' commission, appointed to study possibilities for achieving savings through functional consolidations, recommended merging the two health agencies, but no official action was taken. In 1961, when Mayor Yorty reconstituted the city health commission, negotiations to consolidate the two health departments were renewed.

City and Los Angeles County jails have been discussed from time to time. Consolidation of the fire services was proposed by the county chapter of the International Association of Fire Fighters,[13] at a time when numerous incorporations of new cities posed a threat to the county Fire Protection District organization. If the new cities remained within the district system, the county department would become, in essence, a metropolitan organization. If the new cities chose to form their own departments, the county unit would shrink proportionately. Although the consolidation plan was discussed widely, it was not given official support and did not come to formal action. Los Angeles Chief of Police William Parker proposed on several occasions that the city transfer its responsibility for jails to the county. He cited the duplication of facilities and emphasized that the county had primary responsibility for custody of prisoners awaiting trial. Chief Parker called city officials' attention to the saving that would result to the city budget from the transference, and to the freeing of departmental personnel to concentrate on policing. A 1961 statute, which authorized municipal courts to sentence to the county jail persons arrested for violation of state laws on intoxication, reopened the controversy regarding transfer of jails to county jurisdiction.

Generally speaking, functional consolidation has resulted in a transfer from one or more cities to the county when the municipalities were especially hard-pressed financially and were seeking to make the savings available for other activities. Functional consolidation also has occurred in those instances in which the county has demonstrated a performance standard at least equal to that of the better municipal

COUNTY SERVICE TO UNINCORPORATED AREAS

One of the unique features of Los Angeles County government is its response to the growth of population in unincorporated areas, by providing municipal-type services. In some instances, as in structural fire protection, water service, and street lighting, it has provided service through county administered special districts. In such instances, the special district is primarily a means for collecting taxes from property that benefited from the service. In many other instances, the county provides the service through regular county personnel and supports the cost of the operations from the county general-tax rate.

[13] Los Angeles County Fire Fighters Association; *Metropolitan Fire Protection Authority Act* (1959); Assembly Interim Committee on Municipal and County Government, "Special Districts in the State of California," in *Assembly Interim Committee Reports, 1956–1959,* vol. 6, no. 12 (Sacramento, 1959), pp. 32–33.

departments in the area. In no instance of functional consolidation have city employees suffered loss of jobs.

Expansion, development, and refinement of county administration, to produce a system of governmental services that compares favorably with any large city, occurred over a period of time. That is, the county board did not specifically decide at any certain time that it would offer municipal-type services to the unincorporated areas. The system grew from a long series of decisions made at various times.

In 1912, Los Angeles County created a County Library, which was to be supported by a special tax on property in those areas served by the library system. State law permitted a county board to levy a special tax for library purposes and to collect it in unincorporated areas served by special library districts and in cities that elected to come within the county library system. By establishing branches and bookmobiles, the library brought its services directly to a large part of the county.

Although Los Angeles County had a health officer prior to 1913, the present county Health Department was organized in 1915.[14] Under the leadership of Dr. Pomeroy, this department became a strong organization, serving residents of unincorporated areas at a level of performance equal to that in cities. Regional health offices were placed at locations deemed to be best suited to service a region, and each establishment was staffed and equipped to provide a full public health program, supported by specialized services conducted by the central headquarters.

The Sheriff's Department provided police protection to all unincorporated areas of the county. As population grew and demands for police services increased, the department added personnel and modernized its procedures so that it came to be a police department comparable in all respects to those serving large cities. Substations located in various regional centers directed the basic police work at the community level. By means of a hierarchy of supervision, as well as by sophisticated, integrated communications systems, the central sheriff's office brought the organization into line as a unified police department serving an extensive area. The chief point of controversy that has arisen from time to time between citizens of some rapidly growing unincorporated areas and the Sheriff's Department is the amount of patrol service available to cover large areas. Although the department recognizes that communities differ in their requirements, as they differ in population density and other factors, it feels that it is obliged to

[14] Margaret Gorsuch Morden and Richard Bigger, *Cooperative Health Administration in Metropolitan Los Angeles* (Los Angeles: Bureau of Governmental Research, University of California, 1948), pp. 8–9.

maintain a countywide standard of service, and that it cannot spread county taxes unevenly among areas on the basis of different community needs.

In unincorporated areas where urban development has taken place, the county has improved local streets and roads to a standard comparable to streets in many cities. It has established and maintained traffic signals, traffic lanes, and safety devices. In areas where the need has arisen, it has provided street sweeping.

Fire protection began as a county service in the forested, mountainous lands. In 1906, Los Angeles County appointed a fire warden to direct its mountain fire patrol, working in conjunction with state officials. Gradually, as suburbanization developed, a need arose for structural fire protection in unincorporated areas. Inasmuch as this need was for a standard of service that was higher than any required normally by rural areas, it was reasoned that the costs should be collected from property that received the benefits or was likely to receive them in the near future. Therefore, a statute, drafted by Los Angeles County officials and adopted in 1923, authorized boards of supervisors to establish county fire districts and to levy taxes within them. When it became effective, the Los Angeles board set out to organize a number of districts to serve suburban unincorporated areas. Although the firefighting organization was created within districts, it was placed under the direction of the county Fire Warden, giving the county an over-all command structure for its unified fire services.

Street lighting and water services are provided to a number of unincorporated areas by special districts administered by the county engineer's department. Costs of constructing waterworks and distribution systems are charged to landowners and maintenance expenses are met from charges for sale of water. Although state laws permit waterworks districts to have separately elected boards, those organized in Los Angeles are under the Board of Supervisors.

A sanitary sewer system has been made available to residents of unincorporated areas by the county Sanitation Districts' organization, which is governed by district boards comprising municipal and county officials. There are eighteen county sanitation districts that include some unincorporated area within their territory. Each district exists for the purpose of financing, through taxes upon property, a system of collection sewers. These districts, in turn, are federated in the county Sanitation District System, which maintains a unified system of trunk sewers, a treatment plant, and an ocean-outfall disposal line. Each district contributes to financing the system, which is administered by a central engineering staff. Districts whose service area include unincorporated territory include the chairman of the county supervisors on their governing boards. Thus, the county participates directly in the administration of most districts and in determining policy for the over-all system. The districts' complex administrative system makes it possible for residents of unincorporated communities to receive sanitary sewer services equal to those that are available to city residents.

Garbage and refuse disposal have also been provided for unincorporated areas by some of the county sanitation districts. When home owners installed garbage-disposal equipment connected with the sewers, the districts' services were expanded. Disposal of other refuse, by district pick-up service and cut-and-cover fills, has been available for several years. All district services are supported by property taxes levied within the districts, rather than by the county general tax.

Clearly, the county has responded in a variety of ways to the demands of residents in unincorporated areas for services that relate to urban living conditions. This responsiveness has, in turn, produced a number of tensions that are directly related to the problem of achieving effective government over a large metropolitan area. One set of tensions is exhibited by the residents of the unincorporated areas. Until an area is sufficiently developed to warrant organization of special districts or to cause the county government to establish field offices in or near the area, local residents remain frustrated over their inability to obtain a level of service commensurate with their estimate of needs. In many instances, the county bureaucracy's estimate of countywide needs and interests clash with local residents' ambitions and estimates of local interests and needs.

The Cities React

The cities reacted sharply to the expansion of county services to the unincorporated areas. They charged that the county taxed city property owners in order to support services that were provided only to the unincorporated communities. The first documented allegation of this point was made in 1935 by the city of Los Angeles. In a lengthy report, the bureau of budget and efficiency stated:

> The performance of municipal services by the county indicates a definite duplication of authority previously granted to and exercised by municipalities. It imposes restrictions upon municipalities in the performance of similar functions, and in the final analysis is the principal cause of the existing burden of excessive taxation in such cities.[15]

---

[15] Los Angeles City Bureau of Budget and Efficiency, *A Study of Local Government in the Metropolitan Area within Los Angeles County* (Los Angeles, 1935).

It recommended that all services to unincorporated areas be limited to actual needs and be financed chiefly by taxes and fees from those areas. Looking to the future, and suggesting a policy that the League of California Cities ultimately espoused in a modified form on a state-wide basis, the bureau urged that the state force densely populated unincorporated areas to incorporate or to annex to the largest and nearest municipality. No direct action was taken on this recommendation.

City officials discussed critically, for more than two decades, the county's methods of providing and financing services to urban fringe areas bordering the larger cities. Most of the proposals sought to provide a means for taxing the unincorporated areas on a differential basis, in accordance with their needs for service, or to reorganize the county in such a way that the local areas would have a greater share in determining policies and supporting costs of service. The "fringe-area" problem was not unique to southern California; throughout the nation, many states in which urban development was overflowing municipal boundaries experienced similar difficulties. Los Angeles was also but one of several counties in California faced with this problem, but its situation was the most acute and extensive.

World problems tended to divert attention from the local scene between 1939 and 1946. Influx of population, at the close of World War II, caused a boom in land development and housing in southern California. Although the cities experienced much of this, the unincorporated areas in the eastern and southern portions of Los Angeles County became especially active. County efforts to respond to service demands were equally extensive. It was inevitable that municipal criticism of county activity would be reopened.

The clash between the cities and the counties broke out in legislative skirmishing in the 1951 session. The League of California Cities sponsored Assembly Bill 3217, which required all unincorporated areas that desired to obtain municipal-type services at a level above that provided countywide to establish a tax zone for the purpose of financing the additional cost. The bill was opposed by the Supervisors' Association as being unworkable because the cost of services given a specific area could not be computed. Both sides took intransigent positions,[16] and although AB 3217 passed the Assembly, it was killed in the Senate. The subject, "fringe-area" government, was referred to interim committees of both houses for study.

---

[16] Senate Fact Finding Committee on Local Government, *Report to the Legislature, 1961 Regular Session* (Sacramento, 1961), pp. 13–17; Cottrell and Jones, *op. cit.*, pp. 108–110.

One piece of legislation was produced by the 1951 session that could have relieved the tension somewhat. This was the Community Services District Act, which authorized the formation of multipurpose special districts in unincorporated areas to provide municipal-type services and to tax property therein. Formation of districts was to be voluntary, and initiative was to be with the area that was to receive the services. This plan did not satisfy the organized cities, however, because it was too permissive.

Both legislative interim committees reported to the 1953 legislative session and concluded that county services to unincorporated areas were being subsidized by city taxpayers. The assembly committee reported as follows:

> To a steadily increasing extent, county government has been called upon to perform [municipal type services] in much the same manner as traditionally has been assigned to cities. When extension of services has been made at general county expense for a service primarily of local benefit, it has resulted in inequity to taxpayers in cities maintaining the same services at municipal expense.[17]

The Senate committee estimated that the subsidy by city taxpayers in five counties, Los Angeles, Alameda, Napa, Sacramento, and Kern, amounted to six million dollars annually:

> To the extent that county units of government expanded their operations to meet the demands of the residents of unincorporated urban areas for higher levels of service, county budgets and tax bills were obviously increased. This meant, of course, that the taxpayers were not only required to pay city taxes to provide themselves with municipal services; they were also required to pay higher county taxes to provide municipal-type services to the residents of urban unincorporated communities. Rural dwellers similarly were required to pay higher county tax bills to help provide a level of county service in unincorporated urban areas higher than the level required or received in rural areas.[18]

Both committees endorsed a bill that had been prepared by the Los Angeles County Counsel and was known as the County Service Area Law. This Act, adopted by the 1953 session, authorized counties to

---

[17] California Legislature, Assembly, *Final Report of the Assembly Interim Committee on Municipal and County Government Covering Fringe Area Problems in the State of California* (Sacramento, 1953), p. 6.

[18] California Legislature, Senate, *Report of the Senate Interim Committee on State and Local Taxation,* Part Seven, "Fiscal Problems of Urban Growth in California" (Sacramento, 1953), p. xiii.

provide improved services to unincorporated areas and to charge for those furnished at a level above that prevailing in the county-at-large.[19]

Los Angeles has created no community services district, nor has it made use of the County Service Area Law. Shortly after these plans were authorized by the state, attention centered on other developments in the "fringe areas." The Lakewood community incorporated, the first city to be organized within the county in fourteen years, and was followed by twenty-six others. Although many other fringe-area communities chose to annex to adjacent municipalities, several heavily populated ones remained with the county government.

COUNTY-CITY CONTRACTS

County-city contracts place Los Angeles County in a relatively unusual leadership role. By voluntary action, most of the cities have contracted with the county government to perform a broad array of functions for them. Although other counties in California, and some in other states, have developed this type of intergovernmental relationship, Los Angeles continues to be the leading example.

Experience with county-city contracts in Los Angeles falls into three time periods. During the first, 1908 to 1940, the county accepted city ordinances that transferred a city function, without negotiating formal contracts. The functions transferred during that period were ones the county was required by state law to perform for itself, thereby duplicating city activity. The first cities to avail themselves of the opportunity to contract were newly incorporated small communities. The second period is not subject to precise demarcation in time, but it is characterized by the county's efforts to negotiate formal contracts, in which it increased the charges and placed them on a formula basis. Each contract was negotiated for a single function, however. The third period began in 1954, with the negotiation of a multifunction contract with the newly incorporated city of Lakewood. In this latter arrangement, the county agreed to perform numerous services, including police and fire protection, and spelled out service levels and charges. Although most services were agreed upon by means of single-function contracts, a general-services agreement made a variety of routine aids available to the city at cost. Each of the twenty-nine cities that incorporated between 1954 and 1962 negotiated contracts with the county for a varying number of services. The county government, for

[19] *Cal. Stats.* (1953), chap. 858.

the first time, adopted a specific program of assisting communities to incorporate and demonstrated an active interest in contracting to provide services.

The earliest municipal contract made by Los Angeles County, entered into in 1908, for assessment of property for tax purposes and collection of property taxes, was with the little city of La Verne. Nineteen other cities followed as they incorporated. Other cities that had organized previously also joined. Los Angeles, being a charter city at the time the county began making contracts, was not eligible. This deficiency was overcome in 1913, however, and the central city completed a contract for assessment and collection in 1917.

County tax assessment and collection has been subjected to the least controversy of any of the interlocal contract activities. The county assessor is required by state law to assess property for county and school-district purposes, therefore a separate city assessment is redundant unless a different valuation is desired. The cities save in administrative costs, because the county charge for administration is considerably less in each case than they would have to pay to maintain their own staffs. The chief factor that seems likely to cause controversy is the level of assessment. Los Angeles County has maintained a level of 25 per cent valuation, for many years. Of the seventy-four cities operating in the county at present, seventy-two contract for tax services. Two of the larger suburban cities, Pasadena and Long Beach, have not joined with the county, retaining the authority to determine their own assessment levels for municipal purposes.

Contract relations in health administration began in 1919, when the county made agreements with the cities of La Verne and Pomona. Several additional cities arranged for the county to do laboratory testing for communicable diseases, milk, and water supplies. Between 1923 and 1933, twenty-six additional cities contracted for the county health service.[20] In 1935, the Legislature authorized cities to transfer their health service responsibilities to the county and to contract for the enforcement of municipal sanitation ordinances. Shortly thereafter, thirty-nine cities contracted with Los Angeles County to enforce their municipal health-inspection ordinances, and twenty-one arranged for it to enforce their rodent-control laws. More cities have been added to the contract list as they have incorporated. In this system, the city determines the level and complexity of the standard that will be enforced and pays the cost of inspections made by county health personnel.

[20] Winston W. Crouch, *Intergovernmental Relations* (Los Angeles: Haynes Foundation, 1954), pp. 71–72.

County-city contractual relations for personnel work were first authorized by state law in 1935. Sixteen cities have contracted for a variety of professional assistance in this field.[21] Some have contracted solely for examination work; others have included classification, some have asked for in-service training. Eight have requested full personnel service and have designated the county Civil Service Commission as the city's personnel board. The cities contracting for personnel assistance range in size from Palos Verdes Estates, with forty-four employees, to Burbank, with 1,095 employees.

Other services supplied on a contractual basis include: enforcement of city building regulations, street sweeping, street and road work, traffic-stripe painting, bridge maintenance, enforcement of municipal industrial-waste ordinances, engineering surveys, and animal care. Seacoast cities, such as Redondo, Manhattan, and Hermosa, contract with the county to provide lifeguard services on the municipal beaches.

County-city contract relationships entered a dramatically new phase when the so-called "Lakewood Plan" was developed. This was the first time that the county had undertaken to provide police and fire protection to an incorporated city. In drawing the contracts, the county and city gave attention to defining the levels of performance and to setting reimbursement on the basis of cost to the county for operating each of the services.

Lakewood and the county were equally well satisfied with the new contract plan and each set out to publicize the arrangement. The county established an office of County-City Coördinator in the county Chief Administrator's office and employed Lakewood's first City Administrative Officer to develop it. The new office, a central liaison agency, sought to facilitate communications between city and county officials and provide information relative to incorporation procedures and county-city contract matters. The Coördinator's staff gave technical assistance to community groups contemplating incorporation, by making feasibility surveys and advising about fiscal matters. New cities returned to the county for assistance in making the transition to operational status, usually asking for contract services.

Originally, the Lakewood Plan was described as an arrangement wherein the county provided a complete set of municipal functions at cost, although it never indicated at any time an unwillingness to provide less than a complete set. The emphasis upon selling county services at cost arose in answer to the criticisms levelled at the county for providing municipal-type services to unincorporated areas without

---

[21] The number of contracting cities varies from time to time. In 1961 there were twelve cities, with a total of 2,522 employees.

charging recipients for the full cost. Although most of the cities that were incorporated after 1954 were known as "Lakewood Plan Cities," they differed widely in the number of services they chose to purchase by contract. Pico Rivera, for example, decided to employ its own street-sweeping force after purchasing the county service for a time. Some others employed their own recreation directors.

Downey withdrew from most of its contract arrangements after a brief time and set up its own police, fire, library, and other departments. It withdrew from the county fire and library district systems, retaining only contracts for tax assessment and collection, animal care, and health inspection. Somewhat similarly, Santa Fe Springs withdrew from the police and fire contractual arrangement, although it retained county agreements for some other functions.

The Lakewood Plan has been confined, in practice, to the cities that have incorporated since 1954. No municipality that has been in operation long enough to establish a set of administrative departments has abandoned them and gone over to the contract system. The small city of Signal Hill moved part way in that direction, in 1959, when it transferred its police and fire personnel to the county and contracted for the services. After a few months, however, two members of the Signal Hill council were recalled, in the aftermath of a controversy over the method employed to shift to county administration, and the new council majority cancelled the contract and recruited new police and fire personnel. Even after withdrawing from the police and fire arrangements, the city continued several other contracts that it had had with the county for many years.

The contract plan presents a number of problems for the county government. One result has been to focus attention upon the costs of contract services. In order to set charges for units of service, the county has had to work out data on costs of its regular operations and to develop a policy concerning which elements of administrative costs to include in the charges made to cities. One additional result has been to compel the county administration to tighten its procedures and to give increased attention to analyzing cost factors. Another concern to top administrators has been the planning of the county's physical plant facilities to serve contract cities as well as unincorporated territory. In a contract system in which the cities may withdraw whenever they choose, the county runs the risk that it may locate sheriff's substations, fire stations, road equipment yards, and offices in centers that cease to be the most strategically located for its own purposes. A somewhat equal risk arises from the likelihood that a municipality will withdraw and seek to take over the facilities. In that event, the respective financial interests are adjusted, although the county must then relocate its own administration. The situation presents some risks and uncertainties for the county, especially in planning its capital improvement program for those areas where contract cities are most numerous.

Two other problems have arisen from the general movement to have the county perform administrative services for cities, although these are not specifically contract problems. One involves efforts by some cities to withdraw from the county library system. Downey and Commerce, for example, have withdrawn and established their own programs. In both instances, the city possessed considerable taxable wealth and was able to inaugurate a library program of some substance. The attitude was expressed that their tax contributions to the county Library District exceeded the value of the benefits received; both rejected the equalization theory of tax support for local government services. The second problem is similar, and involves the fire services provided by the county fire districts. Downey and Santa Fe Springs both withdrew from the district and established their own departments. Commerce also threatened to withdraw soon after it was incorporated. All three cities maintained that their tax base was supporting fire services for other portions of the district, where tax resources were less. The situation in Commerce was alleviated somewhat by a change in the state law to permit cities to contribute their share of the costs of a district fire system from sales tax revenues.

Another situation arises from the fact that almost all cities incorporated after 1954 are in the First Supervisoral District, that is, the eastern portion of the county. A small number are in the Second District, which extends along the coastline from Long Beach to Malibu. This situation compels those two supervisors to be especially concerned with adjusting county policy and administration to the needs of new cities. Each of the five supervisors, however, has several cities in his district, and each is aware of the significance of city-county relations and of the shrinkage in unincorporated territory.

Tensions and factionalism have appeared among municipal officials as a result of the county's contract policies. Officials from a number of the older cities, those having few contracts with the county, often have opposed officials from the contract cities in such matters as election to League of California Cities offices. Those of the new group often express themselves as feeling isolated and pressured. Administrative officers of contract cities often have found themselves opposed in their efforts by chief administrators of the conventional municipalities. In reaction to this factionalism and to call attention to the special prob-

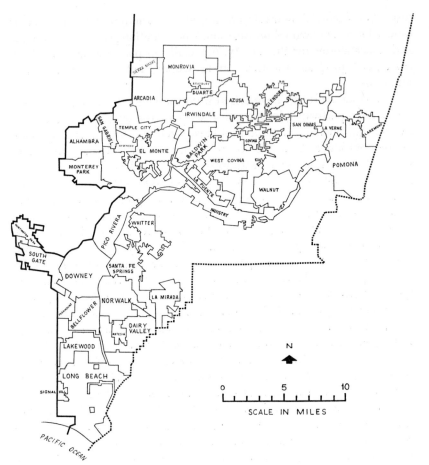

FIG. 7. Incorporated cities in the 1st Supervisoral District,
Los Angeles County.

lems involved in their type of undertaking, the "Lakewood" group
organized as the League of Contract Cities. Their annual conferences,
beginning in 1960 at Palm Springs, have been devoted to publicizing
the contract plan and to problems facing members of the group. Although county officials are not officers of this group, they take prominent roles in the conference programs.

Officials from Downey and Santa Fe Springs have led counterefforts
to dissuade newly organized cities from relying upon county contracts.
Several cities have offered to provide services to neighboring municipalities, either on a mutual-aid basis or on contract. Others have dis-

cussed plans for coöperative purchase and maintenance of heavy street equipment. To further this intercity coöperative activity, a group of officials from eight cities convened and organized the Independent Cities of Los Angeles County. The central theme of this group was to encourage each city to administer its own programs and assist its neighboring cities through mutual-aid agreements. In this self-help endeavor, the organizers proposed to bring about disintegration of the county-city contract system. Spokesmen for the aggregation were strongly antagonistic to both the county government and any integrated formal structure of government for the metropolitan area.

POLITICS OF LOCATING COUNTY FACILITIES

Because of the diversity of its functions and because it has decentralized the location of its facilities, the county participates in making many decisions that are important to public and private leaders in communities throughout the metropolitan region. The county involves itself in matters relating to some of the principal cities, in addition to providing services to unincorporated communities and serving newer cities through contracts. It has done this by consulting local groups on the location of county facilities and branch courts.[22] Municipal officials in most southern California communities have been deeply impressed with the civic center concept and have attempted to draw all public buildings in the particular city into a central complex. In planning for the civic centers, they have been affected by such considerations as upgrading of obsolescent or depressed sections of the central area, providing for off-street parking for the business section, and promoting civic pride. The county government has been an active participant in the negotiations in planning municipal centers in Pomona, Santa Monica, Glendale, Torrance, and to a lesser degree in other, smaller cities. Planning and construction of a tall county office and courts building in Long Beach provided a major example of the county's involvement in the development of a civic center.

The county has also taken an active part in shaping the Los Angeles Civic Center, an integral part of a comprehensive effort to revitalize downtown Los Angeles as the center of commercial, financial, and governmental headquarters for the region. The county government joined the city in planning the location and design of the Civic Center and has been an active force in implementing this plan. Construction

---

[22] See particularly chapters ten through eleven for a more detailed discussion of the decentralization of county facilities.

of a gigantic Hall of Administration, a Court House, and a Hall of Records in the central portion of the civic area, together with the continued operation of a Hall of Justice and other buildings, concentrates the county's headquarters personnel and activities in this location. Construction of a Music Center, under county auspices, further enhances the Civic Center as a regional focal point.

One result of the county's decisions to locate so much of its headquarters activities in the Los Angeles Civic Center is a large demand for parking facilities. The nature of the county functions located there brings in not only large numbers of county employees but also a very large number of citizens who have public business to transact. Because of this situation, the Board of Supervisors has been the principal body to plan, finance, and manage parking facilities in the Civic Center.

Because further concentration of governmental headquarters staffs in the Civic Center would aggravate traffic and parking demands, the county has developed subsidiary centers for several departments a short distance away. Election administration and county schools offices have been located in a warehouse area a mile from the Civic Center. The new county jail is located in an industrial area whose make-up is changing. Another headquarters complex has been developed in an area, approximately a mile from the Civic Center, that has long been obsolescent. The General Hospital, Juvenile Hall, central purchasing and stores, and central administrative offices for Charities, Road Department, and Flood Control are located there. Further eastward, in an undeveloped hilly section in unincorporated territory, the county Fire Department has built a central operating headquarters and the Sheriff's Department has located its training academy and a detention facility.

In planning and developing its headquarters accommodations, the county government has involved itself squarely in the politics of metropolitan development. It has assisted suburban centers to develop their facilities, in order to strengthen their claims as subcenters of service and influence. At the same time it has given substantial assistance to those who wish to see downtown Los Angeles as the headquarters for certain basic groups that control or influence operations in the metropolitan region. Occasionally, as when the county was urged to construct a central convention and trade-fair hall in downtown Los Angeles, the county board has found itself caught between the contending forces. Although supervisoral district boundaries are such that only one district encompasses downtown Los Angeles, considerations involved in developing the county headquarters facilities transcend district constituency interests for each supervisor.

CHOICES FOR THE FUTURE

What is likely to be the future role of the county in the government of the metropolitan area? Two paths of action seem feasible. One is to continue to assist unincorporated "fringe areas" to incorporate as cities, and to encourage them to contract with the county for most of their municipal services. The other is to expand those functions of county government that are region-wide in their impact; to achieve a status in which the county will be a metropolitan unit of government. In the latter choice the county would provide a smaller number of services than it has in the past, but would concentrate upon those functions that it can provide best because of its unique position. Choice of alternatives is not necessarily an "either-or" selection.

At the time the Lakewood community incorporated in 1954, the Board of Supervisors made a policy choice that has had a profound effect upon the pattern of government in this area. It involved encouraging incorporations, by lending the services of appropriate county departments in getting the city government started and by offering to provide services by contract thereafter. Under the state law pertaining to incorporations, no county board of supervisors can prevent a community that has sufficient population and taxable wealth from forming a city. In the Lakewood incident, the county government responded positively to the local leaders' request for assistance. Faced with a situation in which Lakewood was to be lost to the unincorporated-area category, either by incorporation or by annexation to Long Beach, the county chose to befriend the new city and espouse a policy that was calculated to retain a close relationship.

Incorporation of twenty-nine cities in one county in eight years is a remarkable record. Numerous other communities have attempted or discussed incorporation. Predictably, all or most of the territory on the coastal plain of Los Angeles County may either incorporate or annex to established cities in the near future. Efforts at organizing cities in the Antelope Valley and in the portion of the county that lies between the Los Angeles City limits and the Ventura County border indicate that still other parts of the county may incorporate. If this trend continues, what role is left for the county?

The county-city relationship wherein the county provides most of the municipal services for new cities involves some uncertainty and risk for the county. Contract cancellations by single cities at various times can cause considerable readjustment in county administrative organization and programs. Dislocation of county administrative personnel, resulting from changes in the contract system, can be offset, however, by developing other areas of the county. Mountainous regions outside the national forest preserves continue to draw increased settlement, particularly as the county makes them more accessible by building new roads. The Antelope Valley is a large section that will undoubtedly develop further when increased water supplies are available. It is predictable, therefore, that the county can shift personnel and operations to newer areas as the older communities on the coastal plain become municipalities. The transfer will be costly to the county, but the shift appears to be a natural one, brought about by changing demands for local government.

The basic concept of the contract system offers an element of uncertainty as to the permanence of the system itself. Any contract, governmental or private, will continue only so long as the contracting parties believe they enjoy a benefit that exceeds any that can be obtained by an alternative method. The county may find it advantageous to satisfy the requests of its contract cities for a long period, in order to achieve aims that are significant to it. The county has only limited control, however, over the events that determine the future of the system. It can satisfy the contracting cities chiefly by offering superior service. It must charge full costs for its services; therefore, the only method by which it may reduce prices is by reducing the costs of conducting county government. It cannot undertake to reduce the level of performance to some cities in order to offer them reduced prices as an inducement to continue contracts.

The Signal Hill incident indicates another element of uncertainty. Internal political pressures, which are not founded upon such rational factors as comparative monetary costs, may force cancellation of contracts. No contracting government is in a position to protect itself in such situations. If it loses some contracts because of political disturbances, it has a relatively limited field of potential buyers to which it may turn to maintain its administrative organization. The alternatives, if major reductions in the contract program materialize, are to turn to newly developing areas of the county or to transfer the emphasis to functions that are region-wide.

In either of these two choices of action, the county has a considerable degree of control over events. It possesses legal authority to perform many services that are region-wide in their impact: law enforcement (including prosecution, jails, court facilities, and probation administration), general hospitals, charities, regional planning, regional parks, regional recreational facilities (that is, major play areas, golf courses, bathing beaches, marinas, and mountain recreation areas), museums of fine arts and science, auditoriums, music centers, art schools, sports arenas, and airports. Los Angeles County has been conducting programs in these functions for several years and has assembled the necessary administrative talent to develop them further.

The principal limitation upon the county may be a financial one, although the county is in a relatively good position on this score. There is no legal limitation upon the county tax rate upon property. As the metropolitan area grows in wealth, the county tax base grows accordingly and provides a strong support foundation for governmental functions. The county's strength has been improved by the Bradley-Burns Reciprocal Sales Tax Act. It is in a reasonably good condition to finance capital improvements, although the electorate has been reluctant to grant approval. The county's existing bond debt is not large, and the state has imposed no bond-debt limitations. Many of the functions that have region-wide significance are capable of producing revenues and can finance their related construction. The county has considerable experience with lease-purchase financing and with concession leasing.

County functions that are region-wide in impact constitute a basic core that the county may perform regardless of other predictable changes in the pattern of local government. This core program alone makes the county a formidable contender for leadership on the metropolitan scene.

Los Angeles County directs two other programs that are particularly significant for metropolitan affairs: flood control and air pollution control. Both are administered by special districts, governed by the board of supervisors serving in an *ex officio* capacity.[23] In performing its basic responsibility, the Flood Control District, working jointly with the Army Corps of Engineers, has constructed dams and channels to protect the metropolitan area and to make it possible to utilize a much greater portion of the land area.[24] In coöperation with the cities, it has created a storm drainage system that disposes of waste storm waters from the entire area. It has also indicated that it is prepared to take a lead in water reclamation and recharging ground-water resources programs that are highly important in southern California. Although the Air Pollution District has not been fully successful, it has administered strong research activities to discover causes of air pollution and a forceful code-enforcement program.

From a combination of county and special district programs, which

[23] County and district personnel may also transfer from one jurisdiction to the other without loss of status or seniority.

[24] For the programs of the Flood Control District, see Richard Bigger, *Flood Control in Metropolitan Los Angeles* (Berkeley and Los Angeles: University of California Press, 1959).

are directed by the Board of Supervisors and the Chief Administrative Officer, Los Angeles County is firmly established as a regional or metropolitan unit of local government. Whichever path of action is chosen for future development, the county is not likely to be moved from that position of strength—unless it falls behind its competitors in the quality of its political and administrative leadership.

SUMMARY

Los Angeles County began a bid for a leadership role in the metropolitan scene at a time when its existence was being threatened by city expansion. The home-rule movement, which developed such great strength in California, extended to urban counties, as well as to the municipalities. In consequence of adopting a county home-rule charter, Los Angeles was able to initiate a series of events that eventually strengthened it to a point that it could effectively meet the challenges presented by urban developments.

Functional consolidations increased the number of services that the county provided on a region-wide basis. Its policy of offering municipal-type services to unincorporated "fringe areas" tended for many years to induce many suburban communities to remain under county jurisdiction, rather than annex to a city or incorporate. Areas that did incorporate as comparatively small cities chose to obtain a number of services from the county by contract or by remaining in county-administered districts. Development of the packaged full-service contract program, known as the Lakewood Plan, further linked the county and the new cities.

As the county became a large administrative organization, its requirements for competent management and technical personnel increased enormously. It compares very favorably with other governments throughout the United States in quality of personnel and level of administrative performance. Although much of the formal organization for policy-making and management requires improvement, the county has produced a notable record of performance.

Los Angeles County has been challenged by the statewide organization of municipalities to charge more of the cost for servicing unincorporated areas to the property that is benefited. Groups of elective municipal officials oppose the county-city contracts. More and more of county territory is being incorporated as cities, and the county is forced to withdraw direct services, except where the new cities contract for them.

Despite the changes that are being forced by increased urbanization and incorporation of the fringe areas, the county retains a series of functions that are important for the entire region. A number of circumstances give it a favorable opportunity to develop them further. The county seems not to be able to integrate the governmental programs of the metropolitan area, by means of functional consolidation and intergovernmental agreements, as once appeared possible. Nevertheless, it will remain a potent force in the governmental processes of the region. The level of that force will depend upon the skill of county political and administrative leadership.

EIGHT

The Suburbs: Conflict,
Coöperation, Confederation

THE SUBURBAN CITIES in this metropolitan region constitute, in a sense, a "third force" that countervails the two that have been more dominant, in past decades, in the struggle to determine the governmental pattern for the region. Basically, the suburban cities came into being in response to desires of various groups of people who wished to escape the forces unifying local governments and to create institutions that would protect the diversities of urban life that exist in a vast metropolitan community.

SUBURBAN RELATIONS WITH THE CENTRAL CITY

Suburbs in the Los Angeles area, unlike those in many other great metropolitan complexes of the United States, are not the products of any vast migration from the central city. Much of the literature relative to metropolitan problems that has appeared in the United States in recent years has laid great emphasis upon the "escape to the suburbs" by persons who grow to maturity in the central city and move to a more congenial environ as they ascend the economic and social scale.[1] Similarly, much has been written about both the "suburban way of life" and suburban attitudes toward political issues, emphasizing the dichotomy between the city and its suburbs. The

[1] Robert Wood, *Suburbia: Its People and Their Politics* (Boston: Houghton Mifflin, 1959).

conditions under which the central city of Los Angeles and its suburbs developed seem to have produced a different situation.

It may be, as some observers from distant points have remarked, that Los Angeles is not really a "central city," in the sense that the term is often used. In reality, the entire Los Angeles metropolitan area may be a collection of suburbs. Areas within the incorporated limits of Los Angeles, such as Van Nuys, Encino, Brentwood, and Westchester, are indeed suburbs in a sense, although they are not separate from the formal government of Los Angeles. The characteristic pattern of development in the entire metropolitan region has been for population to spread over the land rather than crowd into high buildings in the central area. Spectacular population growth has come to Los Angeles in brief spans of years. There was never a sufficient inducement to attract a disproportionately large share of the migrants to settle in downtown Los Angeles. Although the municipalities have clearly possessed unequal abilities to attract population and industries, most have achieved some growth. Almost all suburbs have attracted and held a share of the human flood. The fact that the city of Los Angeles had a vast land area that was only partially developed and that could absorb large numbers of newcomers without congesting the older, central areas was significant. It was equally important that the city possessed a high proportion of the local water supply.

Mobility of the population, both as to residence and employment, has been a meaningful phenomenon of economic, social, and political conditions in the Los Angeles area for decades. Nevertheless, the mobility pattern does not appear to have been confined to movements from the center to the periphery, at least as those points are defined by municipal boundaries. For reasons discussed previously in Chapter Six, however, several suburban municipalities were organized during the 1920's to protect living conditions in certain communities from the challenges of the big city. San Marino and Beverly Hills are often cited as examples of cities organized to protect residential living standards that were dependent upon large building lots and municipal services geared to the special needs of high-income families. Leaders of these municipalities in later years, like the founders, have believed that the desired standards would be destroyed if the political processes of a large city were to intrude.

ARE THE SUBURBS A UNIFIED FORCE?

Unlike either the central city or the county, the suburban municipalities do not constitute a unified force that contends steadily and con-

sistently to influence decisions on matters affecting the entire metropolitan region. Inasmuch as the suburban group consists of seventy-
three municipalities, each of which has been created to satisfy some
local need and has separate status as a legal institution, one might
expect them to operate in unison only to achieve some very important
common goal that they could not achieve separately. Nevertheless, the
suburban municipalities of Los Angeles county have sufficient experience with coöperative or coalition action to warrant being considered
as a determinant in the process by which the governmental pattern of
the region will evolve.

Disagreements among the suburban municipalities on matters that
have metropolitan impact and that cause them to form into subgroups
or factions to advocate contradictory actions, tend to take on importance equal to that of the areas of agreement. In general, the disagreements tend to arise from actions by some municipalities that result in
unfavorable consequences for others. Another aspect of the suburban
activities that relates to decision-making on metropolitan problems
consists of unilateral actions by some cities to enhance their relative
influence in the area as a whole. The central city has not been alone
in the drive to bring large territory and population under control of
municipal government. When the 1960 federal census was taken, four
suburban cities, Long Beach, Pasadena, Glendale, and Torrance, had
over one hundred thousand population each. Each has been active in
annexing territory. Each supplies an extensive array of municipal
services to its inhabitants through its own set of administrative employees, and each is relatively uninterested in functional consolidation
or coöperative programs. Because of their size, all four have become
influences in metropolitan-area affairs.

An aspect of the suburban municipalities' strength is the strength
of their administrative systems. One of the nation's heaviest concentrations of the manager-council form of government is to be found in the
Los Angeles metropolitan area. Many other cities have appointed chief
administrative officers. Most of the managers and administrators are
trained professionals. Although adoption of fashionable institutions is
no guarantee of strength in governmental processes, the appointment
of professional administrators indicates interest in strengthening the
internal administrative systems of the cities and demonstrates a determination to make local government work effectively. Equally significant is the success of suburban cities in developing municipal waterworks and in securing sources of water, both local and imported. Each
of these trends clearly strengthens the position of the municipalities

as local service enterprises. From the base of strength thus provided, the municipalities are able to exercise considerable influence upon public decisions that affect the metropolitan area as a whole.

AREAS OF AGREEMENT AND DISAGREEMENT AMONG THE SUBURBS

Whether considered as a suburban influence bloc, as a series of alliances comprising several cities each, or, in some instances, as single units, the suburban municipalities possess a negotiating capacity that must be reckoned with, especially when one attempts to calculate which alternative governmental arrangement having a region-wide impact can succeed in achieving its prescribed goals. The municipalities' strength stems, in large part, from the fact that, in the California system of government, no municipal corporation can be altered substantially or eliminated without approval of the local voters.

Twenty-nine municipalities in Los Angeles County have been in existence for less than a decade. Memories of their incorporation efforts are still fresh. Each newly organized municipality represents, to those who assisted in creating it, an achievement and a mechanism by which to define local group goals and determine programs. Citizens of older cities have strong loyalties to their local institutions and have learned by experience to defend themselves as communities. It follows that the persons who control the mechanisms of a specific municipality are in a strong position to negotiate with those who would change the structure of government in the metropolitan area. So long as each suburban municipality possesses sufficient finances to provide services at a level that satisfies a majority of its citizens, and so long as its elective officers and administrators demonstrate a moderately vigorous concern over the performance of local functions, each municipality can deal from strength with those who propose to change the system.

The objectives that the suburban municipalities seem to have in common are more defensive than creative. They relate to the preservation of those values of municipal government that local electors evidently hold in high esteem. Inasmuch as any type of integrated governmental structure for the metropolitan area tends to threaten those values, the suburbs join together to combat any proposals to integrate. The suburbs may differ in the techniques of how best to implement and realize local governmental values, but they appear to be unified in their belief in the values themselves. For example, those cities that provide a considerable number of functions by direct, municipally conducted administration strongly criticize those others that secure services from the county by contract. Yet, each set of municipal officials expresses itself strongly in favor of municipal home rule and the local determination of policies.

If we are to consider the suburban municipalities as an influence bloc that will negotiate decisions about metropolitan affairs, it becomes necessary to determine what subjects tend to draw them into unified action. For this purpose we shall examine the activities of the suburban cities with reference to metropolitan affairs during the period 1947–1961. In determining the attitude or decision of a city, we look to the actions taken, and the attitudes expressed, by its city council, inasmuch as that body is composed of elected representatives of the political will of the community.

Suburban consensus and disagreement may be expressed in terms of a range, or scale, representing the degree of agreement reached on a number of matters that affect local governments in a metropolitan area. It is useful to divide this range into three parts: one, those matters about which there appears to be nearly unanimous agreement, that is, consensus; two, matters about which many suburban cities tend to agree although there does not appear to be consensus; and, three, matters in which there is active disagreement, resulting in groups of cities forming coalitions to oppose the views or actions of others.

Subjects of decisions relating to metropolitan problems about which Suburban Municipalities tend to take a position

Matters about which they tend to have consensus:

1. Integrity of municipal boundaries—not to be changed by state action or by unilateral action of any agency external to the city.
2. Municipal home rule—freedom from state encroachment in a wide range of subjects defined to be "municipal affairs."
3. The value of diversity as a principle of local government in a metropolitan area; for example, freedom of each city to plan and zone land-use within its boundaries.
4. Consolidation or unification of governments in a metropolitan area —acceptable only when approved by majority vote of the residents in areas affected.
5. State collected taxes on automobiles and the alcoholic beverage industry—to be shared with the cities.
6. Mutual aid for fire protection.

Matters about which a large number tend
to be in agreement:

1. Intergovernmental coöperation involving the county and other cites in the following:
   a. Informal joint administrative action.
   b. Contracting with the county for a limited number of services, for example, tax assessment and collection of property taxes.
   c. Formulating plans for allocating ground-water rights and obtaining judicial sanction for arrangements.
2. Intergovernmental coöperation with regional administrative authorities for:
   (1) Flood control (County Flood Control District)
   (2) Water importation (Metropolitan Water District)
   (3) Waste disposal (County Sanitation District system and Los Angeles City contract system)
   (4) Air pollution control (County Air Pollution Control District).
3. Appointed executive to head local administrative systems.

Matters about which the Suburban Cities tend
to differ or to divide into coalitions:

1. Purchase of an extensive range of municipal-type services from the county.
2. The role and purpose of the municipality in a metropolitan area.
3. Extension of municipal controls and obligations through annexation of territory.

THE AGREEMENTS

Four of the five areas of consensus listed pertain basically to relations with the state of California. Three are really variations upon the theme of municipal home rule and therefore are points about which municipal officials throughout the state tend to be in agreement. These points are fully consistent with the Statement of Principles on Metropolitan Problems that the Board of Directors of the League of California Cities adopted in April, 1959. Two excerpts from that statement are especially relevant:

The best interests of the people of this state and nation require the maintenance of strong, healthy cities which have the right of home rule and which provide local governmental devices and perform local govenmental and policy-making functions.

Local municipal affairs, involving policy making, enforcement of laws and regulatory measures, and government activities, are not proper subjects for inclusion in regional or metropolitan government and should be retained by the cities.

A statement of principles adopted by a special conference of the League of California Cities in February, 1962, is also relevant:

> Functions and services performed by a city or a county should not be removed from a city or county and incorporated in a regional or metropolitan district without the consent of the electorate of the city or the county, or a majority vote of the entire membership of the legislative body of the city or county, subject to referendum.

The fifth subject of agreement among the suburban cities concerns a method of distributing tax sources, a subject that has become very important to continuance of the cities' programs. It too finds support among cities throughout the state.

The sixth subject, mutual aid for fire protection, relates to intergovernmental relations at the metropolitan-region level, and is the product of joint efforts on the part of federal, state, and local officials. In Los Angeles County, the cities have grown accustomed, over a period of years, to the principle of mutual aid. Although individual cities may have reservations about whether costs and benefits of the arrangements balance, all tend to rely upon mutual aid. When functional consolidation of fire suppression services on a metropolitan scale was proposed, the suburban cities countered with a statement of belief that mutual aid was an adequate alternative.

The second broad area of agreement among the suburban cities involves relations with the county government and with regional administrative authorities, some of which are closely related to the county. It may be observed that those suburban municipalities that do not fully agree with their fellows are not moved to take action to dissuade their associates.

All municipalities agree that, inasmuch as they have the option to purchase services from an outside agency, it is advantageous to contract with the county government for some administrative services. They do not agree fully as to which ones are properly to be supplied in this manner. Seven services rank high in choice by the cities (see table 6). All cities contract for election services from the County Registrar of Voters. Some of the larger ones continue to handle some phases of election administration but receive county assistance on others. All, except Pasadena and Long Beach, contract for assessment of property for tax purposes and for collection of local property taxes. Seventy cities have arranged for the county to keep custody of prisoners sentenced under city ordinances; only Los Angeles, Long Beach, and Santa Monica are exceptions. Sixty-nine have assigned public health protection to the county Health Department under authority of state statutes, and sixty-seven contract with the county department to perform additional health work within their borders and to enforce local health ordinances. Sixty-six cities contract with the county Engineer to have final checks made of subdivision maps. Forty-four receive library service through the integrated county Library System, financed by a district tax.

At the other extreme of the scale, there are several major functions that rank low in choice, ones that municipal officials deem should be performed locally. Inspection of the chart indicates that police protection, fire protection, and public works are the functions for which the fewest number of cities contract. Only twenty-five contract with the Sheriff for police protection, only twenty-six are either members of county fire districts or contract for fire protection, and only twenty-six look to the county Engineer for public works and street work. The majority of the cities believe that these functions should be operated by their own employees under supervision of municipal officials.

The cities have shown a disposition to work coöperatively with certain other regional agencies, in addition to the county. In the field of water supply, most cities are now associated with the Metropolitan Water District of Southern California. Ten—Beverly Hills, Burbank, Compton, Glendale, Long Beach, Los Angeles, Pasadena, San Marino, Santa Monica, and Torrance—are individual members of the district. Cities in other portions of the county, with the exception of those in the San Gabriel Valley, are constituent members of municipal water districts that, in turn, are members of the metropolitan district. The San Gabriel Valley Municipal Water District and the Upper San Gabriel Valley Municipal Water District, comprising cities as well as unincorporated communities, have not affiliated with the metropolitan district. All cities in the Los Angeles metropolitan area are evidently disposed to join with other governmental units in some type of regional organization to assure a water supply.

Similarly, the cities have shown a willingness to work with a regional agency in flood control and drainage. The County Flood Control District has the primary responsibility for flood control. A bond issue, approved by the district voters in 1956, inaugurated a district-city coöperative program in selecting routes and designing and supervising construction of major storm drains. A majority of the cities within

TABLE 6

Services Provided to Cities by the County of Los Angeles
(November 15, 1961)

CONTRACTS	Alhambra	Arcadia	Artesia	Avalon	Azusa	Baldwin Park	Bell	Bellflower	Bell Gardens	Beverly Hills	Bradbury	Burbank	Claremont	Commerce	Compton	Covina	Cudahy	Culver City	Dairy Valley	Downey	Duarte	El Monte	El Segundo	Gardena	Glendale	Glendora	Hawthorne	Hermosa Beach	Hidden Hills	Huntington Park
Assessment and collection of taxes	•	•	•	•	•	•	•	•	•		•	•	•	•	•	•	•	•	•	•	•	•	•	•		•	•	•	•	•
Building inspection services			•	•			•	•		•		•		•		•		•								•			•	
Business license issuance services			•				•					•		•		•		•												
County jail	•	•	•		•	•	•	•	•	•	•	•		•		•		•	•	•	•		•	•	•	•	•	•	•	•
Emergency ambulance service			•		•	•	•	•	•	•		•	•	•		•		•	•	•	•	•		•		•	•	•	•	•
General services agreement			•	•	•	•	•			•		•		•		•		•	•	•	•	•	•	•		•	•	•	•	•
Health services	•	•	•	•		•	•			•		•	•	•		•		•		•	•	•	•	•	•	•	•	•	•	•
Rodent control	•	•					•							•				•												•
Industrial-waste regulation			•		•		•	•				•				•		•	•											•
Law enforcement services			•				•	•				•		•		•		•	•									•		
Business license enforcement			•				•							•		•		•												
Crossing guard service			•				•																							
Motorcycle patrol			•				•					•																		
Traffic-law enforcement			•				•			•				•																•
Pound: animal regulation	•	•		•		•	•			•		•		•	•		•	•	•					•		•				
Sewer maintenance			•														•		•					•	•					
Street maintenance and construction			•				•	•		•		•				•		•		•		•								
Bridge maintenance			•				•	•		•		•				•		•		•										
Street light maintenance	•		•				•	•		•		•				•		•		•		•								
Street sweeping			•				•	•		•		•				•		•		•										
Signing			•				•	•		•		•				•		•		•										
Traffic signal maintenance		•	•		•		•	•		•		•			•	•	•	•		•					•		•			
Traffic stripping and marking			•				•	•		•		•				•		•		•										•
Subdivision final map check (County Engineer)	•	•	•		•	•	•	•		•	•	•	•	•	•	•	•	•	•	•	•		•	•		•	•		•	•
Resolutions pursuant to general services agreement																														
Engineering staff services							•	•		•				•		•		•	•	•									•	•
Master house-numbering map service			•				•	•		•				•		•		•		•									•	•
Personnel staff services					•					•		•															•	•		
Prosecution of city violations			•				•	•		•				•	•	•		•	•	•				•		•				•
Subdivision services (R.P.C.)			•				•	•		•				•		•		•	•						•					•
Tree-trimming service			•				•			•				•		•		•												
Zoning, Planning staff services			•				•	•		•				•		•		•		•										
Other resolutions																														
Company Engineer—appointed City Engineer			•				•	•		•				•		•														•
Road Commissioner—appointed City Superintendent of Streets			•				•	•		•				•		•						•								
Election services	•	•	•	•	•	•	•	•	•	•	•	•	•	•	•	•	•	•	•	•	•	•		•	•	•	•	•	•	
Forester and Fire Warden—appointed Fire Chief			•			•		•	•	•		•		•		•		•	•	•	•	•							•	
Health services (state law)	•	•	•	•	•	•	•	•	•	•	•	•	•	•	•	•	•	•	•	•	•	•	•	•	•	•	•	•	•	•
Sheriff—appointed Chief of Police			•				•	•		•				•		•				•										
Special districts																														
Fire Protection District			•			•		•		•		•		ᵃ		•		•											•	
Library District		•	•		•	•	•	•		•	•	•	•	•	•		•				•					•	•	•	
Lighting and Lighting Maintenance Districts	•	•					•	•															•							
Park, Recreation and Parkway Districts			•				•			•					•			•							•					
Sewer Maintenance District			•				•							•		ᵇ		•	•	•										
Total	7	11	35	8	10	16	11	38	27	6	31	10	10	34	11	13	32	9	29	17	30	11	9	15	8	12	11	9	18	15

Source: County-City Coördinator, Los Angeles County.

ᵃ Fire service provided by contract

ᵇ Sewer maintenance service by contract

TABLE 6 (Continued)

Irwindale	Lakewood	La Mirada	La Puente	La Verne	Lawndale	Long Beach	Los Angeles	Lynwood	Manhattan Beach	Maywood	Monrovia	Montebello	Monterey Park	Norwalk	Palos Verdes Estates	Paramount	Pasadena	Pico Rivera	Pomona	Redondo Beach	Rolling Hills	Rolling Hills Estates	Rosemead	San Dimas	San Fernando	San Gabriel	San Marino	Santa Fe Springs	Santa Monica	Sierra Madre	Signal Hill	South El Monte	South Gate	South Pasadena	Temple City	Torrance	Vernon	Walnut	West Covina	Whittier	Total
•	•	•	•	•	•		•	•	•	•	•	•	•	•		•		•		•	•	•	•	•	•	•	•		•		•		•		•		•	•	•	•	71
•	•	•	•		•							•					•			•		•					•				•			•							30
				•																	•						•				•			•							9
•	•	•	•	•	•			•	•	•	•	•	•	•		•		•		•	•	•	•	•	•	•	•		•		•		•		•		•	•	•	•	70
•	•	•	•	•	•			•	•	•		•		•		•		•		•	•	•	•		•		•		•		•		•		•		•	•	•		56
•	•	•	•	•				•	•		•	•	•	•		•		•		•	•	•			•		•		•		•		•		•			•	•		54
•	•	•	•	•				•		•	•	•	•	•		•		•		•					•		•		•		•		•		•			•	•	•	67
•	•	•	•	•				•			•	•	•			•		•		•							•				•		•						•		33
•	•	•	•		•													•		•							•				•		•					•	•		28
	•	•	•		•													•		•							•				•		•								25
	•	•	•		•													•		•							•				•										15
•					•													•		•							•						•								8
•		•			•													•		•							•						•								7
•	•	•		•								•				•		•		•							•				•		•					•			18
•	•	•	•	•								•	•			•		•		•	•		•				•				•		•			•	•	•			35
			•									•	•						•												•			•		•						9
•	•	•	•		•									•		•	•	•		•							•				•		•					•			26
•	•	•	•		•													•		•							•				•		•					•			22
•	•	•			•													•		•	•						•				•								•		14
•	•	•	•		•							•						•		•	•	•					•				•		•					•			18
•	•	•	•	•										•		•		•		•	•						•				•		•					•			21
•	•	•	•		•							•		•		•		•		•	•						•				•		•					•			30
•	•	•	•	•	•							•		•		•	•	•		•	•	•					•	•			•		•			•	•	•	•	•	66
•	•	•	•	•	•								•			•		•		•	•	•					•				•		•					•	•		29
•	•	•	•		•													•		•	•	•					•				•		•					•			22
											•	•	•		•												•				•										12
	•	•	•		•					•		•						•		•							•				•		•					•	•		38
•	•	•	•		•													•		•	•	•					•				•		•					•			24
	•	•	•		•															•	•	•									•		•					•			16
•	•	•			•													•		•	•	•					•				•		•					•			22
•	•	•	•		•									•				•		•	•	•					•				•		•					•			26
•	•	•	•		•													•		•	•	•					•				•		•					•	•		22
•	•	•	•	•	•		•	•	•	•	•	•	•	•		•	•	•	•	•	•	•	•	•	•	•	•	•	•	•	•	•	•	•	•	•	•	•	•	•	72
•	•	•	•		•													•		•	•	•					•				•		•					•	•		26
•	•	•	•	•	•			•	•	•	•	•	•	•		•		•		•	•	•	•			•	•		•		•		•		•		•	•	•	•	69
•	•	•	•		•													•		•							•				•		•					•			25
•	•	•	•		•									•				•		•	•	•					•				•		•					•			26
•	•	•	•	•	•			•	•		•							•		•	•	•					•	•	•		•							•	•		41
	•	•	•		•													•									•				•							•	•		14
•	•	•	•		•										•												•			•			•						•		11
•	•	•	•		•									•	•		•			•	•	•									•								•	•	27
34	34	35	32	15	34	2	2	12	9	12	8	15	10	28	10	36	3	33	8	11	21	33	37	32	10	9	7	27	7	9	10	35	9	8	35	10	6	31	14	7	1278

the area have been involved in the integrated regional storm-water disposal program.

Almost all cities participate in one of two metropolitan sewage-disposal administrative systems. All but seven are members of one or more county sanitation districts. The districts, in turn, are associated together in the County Sanitation Districts administrative system. Four cities, San Fernando, Burbank, Glendale, and Santa Monica, are not members of the county district system, but contract with the city of Los Angeles to use the system maintained by that municipality. Those contracting with Los Angeles do not participate directly in determining policies for that system, although they share in the maintenance costs and have twice shared in financing the reconstruction of treatment and disposal facilities. Only two small residential cities, Hidden Hills and Rolling Hills, do not belong to either system.

It may be concluded that the suburban cities tend to agree that there are certain local government functions that may be performed advantageously in an administrative context larger than any individual city. In almost every instance, however, they retain either a degree of control over decision-making or participate in the formulation of policy. The functions that rank high, within the framework outlined, are election administration, property assessment and tax collection, jail custody of certain prisoners, health protection and services, library service, water supply, drainage, and sewage disposal.

THE DISAGREEMENTS

In the third category of subjects about which the suburban municipalities take a position, there are disagreements that tend to produce action that in turn influences decisions on metropolitan issues. Each of these disputes has arisen over policies relating to control of the newly developed urban fringes.

During the period under study, 1947–1961, the sharpest division has arisen over the purchase of numerous municipal-type services from the county, the so-called Lakewood Plan. Consequences of this disagreement have been manifested in a variety of ways. The Los Angeles County Division of the League of California Cities has been riven often by controversy on this subject. Representatives of the contract cities often alleged that they were discriminated against in the division's program and that the organization was controlled by the cities that favored municipal performance of most functions.[2] While continuing in the League, the contract cities have formed a Contract

---

[2] This was contradicted, in part, by the selection of Councilman Iacoboni of Lakewood as the division president in 1961.

Cities Seminar; and the anticontract group have set up the Independent Cities of Los Angeles County.

Appointed administrators in several municipalities are in active opposition to the county-city contract plan. Nevertheless, there is no apparent correlation between the activities of the elected officials and those of the appointed administrators in this matter. That is to say, the city manager or administrator whose mayor or council members are active in one of the intercity groups is not always identified prominently with the same point of view. Similarly, some managers and administrators have been more outspoken or active, but their councilmen have not usually exhibited the same degree of prominence in the discussion.

Most of the action that has arisen from the discussions among the appointed administrators has been to develop means for informal intercity coöperation. Often this coöperation has involved offers to loan or lease heavy equipment required for street work or to "pool" informally equipment owned and used by adjacent cities.

Opposition to the county-city contract plan appears to be based largely upon the fear that the plan will enhance the position of the county as the coördinator of local government in the metropolitan area. Opponents maintain that the county gives, in effect, a hidden subsidy to the contract cities, to induce them to remain within its administrative system. It is alleged also that this system produces adverse results for the noncontracting cities, inasmuch as county government is financed by taxes collected in cities as well as in unicorporated areas, and therefore the noncontracting cities are being forced to help subsidize the others.

To counteract this allegation, the county has established a policy of charging a prorated share of the indirect, as well as the direct, costs of supplying services to cities. It is not fully clear, however, how rigorously the county administration has pursued cost-benefit analysis of its operations and capital outlay in order to allocate charges to the general county budget and the city-contract services. Inasmuch as personnel assigned to contract services are part of the total county government work force, and most equipment and facilities are also used jointly by county and contract-city operations, there is room for controversy over the assignment of charges. It may be valid to speculate that the contract cities are being charged more than their share of the costs, or, on the contrary, that a partial subsidy exists. There are enough unresolved factual points to stimulate controversy and to cause groups opposed to the county government to employ a political strategy claiming that hidden subsidies exist.

The county-subsidy issue has divided the county government and the cities for approximately thirty years. In its original form, it involved direct county performance of municipal-type services for unincorporated areas. The city spokesmen argued, at that time, that their taxpayers financed similar services within the cities and also were required to pay a portion of the costs of supplying the unincorporated areas, through county taxes. The Los Angeles City Bureau of Budget and Efficiency and the mayor complained of this in 1935 and on several subsequent occasions.[3] In 1951, the Los Angeles County Division of the League of California Cities made an analysis and published its findings that a subsidy did exist.[4] The statewide League also took up the attack, aiming its fire at several counties, as well as at Los Angeles.[5] Legislative committees were drawn into the controversy and sought ways to meet the problem.[6]

The significance of the county-city controversy concerning the unincorporated areas, at that time, is highlighted by the data set forth in table 7. During the 1947–1953 period, population growth took place at a more rapid rate in the unincorporated areas served by the county than in the incorporated cities. Although the cities' population showed a numerical increase, their portion of the total county residents declined.

Incorporation of Lakewood in 1954 marked the beginning of a new trend, as the cities expanded their control over urban portions of the county. During the subperiod of 1954–1961, when there were numerous incorporations and annexations, the population living in the unincorporated area declined 4.151 per cent, whereas the population served by the cities grew 43.950 per cent.

Relating population changes to area—or jurisdiction—changes, we find that the suburban cities increased significantly in area after 1954, as is illustrated by table 8. Inspection of this table discloses that, during the subperiod of 1947–1953, the suburbs acquired only 0.743 per cent of the county's land area, and their share of the county's population total increased only 0.721 per cent. In the period after 1954, however, the suburban group added 5.138 per cent of the county's land

[3] See discussion on pp. 196–199.

[4] League of California Cities, Los Angeles County Division, County-City Relations Committee, *Report* (Los Angeles, 1951).

[5] League of California Cities, Committee on Intergovernmental Relations, *A Study of the County Subsidy of Municipal-Type Services to Urban Unincorporated Areas* (Berkeley, 1951).

[6] California Legislature, Assembly, Interim Committee on Municipal and County Government, *Financing Local Government in Los Angeles County* (Sacramento, 1952).

area to its jurisdiction and raised its share of the county's population total by 9.861 per cent.

When several communities decided to incorporate and chose to contract for most of their municipal functions, the county-subsidy issue shifted to the subject of cost allocation. In large part, it seemed that the cities' previous demands had been met by the Lakewood Plan and other county actions. Urbanized fringe areas were incorporating or annexing to established cities and were paying directly for municipal-type services. After 1954, the cities tended to divide over the new issue along lines separating the contract group from those that wished to perform the majority of their municipal services themselves.

The stand taken by those opposed to the contract arrangement suggested an interesting implication. If the county were actually subsidizing some cities, enlightened self-interest ought to induce the other cities to avail themselves of the subsidy also. Had a sufficient number of cities accepted this hypothetical choice, the subsidy issue would have disappeared, because a type of functional consolidation would have been achieved, and the county would have become the metropolitan administrative agency. Vested interests in long-established local institutions, however, caused the older cities to reject the supposed inducements of the county's contract system.

The so-called old-line cities, those that prefer to retain municipal control and performance and that criticize the county-city contract plan, advance three major contentions. One, they assert that the economists' theory of economy of scale—that a larger organization is able to add units of output at diminishing costs per unit and perform more efficiently than can smaller organizations—is not proven true in this situation. Some cities have measured their dollar costs of operating selected functions and contend that they can perform several functions, such as street cleaning, more cheaply than can the larger county organization. Two, they postulate that the city administrative organization is more responsive to local wishes and is more sensitive to local demands for service than is a large county organization that must serve a larger area and a greater variety of interests. Third, they declare that the municipality is best able to offer its citizens access to the government in order that they may make known their desires regarding the type and level of services to be provided. These propositions have become articles of faith undergirding the political position of the suburban leaders.

A second issue about which the suburban cities tend to divide concerns the question of whether or not urbanized unincorporated territory that has tended to look to the county for municipal-type services

TABLE 7
GROWTH OF POPULATION IN LOS ANGELES COUNTY AND SELECTED AREAS

Area	April, 1947		October, 1953				October, 1961			
	Population	Per cent	Population	Per cent	Numerical change	Per cent change	Population	Per cent	Numerical change	Per cent change
City of Los Angeles	1,890,000	50.427	2,089,189	44.012	+199,189	+10.539	2,561,674	40.713	+ 472,485	+22.615
All other cities	1,183,104	31.567	1,532,698	32.288	+349,594	+29.548	2,652,036	42.149	+1,119,338	+73.030
Total all cities	3,073,104	81.994	3,621,887	76.300	+548,783	+17.857	5,213,710	82.862	+1,591,823	+43.950
All unincorporated areas	674,858	18.005	1,124,985	23.699	+450,127	+66.699	1,078,278	17.137	− 46,707	− 4.151
Total County of Los Angeles	3,747,962	99.999	4,746,872	99.999	+998,910	+26.652	6,291,988	99.999	+1,545,116	+32.550
Southeast area										
Cities	284,706	76.453	300,903	74.456	+16,197	+ 5.689	372,701	85.127	+71,798	+23.860
Unincorporated	87,686	23.546	103,229	25.543	+15,543	+17.725	65,115	14.872	−38,114	−36.921
Total	372,392	99.999	404,132	99.999	+31,740	+ 8.523	437,816	99.999	+33,684	+ 8.334
San Gabriel area										
Cities	104,410	78.563	133,377	76.482	+28,967	+27.743	155,529	79.158	+22,152	+16.608
Unincorporated	28,489	21.436	41,012	23.517	+12,523	+43.957	40,948	20.841	− 64	− 0.156
Total	132,899	99.999	174,389	99.999	+41,490	+31.219	196,477	99.999	+22,088	+12.665
Pomona area										
Cities	37,683	86.528	58,538	90.125	+20,855	+55.343	99,572	94.868	+41,034	+70.098
Unincorporated	5,867	13.471	6,414	9.874	+ 547	+ 9.323	5,386	5.131	− 1,028	−16.027
Total	43,550	99.999	64,952	99.999	+21,402	+49.143	104,958	99.999	+40,006	+61.593

SOURCE: Los Angeles County, Regional Planning Commission, *Population and Dwelling Units*, Bull. 23 (July, 1947); Bull. 42 (Oct., 1953); Bull. 74 (Oct., 1961).

TABLE 8

GROWTH OF AREAS AND POPULATION, 1947–1961

	April, 1947				October, 1953				October, 1961			
	Area (sq. mi.)	Per cent of total	Popula- tion	Per cent of total	Area (sq. mi.)	Per cent of total	Popula- tion	Per cent of total	Area (sq. mi.)	Per cent of total	Popula- tion	Per cent of total
County	3,951.980	.....	3,747,962	99.999	......	.....	4,746,872	99.999	......	.....	6,291,988	99.999
Los Angeles City	452.645	11.453	1,890,000	50.427	453.902	11.485	2,089,189	44.012	457.773	11.584	2,561,674	40.713
Suburban cities	282.660	7.152	1,183,104	31.567	311.991	7.895	1,532,698	32.288	515.074	13.033	2,652,036	42.149
Total cities	735.305	18.605	3,073,104	81.994	765.893	19.380	3,621,887	76.300	972.847	24.617	5,213,710	82.862
Unincorporated area	3,216.675	81.395	674,858	18.005	3,186.087	80.620	1,124,985	23.699	2,979.133	75.383	1,078,278	17.137

SOURCE: Area figures are based upon data supplied by the Los Angeles County Engineer's Department. Population figures are based upon data supplied by the Los Angeles County Regional Planning Commission, *Population and Dwelling Units*, Bull. 23 (July, 1947); Bull. 42 (Oct., 1953); Bull. 74 (Oct., 1961).

should be induced to incorporate as new cities or be annexed to existing ones. Either alternative would bring the communities into the
municipal camp and might conceivably reduce the influence of the
county government. Individual cities have demonstrated preference
according to what their official leaders perceived to be advantageous.
Some are unable to expand their area because they are surrounded by
other municipalities. Some cities' policy is to restrict annexation, unless
the area to be annexed clearly contains a tax base or natural resource,
such as ground-water supply, that will give the annexing city additional strength. Other cities will accept annexations only if the property owners involved pay a substantial fee, to cover estimated costs of
making the city's administrative system available to the new area. Still
others are anxious to extend their influence and control over adjacent
areas and therefore resent and oppose the efforts of leaders in the unincorporated areas to set up independent city governments.

As we have suggested previously, the data indicates that there are
two relatively distinct subperiods in the postwar era of suburban
growth. Between 1947 and 1953, there were several annexations, but
there were no new incorporations. Between 1954 and 1961, there was
brisk activity in both procedures. Therefore, it might have been predicted that the sharpest divisions would take place between the municipal protagonists during this latter period. Table 9 suggests the basis
for suburban conflicts. A number of cities exhibited a relatively low
interest in annexation. In the full period of 1947–1961, there were

TABLE 9

SUMMARY OF MUNICIPAL AREA CHANGES
IN LOS ANGELES COUNTY, 1947–1961

Type of change	Number of cities	
	1947–1953	1954–1961
Incorporations	0	25
No change in area	14	8
Loss of area	2	1
Gain (in square miles of area)		
0.01–0.50	15	16
0.51–1.00	5	5
1.01–2.00	6	4
2.01–3.00	1	3
More than 3.00	2	8

SOURCE: Unpublished data supplied by County Engineer, Los Angeles County.

twenty-three cities that showed little interest in this procedure, sixteen being ones that incorporated prior to 1954, and seven, ones that organized after that date. Six made no annexations whatever, notably because they were surrounded by other municipalities, and had little or no choice.[7] Three others made no annexations in 1947–1953, but did add small amounts in the second subperiod. Two others reversed the timing. Beverly Hills may be added to the group of sixteen, even though it did annex a few tracts. Although it is almost surrounded by Los Angeles, it acquired a few parcels of unincorporated territory in the Santa Monica Mountains and received two small bits by transfer from Los Angeles. Four cities showed relatively little interest in annexation in either period, although they were not entirely negative to the procedure.

The behavior of the sixteen cities that demonstrated low interest does not give a satisfactory clue, however, to the attitude they might exhibit towards legislation that would alter the rules governing either annexation or incorporation. None of them suffered any defeat or frustration by another city in an annexation skirmish. Likewise, none seemed to covet territory that was taken by a new incorporation. It might be predicted, however, that officials in this group would be relatively unimpressed with the value of annexation, and might be sympathetic to increasing the number of cities in the metropolitan area.

Another group of cities, typified by Pasadena, has come to regard annexation as a procedure to be used sparingly and selectively. They discourage annexations by setting a schedule of fees. The action pattern followed by this group does not disclose the policy makers' opinions regarding annexation as it relates to metropolitan problems and apart from the individual city's interests. Conceivably, officials in these communities may favor new incorporations, except where an established city would gain substantial tax resources, protect its water rights, or advance its corporate interests in some similar manner by annexation.

Annexation causes intercity conflict when a community incorporates in order to block another's effort to expand, or when two established cities seek to annex the same parcels of land. Table 10 indicates that in the pre-Lakewood era of 1947–1953 there was relatively little conflict; no community incorporated, and only fourteen cities annexed more than a half square mile of territory. In the next subperiod, however, there were twenty-eight incorporations, and twenty cities an-

---

[7] Avalon, though included in the list, is not considered because it is on an island off the mainland and therefore is not involved in the relationships in the metropolitan area.

TABLE 10

CITIES DEMONSTRATING LOW INTEREST IN ANNEXATION

City	Area annexed in square miles		
	1947–1953	1954–1961	Total area annexed
Artesia[a]			
Avalon			
Bell Gardens[a]			
Bradbury[a]			
Cudahy[a]			
Hermosa Beach			
Manhattan Beach	0.000	0.000	0.000
Maywood			
Paramount[a]			
Rolling Hills[a]			
Santa Monica			
Signal Hill			
South Pasadena			
Temple City[a]			
Sierra Madre	0.003	0.000	0.003
Palos Verdes Estates	0.000	0.007	0.007
Huntington Park	0.019	0.003	0.022
San Marino	0.011	0.019	0.030
Montebello	0.000	0.043	0.043
San Fernando	0.052	0.000	0.052
El Segundo	0.000	0.156	0.156
Redondo Beach	0.038	0.122	0.160
Lynwood	0.275	0.181	0.456

SOURCE: Computed from unpublished data supplied by County Engineer, Los Angeles County.
[a] Incorporated after December 31, 1953.

nexed more than a half square mile. We would expect, therefore, to discover considerable intercity conflicts during this latter time.

To demonstrate which suburban areas experienced the greatest amount of intercity tension, we have (a) ranked the pre-1947 cities in order of amount of territory annexed (table 11), (b) ranked the cities incorporated between 1954 and 1961 in order of size of area at time of incorporation (table 11), and (c) grouped the clusters of high-activity cities (table 12). The data reveals five major centers of activity and tension (see table 12). Three older cities, Long Beach, Whittier, and Pomona, were high in annexation activity throughout the entire postwar era of urban growth.

The largest number of new cities is to be found in the southeast part of the county, between Long Beach, ranked second among the

TABLE 11

New Cities and Cities Annexing More Than 1 Square Mile,
in Rank Order of Area

	Annexations			Incorporations, 1953–1961	
Rank	Annexing city	Area annexed (in sq. miles) 1953–1961	Rank	New city	Area at time of incorporation (in sq. miles)
1	Whittier	5.819	1	Downey	11.785
2	Long Beach	5.777	2	Irwindale	9.477
3	Monrovia	5.269	3	Duarte	9.477
4	El Monte	3.996	4	Norwalk	9.095
5	West Covina	3.734	5	Dairy Valley	8.450
6	Pomona	3.566	6	Walnut	7.737
7	La Verne	3.448	7	Pico Rivera	7.604
8	Azusa	2.746	8	Lakewood	6.994
9	Glendora	2.714	9	Commerce	6.311
10	Covina	2.399	10	Baldwin Park	6.127
11	Hawthorne	1.526	11	Bellflower	6.074
12	Inglewood	1.458	12	Santa Fe Springs	6.042
13	Bell	1.244	13	Industry	5.508
14	Torrance	1.030	14	San Dimas	5.464
			15	La Mirada	4.748
			16	Paramount	4.285
Rank	Annexing city	Area annexed (in sq. miles) 1947–1953	17	Temple City	3.604
			18	La Puente	3.204
			19	Rolling Hills	2.953
			20	Bell Gardens	2.398
1	Glendale	8.929	21	Rosemead	2.241
2	Long Beach	6.489	22	Bradbury	1.996
3	Compton	2.557	23	Lawndale	1.897
4	Pomona	1.557	24	Artesia	1.614
5	Monterey Park	1.444	25	Hidden Hills	1.300
6	Pasadena	1.400	26	Rolling Hills Estates	1.249
7	Whittier	1.302	27	South El Monte	1.124
8	Gardena	1.064	28	Cudahy	1.060

Source: Unpublished data supplied by the County Engineer of Los Angeles County.

annexing cities in the entire county both in 1954–1961 and in 1947–1953, and Whittier, ranked first in 1954–1961 and seventh in 1947–1953. Five in this group score high in size of area, when first organized. The southeast part of the county was devoid of incorporated cities prior to 1954. Long Beach, Compton, Bell, and Whittier were the only established cities that succeeded in making much inroad into it by annexation.

Compton was highly active in the first subperiod, but made only a modest extension in the second. Whittier was active in both subperiods. Despite its defeat when it tried to annex a huge residential area that lay between its borders and the county line, it was able later to annex smaller portions. Great tension developed throughout the surrounding area, however, as a consequence of Whittier's efforts.

Long Beach was frustrated, first, in its campaign to annex the Lakewood housing development, by that community's incorporation. Next, establishment of additional new cities, such as Norwalk, Bellflower and Dairy Valley, blocked its extension to the north and northeast. Its growth was, therefore, confined to an area that lay between the city's 1947 boundaries and the Orange County border near Seal Beach and Los Alamitos.

Tension developed also between some of the newly organized cities in the southeast area when Santa Fe Springs, Downey, and Pico Rivera sought to extend their influence by annexation. "Islands" of unincorporated area were surrounded by new cities. In some instances, the "islands" were so small in area that there was little possibility of their incorporating separately; therefore, when the section developed, annexation became appropriate. Several annexation struggles took place also in the subareas upon which Whittier, Pico Rivera, Santa Fe Springs, and La Mirada bordered. In another subarea, Downey sought to annex a community that was soon afterward included in the new city of Cudahy. The new municipalities most successful in achieving annexation objectives were Santa Fe Springs and Downey.

The eastern part of the San Gabriel Valley ranked second in amount of competition for municipal area in 1954–1961, although it showed little activity in the previous period. Population estimates and building reports indicate, however, that it was developing rapidly in both intervals. Four cities that existed prior to 1954 ranked high in the countywide list for annexation activity; and seven new cities were formed, three encompassing relatively large areas.

The San Gabriel Valley is large enough for its municipal-growth pattern to show subclusters. Monrovia and Azusa are located at the north end of the valley along the base of the San Gabriel mountains. Three new cities, Irwindale, Duarte, and Bradbury, lie between the two expanding older cities. One of the motivations for the incorporations was the desire to prevent either of the older cities from extending its control. Covina and West Covina, which lie at the valley's southern end, were actively annexing in both periods, ranking high in the second. In this portion of the valley, several pairs of municipalities competed: Covina–West Covina, West Covina–Walnut, La

Puente–Industry. Considerable intercity tension resulted from a contest to acquire and control areas that were developing or were considered potentially ripe for development.

Three lesser clusters of competing municipalities are located in the central portion of the San Gabriel Valley, in the Pomona Valley, and

TABLE 12

CENTERS OF INTERCOMMUNITY TENSION OVER AREA EXTENSION

Cities annexing	Rank 1947–1953	Rank 1954–1961	New cities	Rank	Area of county
Long Beach	2	2	Lakewood	8	Southeast
			Bellflower	11	
			Artesia	24	
Compton	3	...	Paramount	16	
			Dairy Valley	5	
			Norwalk	4	
			Downey	1	
Bell	...	12	Bell Gardens	20	
			Cudahy	28	
Whittier	7	1	Pico Rivera	7	
			La Mirada	15	
			Santa Fe Springs	12	
Monrovia	...	3	Irwindale	2	East San Gabriel Valley
Azusa	...	8	Duarte	3	
			Bradbury	22	
West Covina	...	5	Baldwin Park	10	
			La Puente	17	
			Walnut	6	
			Industry	13	
El Monte	...	4	Temple City	17	Central San Gabriel Valley
			Rosemead	21	
			South El Monte	27	
Pomona	4	6	San Dimas	14	Pomona Valley
La Verne	...	7			
Claremont[a]	...	...			
Inglewood	...	12	Lawndale	23	Centinella Valley
Hawthorne	...	11			
Torrance	...	14			
Gardena	8	...			

SOURCE: Unpublished data supplied by the County Engineer of Los Angeles County. Ranks are taken from table 11.
[a] Claremont, although unranked, has done some annexation.

in the Centinella Valley and its southern extension. El Monte is the core of the first cluster, being located in the midst of a rapidly developing residential and small-business section. Adjacent to it, three new cities have organized, each ranking relatively low in territorial size.

Pomona forms the industrial and commercial center of the second cluster, although La Verne has been almost equally active in annexing adjacent lands to extend municipal control over a section where citrus acreage has suddenly given way to subdivisions. A very active three-way annexation competition has gone on in the Pomona Valley, between Pomona, La Verne, and Claremont. The San Dimas community, which had long drawn its public services from the county government, incorporated in 1960 to protect itself against this intercity competition. A new city of Walnut formed, on the southwest boundary of Pomona, barring both Pomona and West Covina from extending into that developing section.

The third cluster includes the cities of Inglewood, Hawthorne, and Torrance. A relatively small amount of unincorporated land remained in this area, as compared to other sections of the county. Nevertheless, Lawndale incorporated in 1959 to protect its community identity after Hawthorne and Torrance had made annexation inroads. Proposed incorporations of Hahn and Lennox both failed.

Controversies over the county-subsidy issue and struggles between the annexationists and the incorporators have called attention to broad policy matters that might not otherwise have received much consideration. From the claims and counterclaims of these arguments, some very tentative outlines of thought regarding the proper role and purpose of municipal government in a metropolitan area begin to emerge. It is contended that a community that has sufficient population and taxable wealth to require municipal-type services should be pressed to incorporate as a municipality, and that it ought to provide those services through machinery it controls directly.

This notion tends to raise a series of questions that are not yet resolved in the Los Angeles area. What is the minimum population a community should have in order to justify incorporation? What should be the minimum financial base at the time of incorporation? The suburban cities' contention seems to imply that there is a practical minimum below which a viable municipal government could not be supported. Should a community seeking to incorporate have a balance of residential, commercial, and industrial elements, in order to have an adequate financial base to support its functions? Is such a make-up also essential for a balanced political and social organization?

Advocates of municipal government have shrunk from the challenge to enunciate criteria for incorporation in the metropolitan environment, because they have been fearful that the necessity for devising machinery to enforce the criteria would enhance the role of the state or the county. In the absence of any clear concept of an alternative, they have assumed that only a state administrative board or office, or the county Board of Supervisors, could enforce a set of criteria governing incorporation. The local political process by which incorporations are manipulated by means of petitions and referenda does not provide any mechanism for enforcing policy criteria. It has not seemed plausible, either from a legal or a political basis, that the existing local governments might be able to devise policies and procedures for their enforcement for communities outside their own borders. Nevertheless, the group of municipal officials that espouses the theory of the vigorous "independent" municipality cannot afford to weaken its political strategy by condoning the incorporation of communities that are either financially weak or politically imbalanced. Any municipality that cannot maintain a popular image as a vigorous, viable municipal government is a source of embarrassment. The position taken by the strong-city advocates is only tenable so long as they and their associates can meet the terms of their own proposal.

"Defensive incorporation" presents the chief challenge to the theory of the independent city. Incorporation is generally the result of a community decision that has been made after comparing the costs and benefits of a municipal-type government with county-district-type government. Nevertheless, the community that incorporates because of a defensive strategy tends to disregard the costs and to focus upon only one benefit. This latter stratagem is likely to produce a municipality that is largely agricultural or chiefly industrial and has but a small nighttime population. It may also produce a relatively small dormitory suburb that declines to assist in meeting region-wide problems, or an oddly shaped municipality.

Dairy Valley illustrates the defensive incorporation to protect an agricultural interest. In the 1950's, population pressures in the southeast portion of the county, where this community is located, caused land values to rise to levels that attracted some owners to sell to tract subdividers. Residential groups also began to put pressure on the county regional planning commission to change zoning regulations to assist urban development. Complaints about flies and cattle odor mounted during the summer season. The business community in Artesia, the commercial center of the area, proposed to incorporate the combined communities. To protect the agricultural land from encroachment, the dairy operators used the incorporation device, forming a city government in 1956. The population was 3,505 in 1960, but it was lightly distributed over 8.6 square miles. In 1961, Dairy Valley still was one of the least densely populated cities in the county. Although the assessed valuation of property in 1961 was only $17,993,830, a figure in the lower quartile of the cities, its per capita property-tax resources earned it a much higher ranking. The city levies no property tax, however, but finances its program by sales taxes and use taxes and state subventions. In sales-tax income, Dairy Valley ranks above the county average. It appears, then, that this city is financially able to support a minimum-level city government. Although the municipality was organized primarily to protect dairy operations, it provides the local decision-makers a mechanism by which they can withhold the land from piecemeal development and await a propitious time to convert to intensive urban land use.

An interesting comparison can be made between Dairy Valley and the neighboring city of Artesia, which was once a dairy community, but which has transformed rapidly into a residential one. In 1960, Artesia had a population of 10,013 in 1.614 square miles, or a density of 6,440 persons per square mile, as compared to Dairy Valley's 408. However, property-tax resources in Artesia in 1961 were only $9,389,-080 gross, and $903.92 per capita, as compared to Dairy Valley's $17,993,830 gross and $5,029.02 per capita.

Five of the newer cities were organized to protect residential developments from commercial and industrial encroachments. Rolling Hills and Rolling Hills Estates, located in the Palos Verdes Hills, are exclusive residential enclaves for high-income families. Both were created to protect the residential community from land uses for which zone-change applications had been made to the county Regional Planning Commission. Both also aimed to vest control in local decision-makers, in the confident expectation that the latter would reject efforts to bring about lower-cost housing development in the area. In 1961, Rolling Hills had an estimated population of 1,781 in an area of 2.953 square miles, or a density of 603 persons per square mile; Rolling Hills Estates had 4,498 in 1.249 square miles, or a density of 3,601 per square mile. Both have relatively low property-tax bases: $7,759,000 gross or $4,356.57 per person, and $10,511,410 gross or $2,336.91 per person, respectively. Both must rely upon property taxes to support municipal government, inasmuch as there is almost no commercial or shopping activity in either city to yield a sales tax. Rolling Hills ranks sixty-fifth, and Rolling Hills Estates fifty-fifth, in the county in yield of sales taxes.

The city of Hidden Hills, located on the northwest border of Los

Angeles near the Ventura County line, is an exclusive residential suburb patterned after Rolling Hills. Its developer was instrumental in having the area incorporated to protect its high-type residence status and to prevent the city of Los Angeles from annexing it. It has an estimated population of 1,200 residing in 1.254 square miles.

Bradbury, a residential suburb in the San Gabriel Valley, has the smallest population count, one of the smallest land areas, and the lowest gross property-tax base among the cities of the county. It had an estimated 648 inhabitants in 1961 and a property-tax base of $2,377,640, so its per capita wealth was a modest $3,680.56. Its sales-tax income in 1960 was negligible. The city of Walnut is less compact and less fully developed than the other four residential cities. It has an estimated population of 988 in an area of 7.875 square miles and a density of 125 persons per square mile, thus ranking sixty-seventh in the county. Its property tax base was only $2,290,670 in 1961, with a per capita figure of $2,318.49, which was relatively low. It also ranked very low in sales-tax income.

Each of these residential cities provides a limited number of municipal services, chiefly those supplied by the county through contract. Neither city participates to any great extent in the affairs of the metropolitan region, although individual council members from Rolling Hills and Rolling Hills Estates have been active and perceptive. For the most part, these five municipalities are limited-purpose governments.

Three new cities that are predominantly, though not exclusively, residential communities present a more disturbing picture. They were not formed as defensive incorporations, in the usual sense in which the term is used. They all had records of resisting annexation to communities that were stronger in resources. Lawndale, located in the western section of the metropolitan area, has a population density of 10,384 per square mile. Yet, its assessed valuation is only $701.67 per person and its sales-tax income a mere $1.56 per inhabitant, giving it one of the lowest rankings in the county on both sets of tax resources. Cudahy, which is located between Vernon and Downey in the east-central section, has an equally discouraging prospect. Its population density is 10,778 persons per square mile and its assessed valuation of property is only $740.07 per person. Inasmuch as this city was incorporated in 1961, no sales-tax figures were available for it. Duarte, located in the San Gabriel Valley, is in only a slightly better condition. Inasmuch as it incorporated an area three times the size of Lawndale or Cudahy, this city has only a moderate population density: 2,128 per square mile. Its assessed valuation, however, is $898.23 per inhabitant and its sales-tax income was $5.21 per person, ranking it in the low-resource category.

Both Duarte and Cudahy have had turbulent political conditions in their beginning years. Gambling interests made a vigorous effort to establish draw poker in Duarte in 1961 and similar efforts were made in Cudahy, although the issue did not come to a vote in the latter city. Duarte has been troubled by recall elections, vote-fraud investigations, and by turmoil among its elected officials.

Three new industrial cities illustrate characteristics that are extremely different from those of the new residential suburbs. Industry, Commerce, and Irwindale have low density of population, high per capita value for property taxes, and high per capita returns from sales and use taxes. They tend also to be among the larger cities in land area. The cities of Industry and Commerce were formed chiefly to protect industrial sites from encroachment by residential subdivisions and to prevent other cities from enhancing their property-tax bases by annexing industrial sections piecemeal. The city of Industry is only partially developed as an industrial center; it has a large potential for further development as industrial-site requirements increase in the metropolitan region. In 1961, its estimated population was 813 and its property evaluation for tax purposes was $34,036,700 or $41,865.56 per person. The original boundaries of Industry were drawn in a manner to exclude residential tracts that were being developed in the eastern section of the San Gabriel Valley. Nevertheless, this city has been one of the most aggressive new municipalities, having annexed 4.367 square miles in its four years of existence. Furthermore, the areas acquired stretch in long, narrow corridors along railway lines where industrial development is potential. The city of Commerce is also an industrial municipality, but its land area has been developed for a longer period than has that of Industry. Prior to incorporation, it was referred to as the Eastside Manufacturing District, a community that had long preferred to draw its police and fire protection from the county and to avoid encouraging any demand for other local governmental services. Sponsors of this incorporation became alarmed by efforts to annex portions of the area to adjacent cities. They were persuaded also that they could reduce property taxes for support of fire protection by incorporating and thereafter withdrawing from the county Fire Protection District. Commerce had an estimated population of 9,986 in 1961 and an assessed valuation of taxable property of $180,308,500. It was by far the wealthiest new city and ranked seventh among the cities in the county in taxable property, although its per capita wealth, $18,056.13, gave it a lower ranking than Industry. Both new cities have been able to avoid any property tax for municipal purposes, however, supporting the cost of government by the sales tax and state subventions. Commerce reflects a type of political imbalance that may be predicted for defensive industrial city incorporations. Resident voters have been at odds with the representatives of the corporate industrial owners on matters relating to taxes, public works, and service programs. This tension has been reflected in City Council elections and in efforts to recall council members.

A slightly different type of defensive incorporation is illustrated by Irwindale, although the results of incorporation were similar to those in Commerce. The initial sponsors of the incorporation were representatives of sand and gravel quarry companies whose business operations were being threatened, both by adjacent cities' efforts to annex portions of the area and by tract-residents' agitation that the county curtail the quarries. The preponderant number of residents were Spanish-American families, many of whom worked for the quarries, but who after the city was organized found themselves in conflict politically with the companies over taxes, services, and regulatory matters. Irwindale was estimated in 1961 to have 1,540 persons residing in an area of 9.493 square miles, a density of 162 persons per square mile. Its assessed valuation was $13,370,230 or $8,681.97 per person. At the same time, it had an income from sales taxes and use taxes equalling $375.64, a figure that was the third highest in the county. In spite of its favorable financial position, Irwindale has been unstable politically because of the tensions between the quarry companies and the residents.

Although not all the new cities that were organized for defensive purposes have deficiencies in financial resources, each presents some problem of imbalance. Some cities have large populations and few resources. Others have small populations and large financial resources. In each instance the predominant desire was to ensure that decisions regarding land-use zoning would be made at the local or municipal level rather than at the metropolitan or county level. Where the major preoccupation was with land use, financial and political imbalances appeared. Had there been more attention given to criteria for strong, well-balanced municipalities, the series of new cities might have been strengthened.

STRENGTHENING SUBURBAN CITY GOVERNMENT

Most suburban cities in Los Angeles County have shown a considerable interest in strengthening their governmental institutions in order to perform effectively as local service enterprises. This interest has often been kept separate from considerations of municipal area, financial strength, and political balance. The first evidence of this interest is the number of freeholder charters adopted. Freeholder charters illustrate the doctrine of home rule—one based upon the belief that each city is a social and economic unit and has its individual problems of self-government. From this doctrine, it follows that the citizens of individual cities are in a better position than members of the state legislature to decide organizational and functional requirements. The charter is a device that permits the city to achieve primary responsibility in municipal affairs.

Fourteen cities in Los Angeles county, including the central city, have adopted home-rule charters (see table 13). This number constitutes approximately one-fifth of the total of home-rule charter cities and is the largest group in any single county in the state.

Changes in the state general law that permit noncharter cities to choose from a number of alternative forms of government have tended to take away one of the distinctive advantages of the charter method. Nevertheless, charter cities continue to have greater freedom than do noncharter cities in determining policy on matters that are "municipal affairs."

The home-rule movement offers considerable evidence of the impact of the independent attitude that is exhibited in the suburbs. For

TABLE 13

HOME RULE CHARTER CITIES IN LOS ANGELES COUNTY

City	Date charter(s) adopted
Alhambra	1915
Arcadia	1951
Burbank	1927
Compton	1925
Culver City	1947
Dairy Valley	1959
Glendale	1921
Inglewood	1927
Long Beach	1907, 1921
LOS ANGELES	1889, 1925
Pasadena	1901
Pomona	1911
Redondo Beach	1935, 1949
Santa Monica	1907, 1947
Torrance	1947

the most part, the larger cities constitute the home-rule group. Those with larger wealth and larger population have tended to be most restive under state law limitations and to advocate that cities need an opportunity to experiment with their administrative and political institutions. Furthermore, the chartered cities tended to be the most resistive to efforts by the central city to integrate the metropolitan area by annexation in the 1920's.[8] Other evidence indicates that they have also been the least interested in functional consolidation and contractual relations with the county.

The council-manager form of city government emerged in California through the home-rule movement. Glendale, Alhambra, Pasadena, and Long Beach were among the pioneering cities in the state and nation to adopt this plan for an appointed executive.[9] The greatest growth in employment of the manager-council plan in Los Angeles suburban cities came with the increase in municipal government activity after 1945 (see table 14). This was a response, in part, to the increased demands made upon the city governments by a rapidly increasing population. It was due also to a desire to strengthen the city governments to meet the potential challenge offered by the county and other units. The League of California Cities and its subgroups generally favored the manager-council plan and assisted cities that wished to consider adopting it. Although it did not officially advocate adoption of the plan, the League staff helped municipal officials to draft ordinances and select appointees. The number of California cities that had operated under the plan gave other cities examples to study. Furthermore, implementation of the manager plan was facilitated by the fact that a supply of trained administrators existed within the state. Several cities drew their first managers from the ranks of assistants in neighboring cities. Several also proselyted managers from cities in other sections of the state.

Many city councils that were loath to delegate the full array of formal authority to a manager, or who found the title "manager" politically objectionable, appointed an administrative officer to coördinate the city administration and to relieve the council of innumerable details of supervision. Responsibilities assigned to these city administrative officers differ widely between cities. Some administrators operate, in fact, in a manner similar to city managers, in their relations both

---

[8] See pp. 157–158.

[9] Glendale adopted a manager-council plan for ordinance in 1914, and re-enforced the arrangement by including it in the charter when the latter was adopted in 1921. South Pasadena was one of the first general-law cities in Los Angeles County to adopt the manager plan, although it did not choose a home-rule charter.

TABLE 14

CITIES IN LOS ANGELES COUNTY HAVING CITY MANAGERS
OR ADMINISTRATIVE OFFICERS

Manager-council cities	Date of adoption	Cities employing administrative officers	Date of adoption	Cities having neither plan
Alhambra[a]	1916	Azusa	1956	Avalon
Arcadia	1951	Baldwin Park	1957	Maywood
Artesia	1959	Bell	1958	Palmdale
Bell Gardens	1961	Bellflower	1958	Palos Verdes
Burbank[a]	1927	Beverly Hills	1952	Estates
Claremont	1948	Bradbury	1957	Walnut
Compton[a]	1925	Commerce	1960	Hidden Hills
Dairy Valley[a]	1956	Covina	1955	
Downey[b]	1956	Cudahy	1960	
El Segundo	1956	Culver City	1949	
Glendale[a]	1914	Duarte	1957	
Glendora	1955	El Monte	1947	
Hermosa Beach[b]	1956	Gardena	1959	
Hawthorne	1948	Huntington Park	1957	
Industry	1957	Inglewood	1946	
Irwindale	1957	Lakewood	1954	
La Puente[b]	1956	La Mirada[b]	1960	
La Verne	1956	Lawndale	1960	
Long Beach[a]	1921	Los Angeles[a]	1951	
Lynwood	1945	Montebello (called		
Manhattan Beach[b]	1948	City Coördinator)	1957	
Monrovia	1949	Norwalk	1957	
Monterey Park[b]	1948	Pomona	1949	
Paramount	1957	Rolling Hills Estates	1958	
Pasadena[a]	1921	Rosemead	1959	
Pico Rivera	1958	San Fernando	1952	
Redondo Beach[a]	1949	San Gabriel	1943	
Rolling Hills	1957	Sierra Madre	1950	
San Dimas	1960	Signal Hill	1960	
San Marino	1952	South El Monte	1961	
Sante Fe Springs	1957	South Gate	1958	
Santa Monica[a]	1947	Vernon	1952	
South Pasadena	1920			
Temple City	1960			
Torrance[a]	1948			
West Covina	1955			
Whittier[b]	1949			

SOURCE: California Secretary of State, *Roster of Federal, State, County, City and Township Officials,
1961* (Sacramento, 1962).
    [a] Plan implemented through home rule-charter.
    [b] Plan implemented by ordinance approved by votes in local referendum. All others implemented
by ordinance without referendum to the local voters.

with administrative departments and with the city council. Other administrators are permitted relatively little supervisory control over the city's administrative operations, and act chiefly as a liaison between the council members and the administrative staff. Nevertheless, through budget preparation and administration and through close relationship with the council, experienced city administrators exert influence to strengthen administrative performance.

Both plans spread very rapidly among the cities of Los Angeles County in the 1950's. By 1962, all but six of the incorporated cities had adopted one of these plans (see table 14). Development of the two systems has been an important factor in strengthening attitudes of independence in the suburbs. The basic concept of both plans emphasizes the desirability of an administrative staff performing municipal functions under the direct supervision of the chief central administrator. Although many managers vigorously endeavor to negotiate with county and state officials for benefits to enhance their own city's program, the basic element that determines a manager's success in his total job is likely to lie in the control that he exercises over the city's administration. Therefore, members of the city manager profession have been preoccupied with internal management control mechanisms and procedures, supervision of employees, and measuring and improving administrative performance.

The incentive system that is inherent in the manager-council and administrative-officer systems has enhanced the attitude of municipal independence. The career manager, or administrator, is understandably sensitive of his professional reputation, which depends upon his control over, or influence upon, the administrative institutions with which he is identified. Status in the management profession is not uniformly related to the size of the administrative organization supervised. Nevertheless, professional prestige does go to those who have guided administrative units whose size is at least in the median rank. This arises because the skills that the management profession approves tend to be most effectively demonstrated in moderately large and complex administrative environments. With regard to internal administrative relationships, the manager or administrator has strong incentives to build up pride of organization and local identification among the employees that he directs. In cementing his relationship with the city council and the community, the manager has even greater incentive to emphasize pride in, and loyalty to, the city's administrative apparatus. This causes him to endeavor to substantiate claims that the local city organization can perform functions more adequately and meaningfully than can any other organization, real or proposed.

In the rivalry between the county of Los Angeles and the suburban cities, the appointed managers and administrators have played a role that has been relatively unpublicized but that has strengthened the stand taken by the elective leaders. The managers' department of the League of California Cities has devoted large portions of its meetings to discussions and papers on the several roles that city managers ought to perform in cities in the metropolitan areas. Considerable emphasis has been placed upon perceiving and understanding the consequences of intergovernmental relationships as well as of local operations, within the context of a metropolitan-community environment.

THE BIG SUBURBS: POLARITIES OF LOCAL INTEREST

Several of the suburbs have demonstrated remarkable success in achieving their goal of becoming relatively large, populous municipalities. Six cities, Long Beach, Glendale, Pasadena, Torrance, Burbank, and Pomona, have grown to encompass more than fifteen square miles. The first four named have also exceeded the one hundred thousand figure in population, according to the 1960 federal census. Each of these cities has exhibited several traits of independence in the metropolitan scene; each has been cool towards the county's efforts to coordinate administration on a metropolitan scale, and five have been active in opposing the central city's efforts to expand its influence. However, only three were among the organizers of the Metropolitan Water District. Any proposal to alter the structure of local government or to modify the pattern of intergovernmental relations in the region must take into consideration the attitudes of the leadership, official and unofficial, in these cities.

LONG BEACH

Long Beach is the second largest city in Los Angeles County. In 1960, it had 323,996 inhabitants in an area of 46 square miles. Its economic base included an assessed valuation of taxable property estimated at $664 million, and a large oil-producing industry. A portion of the petroleum deposits lie under city controlled lands, and royalties from exploitation are devoted to supporting municipal recreation and commercial harbor facilities.

Long Beach exercises an important influence upon the region's economy through its management of its harbor facilities. Not only does it have an impact upon shipping and ancillary industries, but because of its harbor development, Long Beach has obtained one of the principal naval bases on the Pacific coast and a major naval shipyard, which employs a large work force.

Municipally controlled beaches and small-boat marinas make Long Beach one of the principal outdoor recreation areas in the metropolitan region. A municipally operated convention hall has made it one of the three or four major convention and tourist centers of the state. These interests, which undergird the tourist industry, and which the city government has vigorously developed with the support of local financial interests, have often brought the community's leaders into sharp political conflict with those groups that propose to develop regional facilities in central Los Angeles. Efforts by Los Angeles City government and private groups to attract trade fairs, major conventions, and commercial sporting events have been watched jealously. When promoters of regional developments have urged the county government to build convention halls or similar undertakings, Long Beach political groups have successfully opposed them.

This was one of the first cities in the region to adopt a home-rule charter and to select a city manager. In the earlier years, it had a record of political upheavals and dismissal of managers, but for the past twenty years, it has made effective use of this form of city government. Throughout its municipal history, Long Beach has demonstrated a strong interest in retaining control over its municipal affairs. It has declined to contract with the county for any major function. Unlike most other cities in the county, it has not contracted for assessment or property tax collection. It has also chosen to continue its own health department.

At the same time, Long Beach has been highly successful in persuading the county government to provide services. Because of the heavy concentration of population and economic activity in the city and its environs, the Superior Court has conducted a branch court there for several years, with five divisions assigned. A municipal court district serves the needs at the lower judiciary level. The county now operates one specialized and one general public hospital in this city. Most county administrative departments have maintained offices in Long Beach for several years. A multistory courts and office building, opened in the civic center in 1961, serves as a regional center for activities in the entire southern part of the county. The building is the largest administrative center outside the county headquarters complex located in central Los Angeles. Political leadership in Long Beach gives much evidence of being intent upon making this city the major influence in the southern part of the county. The effort is aided strongly by two daily newspapers.

Long Beach has steadily demonstrated an active interest in expanding its area and bringing additional population and land under its control. It raced Los Angeles to annex portions of Terminal Island in 1905, and it opposed that city's efforts to seize control of the San Pedro–Wilmington harbor area. Unsuccessful in thwarting the larger city's harbor plans, it acquired enough waterfront area to build its own harbor. Thereafter, it turned its attention to annexations. First, it consolidated with the small town of Belmont Heights and annexed tracts adjacent to Alamitos Bay. It also acquired tracts on its northern boundary and below Signal Hill. A narrow strip of annexed land, which extended to the Orange County line, successfully blocked any encroachment by other cities upon the Long Beach "preserve" northeast of its city limits. By 1910, Long Beach had quadrupled its original land area and produced a population growth statistic of 690.3 per cent for the decade of 1900–1910,[10] the greatest population growth in the nation.

During the decade of the 1920's, Long Beach made a spectacular extension northward. However, it also suffered three major disappointments. The oil companies that developed the great field on top of Signal Hill thwarted the city's desire to annex the area after development took place and succeeded in having the area incorporated as a separate city. Long Beach sought to prevent Los Angeles and Compton from moving into the Dominguez area, where industrial and petroleum developments were contemplated. After a long controversy in the courts, it was forced to disincorporate two tracts. Thereupon, official representatives from Long Beach and Los Angeles, together with groups representing harbor business interests, agreed to a moratorium upon annexation in the Dominguez area and a plan to develop railroad classification yards, which facilitated freight service for the entire harbor. In this same decade, Long Beach suffered another setback, and this defeat in 1923 paved the way for a further disappointment in the 1950's. Anticipating that a large acreage owned by the Bixby family and the Montana Land Company would soon develop, the city sought to annex it while it was still relatively uninhabited and held by a few owners. Objections filed by the major owners caused most of the acreage to be excluded under state law, however, on the point that it was agricultural land. The city was left with a "shoestring strip" circumscribing the borders of the area, but its leaders anticipated that this would provide an advantageous position from which to annex parcels of the excluded area as they developed. Twenty years later, this

---

[10] Richard Bigger and James D. Kitchen, *How the Cities Grew* (Los Angeles: Bureau of Governmental Research, University of California, 1952), p. 213.

section figured in the Lakewood annexation and incorporation battles. (See Figure 8.)

Long Beach enjoyed a great development boom during the war years of 1939–1945. United States Navy fleet, air, and supply facilities burgeoned. The Douglas Aircraft Company located a big plant in the Lakewood section, and the Air Force developed the municipal airport as a training and ferrying base. Most of these developments continued to make important impacts upon the area's economic activity after the war ended.

In the post-war era, spectacular housing developments took place adjacent to Long Beach, reawakening interest in expanding the city's jurisdiction. With a relatively strong municipal administration, backed by a stable political regime, and with an attractive financial condition resulting from tideland oil revenues, Long Beach leaders felt they were

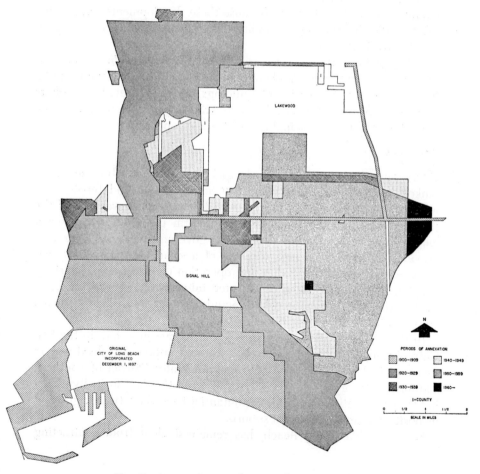

FIG. 8. Annexations to the city of Long Beach.

in a strong position to bid for the new neighborhoods. Several tracts were annexed in the Lakewood section; the city adopted the tactic of inviting relatively small parcels to join, hoping thereby to avoid large pockets of opposition voters and to so divide the community that incorporation of a new city would be made difficult. This strategy was countered successfully in 1954, however, by those who fought to incorporate the new city of Lakewood, which encompassed the larger portion of the huge housing tract developed by the Boyer company. Efforts by land developers, a gas company, and a privately owned water company enabled annexation opponents to triumph.

In the area north of Lakewood, three new cities, Norwalk, Bellflower, and Dairy Valley, blocked any farther extensions by Long Beach. Thus, the county's second city met the same reaction that Los Angeles had experienced in the late 1920's.

Long Beach has added some tracts between its borders and the Orange County line. Perhaps because these developments were somewhat smaller in scale, crises similar to that which took place in Lakewood have been avoided.

Although Long Beach's area-growth has reached its climax, population growth continues. A change in housing patterns, from single-family dwellings to apartment buildings, already in evidence, offers promise of further increase. Evidently this city will remain a strong second among the municipalities of the metropolitan area.

PASADENA

Pasadena, long one of the principal independent suburban cities, ranked fourth in the county in 1960 in population and territory. It was the second city to adopt a home-rule charter and was one of the state's pioneers in the manager-council form of government. For a long period, it has had a strong city government. As indicated in previous chapters, Pasadena was one of a small group of cities that accepted municipal ownership and operation of water and electricity supplies. To protect its ground-water interests, it annexed a large tract in the Arroyo Seco and later acquired other water-bearing lands on the eastern side of the city.

In the 1920's Pasadena constructed a large masonry dam in the San Gabriel Canyon above the city of Azusa and impounded flood waters for municipal use. When the Metropolitan Water District of Southern California was organized, the city transferred the dam to it. By assisting the organization of the Metropolitan District, the city strengthened its position as an independent suburb.

Pasadena, like Long Beach, has remained aloof from contracting with the county for services, purchasing aid only for ambulances, election services, and jail care. It has chosen to administer its own tax assessment and collection, health services, and other functions. For a number of years, the Superior Court has assigned divisions to this city as part of the general court decentralization program. The county government has assigned only a few administrative offices and maintains a small courts and office building in the civic center.

Unlike Long Beach, the city of Pasadena is not extensively involved in activities that have a regional impact. The annual Rose Parade and Rose Bowl football game on New Year's Day are the major exceptions. Both events require an elaborate system for coördinating traffic movement and policing on January first.

For many years this city was characterized as a residential community with a relatively large percentage of high-income families. Its educational institutions and cultural activities drew people from the region and elsewhere. In the 1940's, the general economic characteristic of the city began to change. Light industries, many of which were involved in national defense research and development activity, multiplied and caused wage-earning categories of the population to increase. However, the total population increase between 1950 and 1960 was only 9.9 per cent, a relatively modest figure when compared with those for other municipalities in the Los Angeles region.

Pasadena has more than quadrupled its original land area; the expansion was accomplished chiefly in three periods. Between 1909 and 1914, it annexed tracts along the Arroyo Seco to keep Los Angeles from acquiring them. When the county Flood Control District constructed a dam at Devil's Gate, the entire Arroyo area was stabilized for further residential development. Since Pasadena's water supply came from this canyon, it annexed a section extending well up into the San Gabriel mountains.

The expansion in the 1920–1930 decade brought in Lamanda Park and tracts on the eastern side of the city, all relatively heavily populated. The chief argument used to encourage annexation was that the city could provide high quality municipal services because its manager-council government was unusually efficient.[11]

In later decades the city extended its boundaries in two directions: farther into the mountains along the Arroyo Seco, and eastward. This growth filled in gaps that had been left by earlier annexations. In many instances, the additions were related to water needs; the city's water system proved attractive to many fringe areas.

---

[11] *Ibid.*, p. 198.

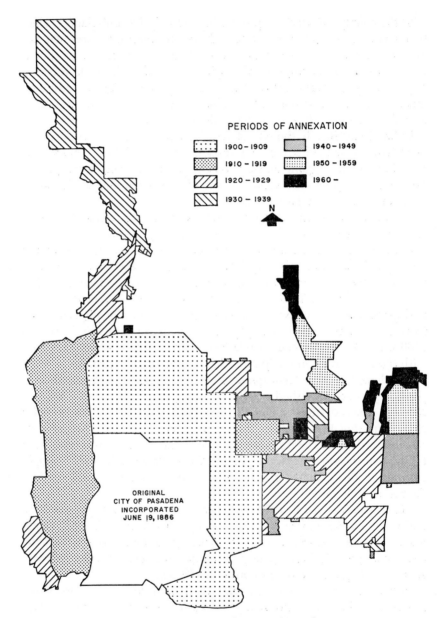

Fig. 9. Annexations to the city of Pasadena.

Two heavily populated areas adjacent to Pasadena have long resisted annexation, even though their water supply has been short at times. Altadena, located at the base of the mountains above Pasadena, has considered both annexation and incorporation periodically since 1914. Thusfar, its voters have rejected both alternatives. La Canada, located across the Arroyo Seco from Pasadena in a highland valley, has rejected annexations to Los Angeles, Glendale, and Pasadena, although it has undergone extensive urban development. In 1951, groups in La Canada and Altadena that were opposed to annexing to Pasadena organized the Foothill Municipal Water District and caused it to join the Metropolitan Water District system. By means of special districts, organized and operated under the county government, both foothill communities have secured urban-type services and have fortified themselves to resist annexation and incorporation.

GLENDALE

The city of Glendale is a newer municipality than Long Beach or Pasadena, having incorporated in 1906. After 1910 it grew steadily in area and in population. It was one of the state's pioneers in municipal ownership of water and electricity and was the first in southern California to adopt the manager-council plan of government, having adopted it by ordinance in 1914.

Glendale was involved in considerable controversy with Los Angeles in the 1920's, rejecting overtures to consolidate, and losing litigation to withdraw water from the Los Angeles river basin. It was a charter member of the Metropolitan Water District. Despite these earlier differences with the central city, Glendale has maintained coöperative agreements with Los Angeles for many years to purchase electric power and to connect with the sewage-disposal system. Because the business and civic center of Glendale is only a short distance from downtown Los Angeles, there has been less justification for the county to establish branch courts and administrative offices here than in Long Beach. County health and welfare departments do have major branches, however.

This suburban city has exhibited strong local pride consistently in its relations with the county, the central city, and its suburban neighbors. A daily newspaper and civic groups emphasize the suburban interest, setting the community apart from its larger neighbor, Los Angeles.

Glendale's area expansion has been steady. In 1917, after two unsuccessful attempts, it consolidated with the small city of Tropico, which had previously served as a buffer between it and Los Angeles.

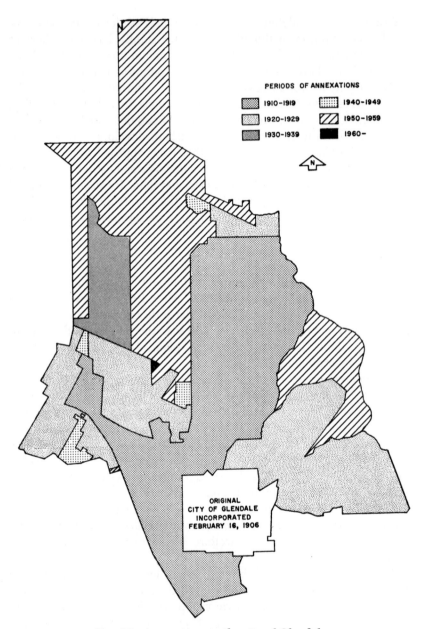

PERIODS OF ANNEXATIONS

1910-1919   1940-1949
1920-1929   1950-1959
1930-1939   1960-

ORIGINAL
CITY OF GLENDALE
INCORPORATED
FEBRUARY 16, 1906

FIG. 10. Annexations to the city of Glendale.

Later annexations extended Glendale's boundaries westward, close to Burbank boundaries, and eastward to Pasadena. Northward expansion has been through the Verdugo Valley, where much of the city's ground-water resources lie. The foothill areas of Montrose and La Canada, north of the Verdugo Valley, have grown steadily, and as they grew, much tension resulted from controversies over annexation to Glendale and to Pasadena. Creation of the Foothill Municipal Water District in 1951, however, has checked the city's expansion.

TORRANCE

Youngest of the larger suburbs, Torrance is a Cinderella of the post-war urban development era. Originally designed as a planned in-dustrial community, it remained modestly developed for twenty years after incorporation in 1921. Steel plants and other industries located there, but no development boom resulted. Although oil fields were drilled nearby, this activity did not cause Torrance to prosper. It was a city of modest residences and of moderate-size industry.

Three large annexations of land that was chiefly in agricultural use added a large amount of area to Torrance during the first ten years of the municipality's history. The Meadow Park Annex, accomplished in 1927, extended south and westward of the city center, across an agricul-tural belt, to reach around the southern boundary of the city of Re-dondo Beach and give Torrance an ocean frontage.

The population explosion that took place in southern California after 1945 affected Torrance heavily. Between 1950 and 1960, its population expanded from 22,241 to 100,603—a growth of 352.3 per cent. The rate was the fifth highest in the county. Most of this growth took place within the area of the original city and the earlier annexations, al-though Torrance did annex two relatively small tracts in 1956, and resulted chiefly from subdivision developments that transformed mar-ket gardens and farms to urban housing. The section of the city that overlooked the ocean, consisting of open fields when annexed, became the site of an extensive apartment project.

Even more than the other larger suburbs, Torrance lacks physical unity as a municipality. Outlying portions, even though existing as parts of the official city for several years, have not been related mean-ingfully to the city's center. Although the original city was laid out on a planned basis, the annexed portions were not developed as exten-sions of the original plan but rather as separate concretions.

Like some other rapidly growing suburban cities, Torrance experi-enced an exhibition of citizen participation in volunteer community

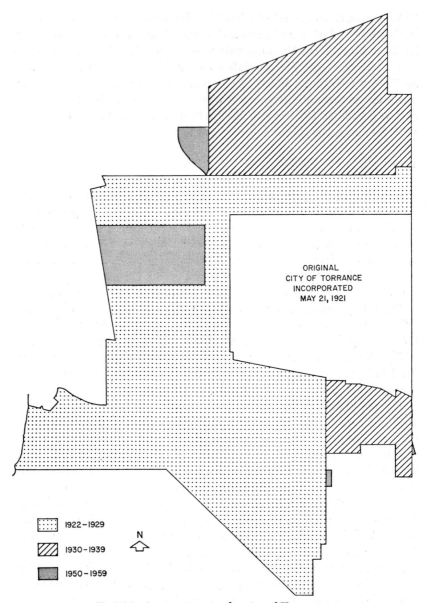

FIG. 11. Annexations to the city of Torrance.

activities. Interest in civic affairs was aroused by the discussion and adoption of a home rule charter in 1947. In the following year, the manager-council plan was placed in operation. Because of the extent of citizen participation in community affairs, the National Municipal

League awarded Torrance designation as an "All-American City in 1956"—a title shared with ten others.

In its relationship with the county and other regional governmental agencies, Torrance differs slightly from the other large suburbs. It contracts with the county for ten services, slightly more than the others. Nevertheless, its leaders are in the group that criticizes Lakewood Plan county-city contracts. The principal county establishment in the Torrance area is the Harbor General Hospital, which is being developed as a permanent regional facility. Torrance is a comparatively recent recruit to the Metropolitan Water District; it was a late starter as a municipal water enterpriser. It has participated in the county sanitation district system for a much longer period. Other evidence of its efforts to perform the role of a major city include its operation of a municipal bus line and development of a municipal airport with federal assistance.

SUMMARY

The seventy-three suburban cities in Los Angeles County constitute a "third force," countervailing the efforts of both the central city and the county to unify the region. They have demonstrated strong opposition to proposals that would integrate the government of the metropolitan area by superseding municipalities with a general-purpose unit at the regional level. However, they have shown a tendency to coöperate with most regional authorities that perform single functions. In water and sewer administration, they demonstrate a willingness to join a federated metropolitan organization in which each municipality is represented in policy making.

The suburbs also disagree over the use of annexation to bring newly developing urban areas under municipal government. Although most of them have annexed some territory, many have acquired relatively small tracts. The conclusion is that most cities would prefer to have the newly urbanized sections on the fringes of the metropolitan area incorporate as new cities. The growing number of cities enhances the political strength of the municipal interest group, the League of California Cities.

Individual suburban cities have strengthened their internal organization in order to give a more effective performance as a community service organization. Individually and collectively, they have taken strong stands on matters relating to municipal home rule. Their strategy has been defensive in part but also aggressive in demonstrating an ability to perform services and to promote belief in the doctrine of local self-government.

Six of the suburbs, much in the same manner as the central city, have annexed considerable amounts of territory, have assured water supplies under local control, and have worked aggressively to establish their position as regional centers of commerce. Four of these cities have achieved a population figure in excess of a hundred thousand.

By developing several bases of strength, the suburban cities have placed themselves in a position to bargain with those who would reorganize the structure and the relationships of local government in the metropolitan area. At the minimum, they are able to exercise a veto upon efforts to integrate. Certainly, they are able to influence any positive arrangements that may be developed.

PART III
DECENTRALIZATION—MANY DECISION CENTERS

NINE

Decentralization of Social
and Economic Activities

A THEORY of urban development, respected in the United States for several decades, explained that any city tends to expand radially from the oldest part, usually the central business district.[1] Although urban growth generally conforms to this pattern, population may, at the same time, scatter in many directions, with subsequent formation of population clusters in widely separated areas. A concentration of population in urban centers has been paralleled by large-scale decentralization to the outlying parts of those same centers.

These trends in population movements are not unique to Los Angeles. Consequences emanating from the development of urban areas and the subsequent "flight to the suburbs" have been felt throughout the nation, if not throughout the world. However, nowhere has the impact of these countervailing forces been more evident than in the Los Angeles metropolitan area.

---

[1] See Ernest W. Burgess, "The Growth of a City," in Robert E. Park, Ernest W. Burgess, and Roderick D. McKenzie, *The City* (Chicago: University of Chicago Press, 1925), pp. 47–62. For a discussion of criticisms directed toward the Burgess theory of urban growth, see James A. Quinn, "The Burgess Zonal Hypothesis and its Critics," *American Sociological Review*, V (April, 1940), 210–218, and Homer Hoyt, *The Structure and Growth of Residential Neighborhoods in American Cities* (Washington, D.C.: Federal Housing Administration, 1939). See also Chauncy D. Harris and Edward L. Ullman, "The Nature of Cities," *Annals of the American Academy of Political and Social Science*, CCXLII (Nov., 1945), 7–17.

GROWTH OF THE SUBURBS

The urbanization of Los Angeles County coincided with a nation-wide population shift from rural to urban areas, beginning in the latter part of the nineteenth century.[2] Growth of the Los Angeles area to metropolitan proportions, and to a key social, economic, and cultural position, was accompanied by an accretion of separate, identifiable communities. Suburbanization, stimulated by the desire to enjoy the amenities of outdoor living, received its final impetus with the advent of the automobile and the development of an intricate freeway system that freed the population from dependence upon static transportation systems, expanded areas of potential settlement, and reduced travel-time in communting.[3] The downtown area of Los Angeles was soon surrounded by independent municipal corporations; this proliferation of separate identifiable communities has now reached the point that Los Angeles City is ringed by no less than seventy-two independent municipalities. Of even greater significance is the fact that the central city, despite its legal unity, is itself divided into some fifty place-name communities that exhibit a sense of cohesiveness that tends to distinguish them from the giant municipality to which they are bound by law.

Development of the downtown section, the nucleus of original settlement, proceeded far in advance of similar growth in other parts of the county. The first city and county administrative offices, the first post office, the first hotel, the first hospital, the first chamber of commerce, and the first medical school were some of the institutions located within the central area. The central business district gradually evolved to be the focal point of wholesale trade, financial transactions, transportation facilities, entertainment, and governmental and related activities. Central Los Angeles has retained its dominant position in relation to the Los Angeles metropolitan area; yet, the trend toward decentralization has made its impact.

Large suburban shopping centers tended to encourage this trend. Department store sales in the downtown area, which in 1929 had accounted for 75 per cent of the total retail sales in the Los Angeles metropolitan area, dropped to 54 per cent by 1939, and to 28.6 per cent by 1953. The downtown portion of total retail sales in the Los Angeles

---

[2] See Leo F. Schnore, "The Timing of Metropolitan Decentralization," *Journal of the American Institute of Planners,* XXV (Nov., 1959), 200–206.

[3] See Wilbur C. Hallenbeck, *American Urban Communities* (New York: Harper, 1951), pp. 201–223. For an interesting analysis of the nature and implications of suburban developments, see Robert C. Wood, *Suburbia* (Boston: Houghton Mifflin, 1959).

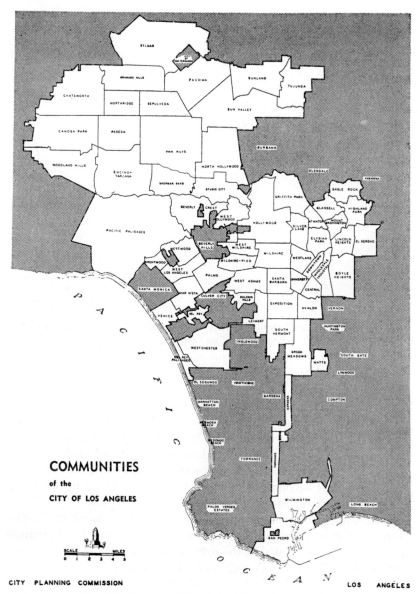

FIG. 12. Communities of the city of Los Angeles.

metropolitan area declined to 18.2 per cent in 1959.[4] Increased cost of doing business in the central area, partly caused by traffic congestion and lack of convenient parking space, contributed to the situation.

[4] Los Angeles Central City Committee and Los Angeles City Planning Department, *Centropolis, 1980* (Los Angeles, 1961), p. 42.

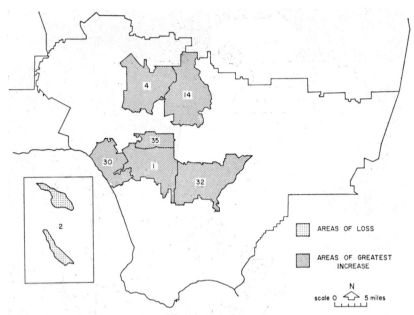

AREAS OF LOSS

AREAS OF GREATEST INCREASE

scale 0 ⌃ 5 miles

Fig. 13. Los Angeles County statistical areas showing greatest population change, 1930–1940 (data from Los Angeles County Regional Planning Commission).

Decrease in the central area's population, though slight, has been fairly constant in recent years and has been still another feature in the change that is taking place. This trend first appeared in the 1950 census, but it has continued after 1950 and has spread to the adjacent communities on the northeast and east (see tables 16 and 17). This centrifugal shift becomes meaningful when it is viewed in relation to the growth patterns of other county regions. The greatest population growth during this period occurred in the fringe areas of Encino, Norwalk, Citrus, Long Beach, Whittier, Inglewood, and San Fernando, most of which are located at the extreme outskirts of the county, some distance from the central downtown business district.

Four of these (Norwalk, Citrus, Whittier, and San Fernando) were listed as areas of major population change for the first time in 1960. Conversely, the tremendous 1940–1950 population growth experienced in Adams, Burbank, and Compton, located in closer geographical proximity to downtown Los Angeles, came to an end and population was stabilized in those areas after 1950. These figures reflect the well-known pattern of urban growth, whereby population moves farther

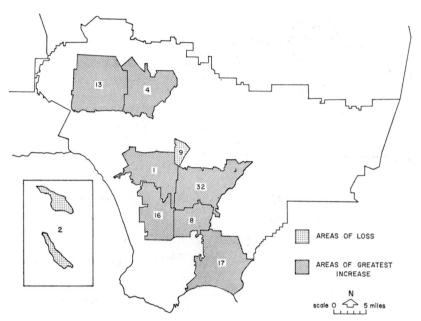

Fig. 14. Los Angeles County statistical areas showing greatest population change, 1940–1950 (data from Los Angeles County Regional Planning Commission).

and farther from the central business district as available land in closer physical proximity diminishes.

A significant outcome of the growth pattern has been the development of separate community areas within the larger county. Some have become legal entities, as we have seen. Communities also exist in the absence of any legal basis; their unity is often the product of a sense of identification and cohesion that is produced by local institutions whose orientation is directed toward the limited geographic area they are designed to serve. The individual citizen is likely to exhibit a greater sense of allegiance to the small community area in which he lives than to the larger legal entity, such as the county or the metropolitan city, of which he is a part.

The formation of densely settled population clusters, scattered throughout the county, has magnified the problem of governing this area and providing effective public services to its citizens. At the same time, geographic decentralization and the increasingly self-sufficient nature of suburban communities, located some distance from the seat of local government, have combined to foster a sense of "localism."

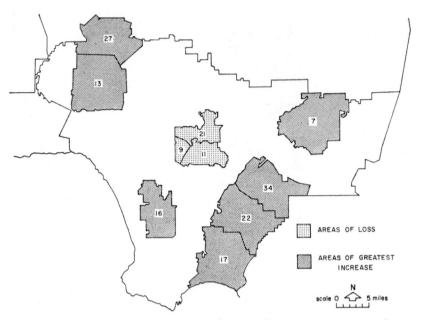

FIG. 15. Los Angeles County statistical areas showing greatest population change, 1950–1961 (data from Los Angeles County Regional Planning Commission).

A parochial spirit has developed that is seemingly incompatible with the political feasibility of instituting comprehensive governmental reorganization to facilitate the prompt, effective execution of public duties and responsibilities. This apparent contradiction represents the essence of "the metropolitan problem."

The practical significance of the relationship between localism and problems of governing a metropolitan area warrants some analysis of the "community" phenomenon. Precisely what is meant by a community? What are the essential characteristics that serve to distinguish the mere physical grouping of population from a true community?

IDENTIFYING COMMUNITIES

The community concept is an extremely nebulous one. It can be said that a community is generally characterized by a group of people, some type of geographical orientation, and one or more major interests held in common.[5] However, these criteria are not, in and of themselves,

_____

[5] Jefferson B. Fordham, *A Larger Concept of Community* (Baton Rouge: Louisiana State University Press, 1956), p. 4.

TABLE 15

Los Angeles County Statistical Areas[a]
Showing Greatest Population Change[b]
1930–1940[c]

Statistical area	Population in 1930	Population in 1940	Population change	Percentage of total change
South East	232,065	284,564	52,499	9.10
Adams	281,129	333,560	52,431	9.08
Burbank	33,789	77,516	43,727	7.58
Wilshire	114,058	151,086	37,028	6.41
Santa Monica	81,268	117,801	36,533	6.33
Glendale	125,678	161,607	35,929	6.23
Avalon	1,986	1,933	−53	−0.01

Source: Population figures from *Quarterly Population Dwelling Units Bulletin* (for years cited), published by the Los Angeles County Regional Planning Commission.

[a] in 1938 the Los Angeles County Regional Planning Commission divided the county into a number of statistical areas. These areas, each of which represents a group of census tracts, were devised for the purpose of instituting a manageable, county-wide system of relatively permanent areas by which population and housing changes could be regularly reported.

[b] Greatest population growth is defined as an increase of 5 per cent or more of the total population increase in the county. Any decrease in population is also considered to be a major population change.

[c] Total county population, 1930: 2,208,492; total county population, 1940: 2,285,643; total county increase, 1930–1940: 577,151.

TABLE 16

Los Angeles County Statistical Areas[a]
Showing Greatest Population Change[b]
1940–1950[c]

Statistical area	Population in 1940	Population in 1950	Population change	Percentage of total change
Long Beach	169,513	268,505	116,992	8.56
Burbank	77,516	186,847	109,331	8.00
South East	284,564	393,791	109,227	8.00
Inglewood	78,820	174,415	95,595	7.00
Encino	37,312	117,988	80,676	5.91
Compton	48,679	127,868	79,189	5.80
Adams	333,560	401,817	68,257	5.00
Avalon	1,933	1,630	−303	−0.02
Central	133,351	129,578	−3,773	−0.28

Source: Population figures from *Quarterly Population Dwelling Units Bulletin* (for years cited), published by the Los Angeles County Regional Planning Commission.

[a] See note a, table 15.

[b] See note b, table 15.

[c] Total county population, 1940: 2,785,643; total county population, 1950: 4,151,687; total county ncrease, 1940–1950: 1,366,044.

TABLE 17

Los Angeles County Statistical Areas[a]
Showing Greatest Population Change[b]
1950–July, 1961[c]

Statistical area	Population in 1950	Population in July, 1961	Population change	Percentage of total change
Norwalk	109,659	355,195	245,536	11.69
Encino	117,988	303,232	185,244	8.83
Citrus	46,276	208,756	162,480	7.73
Long Beach	286,505	429,315	142,810	6.80
Inglewood	174,415	310,819	136,404	6.49
Whittier	68,368	196,426	128,058	6.09
San Fernando	53,557	169,857	116,300	5.53
North East	162,654	160,605	−2,049	−0.09
East	238,653	214,682	−23,971	−1.14
Central	129,578	92,990	−36,588	−1.75

Source: Population figures for 1950 and 1960 taken from *Quarterly Population Dwelling Units Bulletin*, published by the Los Angeles County Regional Planning Commission; figures for 1961 are projected by the Planning Commission.

[a] See note *a*, table 15.

[b] See note *b*, table 15.

[c] Total county population, 1950: 4,151,687; total county population, July, 1961: 6,251,204; total county increase, 1950–July, 1961: 2,099,517.

a sufficient basis for determining the presence or absence of a community in any given geographical area. The truly distinguishing feature of a community is a mental attitude, a sense of loyalty and identification directed toward a specific area. It is this state of mind that is so difficult to define or pinpoint with any reasonable degree of accuracy.

In the light of this recognized limitation, it is suggested that the problem of identification be approached indirectly through an analysis of local institutions whose establishment and operations may reflect a deeper community consciousness—a concentrated population-grouping bound together by a community of interests emanating from needs and requirements associated with a fairly limited geographical area. Greater light may be cast upon the entire concept of community decentralization by investigating the decentralization patterns that are assisted by such institutions as local chambers of commerce, community coördinating councils, neighborhood newspapers, community churches, local service clubs, city and county branch offices, and retail and service business establishments. These institutions are analyzed with a view toward determining the extent to which their establishment, activities and general frame of reference center around the limited geographic area in which they are located. Decentralized institutions may not be synonymous with the community frame of mind; nevertheless, they are a source of community identification and play no small part in strengthening an allegiance toward limited geographic areas.

As population in suburban areas has grown, governmental, business, and social organizations have decentralized their operations to serve the needs of this expanding population. Business establishments originally located exclusively in the central business district set up branches in suburban areas in order to maintain their economic supremacy against suburban competitors. Today, all five major department stores, most of the eleven variety stores, and several of the twenty-two general merchandising stores in the central business district conduct one or more branch store operations. Banking institutions have decentralized to the point that there are over five hundred offices and branches in the county. The municipal Water and Power Department has a total of twenty-three suboffices and establishments; the Southern California Edison Company has forty-six branch offices; the Pacific Telephone and Telegraph Company similarly serves the area from fifty local units, spaced according to population and customer convenience in paying bills. Community newspapers, focusing their coverage on news items of local interest, have grown steadily. Suburban areas have also been the most active in organizing new churches and hospital institutions.[6] Departments of the Los Angeles City and Los Angeles County governments have engaged in similar decentralization programs to serve the needs of outlying areas. These developments, when viewed together, reflect a recognition of the fact that Los Angeles County, with a population of over six million persons distributed over 4,083 square miles and divided into over one hundred separate communities, can no longer be served adequately from one metropolitan center.

Extensive programs of planned decentralization by public and private institutions indicate the presence of concentrated population groupings large enough to warrant the investment involved in constructing and staffing branch facilities. They reflect the trend toward population dispersal and, at the same time, facilitate it by providing essential services at convenient locations. In this manner, the neighborhood shopping center, banking institution, business offices of various

---

[6] See Beatrice Dinerman, *Hospital Development and Communities: Hospital Development in the Western and San Fernando Valley Areas of Los Angeles County* (Los Angeles: Bureau of Governmental Research, University of California, 1960).

utilities, and local police station are closely interwoven into the daily pattern of community life.[7]

It is difficult to overemphasize the degree to which decentralization of social, economic, and governmental institutions has contributed to the development of a community identity in the suburbs. A number of early settlements had an initial basis for cohesion. One example was Compton, founded in 1867 as a Methodist Church enterprise pledged to teetotalism. Whittier was established in 1886 by a group of Quakers from Indiana, Iowa, and Illinois. Long Beach, Bell Gardens, and Palmdale were similarly composed of homogeneous settlers from a specific area or social group. However, subsequent migrations by more heterogeneous population groups tended to blur these distinctions as a basis for unity. It is submitted that the continued cohesion and separate status of these communities are, in large part, the product of decentralization programs executed by public and private institutions.

INSTITUTIONAL DECENTRALIZATION AND LOCALISM

BUSINESS DECENTRALIZATION

The trend toward decentralization in public and private spheres has strengthened the unity of communities by bringing an active social and economic life to the suburbs. Suburban residents are provided with all of the amenities of urban living; they are no longer totally dependent upon the central downtown area for economic livelihood, shopping convenience, and an active social environment. Perhaps no single group has had a more potent impact upon the face of community decentralization than commercial business interests.[8] Perceptive to the tremendous profit potential in rapidly expanding suburban communities, commercial establishments have followed closely at the heels of population migrations to the suburbs. Retail stores dealing in drugs, groceries, and general merchandise initiated the movement to newly populated areas, forming the nucleus of a large number of shopping centers presently scattered throughout the county. Department stores, banking institutions, and utilities soon followed suit.

Business decentralization has progressed to the point that the entire county is covered by a maze of concentrated commercial enterprises

---

[7] For an interesting analysis of the types of local facilities used most frequently by local residents, see Donald L. Foley, "The Use of Local Facilities in a Metropolis," *American Journal of Sociology*, LVI (Nov., 1950), 238–246.

[8] See Edward F. Staniford, *Business Decentralization* (Los Angeles: Bureau of Governmental Research, University of California, 1960).

TABLE 18

BUSINESS DECENTRALIZATION IN LOS ANGELES COUNTY
SELECTED BUSINESSES

Retail stores	Number of branches in county (as of October, 1961)
J. J. Newberry	45
J. C. Penney's	40
S. H. Kress	16
Sears Roebuck	14
Broadway	11
Bullock's	7
May Company	6
Banking institutions	
Bank of America	224
Los Angeles Security First National	143
Public utilities	
Pacific Telephone and Telegraph	50
Southern California Edison Company	46
Southern California Gas Company	32
General Telephone Company	26
Los Angeles City Department of Water and Power	23
Southern Counties Gas Company	16

SOURCES: Private communications from the businesses.

or shopping centers.[9] These centers are composed of branches of various business establishments formerly operating exclusively in the central area of the city, in addition to enterprises identified solely with the suburbs in which they are located. Shopping centers range from small neighborhood operations comprising five acres or more, composed of ten to fifteen stores, and serving some ten thousand persons, to large regional centers covering forty acres or more, encompassing fifty to one hundred stores (usually including one or more major department stores) and supplying a population of one to three hundred thousand. A Los Angeles *Times* survey listed a total of 313 shopping areas as of 1959, forty-one of which had one or more department stores in their cluster, giving them the status of regional shopping centers.

Merchandise distributing centers have become so numerous and so varied that they may now be classified into several different categories,

[9] For a comprehensive listing of materials available on the subject of planned suburban shopping centers, see Jack D. L. Holmes, *A Selected and Annotated Bibliography of Shopping Centers* (Austin: Bureau of Business Research, University of Texas, 1957).

depending upon their location, the size of their clientele, the geographical area covered, and the type of business establishments located within their boundaries. *Neighborhood shopping centers* were the first commercial developments to arise in the suburbs. Initially established in a piecemeal fashion to serve the needs of the immediate community in which they were located, these neighborhood centers continue to be numerous and widely scattered throughout the metropolitan area. Such centers include the small, "neighborhood-type" store dealing in groceries, drugs, and notions. Another category, *suburban business districts,* represents the central business areas of older, well-established municipalities other than the city of Los Angeles. These districts resemble the Los Angeles downtown shopping area in terms of their substantial growth, their central location in relation to the area they are designed to serve, and the wide variety of goods and services they provide. *Strip or marginal trading areas* is the name given to a number of unplanned, sporadic community developments arising along radial thoroughfares connecting suburban shopping centers with the central business districts.

Decentralized business establishments view the community as the focal point of their services, irrespective of political boundaries. The population of a community, in terms of its size and character, is a primary factor to be considered when judging the economic feasibility of establishing a branch operation and selecting a site for it. Decentralization is an expensive operation, not to be undertaken unless the area chosen is inhabited by a large enough potential clientele to warrant accepting the investment risks involved. Equal consideration is given to the character of the community, including analysis of income level, type of housing units, size of the average family and ages of its members, and social status. Data of this type is used in justifying proposed branches and in determining the size of the store and the quality of its merchandise. Estimates of mileage and driving time for potential customers also enter into the analysis. Variety stores, for example, consider a twenty-minute driving limit as maximum and anticipate drawing customers from a radius of one to five miles. Department stores estimate maximum mileage to be twenty, and driving time from thirty minutes to an hour.

Business decentralization is the outgrowth of a natural desire on the part of the corporate managements to expand their margin of profit by widening their potential range of customers. Operation of these economic forces, however, has played no small part in strengthening the cohesion and identification of areas to which businesses have decentralized. Business decentralization has contributed to the self-sufficiency of communities, by providing suburbanites with access to attractive shopping centers where they are able to obtain both the necessities and luxuries of life at a convenient, nearby location, thereby avoiding the traffic and congestion characteristic of the downtown shopping area. Products, services, and greater employment opportunities are now available to the suburbanite in close proximity to his residence. The local shopping center, through frequent usage, comes to embody a sense of close community identification produced by consistent contact with community residents. It further strengthens community cohesion by tending to limit the resident's movement between the community in which he resides and surrounding communities. In this manner, a highly localized geographical area becomes the focal point of the citizen's daily life.

RELIGIOUS ORGANIZATION DECENTRALIZATION

As business decentralization furnishes the material sustenance of a community, establishment of local churches contributes to the spiritual requirements of suburbanites.[10] Churches, like other institutions, have sought to meet the demands of an increasing population and have been forced to accommodate their organizations to neighborhoods of changing economic and ethnic composition.

Membership expansion is an historical, and doctrinal, goal of most religious groups. The necessity of keeping pace with a rapidly expanding and mobile population represents an area of deep concern for all religious groups. Population shifts invariably present problems affecting the pattern of church development and raise questions concerning the location of facilities. A population exodus from the central area jeopardizes the future of centrally located congregations with a dwindling membership. Any change in the original character of a neighborhood requires equally significant decisions as to whether to integrate new residents into the congregation or to abandon the area. Expansion of religious groups, and its attendant problems, is thereby closely dependent upon patterns of metropolitan growth.[11]

Differences in the nature and extent of the various denominations' expansion programs may be explained, in part, by variations in their proselyting policies. Some denominations, such as the Mormons, em-

---

[10] Robert Warren, "Religious Organization and the Development of the Urban Community" (unpublished manuscript, Bureau of Governmental Research, University of California, Los Angeles, 1959).

[11] See F. Stuart Chapin, "The Protestant Church in an Urban Government," in Paul K. Hatt and Albert J. Reiss, Jr., eds., *Cities and Society* (Glencoe: Free Press, 1957), pp. 505–515; and Rose Hum Lee, *The City* (Philadelphia: J. B. Lippincott Co., 1955), pp. 341–363.

phasize the conversion of persons holding different faiths; others, such as the Presbyterians and Methodists, depend upon contacting persons who already have a preëxisting affiliation or identification with the faith in order to expand existing congregations or form new ones. Expansion of Jewish congregations is not based upon increases in converted members, because this faith does not depend upon proselyting. Rather, new facilities are generally constructed to serve those areas in which there has been an increase in resident Jewish population.

Despite these policy differences, however, all religious groups have participated in the trend toward decentralization by forming new congregations and building new facilities in growing suburban areas. Areas of greatest population growth have become the most productive sections for church expansion, irrespective of particular proselyting policies; church development has taken on a definite suburban character. The most impressive emergence of the Mormon church during the postwar period has taken place in the rapidly growing San Fernando Valley; a predominant number of Jewish and Catholic congregations have also located in that valley. Over one-half of the United Lutheran Synod parishes in the county have been organized since 1946, and almost all of these are located in suburban areas.

The close relationship between religious organization and patterns of population distribution has forced several denominations to base their expansion plans upon intensive analyses of population-trend forecasts. All recognize the advantage of being able to purchase appropriate sites in advance of actual population growth. The institutionalization of this type of research within church organizations is exemplified by the Department of Research and Planning established within the Comity Commission of the Southern California Council of Churches in 1946. The commission was formed initially in 1931 to limit interdenominational rivalry among Protestant groups by providing an orderly pattern of church extension for its members in selecting new building sites. All members, which presently include representatives from nine denominations,[12] agree to accept the commission's decisions in matters of locating new church units. Essential data for the formulation of such decisions is supplied by the Department of Research and Planning, which is charged with developing general studies of area growth trends, maintaining liaison with private developers and government planning bodies, and assisting in site selection and development. The department uses as a planning tool a united community religious

---

[12] Christian Church, Church of the Brethren, Congregational, Evangelical and Reformed, Evangelical United Brethren, Methodist, Presbyterian U.S.A., Reformed Church in America, and United Presbyterian.

census developed as a statistical aid to church extension planning. When a census is requested, the department supplies a director and invites all church groups in the area to participate. Participants provide census takers and share the costs on a proportionate basis. These studies play an important part in realizing the concept of "churching an area." For example, a house-to-house survey conducted in nineteen southern California communities revealed that 73.5 per cent of those interviewed were related to one of the major faiths. Protestant denominations accounted for 52.8 per cent of those queried, Catholics for 17 per cent, and persons belonging to the Jewish faith for 2.7 per cent. Drawing upon this study, the department recommended adoption of the criterion that an adequately churched urban area requires four Protestant churches and one Catholic church for every fifteen thousand inhabitants.

The establishment and perpetuation of a parish church develops a sense of community among its membership by offering symbols of faith. It further enhances identification with the community as a whole by providing physical facilities and by enabling residents to associate with other members of the community holding a similar faith. This nonreligious, *geographical* identification is further stimulated by the increasing amount of nonreligious social service and educational programs provided by religious establishments for their members. In the area of education, the Catholic Church is the most active of the various faiths, maintaining a complete academic school system in competition with the public schools. Other religious faiths operate educational programs on a lesser scale. The United Lutheran Synod of Los Angeles County maintains five day-schools. Courses in the history and philosophy of religion are regular aspects of many programs offered by Protestant congregations. The close interrelationship between Jewish religion and culture gives the educational programs of Jewish groups a more cultural orientation. Educational programs offered as an aspect of church membership are supplemented by additional nonreligious activities in recreation and social service.

The close relationship between identification with a religious faith and the community in which it is practiced is further exhibited in widespread attempts to provide a sufficient number of religious facilities to allow members to have easy access. The Southern California Council of Churches recommends that a church site be located as close to the center of the community or neighborhood as possible. If the population is sparse, it should be placed on an interneighborhood boulevard, though this type of location tends to weaken neighborhood loyalty to the denomination and handicaps constructive community efforts.[13] The actual steps taken to develop identification with a geographic community per se depend upon the individual congregation, though all religious groups encourage participation in general community affairs.

Community identification represents a composite of common interests that distinguish given population groups. The ability of an individual to practice his faith actively within the confines of his community emerges as an exceedingly significant source of such identification.

DECENTRALIZATION OF THE PRESS

The increase of suburban population has been accompanied by a rapid growth in community newspapers designed to inform residents of local developments. With the exception of the Los Angeles *Times* and the *Herald-Examiner,* which are metropolitan-wide papers, the 212 newspapers operating in Los Angeles County (exclusive of special periodicals such as industrial, labor and college papers) are considered to be community enterprises. The number of metropolitan-wide papers circulating in the county has remained, through the years, small and relatively constant. Community newspapers, on the other hand, have grown steadily in number and influence. Virtually every local-name area in the county, including municipalities, unincorporated place-name areas, and communities within the city of Los Angeles, is served by one or more local newspapers.

The community press[14] differs from its metropolitan-wide counterpart in terms of its audience, the nature and scope of its coverage, and the public image it creates. The metropolitan daily is directed toward capturing the widest possible audience and providing extensive coverage of national and international events. It is organized into a number of departments that are responsible for special features appearing on a regular basis. Its public image has a partisan flavor, emanating from the presentation of definite editorial policies with respect to issues and candidates.

The community newspaper is designed to secure the readership of persons residing in limited geographic areas within the metropolis. It relegates national and international events to positions of secondary

---

[13] James T. Smith, *The Church and the Planned Community,* Southern California Council of Churches, Department of Research and Planning (mimeo.), p. 6.

[14] For an extensive analysis of the community press phenomenon, see Morris Janowitz, *The Community Press in an Urban Setting* (Glencoe: Free Press, 1952). A related study of the impact of the community press in Los Angeles County was made by Judith N. Jamison, under the auspices of the Bureau of Governmental Research, University of California, Los Angeles.

importance, and focuses primary attention upon details of community life. Local-interest stories, including social items, human-interest features, and reports of local organizational activities, are essential aspects of community-press coverage that are not found in the metropolitan counterpart. The community newspaper generally stands independent of political party affiliations and therefore refrains from taking a definite stand on partisan issues. These differences in coverage and approach have tended to limit the potential competition between the metropolitan-wide press and community newspapers. The community press is perceived as a valuable supplement to the metropolitan daily, rather than as a competing source of news.

The growth of community newspapers in Los Angeles County, as in other urban areas, is dependent upon two major prerequisites: an adequate financial base and a large enough potential audience to justify the necessary capital investment. The rapid increase of suburban population and the subsequent decentralization of retail business establishments to meet the needs of this newly dispersed clientele have provided these prerequisites in abundance. As suburban communities, particularly those located some distance from the central area, became densely settled, aspiring publishers found a geographically concentrated potential audience with a natural interest in local developments. Rapidly growing retail business establishments, which accompanied population dispersal to the suburbs, provided an adequate advertising revenue for the community press. The relationship between the growth of community newspapers and population expansion is reflected in table 19.

Variations and distinctions among community newspapers indicate that the general category, termed "the community press," lends itself to further classification based upon such factors as frequency of distribution and size of the circulation area. Some publish daily editions, others are weekly papers, and still others publish biweekly. There are comparatively few dailies circulating in the Los Angeles area, but, significantly, they have three major characteristics in common. First, most of them have been in existence for comparatively long periods of time. Out of a total of twenty-four dailies operating in Los Angeles County in 1961, seven were established before 1900 and eleven came into existence between 1900 and 1920. For the next quarter of a century, only five additional dailies were established. Since 1950, one more has joined the ranks.

Second, community daily newspapers are generally found within the boundaries of long-established municipalities. Nineteen of the twenty-four are published in the municipalities of Alhambra, Beverly Hills,

TABLE 19

Growth of Population and Newspapers[a] in Los Angeles County, Selected Years, 1850–1960

Year	Population	Number of newspapers
1850	3,530	0
1880	33,381	4
1890	101,454	15
1900	129,734	22
1910	426,274	47
1920	936,455	69
1930	2,208,492	120
1940	2,785,643	140
1950	4,151,687	197
1960	6,038,771	212

Sources: N. W. Ayers and Sons, *Directory of Newspapers and Periodicals;* U.S. Census of Population, 1960, *California Number of Inhabitants,* PC (1) 6A, California.
[a] Exclusive of special periodicals such as industrial, labor, and college papers.

Burbank, Culver City, Glendale, Huntington Park, Inglewood, Long Beach, Monrovia, Montebello, Monterey Park, Pasadena, Pomona, Redondo Beach, Santa Monica, West Covina, and Whittier. Each of these cities is served by one daily, with the exception of Long Beach and Pasadena, which have two. All were incorporated before 1925 and are heavily populated. Three have populations in excess of one hundred thousand and seven are populated by more than fifty thousand. No municipality served by a daily newspaper is inhabited by less than twenty-five thousand persons. The remaining five dailies are published in the Los Angeles City communities of Hollywood, North Hollywood, San Pedro, Venice, and Wilmington. These communities, like the independent municipalities, were settled relatively early in the history of Los Angeles County, and all continue to be densely populated.

The third characteristic of each of the dailies operating within Los Angeles County is a relatively large following of advertisers and subscribers. All have a paid circulation that, with few exceptions, exceeds ten thousand subscribers. In some instances, clientele ranges as high as fifty thousand to one hundred thousand, in areas where the daily circulates beyond the limited boundaries of a single community.

Circulation coverage tends to distinguish some community papers from others. Most local ones circulate within a single community, although several have a clientele that covers a much broader geographical area. The *Herald-American,* for example, though published in the city of Compton, circulates in no less than ten communities. The San

Gabriel *Valley Tribune* enjoys an equally broad circulation, as does the *Valley Times*. Similarly, the Beverly Hills *Citizen* supplements its regular daily issue with seven separate Thursday editions, each of which covers a community outside the city of Beverly Hills. Consequently, a selected number of community newspapers exercise a more "regional" influence than the term "local press" would imply.

These distinguishing characteristics, though significant, should not detract from the fact that all community newspapers place a heavy emphasis on local activities, as compared with the metropolitan-wide press. This emphasis has had an impact on the suburbanite. Local residents are provided with a source of news that focuses its attention almost exclusively upon individuals and institutions associated with a limited geographic area. In exposing the suburbanite to information about his community, the press stimulates his interest in local events and promotes a sense of identification and loyalty to the area in which the events occur.

The process of stimulating local identification includes many features. The newspaper masthead, which often bears the name of the community it is designed to serve, reflects this intent. The content of the paper directs attention toward items with which suburban residents may easily identify. Detailed reports of municipal services, social activities, and personal items capture the readers' interest. The comparatively small geographic area of the suburb increases the possibility that the suburbanite is personally acquainted with the individuals appearing in the social column or is a participant in organizational events reported. Ability to identify himself with persons and events reported in the local press promotes in the reader a sense of local pride, which is essential if the residents are to have a sense of community solidarity and cohesion.

The process is nurtured further by the publicity that the local press bestows upon other suburban institutions. Local voluntary associations are strongly supported by the local press, and their activities receive extensive coverage. Merchandising items offered by local retail establishments give the local newspaper its financial backbone and take a considerable amount of its space. The resident is encouraged to patronize the community shopping center and to take a greater interest in local organizational activities. In both instances, the process is one of directing the sights of the suburbanite "inward" toward the community in which he lives, as opposed to the larger metropolis and the concerns of that broader region.

The local press' role as a vehicle for maintaining and strengthening community cohesion is evident in its avoidance of divisive issues.

Community newspapers generally refrain from "crusading" for any cause or program that might produce intracommunity conflicts and, possibly, alienate a major segment of its clientele. Controversies in which the community has reached a consensus and stands opposed to some external threat, on the other hand, receive widespread coverage.

The community press is a key local institution that both reflects and nurtures the local orientation within which it operates. The local newspaper was established initially to serve interests that were predominantly commercial. However, given the nature and scope of its news and advertising coverage, it inevitably emerges as a vital force to enhance and perpetuate the community.

Voluntary Organizations and the Community

Voluntary organizations with community orientation pervade every section of the Los Angeles metropolitan area. If one can visualize a map of the county denoting the location of each chamber of commerce, coördinating council, and related service organization, one would see a distinct clustering of such community associations within the numerous local, place-name areas that comprise this political entity. Virtually every local-name community in the county, irrespective of legal boundary lines, has, within its border, an independent community coördinating council, chamber of commerce, Kiwanis Club, Rotary, or similar voluntary organization.

Most organizations of this type are established in response to a felt need, on the part of their leaders, for programs aimed at community betterment. In almost every case, the leaders define problems and issues in terms of the place-name area which the association is designed to serve. In a large number of cases, the organization has been established for the express purpose of strengthening community identification by providing the designated area with a representative body that would focus its attention exclusively upon problems and requirements of the limited geographic environment. A number of areas formerly affiliated with associations in adjacent communities have subsequently dissolved their relationship with the parent body and formed their own associations, with a view to asserting their separate area identities. Once established, organizational programs focus upon activities that are expected to achieve a greater amount of local improvements; the community serves as the matrix from which a majority of the organization's functions and projects emanate.

The internal structure of most community organizations, which generally includes an elected executive board and a number of special committees, follows a common pattern and is of no special significance in itself. The important feature is the type of individual responsible for performing managerial functions. Most of those serving in an executive capacity, that is, as officers or as members of the governing board, are either residents or businessmen in the community served by the organization. The governing bodies of community organizations are therefore composed of individuals who are motivated by a highly personalized concern for the future of their respective locality. Members, as well as the leadership, are drawn from a localized area, with a majority of the total composed of residents or businessmen closely associated with community affairs.

It is interesting to note that each community organization is characterized by fairly well-defined jurisdictional boundaries, despite the absence of any formal procedure for delimiting their respective spheres of influence. The coverage of each association is arrived at almost automatically and without formal or informal discussions with leaders of adjacent community organizations. Yet incidents of jurisdictional disputes among two or more like organizations claiming jurisdiction over the same geographical area are rare.[15] Similarly, overlapping membership rarely occurs. Two adjoining chambers of commerce seldom draw their membership from the same streets, and, in many cases, membership areas of one chamber are separated from those of a neighboring organization by several noncommercial blocks from which neither draws any members. The satisfactory operation of numerous adjoining community organizations, in the absence of any prior formal agreement, would seem to reflect the presence of community areas that are psychologically separate, despite an ecological cohesiveness and, in many cases, a legal unity. An individual tends to gravitate toward the particular community with which he identifies his interests most closely. This attitude will determine his decision to affiliate with one organization, as opposed to an identical type located in an adjoining community. From a technical point of view, lines that separate community organizations from one another are arrived at arbitrarily, in the sense that they are not products of any objective analysis, are often not explicitly stated, and are determined and perpetuated without formal decision-making. Yet organizational boundary lines manifest a highly rational pattern, in that they reflect a community of interests bound together by problems and characteristics associated with fairly specific geographical areas.

Is there a relationship between the intensity of an individual's loyalty to a particular area and the size of that area? Or, expressed

---

[15] One outstanding exception is the recent disagreement over the jurisdictional boundaries of Pacoima, Panorama City, Mission Hills, and Granada Hills.

another way, is there a geographical limit beyond which close personal identification and loyalty cannot be achieved? An individual might well experience a considerable degree of difficulty in identifying his own personal welfare with the concerns of too broad a geographical area. Affairs of the smaller community in which the same individual resides, having a more direct impact upon his personal welfare, are clearly felt and easily recognized. An individual may experience a strong sense of personal involvement over a situation of gang warfare in close proximity to his residence or place of business, which he could not possibly experience when problems of juvenile delinquency are presented to him within the framework of a broader region. In the latter instance, personal repercussions are indirect, at best, and the individual's reaction could not possibly be as intense. This may explain the rationale behind the existence of numerous independent organizations performing identical functions within the municipal boundaries of Los Angeles, while another municipality such as Culver City, for example, is adequately served by a much smaller number of organizations covering the entire municipality. It would seem that residents of Culver City are psychologically capable of recognizing an areawide community of interests within an area of eight square miles. Apparently, this same type of loyalty and identification cannot be realized by the inhabitants of the city of Los Angeles, scattered over an area of 457 square miles.

COMMUNITIES HAVE PERSONALITIES: THE COMMUNITY COUNCIL EXPERIENCE

The concept of the community is based upon the assumption that each community possesses certain characteristics that serve to distinguish it from adjoining territory; a "personality" that is somehow different from that of neighboring areas. That these distinctions do, in fact, exist is illustrated by the degree to which special traits associated with certain areas affect the operation of community coördinating councils serving those areas.[16] Observations regarding the manner in which council representatives interpret the nature of their communities apply, in large part, to other local organizations.

Why are certain areas more community-oriented than others? Are

---

[16] See Beatrice Dinerman, "Community Coordinating Councils in Los Angeles County" (unpublished manuscript, Bureau of Governmental Research, University of California, Los Angeles, Jan., 1960). For a historical analysis of the coördinating council movement, see Jack D. Mezirow, "The Coordinating Council Movement in Los Angeles County" (unpublished Ph.D. dissertation, University of California, Los Angeles, March, 1955).

there certain essential ingredients present in community-minded areas that are lacking in others?

Community coördinating councils, a relatively widespread form of social organization, have a twofold purpose. First, they seek to stimulate active "grass-roots" participation in community affairs by serving as forums through which residents are encouraged to offer viewpoints and suggestions regarding local problems. Second, being composed largely of representatives from preëxisting local organizations, they attempt to unify the efforts of numerous independent associations operating at the community level.

The growth and development of coördinating councils throughout Los Angeles County is facilitated and encouraged by the Los Angeles County Department of Community Services. The entire county is divided into eleven administrative regions, and each region is served by an area consultant servicing approximately eight to ten councils. The consultant, operating in an advisory capacity, helps to organize and develop councils by coördinating the work of the several private and public agencies, committees, and organizations that seek to strengthen community life in each area.

The Department of Community Services has developed its own criteria for identifying a community, for the purpose of determining an optimum base on which to form a coördinating council. These include specific ecological, geographical, and psychological aspects (for example, does the individual recognize it as a community?). Political identification, the sharing of certain important institutions (for example, transportation, newspapers, schools, police, markets, recreation, parks, public service), and common community problems are also included.[17] Community characteristics deemed essential to successful council operation include a reasonably stable population, a substantial segment of community population affiliated with some type of community organization, a strong leadership corps, and a community attitude favorable to the acceptance of assistance.[18] The degree to which these ingredients exist in any given area will, according to the department, determine the degree of community consciousness inherent in the area and the relative success or failure of council operations.

Departmental representatives tend to attach certain identifying labels to various council areas within their jurisdiction. These labels generally reflect the major traits or characteristics that, when taken

---

[17] Los Angeles County Department of Community Services, *Staff Produced Administration Studies* (Los Angeles, 1960), p. 11.

[18] *Ibid.*, p. 14.

together, give each community an identity of its own. They are based upon such tangible factors as income groups residing in the area, assessed valuation, or age of the community; they may also reflect traditional and, at times, subconscious attitudes that are held by community residents toward certain specific issues.

The concept of a community "personality," which has a direct effect upon the operations of coördinating councils, may be clarified through several specific examples. Departmental representatives identify Lakewood as a bedroom community that contracts with Los Angeles County for its municipal services. They attribute their difficulties in building the Lakewood Coördinating Council into a truly significant community organization to an inability to create a genuine community-consciousness in an area that looks to the county rather than to the city for governmental services. Active local governmental organization seems to be one essential prerequisite for community-consciousness. Long Beach, on the other hand, is identified as an "in-grown community," strongly resenting the introduction of ideas that seem to come from outside its municipal limits. As a result, departmental representatives, in their capacity as county agents, must proceed with extreme caution in their relations with the Long Beach Community Council, for fear of being branded as "county dictators." Similarly, efforts to establish a coördinating council in Pasadena have been unsuccessful due to an aversion on the part of municipal residents to anything that smacks of the county government.

The status of local government, though important, is not the only factor that serves to distinguish areas from each other and to influence the operation of community councils. The Lennox Community Coördinating Council, for example, though located in unincorporated county territory, is a well-disciplined, serious council whose strength, according to the area consultant, stems from "deep American traditions of sanctity of church and home." Communities that are part of the city of Los Angeles and that still exhibit a strong sense of community identification include Woodland Hills, North Hollywood, and Venice. The Venice Community Council, for instance, reflects a solid identification with the local-name community, "making it possible to involve the entire area in crisis situations." The geographical location of Woodland Hills on the fringe of the city is, according to the consultant, responsible for a strong community consciousness emanating from a need to provide this new, sprawling, sparsely populated area with a community identity. The North Hollywood Council, established in 1935, evolved into a commendable council operation from its initial need, as a new area, to gain a cohesive feeling during a period of rapid population growth. The adjacent community of Van Nuys, on the other hand, despite a similar pattern of population growth, has a less effective coördinating council, due to the presence of *too many* well-organized groups that retain a primary loyalty to their respective organizations and give the council a secondary position in their scale of values.

In general, however, those community councils that are cited by departmental representatives as successful ventures are ones serving older municipalities. Councils that are deemed unsuccessful or mediocre are found predominantly in either unincorporated county territory or communities within the legal boundaries of the city of Los Angeles. This would seem to argue that traditional-type cities possess a degree of community identity and loyalty, as reflected in active council participation, that is often lacking in unincorporated areas or in communities situated within the boundaries of a giant municipality. This suggests a possible correlation between community activity, municipal corporate status, and size of the municipality.

Income is another important factor. Area consultants generally agree that the relative success of a community council depends largely upon the attitudes expressed by the area's predominant income group. Community councils are generally more successful in getting active participation in middle-income communities. Residents of wealthier areas refuse to recognize the existence of any problems requiring council action; whereas those in low-income communities recognize certain deficiencies in their areas but fail to exhibit any real concern.

A community "personality," as reflected in the activities of community coördinating councils, is the product of a large number of interrelated variables. These variables, operating in specific community situations, arise in slightly different combinations.

DECENTRALIZATION: IMPLICATIONS FOR THE ORGANIZATION OF LOCAL GOVERNMENT IN METROPOLITAN AREAS

In later chapters, we shall discuss the tasks involved in designing an administrative organization to cope with the problems of governing a metropolitan area, and the distribution of responsibility for the execution of essential public services among two or more levels of government. For the moment, let us concern ourselves with examining the relationship between institutional decentralization and the feasibility of altering the face of local government within a metropolitan context.

The concept of localism, a permanent feature of our political tradition, is reflected in adverse reactions toward any proposed system that smacks of centralization or seeks to increase further the size of what is already deemed to be "big government." It is charged that a metropolitan government would be unwieldy and unresponsive. Public officials would be far removed from the citizens they are designed to serve. Services provided by a single centralized agency remote from the scene of day-to-day performance would inevitably fall short of local requirements. Politically, these sentiments tend to obviate the possibility of transferring *all* substantive local powers to a metropolitan-wide authority. When a metropolitan government is discussed, it is generally done so in terms of a *federated* system based upon a federation of existing local units coördinated under a single authority with jurisdiction over matters of regional interest. Existing local units would continue as they now are in relation to their local functions; only the metropolitan aspects of certain functions would come under the jurisdiction of the metropolitan authority. Local sentiments and authority are thereby preserved through a retention of power over matters deemed to be of a purely local nature. Yet, even these proposals would require local units to relinquish power and responsibility over certain functions that formerly fell within their province.

Institutional decentralization has played no small part in intensifying "localism" by giving substance to this highly intangible concept. One may validly speculate as to whether or not institutional decentralization, by focusing attention upon a limited geographic area and providing this area with a number of local institutionalized services, has strengthened what many feel to be an already exaggerated sense of community identification.

Community consciousness finds expression, sometimes, in extreme forms of behavior that approach the ridiculous. An excellent example of community pride thwarting a rational program is afforded by an effort on the part of Los Angeles City officials to implement a program of uniform community signs for the San Fernando Valley. This program was initially recommended by the city Traffic Department to help reduce the uncertainty of driving in unfamiliar areas by identifying all established communities by means of uniform markers. Place-name definition is essential to adequate city planning, traffic control, civil defense, statistical surveys, marketing, and merchandising. Nevertheless, implementation of this relatively simple program has been delayed for two years because Valley residents have been unable to agree on the precise boundaries separating their respective communities. It was announced, at the outset, that the city government would refrain from dictating the boundary locations of Valley communities, that the Valley residents themselves would make the decisions. Although there is widespread "theoretical" approval of this sign program, conflicting territorial demands have prevented its implementation.

Institutional decentralization, by providing the amenities of both urban and suburban living to the residents of Greater Los Angeles, seemingly produced an atmosphere of complacency that is incompatible with demand for comprehensive changes in the machinery of local government. This situation is exemplified by the community chamber of commerce point of view toward governmental change. A recent study,[19] based upon an investigation of views held by local chambers of commerce leaders toward governmental change in the Los Angeles area, revealed that 54 per cent of the chamber managers noted weaknesses in the present governmental system but were anxious to work for improvements; 23 per cent were favorable to establishing a metropolitan authority; and 22 per cent were strongly in favor of existing arrangements. In other words, a proposed radical revision, such as a metropolitan-wide authority, would probably face opposition by three-fourths of the local chamber leadership. The major reasons given in justifying the viewpoints are even more revealing. They included fear of losing local autonomy and home rule, belief that "big government" generally is dangerous, and uncertainty as to whether a centralized governmental structure would provide adequate attention to community needs. Those favoring revisions were disturbed chiefly by existing deficiencies in local legislative bodies and poor legislative understanding of community needs. Little reference was made by any of those interviewed to positive advantages that might accrue to the metropolitan area through areawide administration and control.

Further insight into the operation of localism may be obtained by referring, once again, to community coördinating councils. This type of voluntary organization has sought to superimpose a *geographical* loyalty upon preëxisting *functional* or *organizational* loyalties that were characteristic of its constituency. The local chamber of commerce equates community betterment with improved business conditions; the parent-teachers association feels a community is sound if it is provided with adequate school facilities; the NAACP views community betterment in terms of improved race relations. Community councils seek to unify the efforts of these related, yet diverse, loyalties and interests behind the common bond of community betterment. Attention is shifted from the welfare of specific segments of the com-

---

[19] See Beatrice Dinerman, "Chambers of Commerce in the Modern Metropolis," *BGR Observer* (Los Angeles: Bureau of Governmental Research, University of California) (Sept., 1958).

munity and brought to focus upon the welfare of the community as a whole. The practical application of this theoretical justification for council existence tends to produce an innocuous and, many feel, insignificant type of association. Individual community organizations base their participation in coördinating councils upon a prior agreement guaranteeing each member organization complete independence. Delegates from the member associations appearing before the community council cannot bind their respective organizations but must vote as individuals. Similarly, a council delegation appearing before local governmental officials cannot speak as a true representative of an autonomous body, since consistent and dependable backing by organizations affiliated with the council is not always forthcoming. Therefore, councils are forced to direct their programs towards education rather than action.

The implications of this situation are thought provoking. An individual's loyalty to the chamber of commerce, PTA, or to any other organization representative of his own interest group, tends to take precedence over his loyalty to a community-wide organization. It points up the fragmented nature of supposedly unified community areas.[20] Even within a small local-name area, it is difficult to gain community-wide consensus, since each community is fragmented by diverse functional and organizational loyalties. Finally, and perhaps of greatest importance, given the difficulties involved in obtaining consensus within a small community area, one becomes even more dubious about the possibility of instituting programs directed toward stimulating a broader *regional* loyalty covering an entire metropolitan area.

COMMUNITY IDENTIFICATION: SOME QUALIFICATIONS

Great emphasis has been placed upon the fragmented loyalties of Los Angeles residents, as exemplified by the growth of distinct communities served by locally oriented community associations. These associations, by focusing attention upon a limited geographic area, tend to detract from efforts to institute regional loyalties. However, the conclusion that community organizations are a direct reflection of a deep and widely held sense of community identification is, in fact, a premature one. The dynamics of community operations reveal a number of additional factors that must be considered in any meaningful analysis. Can one validly conclude that a community organization is formed because a community consciousness already exists? Are

---

[20] For an interesting discussion of several principles of group unity, see Amos Hawley, *Human Ecology* (New York: Ronald Press, 1950), pp. 206–235.

community organizations the product of this prior identification or is community identification a product of manipulations by organizational leaders?

Leaders of community organizations in Los Angeles County generally agree that a true sense of community consciousness is rarely present prior to the establishment of the association. To be sure, every community has a nucleus of leaders providing initial stimulation for the establishment of organizations. However, the presence of this leadership corps cannot logically be equated with widespread community identification, since only a small percentage of the total population is involved. One of the major problems facing local organizations is the lack of participation. Constant efforts to encourage a broader membership participation have not been overly productive. Even if we assume that a true sense of community identification motivates this nucleus of participants, "community spirit" would still be limited to a small portion of the local population.

Further questions arise when we analyze the factors that motivate the behavior of participants. In a small number of cases, the motives are political in nature, with the community organization being utilized as a vehicle through which the individual receives the publicity and acclaim necessary for election to public office. In a larger number of cases, participation may be motivated by a psychological need to achieve a leadership role and receive the respect and recognition it entails. While the avowed purpose of all service organizations is community betterment, it is common knowledge that many persons join in order to increase their professional or social contacts. Therefore, the degree to which active community participants themselves exhibit a close community identification is questionable.

It should be noted that personal identification is being equated with active participation in community affairs. It may well be that every individual possesses a certain degree of loyalty to the area in which he resides; however, the intensity of this loyalty can only be measured through specific observable acts such as participation.

The existence of a concentrated population grouping within a specific area is not necessarily synonymous with a community. The term community implies a unity of purpose and shared interests that are clearly recognized by the inhabitants of the area in question. That these shared interests exist in almost every area cannot be denied. However, many individuals are preoccupied with personal and professional problems not directly related to the area in which they reside. Impinged upon by an array of loyalties and interests outside the scope of their community per se, they either fail to recognize a community loyalty or fail to express it in the form of active participation in programs directed toward community betterment. A true community cannot exist in the absence of such recognition on the part of its inhabitants. Community spirit is the product of conscious, deliberate efforts on the part of a local leadership corps stimulating the latent community consciousness. Given the fact that loyalty to a given community is the product of conscious manipulation, one can validly speculate about the feasibility of engaging in similar efforts to produce loyalty to an entire metropolitan region.

Proponents of a metropolitan-wide governmental body that would be unimpeded by traditional political boundaries denounce municipalities as obsolete entities in a metropolitan environment. However, it is evident that, in the minds of community leaders, communities and concepts of localism are far from obsolete. Business decentralization is a tangible reflection of the presence of densely-settled population clusters. A full religious life has similarly been brought to the doorstep of suburban residents. The local point of view is vociferously proclaimed through numerous community newspapers. The establishment and activity of local improvement associations reveal that residents feel a need for local voluntary organizations whose primary concern is community betterment. This emphasis upon bringing public and private facilities closer to the people may be considered as substantial evidence that there is need for a more localized governmental structure. The proliferation of decentralized institutions, and the localized sentiments they help to engender, must be reckoned with in any reorganization of local government in the Los Angeles metropolitan area.

CENTRIPETAL INFLUENCE: A COUNTERWEIGHT

Despite the growing importance of suburban communities, the downtown Los Angeles area continues to be the focal point of activity for governmental departments, financial institutions, and large enterprises. It still attracts a considerable number of suburban shoppers and retains its position as the fourth largest business center in the nation and the chief commercial center west of the Mississippi. The National Retail Merchants Association indicates that its members plan to decrease their emphasis on suburban branches and to revitalize their parent stores in the downtown area.

Downtown Revisited

Residents of Los Angeles are seeing a considerable resurgence of the central business district. Downtown business groups, deeply aware of the competing trends, are engaged in individual and coöperative efforts to transform this district into a more attractive trading area.[21] Retail stores are modernizing their facilities under the coördination of the Downtown Businessmen's Association. The governments of Los Angeles City and Los Angeles County are also actively involved in this movement. A Central City Committee, appointed by Mayor Norris Poulson in June, 1957, prepared a master plan for the central business district in coöperation with the City Planning Commission and downtown business interests.

The Bunker Hill redevelopment project, seeking to convert an older residential section adjacent to the central business area into a modern center, is an outstanding effort. This $315 million project includes high-rise apartments, office buildings to accommodate a working population of fifty thousand, an elementary school, a playground and other recreational facilities, a modern centrally located shopping center, motel units, and off-street parking facilities. This planned development, located in the heart of the central business district, is expected to precipitate a return to the city.

Modifications in the Municipal Building Code, instituted in 1956, caused some significant changes in Los Angeles' growth pattern. Availability of attractive land on the outskirts of the central city, coupled with building restrictions that kept the maximum height of structures to 150 feet, caused Los Angeles previously to grow horizontally rather than vertically. Modern technological advances in building techniques have made it possible to overcome most of the previous objections to high-rise construction. High land valuation has made it essential that additional office space be provided in new buildings to permit economic and profitable operations.

This projected resurgence of the downtown business district is evident in the following table, which illustrates the significant decline, by principal use categories, in net floor space in the central business district from 1930–1960 and indicates anticipated changes projected through 1980 (see table 20).

SUMMARY

The contemporary Los Angeles scene is the product of interaction between the countervailing forces of urbanization and suburbanization. The growth of suburban fringe areas has been nurtured while the central area has been experiencing a gradual but perceptible decline

---

[21] This attempt to revitalize the downtown area is not peculiar to Los Angeles; Austin, Kansas City, Dayton, Miami, Grand Rapids, and Boston are among other major cities engaged in programs of downtown revitalization.

TABLE 20

LOS ANGELES CENTRAL BUSINESS DISTRICT[a]

NET FLOOR AREA CHANGE BY USE CATEGORY

SELECTED YEARS, 1930–1980

Use	Floor area in square feet						
	1930	1955	Per cent change 1930–1955	1960	Per cent change 1955–1960	1980 (projected)	Per cent change (projected) 1960–1980
Government and quasi-public	1,931,548	2,580,747	25.2	3,451,350	33.7	4,000,000	15.9
Hotel	6,120,466	5,600,769	−8.5	5,389,317	−3.8	7,080,000	31.4
Institutional	2,350,438	2,141,471	−8.9	2,070,079	−3.3	3,658,000	76.7
Manufacturing and wholesale	3,560,564	3,239,660	−9.0	3,175,655	−2.0	2,500,000	−21.3
Office	10,844,594	11,421,176	5.0	12,424,067	8.8	24,145,000	94.3
Parking, inside[b]	1,582,473	1,812,014	14.0	2,227,129	22.0	5,500,000	147.0
Retail	6,539,336	5,985,136	−8.5	5,504,283	−8.0	5,917,000	7.5
Service	2,676,241	2,470,928	−7.7	2,449,775	−1.0	4,366,000	78.2
TOTAL	35,605,640	35,351,901	−1.0	36,691,655	4.0	57,166,000	55.8

SOURCE: Los Angeles Central City Committee and Los Angeles City Planning Department, *Centropolis, 1980* (Los Angeles, 1961), p. 29.

[a] Boundaries as established for a land use survey completed by the Los Angeles City Planning Department in January, 1960.

[b] Inside parking includes parking structures and parking space provided within a building as an accessory to another use.

in population. The increasing importance of communities surrounding the core city has been accompanied by a similar decentralization on the part of private and public institutions designed to provide essential social and economic services.

These developments have contributed to the division of Los Angeles County into a number of separate, relatively self-sufficient community areas, both incorporated and unincorporated. The suburbanite now has access to attractive shopping centers and participates in an active social environment within the confines of the suburb in which he lives. Accordingly, suburban dependence upon the central area of the region has diminished.

A significant by-product of this institutional decentralization has been the enrichment of community identification in the suburbs. De-centralization of social and economic activities, in focusing greater attention upon limited geographic areas, has contributed to the unity and cohesion of fringe communities. The citizen is likely to exhibit a greater allegiance to the suburb in which he lives than to the larger legal entity of which he is a part. Such "localism" has definite implica-tions for any attempt to institute comprehensive governmental re-organization on a metropolitan-wide scale.

In the midst of this contemporary trend toward dispersion, however, countervailing forces looking toward greater integration may be detected. Downtown Los Angeles has retained its position as a govern-ment, financial, and retail center; many suburbanites are still dependent upon the central area for their economic livelihood. Downtown busi-ness interests, in coöperation with public officials, are making a serious effort to revitalize the core area and halt the onslaught of blight and obsolescence.

TEN

Decentralization by Local Governments: The Overview

PUBLIC OFFICIALS who are responsible for providing essential services have come to recognize that the patterns of population growth influence the nature, functions, and location of local governmental agencies. The citizen, increasingly aware of the growth of public services, often fails to recognize that his decision to move himself, his family, and his belongings to another neighborhood, city, county, or state creates problems for the governmental administrator and contributes to the demand for new public policies. Patterns and techniques of decentralizing the governmental machinery emerge as new issues in local public agencies charged with serving a large, dispersed, mobile population.

Investigations pertaining to the operation of decentralization principles and practices at the local level of government are rare.[1] The reasons behind this apparent dearth are exceedingly significant. Many local jurisdictions, aside from the traditional police and fire stations, have not seen fit to decentralize their administrative programs. In the majority of instances, local governments do not encompass a geographical area of sufficient size to warrant doing so. Furthermore, the physical topography of many local jurisdictions is such that the unit may be considered as an integral whole, rather than as a series of relatively

---

[1] For two excellent studies of decentralization with particular reference to the federal level of government, see James W. Fesler, *Area and Administration* (University, Alabama: University of Alabama Press, 1949), and Herbert Kaufman, *The Forest Ranger* (Baltimore: Johns Hopkins Press, 1960).

isolated, unconnected nuclei. The size and geographic dispersion of Los Angeles, on the other hand, promotes decentralization.

Los Angeles City and Los Angeles County officials have embarked upon positive programs of administrative decentralization to carry administrative activities to the people, attempting to meet the challenges raised by population dispersal and growth of communities. City and county programs alike have passed from being uncoördinated, departmental efforts to ones carefully planned, executed, and controlled by central management and planning agencies. The trend is to bring local government within easy reach of the people.

DECENTRALIZATION: A WORKING DEFINITION

Before analyzing administrative decentralization in Los Angeles City and Los Angeles County in some detail, it is essential to discuss the meaning of decentralization. The term is used extensively in public-administration literature with reference to a myriad of situations, ranging from internal management practices to the distribution of functional responsibilities among levels of government. It can have a number of different, often contradictory meanings. One relates to the purely physical aspect of decentralization, that is, the physical location of branch offices operating under the direction and supervision of a central agency. If we interpret decentralization in terms of an abundance or scarcity of branch facilities, a state agency operating through numerous, widely dispersed branch offices might, in actuality, show a more decentralized administrative pattern than a large local unit of government whose coverage was impeded by an inadequate number of branches.

A distinction between "administration" and "control" is also crucial to an interpretation of decentralization. A particular service may be performed in a decentralized manner if it is provided directly to the public from branch offices. However, the administrator performing the service may operate under the rigid supervision of a central management that determines and enforces policies affecting the execution of this function.

The extent to which a particular function is administered in a decentralized manner depends, in part, upon the frame of reference used. Countywide administration of a function can be looked upon as decentralization from the point of view of the state. Municipal control and administration is equally decentralized, from the county point of view.

Decentralization must be considered in the light of intra-agency or intradepartmental administration. A local agency may be characterized by extreme internal centralization, through a failure to delegate substantial functional autonomy and administrative discretion to its agents in the field.

The problem of terminology is a very real one. Any definition that is based upon one aspect of decentralization to the exclusion of others may be judged incomplete and untenable in certain circumstances. The definition problem becomes especially acute when one considers the emotional overtones that have been attributed to this term: the use of the word "decentralization" brings to mind the old town meeting where policies governing the community are made by those most directly affected and every citizen enjoys active participation in the public life of his community. "Centralization," on the other hand, conjures up to some persons visions of an omnipotent giant, bent upon destroying citizen rule through arbitrary control over public life at the community level.

In this chapter, we seek to formulate a "working definition" to serve as a framework for examining the process of decentralizing administration within two large local governments. The definition employed is based upon two major areas of concern: the arrangement of physical establishments to maximize public accessibility to the governmental machinery; and management policies that affect the internal administration of various departments and seek to secure responsible, coördinated action while encouraging field office personnel to make essential decisions. The first criterion views decentralization within a geographic framework. A definition that equates the subject solely with the geographic dispersion of public facilities is oversimplified, however. What is the nature of administrative relationships between central headquarters and branch offices? How much authority is delegated to branch personnel, in terms of the number and kinds of decisions permissible without central approval? How extensive is central supervision and what are the techniques of control utilized to assure uniform application of centrally established policies? How significant is the communication process as a vehicle for coördinating branch operations? The amount of discretion allocated to branch personnel is the second essential criterion. In a sense, it is the more important of the two, since construction of a branch-office building is a mere *reflection of* decentralized operations. Decentralized performance of services can be executed in the absence of separate facilities to house field personnel. Yet, in most instances, extensive decentralization involves a duplication of responsibilities normally executed at central headquarters. This produces a need for adequate building space to house personnel and equipment and serve as a permanent site to which the citizen may address his inquiries. Decentralization, as viewed within this context, is defined as *a delegation of authority and responsibility for making decisions, within established standards, from a central organization to its subunits in the field, usually accompanied by the provision of separate branch establishments at some distance from central headquarters.*

THE SETTING: DEMOGRAPHY AND TOPOGRAPHY

Decentralization of governmental operations in Los Angeles city and county has been dictated by the size of the area, its topography, and the dispersed pattern of population. The county covers 4,083 square miles—some eight hundred square miles more than the combined areas of Delaware and Rhode Island. It is further characterized by varied topography. A motorist traveling from the ocean beaches to the Antelope Valley and Mojave Desert passes through several mountain ranges, such as San Gabriel and Santa Monica, that effectively separate segments of the county from each other. The city comprises over 457 square miles and its topography is also segmented by hills. As we have seen in chapter six, its boundaries are irregularly shaped.

Physical communication between local government agencies in the Los Angeles Civic Center and outlying communities became a serious barrier to the effective provision of essential services because of sheer physical distance, as well as downtown traffic congestion. If one circumscribes a gigantic circle, using the Civic Center–downtown-area as its center, a radius of approximately twenty-five miles virtually covers the farthest points within Los Angeles City. In the northwest, the circle reaches unincorporated county territory at the upper edge of the San Fernando Valley; in the south it extends to the Wilmington–San Pedro area. Citizens residing in these outlying areas would find it difficult to conduct all their business with city officials in the downtown Civic Center.

County residents face similar problems. Lancaster and Palmdale, situated in the Mojave Desert behind the San Gabriel Mountains, and Santa Catalina Island, separated from the mainland by nearly thirty miles of ocean, are extreme examples wherein distance and topographical barriers serve to isolate citizens from the county headquarters in downtown Los Angeles. Much of the remainder of the county, though not affected so drastically, is nevertheless, by virtue of distance and traffic congestion, only slightly less remote from the governmental center.

Examples of difficulties in serving these outlying areas abound.

Prior to 1936, the Lancaster–Palmdale area was served by the Sheriff's deputies from the County Hall of Justice. Officers alerted to some danger while stationed at headquarters would race some ninety miles through the mountains to respond. Needless to say, the victim was already victimized, the lawbreaker was often long out of the immediate area, and the deputy had a long and tedious drive back to the Sheriff's office. This situation was alleviated in 1936 when a branch station was established in Lancaster.

Public officials responded to the challenges of metropolitan growth by formulating plans based partly upon retaining certain features of centralization, coupled with the establishment of branch offices to serve the needs of outlying community areas. This and the following two chapters are devoted to an examination and appraisal of their efforts.

EVOLUTION OF DECENTRALIZATION PROGRAMS: LOS ANGELES COUNTY

Los Angeles County took the first step toward administrative decentralization in 1911 when it established a branch office of the County Public Defender in Long Beach. By 1925, other county departments operating on a partly decentralized basis included the District Attorney, Health, Sheriff and Probation. Decentralization continued for the next several decades, and affected a number of additional county departments.

THE QUEST FOR SIMPLIFICATION AND INTEGRATION

Early programs were executed in an uncoördinated, piecemeal fashion, without reference to any preconceived master plan. Each department decided according to its own evaluation of the nature of the problems and responsibilities involved in carrying out its prescribed functions. When a department decided upon a degree of decentralization, it chose its own branch sites. As more and more departments decided upon this procedure, the county was soon blanketed by a literal maze of crisscrossing departmental jurisdictional lines. Any one place might fall within the branch-office jurisdiction of five or six different departments, each operating from a different location.

It is difficult to determine the precise moment when the need for greater simplification and integration of decentralization programs became evident to county management. During the late 1930's, serious thought was given to discovering some solution to the problems resulting from unplanned, scattered, piecemeal decentralization. By 1941,

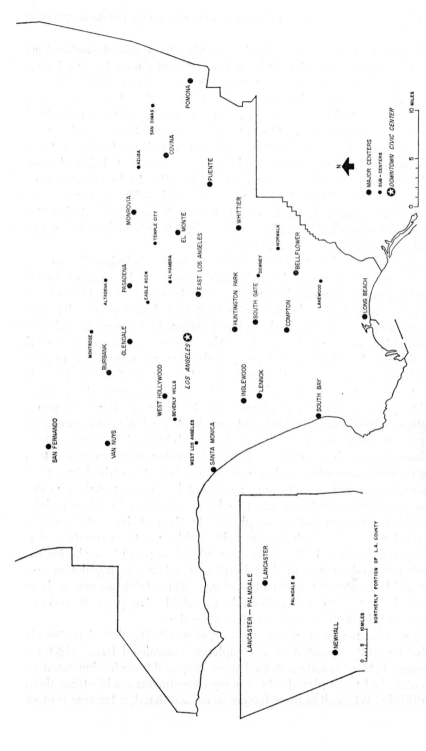

FIG. 16. Branch administrative centers, county of Los Angeles, 1962.

official reports made occasional references to proposed studies that sought to integrate widely dispersed departmental branches at selected sites. Gradually the concept of branch civic centers crystallized.

Studies conducted during the early 1940's analyzed the patterns of county decentralization from an economic standpoint and emphasized the fiscal-economy theme. One report focused attention upon the economies that might be derived by replacing rented quarters in outlying locations with county-owned buildings. It recommended that clusters of county agencies most suitable for combination be brought together at a single location. Citizen convenience and public economy were felt to go hand in hand. However, it soon became evident that the quest for simplification and integration had to extend beyond an initial concern with economies per se.

A number of determinations had to be made, including the size of service area to be assigned each branch, functions to be accommodated, and the most desirable location for each branch center. The service area or range had to be determined for each function on a basis of (a) mileage to be covered, (b) population to be served, and (c) available transportation facilities. The departments involved varied with respect to their clientele, responsibilities, procedures, techniques, and existing decentralization programs. They also differed in the criteria used for determining their workloads. For example, the work of libraries was generally considered to be directly proportionate to population, while Charity Department case loads tended to fluctuate with economic or seasonal conditions. Responsibilities of the Agricultural Commissioner, however, have little relationship to either population or economic conditions. It became obvious, from the earliest investigations, that complete uniformity could not be superimposed upon departments whose field organizational requirements differed so widely.

The picture was further complicated by the fact that certain county agencies were already housed in field establishments on county-owned property. Tentatively these were considered as possible nuclei for future centers by virtue of their location in relation to population and available transportation facilities. Some field establishments, such as material yards, were objectionable to neighboring property owners, however, due to the type of activity engaged in.

Consideration was also given to the possibility that departments that currently operated on a completely centralized basis might require a field organization in the future. Proposed branch administrative centers had to be placed where many departments could utilize them fruitfully. When all of these factors were considered, it became evident that the subject was much more complex than economy in property management.

PLANNED DECENTRALIZATION

The trend toward planned decentralization received its most important impetus in April, 1944, when the county board adopted a resolution by Supervisor Oscar Hauge of Long Beach directing the Regional Planning Commission and the Bureau of Administrative Research[2] to investigate the possibility of further decentralizing county functions and services. These bodies were directed to go beyond a plan for the physical location of branch offices and to determine what departments or functions should be decentralized and the manner in which it should be done. This gave the planners the top-level policy that they required.

The Bureau of Administrative Research was assigned responsibility for evaluating costs and operations. It examined the relative economy of branch and central operations, judged in terms of the total cost and by comparison of personnel, housing, equipment, and transportation expenses. Certain intangibles, such as costs to the citizen at large estimated in terms of time and convenience for those conducting public business, the value of county buildings as neighborhood civic assets, and the desirability of bringing county government closer to the people, were considered. The Bureau also calculated *minimum* workloads for branch operations (the point at which it becomes uneconomical to establish a branch office), and *maximum* economic workloads for *central* headquarters (the point at which it becomes imperative to shift a portion of the function elsewhere). Sixty-one functions of county government were scrutinized.

Conclusions of the study evolved around two major questions: should a given function be executed on a decentralized basis; and should functions requiring decentralization be located in branch civic centers or in detached district offices? Each function analyzed was assigned to one of seven categories, depending upon the degree of decentralization recommended and the preferred type of sites for the branch offices. A total of thirteen potential branch civic-center locations was listed. From this analysis it was concluded that each branch civic center should serve an area with a five-mile radius.

The Regional Planning Commission sought to prepare preliminary

---

[2] The Director of the Bureau of Administrative Research reported directly to the Chief Administrative Officer. This bureau has since been revamped as the management division in the office of the Chief Administrative Officer.

plans for branch civic center sites, make site selections, prepare an economic analysis for each site, and set forth a projected schedule for developing the branches. Its staff analyzed the types as well as the number of quarters needed: offices, laboratories, services and maintenance facilities, and warehouses. They sought answers to many questions. What combinations of branch offices had to be located near each other? What offices had to be remote for special reasons? What special facilities were required? How much off-street parking was needed for each site? How much garage space should be allowed for departmental vehicles? Were there any unusual building requirements to be considered, such as height or special types of insulation or plumbing?

An equally difficult problem involved determining which county facilities should be located within the boundaries of incorporated cities. In some instances, it might be possible to serve city residents from branch offices located in unincorporated areas, although in others a city location would better serve residents of both incorporated and unincorporated territory. Where possible, the planners hoped to have the county participate in existing municipal civic centers. In some instances, such as the city of San Fernando, the county had already established branches for the county Library, Justice Court, Health Department, Charities Department, and Agricultural Commissioner. Some county branches occupied quarters in the same building with municipal offices. Of the ten branch county centers recommended by the Regional Planning Commission in its preliminary program in 1943, five were to be located within incorporated cities.

Recommendations of the Planning Commission and the Bureau of Administrative Research provided a foundation for planning the county's decentralization program. The data uncovered caused central management and top-level departmental personnel to examine existing operations and projected needs carefully.

ADMINISTRATIVE SERVICE AREAS

As an additional major step, the Planning Commission decided to divide the county into a number of geographical areas and to develop a "master map" in order to gain an idea of the relationship between geographical boundaries and departmental service areas. This facilitated analysis of boundaries in relation to population distribution and anticipated population growth.

The proposed administrative service-area boundaries that emerged from this study were closely related to the census tracts and statistical areas established for the entire county in 1940 in collaboration with the Regional Planning Commission, the Los Angeles Chamber of

Commerce, and the Bureau of the Census. The planners concluded that a new "master level" of countywide administrative boundary lines should be developed to encompass the total county area, including Los Angeles City. On the basis of these considerations, the previously recommended pattern of thirteen branch county centers was abandoned in favor of one comprising twenty-eight administrative service areas that would blanket the entire county. Each proposed area would be served by a major branch center and, in some cases, one or more subcenters. The final boundaries recommended coincided closely with those of the population statistical areas.

It soon became evident, however, that administrative service-areas, adopted as the solution to the problem of attaining a more "logical" administrative structure, could not be applied with equal validity to all operating departments. The planners had aspired to bring virtually every county department within the framework of the administrative service-area pattern. Some departments, however, did not perform the type of functions that could be assigned to standardized administrative areas. The probation, history, science and art, and forester and fire warden departments were among those considered to be of a special-purpose nature. Although there was strong support for coördinated decentralization at common sites for most county departments, such specialized activities as probation camps and correctional institutions could not be reconciled with this proposal.

Top management of county departments that already operated on a decentralized basis were lukewarm to the administrative service-area plan. Brief consideration of a suggestion to appoint area coördinators further hardened departmental resistance. Though granting tacit approval to the administrative service-area plan, the board of supervisors never formally established the areas, although maps were distributed widely and received much public attention. The plan is currently utilized as a general guide in determining the locations of branch county centers.

THE BRANCH CIVIC CENTER CONCEPT

The decentralization program conceived by the Regional Planning Commission was really a two-pronged affair, consisting of administrative areas *and* branch civic centers. The latter concept was destined to have a potent impact on county administration, although it was not designed to stand independent of administrative service-areas. In essence it calls for the grouping of public offices and facilities on a common site or in immediate proximity to one another. From the planners' viewpoint, each center requires a specific geographical jurisdiction that does not overlap or conflict with the respective jurisdictions of other centers. After determining the scope of each administrative service area, a center grouping offices and other facilities could be planned. At present, Los Angeles County operates twenty-four major administrative centers and thirteen subcenters.

The civic center program was not without tensions and difficulties in its embryonic stages. Several departments had not considered a decentralization program and had no policy with respect to it. Several others, equating decentralization with the modification of existing administrative jurisdictional boundary lines, were suspicious that the consequences might be undesirable. Many programs had been laboriously worked out and the possibility of interrupting hard-won budgeted commitments produced strong resistance. On the other hand, some departments were eager to move into new branch civic center quarters. This dichotomy between the "ideal" of the planners and the "operational problems" of individual departments was a recurring theme throughout the period of initial planning for greater decentralization of county government.

EVOLUTION OF DECENTRALIZATION PROGRAMS: LOS ANGELES CITY

STEPS TOWARD PLANNED DECENTRALIZATION

Los Angeles City faced problems, similar to the county's, of providin public services efficiently and conveniently over a large geographical area that encompassed widely dispersed population centers. Several decades ago, it was recognized that the main civic center in the downtown Los Angeles area was inadequate to serve the entire city. Central-area traffic congestion, transit problems, an ever-increasing volume of public business, and limited physical facilities forced a recognition of the need for establishing branch civic or administrative centers. Losses in time and money became apparent as central offices sent their personnel to outlying areas of the city.

A systematic, top-level study of the matter was not made, however, until 1946, when the City Planning Commission undertook a survey of potential site locations. A special city coördinating board, composed of the principal department heads, the City Administrative Officer, and the mayor, discussed the problem and requested the planning commission to prepare a report relative to grouping branch public facilities in various parts of the city.

Several municipal departments had begun to decentralize early in the century. In 1909, the building and safety department established a branch office in San Pedro. By 1925, branches of the departments of police, health, and water and power were operating in several outlying districts of the city. The task facing municipal authorities in 1946, like that facing county officials, was the preparation and execution of a scheme that would coördinate decentralized facilities scattered throughout the city. The rationale behind this program was similar to that in the county; that is, economy of operations by reducing rentals, economy of maintenance, and citizen convenience. It was also anticipated that coördination between departmental headquarters and field personnel would be improved.

The Planning Department completed its study of branch administrative centers in the San Fernando Valley before proceeding to investigate the feasibility of other appropriate locations. Following consideration of this proposed program, the City Coördinating Board concluded that it was highly desirable to group related public facilities on appropriate sites to form branch or community civic centers. It also declared a policy that the city would welcome county, state, and federal jurisdictions to locate certain of their branch offices on the same sites.

In 1950, the Planning Department completed a master plan of branch administrative centers in which it recommended a total of twelve to be located in widely separated parts of the city.[3] Areas in greatest need of branch facilities were designated largely on the basis of estimates of population density and distribution. The department concluded that a reasonable radius for an area to be served by a major branch center would be three miles; that by a minor center, two miles. Many citizens could walk to the nearest center; others could drive there in five or ten minutes; even those dependent upon public transportation could reach their destination in less than thirty minutes.

A number of city departments were housed in individual buildings located within various Los Angeles communities. Three communities, Van Nuys, West Los Angeles, and San Pedro, had municipal buildings in which several city departments were situated. These were the nuclei for future branch administrative centers and were accorded much weight because it was considered advisable, from an economic standpoint, to utilize existing buildings wherever possible.

City departments, like those of the county, were surveyed in order to evaluate current as well as prospective needs and to allow for contemplated expansion. The city's approach to ascertaining future departmental needs differed markedly from that of the county. Time

[3] See Los Angeles City Planning Commission, *Branch Administrative Centers* (Los Angeles, 1950).

limitations, and difficulties in obtaining comprehensive data on departmental floor-space needs, prevented the city planners from preparing a detailed survey. Site selections were narrowed on the basis of approximations from available departmental data. The city planners also utilized a design approach that emphasized architecture and physical layout. The most significant departure from the county approach was that no overlay grid of administrative service areas was prepared. City planners had witnessed the county's difficulty in comparing and reconciling the many departmental service boundaries, and concluded that any attempt to utilize a superimposed grid of administrative boundaries was likely to be unsatisfactory.

The final master plan, based upon these studies and projections, proposed twelve branch administrative centers, to include nine major and three minor centers. The principal distinction between the two categories is that major centers include a municipal building that houses a large and varied number of city departments, whereas minor ones generally comprise a number of separate buildings for individual agencies grouped on a single site.

The present system of administrative centers conforms to the concepts of the master plan, but there have been a number of modifications. The number of major centers has been decreased and the number of minor ones has been increased. Currently, the city operates four major centers[4] (now called "regional centers") and nine minor ones ("district centers"). Regions have been selected by dividing the city into four "natural areas": San Fernando Valley, Western, Wilmington–San Pedro, and Downtown. These areas are based upon such factors as topographical features, land use, and distance from other regional centers. Each so-called natural area is assigned one administrative center and several district centers. San Fernando Valley and Downtown have three each, Western has two, and Wilmington–San Pedro one (see fig. 17).

Special mention should be made of the regional center in Van Nuys, because it has been the site of the most extensive branch operations. City planners recognized that the San Fernando Valley, particularly the Van Nuys section, was growing at a rate that surpassed any other portion of the city. Their projections indicated that the Valley would be one of the most populous and, from a governmental standpoint, active regions in the city. Consequently, the Van Nuys regional center was planned to be second only to the civic headquarters in downtown Los Angeles. This center is unique as a municipal case of governmental

---

[4] The downtown Civic Center is considered to be one of the four regional centers.

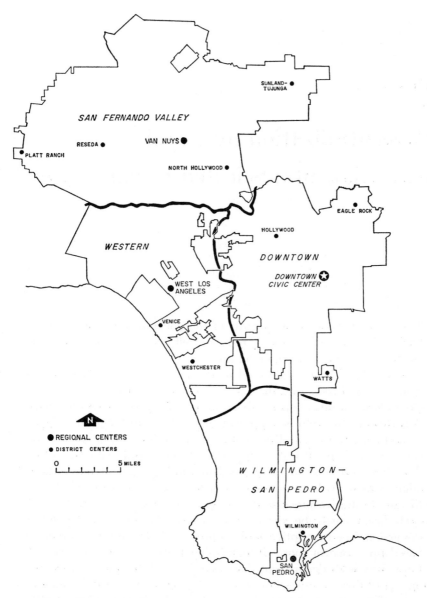

FIG. 17. Branch administrative centers, city of Los Angeles, 1962.

decentralization. No other branch administrative center in Los Angeles has equal facilities. Departments presently operating from it include those of City Attorney, Civil Service, Fire, Police, Health, Planning, Public Defender, Social Service, Building and Safety, and Public Works.

ELEVEN

Decentralization by Local
Governments: Selected Departments

THE DECENTRALIZATION PROGRAMS of the governments of Los Angeles
City and Los Angeles County represent efforts to meet the conflicting
demands of constituents and yet remain effective providers of services.
Branches have been established in various locations to reduce inconvenience to citizens and increase administrative efficiency. The principle of decentralization has been so fully accepted that only a few
departments now find no employment for it, and if long-range departmental plans are true indications, the trend will be towards even more
extensive and sophisticated employment. Twenty-six city and county
departments and agencies engaged in varying types of decentralized
administration will be considered in this chapter. The complexity of
the administrative process and the numerous aspects from which decentralization may be viewed require selection of a focal point for
discussion. The descriptive analysis presented here will use a typology
based upon one or more distinguishing features of the services performed by each department discussed. We will attempt to assess the
impact of these features but will avoid giving highly detailed descrip-
tions of the operations, emphasizing instead the major characteristics
of each program.

It should be noted at the outset, however, that certain characteristics
and problems are common to *all* organizations that undertake to decentralize. Issues that represent common denominators in *all* decentralized administration include: determination of the types of responsibili-

ties to be assigned to field personnel and of the degree of independent judgment to be delegated to them; creation of an adequate communications system; the nature and extent of central supervision over field operations; and maintenance of the delicate balance between the requirements of branch autonomy and central control.

Inevitably some overlap occurs among the departments discussed. Certain features are common to *all* agencies, to a greater or lesser degree: *all* departments, for example, operate within a legal framework, employ a number of professional personnel, and conduct some activities that may be termed "place-oriented." These characteristics are less prominent, however, in some agencies than in others in which their impact upon the decentralization process is more pronounced. This distinction forms the basis for the grouping of certain city and county departments in this discussion.

THE EMERGENCY, UNIFORMED CORPS

FIRE PROTECTION

Operations of the city Fire Department and of the county Forester and Fire Warden Department are similar in a number of respects. The station or company is the lowest level of administration in both—the level at which direct performance of fire-fighting responsibilities takes place. Los Angeles City operates ninety-six stations; the county maintains one hundred and five. Each station or company is headed by a captain who has complete charge over its operations, conducting them within the framework of rules and regulations formulated by authorities at central headquarters. A group of fire stations comprises a battalion, which represents the regional level of administration. The city is divided into fourteen battalion regions; the county into twelve. Each battalion encompasses four to ten stations (five to twelve in the case of the county) and operates under the supervision of a battalion chief. Battalions, in turn, are grouped into divisions. The city has six divisions, and the county has three; each division is headed by a division chief.

Decisions relating to the number and location of fire stations are largely influenced by standards formulated by the National Board of Fire Underwriters, an organization that grades the fire-fighting ability of cities. Adherence to board standards is reflected in fire insurance rates. Factors included are the number of stations within a general area and the amount and kinds of fire equipment needed within a certain response-distance from a heavily populated area.

The need for rapid response has forced departmental officials to reconcile two contradictory administrative requirements. Speedy suppression of fires necessitates a considerable degree of freedom, on the part of lower echelon employees at station and battalion levels, from central supervision and red tape. Station commanders facing a rapidly advancing fire cannot be expected to clear with central headquarters regarding the way the fire is to be fought. The extensiveness of decentralization, however, has produced a highly complicated administrative structure—responsible for day-to-day, routine maintenance of the organization per se, as well as for handling fires on an emergency basis—that demands a high degree of central control, supervision, and coördination. These contradictory requirements have been reconciled, in both departments, by a system that permits station captains to exercise considerable flexibility in coping with fires occurring within their jurisdictions, but that counterbalances this flexibility by a formal chain of command, beginning at the station level and going up through the intermediate echelon to central headquarters. Recruits are constantly reminded of the importance of rigid adherence to this command channel, thereby obviating communication problems that may stem from a failure to report directly to an immediate supervisor. A station captain, for example, though permitted to bypass his battalion chief in seeking advice from a functional specialist at central headquarters, is never under the immediate supervision of that functional specialist, who merely serves in an advisory capacity. Immediate supervisory authority rests with the battalion chief.

Formal methods of communication and control further enhance supervision and coördination. Battalion chiefs make frequent field trips to stations under their command to evaluate fire-fighting performance. Each station captain is required to make monthly reports giving statistics on emergency responses and a summary of fire alarms received. Individual fire reports are required in cases involving damages in excess of $100. Battalion chiefs, in turn, meet with division chiefs for periodic conferences that provide an opportunity to discuss problems concerning the operation of the stations. Instructions are often disseminated at these conferences, and training films are frequently shown. Perhaps the most important communication and coördination device is radio, which links the entire organization, facilitating unified action and control.

The relative success of the city and the county in reconciling the contradictory administrative requirements may be attributed, in large part, to another outstanding characteristic of the fire-fighting function, *esprit de corps*. The fire-fighting force, whose members are distinguishable from other public servants by their physical attire, resembles a military organization in several respects. No single individual is able to stem a major conflagration without assistance from others; fire-fighting, like battle, is a *group* effort executed directly under a commander. Exposed to conditions of extreme emergency and danger, firemen must depend upon coördinated teamwork not only for the successful execution of their responsibilities but also for their own personal safety and survival. These conditions have stimulated the development of a military-type organization characterized by rigid adherence to orders, techniques designed to prevent individual abuses of discretionary authority, strict indoctrination and training, and unfailing obedience to the designated chain of command.

POLICE PROTECTION

Police services, like fire protection, are executed within the framework of a military-type organization characterized by a distinctive uniform, the emergency nature of duties and responsibilities, and performance under a chain of command. Both functions require decentralized provision of services in the interest of speed and efficiency, which produces a highly complicated administrative organization encumbered with problems of supervision and control. These problems are even more acute in police activities than in fire operations. Fire personnel arrive at the scene in a body, an organized company. The policeman, on the other hand, answers requests for assistance and executes his patrol responsibilities alone and in the absence of direct supervision. This additional delegation of responsibility is inherent in the nature of the police function and creates a great need for clear policy directives down from the chief to the individual policemen.

When Los Angeles incorporated as a city in 1850, a single police station supplied all of its protective services. As the city grew, it became necessary to establish other stations to protect outlying areas. During the early part of the twentieth century, Los Angeles was divided into a number of geographic police divisions that have not been altered substantially since. The Patrol Bureau, the basic functional administrative unit, comprises fifteen of these geographic divisions. Each division operates from a police station headed by a captain, who is responsible for commanding station patrol forces and exercising functional control over other police units performing in the area. At present there are fourteen division stations; they are grouped in four geographic areas, each of which is headed by an area inspector or commander. Each station captain is accountable to his area commander, who reports directly to a deputy chief at central headquarters.

The county Sheriff's Department, like the city police force, has divided its jurisdiction into a number of districts, thirteen of which are now quartered in branch stations; three additional stations are scheduled for construction. Each branch is assigned to one of three inspectoral districts, each of which is supervised by an officer whose command duties are comparable to those of a fire department battalion chief. Branch stations, in both city and county jurisdictions, serve as the district headquarters for patrol, detective, and crime prevention unit personnel. They also provide the public with conveniently located offices to which requests for assistance can be directed.

Both departments permit station commanders considerable flexibility in supervising day-to-day police operations. They may redeploy their personnel in response to an emergency situation or request assistance from adjacent stations without prior consultation with central headquarters. Area inspectors are expected to coördinate police programs embracing more than one station, although this discretion is counterbalanced, in both departments, by fairly extensive central supervision. Station commanders are required to forward a constant stream of reports to upper echelons and to attend monthly meetings conducted by area inspectors. Reports and meetings are directed toward such matters as operational problems, personnel items, and requests for policy decisions. Duplicate copies of all reports forwarded by branch stations are received and filed at central headquarters. The area inspector has daily contacts with heads of functional divisions at headquarters, supplemented by more formalized meetings conducted by headquarters personnel.

Decentralized operations instituted by both the police and fire departments of Los Angeles City and Los Angeles County represent efforts to meet the dual requirements of speedy service rendered directly at the location of the crime or conflagration, and centralized supervision and coördination to ensure a reasonable degree of uniformity in functional performance. The trend has been to increase decentralization and to emphasize coördination rather than prescription.

A STRICT LEGAL FRAMEWORK

To a greater or lesser extent, all public employees operate within a framework of legislation, rules, and regulations governing their actions. These legal restrictions are more evident in some functions than in others, however. The relationship between the intensity of this legal framework and the decision-making process as it operates within a decentralized organization is well-exemplified by the Bureau of Public Assistance[1] and the Probation Department.

PUBLIC ASSISTANCE

The county Bureau of Public Assistance has two broad types of responsibilities: programs administered solely by the county in the field of general relief, and state programs administered under state law and under regulations promulgated by the state Department of Social Welfare. The latter include assistance to the aged and to dependent and self-supporting blind, aid to the needy and the permanently disabled, and medical aid to persons on the public assistance roles. The bureau operates through fourteen district offices, twelve of which handle all categories of assistance. The two exceptions are the most populous districts in the metropolitan area, where separate offices are maintained to administer each program. Although district offices are located with a view to serving the needs of concentrated clientele groups, some inevitably have heavier workloads and greater responsibilities than others. In addition to these regular branches, the bureau operates seven suboffices that were established from time to time in response to community need. Because these offices are small and are uneconomical to operate, the bureau hopes to reduce their number in the near future.

Unlike numerous other departments and agencies with field offices, a majority of Public Assistance branches are located outside branch civic centers, in buildings initially acquired by the state when old age assistance was a state responsibility. Professional social workers, keenly aware of the psychological problems faced by handicapped or needy individuals subsisting with public aid, emphasize the need to select inconspicuous sites for welfare offices. Assistance recipients must be given an opportunity to conduct their transactions in an atmosphere somewhat removed from the public eye. Branch civic centers, which are characterized by intensive activity and the presence of large numbers of persons, do not meet this requirement.

Branches have brought the bureau's services closer to its clientele. All case work is conducted there; central headquarters is responsible for general administrative duties, policy development, and supervision.

---

[1] The Bureau of Public Assistance is one of eight divisions in the County Department of Charities. As this discussion is not intended to be an exhaustive analysis of departmental operations, attention is limited to the Bureau of Public Assistance on the grounds that its operations clearly illustrate the relationship between legal restrictions and decision-making in the field. It should be noted, however, that the following departmental bureaus are also decentralized: Bureau of Adoption (two branches) and Medical Social Service (fourteen branches).

Branches also produce administrative advantages. State law requires social case workers to investigate every applicant for assistance and to repeat the inquiry periodically so long as the individual remains on the public assistance roles. Prior to the development of an extensive system of branches, a case worker was obliged to travel long distances from downtown headquarters to any number of outlying communities throughout the county. Decentralization, by placing the case worker in a branch office near his welfare clients, has reduced administrative time and travel expenditures.

Decentralization in the Bureau of Public Assistance, as in other departments and agencies, is based upon a hierarchical organization. Each district is in charge of a director who is responsible for a staff comprising one hundred to four hundred case workers and clerical personnel. Assisting the district director are supervising case workers who guide and review the work of groups of five to six social workers. Headquarters-field supervision and coördination are maintained through conferences and reports, supplemented by additional communications as needed. Instructions and notices are periodically forwarded from the central office to district directors. The latter meet with central headquarters personnel each month and with their own staffs every week. The field offices transmit statistical summary reports, covering such items as applications received, applications granted, and the number of cases handled, to central headquarters weekly and/or monthly. District directors exercise considerable discretion regarding case workloads, office procedures, and district personnel assignments.

The actual operation of this system can be understood, only if it is considered in terms of the legal framework within which public assistance services are performed. The county's Bureau of Public Assistance, operating most of its programs as an agent of the state, is closely circumscribed by state laws that limit administrative discretionary authority. This legal framework does not substantially alter the prerogatives of the district director, who enjoys considerable freedom in managing his staff. It is the social case worker who is most affected. Closely bound by laws, rules, regulations, and detailed manuals, he operates within the confines of a system in which eligibility and procedural questions are clearly and rigidly defined. As a result, most cases are handled in a routine fashion, insofar as eligibility is concerned. Restrictions are compounded further by the heavy case loads assigned to the bureau's social workers. Workloads and the increasing complexity of welfare cases place severe limitations upon the amount of time that may be devoted to each client. The case worker's one major area of discretion lies in his ability to motivate his client to achieve greater "self-help," an ability that helps to distinguish the "exception" from the "average" in the profession. It represents an intrinsic understanding that does not appear in any manual; it cannot be captured and quantified in detailed instructions.

PROBATION

A number of significant comparisons may be drawn between the probation function and public assistance services. Both deal with individuals under extreme stress and require extensive field investigations. Both are closely circumscribed by legally established standards and procedures; both require an ability to manipulate a person's attitudes and behavior. Operating under state and county statutes, the county Probation Department conducts investigations to assist juvenile and criminal courts in determining the proper disposition of persons brought before them, and supervises adults and children placed on probation by the courts. Closely related specialized activities include making suitable living arrangements for juvenile-court wards who are unable to remain in their homes, maintaining local treatment facilities for juveniles, and conducting guardianship and custody investigations for the Superior Court.

Although the department operated branch offices in Long Beach and Santa Monica for a number of years, it did not fully decentralize its probation services until 1953. The motives behind this new policy are essentially similar to those that stimulated decentralization in public assistance administration: clientele convenience and savings in travel time and expenditures. The close relationship existing between the Probation Department and the court system adds another purpose, that of placing probation facilities closer to the court divisions they serve.

The department currently administers its program through ten district offices situated near the points where demands are or will be greatest. Each branch is headed by a director who is in charge of one to five "sections," and each "section" is composed of a senior supervising deputy and nine deputy probation officers. As the workload of a given branch increases, additional deputies and senior deputies are assigned until it reaches a maximum size of five sections, that is, a total of five senior deputies and forty-five deputies. If the case load increases beyond the five-section limit, another branch office is established. There is considerable variation in the geographical area encompassed in branch jurisdictions; the higher the delinquency rate in a given area, the smaller the geographical jurisdiction of the branch.

Branch offices are authorized to perform almost all probation services, including presentence investigation of persons convicted in criminal courts, investigation of juvenile cases to determine the need for juvenile court action, and supervision of adults and juveniles placed on probation. Preparation and filing of case records is done at the branches.

While the department has succeeded in transferring most of its operational activities to the field branches, the unusually heavy case loads and the legal nature of its duties have necessitated strong emphasis upon supervision and upon communication of central management's doctrine. To achieve this emphasis, headquarters conducts monthly conferences for the district directors. These sessions are supplemented by the distribution of operational manuals and a weekly departmental newsletter, all conveying information about departmental practices. However, the essence of central control in the Probation Department, as in the Bureau of Public Assistance, is in the legal framework of legislation, rules, and regulations that govern the actions of departmental employees. Here, too, the one major area of independent judgment open to field employees is the individual's ability to stimulate his client to put forth a greater effort to become a respectable member of society. The department's training program and its operating policies, as exhibited in the contents of its official manuals, are designed to encourage its employees to exercise this type of discretion. For example, Section 601.02 of the *Adult Manual* states: "It is the policy of the department to discourage personal telephone calls from clients to deputy Probation Officers at their home, except where such calls are made in an emergency." The manner in which such contacts are to be discouraged, the definition of precisely what constitutes an emergency situation, and the specifics of meeting this emergency are left to the deputy probation officer. Similarly, Section 602.03 states: "The deputy probation officer should assist the defendant to face the situation honestly and realistically and to assume his responsibility in meeting his problems." Decisions as to how this directive is to be implemented constitute the intangible essence of discretion in administration.

In evaluating the relative merits of decentralized probation activities, a number of major improvements are attributable to this type of administrative organization. Probation services are now available in close proximity to the probationer's residence. Decentralization has facilitated coöperation with community agencies; branches have become vital parts of the communities in which they are located. Travel time for departmental personnel and probationers has been materially decreased. Decentralization has stimulated greater initiative and incentive in field personnel by providing each member of a district staff with a reasonably complete understanding of the total probation situation. As a final by-product, geographical decentralization has aided the departmental recruitment program. Whenever possible, new personnel are assigned to the branch office closest to their houses. This policy has been especially effective in raising the calibre of the department's non-professional personnel.

SERVICES WITH PHYSICAL OBJECTS OF ADMINISTRATION

City and county governments perform a number of services that must, by their very nature, be executed from decentralized bases. In such cases there is a tangible, physical object of administration located in the field, and departmental employees must *go to* these objects in order to perform their duties and responsibilities. The work of the Assessor, the Agricultural Commissioner, the Road Department and the Department of Public Works fall in this category. Here, decentralization is not merely a matter of administrative or public convenience; it is the very essence of the function. Although centralized library or recreation services would constitute poor administrative practice, by burdening the citizen with an undue amount of inconvenience, the theoretical possibility of servicing the population of the county through a single library or park facility exists. This theoretical possibility does not exist in the case of the functions discussed here. Road Department personnel must go to an outlying area if they are to construct and maintain its streets; the Agricultural Commissioner's deputies cannot inspect newly received shipments without going to the port of entry; the Assessor's appraisers cannot fully evaluate property while seated at their desks in the downtown office. It is equally infeasible for the field personnel to operate from a centralized base because of travel costs and time expenditure.

THE ASSESSOR

The County Assessor is responsible for annually identifying, classifying, evaluating, and assessing taxable property. In order to perform these duties, the Assessor's department is divided into a number of specialized divisions, the most decentralized of which is that for residential personal property. This division is charged with assessing household furnishings, farm equipment, and livestock. Each year, deputy assessors call at all places of residence in the county to assess taxable personal property and assist householders in preparing their property statements.[2] For the convenience of the public in filing property state-ments and obtaining assessment information generally, branch offices are located strategically throughout the county. These branches are of two types: permanent and temporary. Four permanent branches house maps and assessment data, serve as general informational centers on a year-round basis, and provide headquarters for field assessors. These permanent offices are supplemented by three additional branches serving the public on a year-round basis but distinguishable in terms of their skeleton staffs, which are usually limited to one or two em-ployees at each branch. In addition to this permanent branch organiza-tion, there are some seventy temporary branch offices that operate dur-ing the peak assessment season, from January to May. The temporary branches are in county buildings or in rented space.

The land and building divisions operate with field staffs but do not maintain any district offices. Both are divided into nine districts, each of which is headed by a supervisor who is responsible for the performance of a number of deputy appraisers. Instructions are re-ceived, reports given, and coördination effected on an informal basis, with appraising crews congregating at each other's homes at scheduled times to receive their assignments and instructions from the foreman.

Decentralized performance is counterbalanced by an equally sig-nificant emphasis upon uniformity in the use of assessment techniques. Maintenance of uniform practices necessitates considerable centralized control over field operations, which is achieved through a number of devices. The work of each appraiser is checked by his foreman, who is in charge of a crew. The foreman, in turn, forwards reports of all assessments made by his subordinates to the central office where staff assistants in charge of equalization over broader geographical areas again verify the appraisals for uniformity and accuracy. Regularly sched-uled conferences are also conducted at the central office, during which field personnel receive instructions, present reports, and discuss tech-niques.

The Agricultural Commissioner

The decentralized program through which the County Agricultural Commissioner executes his mandate is similar to the Assessor's opera-tion in a number of respects. Both functions deal with tangible objects of administration located in the field; both have a workload influenced by seasonal factors; both operate a flexible system of decentralization

---

[2] Phillip Watson, elected assessor in 1962, has discontinued house-to-house appraisals of residential property and instead appraises furnishings according to a formula based upon a percentage of the value of the building.

through which considerable discretion is delegated to branch personnel, within the framework of rules and standards governing their actions.

The Agricultural Comissioner performs a protective function, in that his duties and responsibilities are designed to enforce rules and regulations that protect farmers and the general public in both incorporated and unincorporated areas. He enforces state laws and county ordinances intended to prevent the introduction and spread of agricultural pests; abates injurious insects, rodents, weeds, and plant disease; regulates pest-control operators and issues permits for the application of injurious materials used in pest control; controls and eradicates bee diseases; enforces laws preventing deception in the sale of fruits, nuts, vegetables, honey, eggs, poultry, meat, and nursery stock; and compiles statistics pertaining to crop production, acreage, and related data. The major administrative duties center around inspections, issuance of permits and certificates, and enforcement of quarantine regulations. Inspection assignments have made the field staff the primary force. Since few services are rendered at branch offices, field units—with the exception of the Lancaster branch, which has a permanent secretary— are not manned by a full-time clerical staff. Furthermore, offices are generally open to the public only during limited hours, although telephone communications are taken at any time.

Inspectional duties are distributed among eight divisions, of which five are subdivided into a total of twenty field districts. An inspector in each district is responsible for the entire operation within that jurisdiction. Each district inspector must be a college graduate and have majored in agriculture or a closely related field. The professional status enjoyed by district men enables them to exercise a considerable amount of discretion. With the exception of quarantine inspectors, who have routine schedules, most of the inspectional staff enjoy flexibility in determining their work schedules. An inspector is also permitted to rely solely upon his own discretion in determining whether a shipment will be accepted or a permit issued.

Headquarters-field contacts are frequent; however, they are generally designed to promote informational and instructional purposes, rather than explicitly to supervise and control. Inspection reports and duplicate copies of all permits issued at branch offices are forwarded to central headquarters regularly; but central review is cursory, in a sense, and approval is generally automatic. Field inspectors are often contacted by central headquarters via telephone, to inform them of newly received shipments that must be inspected in addition to regular assignments. Periodically, central agents accompany inspectors on their field trips, but this is generally done at the request of the inspector in cases where a special problem is encountered. Monthly conferences attended by the field personnel are similarly designed to acquaint the inspectors with new rules and procedures.

The relative freedom accorded field inspection personnel is partly the product of their professional status, but its delegation also facilitates enforcement of the rigid legal framework within which they operate. Detailed state legislation, supplemented by county rules and regulations, determines the standards and procedures they must use. These restrictions, in themselves, represent a supervisory tool, in that they carefully define the guidelines that direct the field inspector in meeting his daily responsibilities. The need for central administrative control is thereby diminished, since detailed rules and regulations already limit the range of independent judgment to be exercised by the men in the field, whose professional training makes them familiar with the objectives of the statutory directions.

The Agricultural Commissioner provides an illustration of informality in decentralized arrangements. The field inspector assigned to the Whittier-Downey area, for example, works out of a field office which is, in effect, little more than a store house, with only a caretaker to receive telephone calls. The agent covering El Monte, Monrovia, and Sierra Madre works from a branch office in the Health Center, while the Azusa inspector receives calls through the county building inspector's office. The Covina-Puente representative uses the West Covina county courts building as his base, whereas the San Dimas inspector takes all communications directly from his home.

THE ROAD DEPARTMENT

The county Road Department constructs and maintains all roads and appurtenant facilities in unincorporated county territory and performs street work for twenty-two cities by contract. The scope of its operations includes designing, building, and maintaining highways, residential streets, bridges, pedestrian tunnels, and underpasses, and installing and maintaining traffic signals, street lighting, highway safety lighting, parking meters, and other highway facilities.

The department is divided into ten administrative divisions, three of which are decentralized. The maintenance division performs its work through a series of field crews. Engineering services maintains local offices only for the issuance of permits. The field engineering division, responsible for the construction of mountain roads, utilizes prison labor and therefore administers several detention camps.

The maintenance division, comprising approximately one-half of the total departmental personnel, subdivides its jurisdiction into five road districts, each of which is under the supervision of a district engineer. Operating from a district headquarters facility that houses his clerical and engineering staff, each engineer is responsible for five to seven road maintenance subdistricts. He has fairly broad powers and exercises full responsibility for maintaining all roads and handling all complaints within his district, exercising a wide range of independent judgment relating to various facets of his duties. He initiates many maintenance and road force account projects in his district and transfers personnel among maintenance subdistricts as he deems necessary. The department relies upon him to make decisions regarding the need and timing of road repair work and the technical manner in which the work will be handled. The policy of delegating decision-making authority extends down to the road maintenance superintendents, each of whom is in charge of a subdistrict. Unlike the district engineer, whose decision-making power is justified by his professional status as an accredited engineer, the road maintenance superintendent is a nonprofessional. He is permitted a considerable amount of discretion in his work because he has had considerable on-the-job experience and encounters few technical problems.

Exercise of discretion by field personnel in the road department operates within the framework of a formal headquarters-field communication system. The district engineer is required to forward a work order to central headquarters for every job he undertakes, for the purpose of policy evaluation; approval is generally automatic so far as technical evaluation is concerned. Road maintenance engineers from the central office visit district offices at least once a week. Central headquarters conducts weekly staff meetings, primarily to ensure uniformity between districts, clarify policy determinations, and facilitate informational exchange and discussion. The district engineer meets with his road maintenance superintendents under similar arrangements. District engineers and road maintenance superintendents also operate under a formal code of legal standards governing the adequacy of streets within their respective jurisdictions. Here too, however, discretion is exercised with respect to the manner in which these standards are to be met.

Delegation of substantive authority is involved in the issuance of moving and construction permits. Decentralization of this service has recently been arranged for the convenience of citizens requesting permits or permit information. A permit section of the engineering services division is housed in each of the department's five warehouse areas. Permits issued by these branch offices are reviewed downtown; generally they receive almost automatic approval.

THE DEPARTMENT OF PUBLIC WORKS

The responsibilities of the city Department of Public Works are comparable to those of the Road Department, and like its counterpart, it exercises its duties from decentralized bases. Its decentralization programs are exemplified in the bureaus of engineering and street maintenance.[3] The Bureau of Engineering, which plans, designs, and constructs public works of all kinds, operates through six branch offices. The issuance of permits has also been delegated to the branch level. Each branch is in charge of a principal engineer, who is responsible for preparing plans and specifications for public works projects within his jurisdiction and for supervising the clerical and engineering personnel assigned to his branch. The Bureau of Street Maintenance is similarly decentralized as five administrative districts, which encompass twenty-two maintenance yards. It is also divided into four functional divisions. The street maintenance division maintains bridges, culverts, tunnels, pedestrian subways, street signs, and some state highways. It is also responsible for resurfacing, reconstructing, and cleaning streets. The street use inspection division enforces city ordinances and state laws pertaining to the use of public ways. The design, maintenance, and planning of landscapes, and the trimming of trees for public safety, are the responsibility of the street tree maintenance division. The fourth division, lot cleaning, destroys weeds on vacant lots and removes and disposes of rubbish to prevent fire or health hazards.

Comparison of the rationale behind decentralization of the two bureaus illustrates the two major reasons for establishing branches: citizen convenience and administrative efficiency. The engineering bureau was decentralized primarily to make its services more accessible to the citizen. Bureau personnel face numerous situations that require face-to-face citizen contact and decentralization has facilitated this contact by enabling citizens to file requests for permits or street-construction work near where the work is to be done. It has also improved relationships between citizens and officials because it enables the

---

[3] As this discussion of decentralization is not an intensive analysis of departmental practices, attention is limited to decentralization programs in the bureaus of Street Maintenance and Engineering. The following departmental bureaus are also decentralized: Bureau of Contract Administration (one branch, plus office space in five of the six branches of the Bureau of Engineering) and Bureau of Sanitation (five branches).

professionally qualified district engineer to keep close contact with his area and its citizens, and provides him with a greater understanding of public-works needs and problems. The Bureau of Street Maintenance, on the other hand, has decentralized to improve operational efficiency by locating necessary equipment and manpower close to the scene of actual construction.

Public Works headquarters-field communications and control are implemented through a number of devices similar to those employed by the Road Department. District engineers are required to make detailed reports daily to headquarters on the progress of public works projects, in terms of amount of work accomplished and number of man-hours spent. All plans and specifications prepared in the field, and all permits issued at branch offices, require central approval. Central headquarters conducts meetings regularly to communicate policies and management attitudes; the sessions are held more frequently and in a more systematic manner than in the Road Department; as in the Road Department, legal standards provide an additional element of supervision and control. Similarities between techniques of administration and control utilized by the two departments can be deceiving, however; there are substantial differences in the way they apply the techniques. According to Road Department administrators, the exercise of a branch administrator's discretion and freedom from central control over technical evaluations are the keynotes of decentralization. Although branches are required to make detailed reports pertaining to work progress and permits issued, in matters of technical evaluation central approval is generally given routinely. While the Road Department is concerned with uniformity and respect for the legal requirements, its management believes that standardized procedures preclude the need for excessive central review of detail matters. Administrators in the Department of Public Works, on the other hand, emphasize the need for uniformity in granting permits and for rigid supervision to ensure adherence to the legal standards governing public works matters. Central approval is far from being routine; all permits and work orders forwarded by branch offices are checked thoroughly by central headquarters to prevent arbitrary, if unintentional, variations in granting permits and to assure compliance with prescribed standards. These differences seem ones of degree rather than of kind. One department emphasizes branch discretion and the other stresses uniformity and the legal requirements. This distinction is probably explained by the fact that key administrators apply administrative theory differently in comparable situations.

PLACE-ORIENTED FUNCTIONS

Certain functions of city and county government may be termed
"place-oriented," in that clientele must *go to* the facility in order to
utilize the services it provides. Park and recreation and library services fall into this category. The citizen must go to the recreation facility to enjoy the amenities of recreation programs; he must go to a
library to select and borrow the book of his choice. These services are
also distinguishable from other public functions in that they represent
"leisure-time" activities that citizens participate in voluntarily. They
possess few regulatory aspects, nor do they embody a sense of urgency.
Nevertheless, decentralization programs conducted by the recreation
and library departments of city and county government are older and
more extensively employed than those of the other departments analyzed. The city and county library systems operate a combined total
of no less than one hundred and sixty-two branches; city and county
recreation facilities number over four hundred.

Recreation and library officials, alike, view decentralization as an essential aspect of their program because it helps implement the goal of
enhancing "public convenience," in the broadest use of the term. Although a citizen will travel a considerable distance to obtain the building permit he must have in order to build an addition to his house, he
may be unwilling to travel the same distance to select a desired book
or to spend the day at a park or playing field. The leisure-time, non-
regulatory aspects of recreation and library services mean, in effect,
that the citizens must be *stimulated* to utilize these facilities. Decentralization, by placing services within reasonably easy reach of potential
recipients, is an effective means of providing this necessary incentive. Its effectiveness is attested to by the extensive utilization of services provided at branch locations. Many, including the young and the
aged, the handicapped and the wage earner, would otherwise be prevented from enjoying these services. Bypassing, for the moment, the
very real question of the physical impossibility of accommodating a
countywide clientele at a single recreation or library facility, it is
valid to predict that a relatively small number of persons would utilize
these services if they were centralized in a single facility. Stimulating
public usage through decentralization is a significant aspect of city and
county recreation and library programs.

Library Services

Decentralized library services in the Los Angeles area are significant,
both in terms of the number of branches dispersed throughout the

county and the important role played by the regional administrative personnel. The City Library's extension service plan, first conceived and developed by Everett R. Perry, City Librarian from 1911–1933, was set towards a goal of "giving each branch a circle of service of a half-mile radius." [4] The extension library system grew, in approximately thirty years, from a single delivery station to a network of forty-nine branches and one hundred and eight other library outlets.

These additions derived from a variety of transactions. Several incorporated cities, which had public libraries, consolidated with the city of Los Angeles. When unincorporated territory served by a branch of the county library system was annexed, the library was added to the city's system. Library stations established in outlying parts of the city grew and developed with the communities they served until they were replaced by branch libraries. Branch libraries were also established in communities formerly without library service of any kind. The greatest development took place between 1913 and 1928, thirty-one branch libraries having been constructed during this period. Development of new communities produced a steady demand for new branches and stations. Shifts in population and neighborhood changes made it necessary to reëxamine the Library Department's branch library system and building program. In 1950, the department began to reorganize its operations on the basis of recommendations made by the city Bureau of Budget and Efficiency. In doing this, it introduced a regional level of administration in the extension system. The city is now divided into six geographical library regions. Fifty-three branches, seven of which are called regional branches, and eight subbranches[5] are located within these regional boundaries. Each regional and community branch is headed by a senior librarian who is responsible for the entire branch operation. These field administrators have been delegated authority to select books for their branches; to train, supervise, and assign specific duties to branch personnel; to arrange daily and vacation schedules; to supervise the processing of books; to prepare and present annual budget requests; and to supervise the preparation of statistical reports regarding circulation, registration, and book holdings. The six branch libraries that have been designated regional libraries were selected because they were reasonably near the center of their districts and were in locations that would facilitate receiving book deliveries from the central library and distributing them to other libraries in the region.

---

[4] Everett R. Perry, *Handbook of Branch Libraries* (Los Angeles: City Library, 1928), p. 35.

[5] *Subbranches* are open to the public fewer hours per week than regular branches and are headed by persons in a lower professional classification.

Regional libraries perform two major functions. They serve as additional extension agencies to assist the public in making use of library services. Each is provided with a more substantial book fund than regular branches, enabling it to purchase a greater number of selections and to strengthen the resources of the entire district. Regional libraries also serve as administrative centers assisting central headquarters in supervising the numerous branches, and as comprehensive libraries providing direct service to the public.

Regional librarians have achieved a significant position in the administrative system. They exercise considerable review authority over the operation of the branch and subbranch libraries assigned to them; for example, book selection, hiring and assigning of branch personnel, and supervision of the general operation and maintenance of branch facilities. When branch librarians select books from the central order list, although the branch director has ultimate authority, advisory comments from the regional librarian are given careful consideration. Similarly, annual budget requests, though initially drawn up by branch personnel, must receive regional approval before they are considered by the departmental administrator, who is known as the Division Librarian for Branches. Furthermore, the regional librarian is in constant touch with his branches through regularly scheduled field trips.

At the top of the administrative hierarchy stands the central headquarters of the city Library Department, located in the downtown area. The central library also provides the public with a vast collection of circulating and reference volumes. The Division Librarian for Branches, whose office is at central headquarters, exercises final supervisory authority over all branch operations, including regional libraries. All acquisitions are made at cental headquarters, and branch librarians are rarely permitted to purchase a book that is not already available in the central library collection. As a result of this policy, principal librarians in the subject-matter departments at the central library, in effect, make the initial selection for the entire system.

In executing supervisory responsibilities over the extension system, central headquarters places considerable emphasis upon regularly scheduled meetings with regional- and branch-level representatives. These meetings serve a number of purposes. The division librarian for branches conducts a monthly meeting of regional librarians to discuss general problems of branch administration, and a biweekly adult-book order meeting, for the purpose of presenting reviews of books on the order sheet from which branch librarians make selections. This latter meeting is attended by regional and branch librarians, and those in charge of subbranches.

The county Library Department, operating under a similar regional system, currently maintains nine regions, which embrace a total of one hundred and nine branch libraries. The first region was established in 1930 and encompassed the Antelope Valley. The remaining eight are products of post-1950 developments. The administrative operations of the county library system are similar to that of the city system in most major respects. However, there are some differences. For example, in the county system, central headquarters provides no direct services to the public; its functions and responsibilities are limited to administration, supervision, and control of the whole system. Another significant difference relates to the fact that the city's branch book collections are permanent ones selected by the branch librarians for their respective communities, whereas in the county branches, the collections are not permanent but are assigned by the regional librarians. Each county regional library has its own book budget for books and related materials recommended by subject-matter specialists at headquarters. The regional head assigns books to the branches in response to requests from patrons and branch librarians.

PARK AND RECREATION

Los Angeles County began providing park and recreation services in 1911, when the Board of Supervisors created the Board of Forestry and assigned it responsibility for roadside tree planting and maintenance. Park and recreation programs grew steadily from that time. By 1944, the department was operating forty-five park areas and nine beach properties covering 1,075 acres and seven and one-half miles, respectively.[6] Today, the department operates and maintains 137 park areas covering 10,538 acres, and thirteen beach properties encompassing nine miles of land.[7] Administration and maintenance of park and recreation facilities are decentralized on a countywide basis but are directed by a single departmental administrator who is responsible to the Board of Supervisors. Functional programs are assigned to separate divisions.

The recreation division is divided into three districts, each of which is in charge of a director who is responsible for the programs performed within his geographical area. He establishes community recreation programs and evaluates them and their facilities for adequacy and adherence to departmental standards. He is directly responsible for supervising all park installations in his area. He prepares, justifies to

---

[6] Los Angeles County Department of Parks and Recreation, *Yesterday—Today* (Los Angeles, 1960), pp. 2–5, 11.

[7] *Ibid.*, pp. 4–5, 11.

departmental management, and administers the district budget, compiles data and reports, and supervises employees within his jurisdiction. In the departmental hierarchy, he is directly responsible to the superintendent of recreation, who represents another major administrative level in the department's decentralized operations. Two to four recreation supervisors are assigned to each district, depending upon the size of the area and the scope of its operations. Each is responsible for supervising school and park playgrounds, and pays frequent visits to the facilities within his jurisdiction to check staff performance and the adequacy of physical facilities. A playground director administers the scheduled programs at each playground installation.

The park division, headed by a superintendent, is similarly decentralized. It encompasses three maintenance districts, each of which is in charge of a park foreman, who also directs the maintenance personnel. Personnel responsible for maintaining all county recreation facilities—electrical work, plumbing and so forth—operates from two regional service yards, each yard supervised by a master mechanic. District directors, and the supervisory personnel at each successive hierarchical level, enjoy considerable freedom from central control in making day-to-day operating decisions. They are not required to make formal written reports, except when specific information is requested. However, the district recreation director and all supervisors below that level must obtain clearance from their superiors prior to implementing decisions affecting departmental policies. In addition, the district director attends regular staff meetings with the heads of functional sections at headquarters. At these meetings he is briefed concerning departmental policies and is given an opportunity to discuss field problems.

Los Angeles City municipally operated recreation facilities were first offered when the Violet Street playground opened in 1905. By 1926, there were forty-three.[8] Today, the department maintains 112 parks, 113 playgrounds, thirty-six swimming pools, and eleven miles of beaches. Each conventional park or playground is manned by two persons (one man, one woman), who are responsible to a district recreation director. There are eight such directors, each in charge of a geographical area within the over-all city jurisdiction. Each has six major responsibilities: generally to supervise employees assigned to each park and playground facility within his area; to issue permits for public use of recreation facilities; to enhance effective and fruitful public relations with various recreation-oriented community organiza-

---

[8] Los Angeles City Department of Playgrounds and Recreation, *Annual Report, 1925–1926* (Los Angeles, 1926), p. 7.

tions operating within his jurisdiction; to process complaints; to plan additional installations and facilities; and to promote events and activities involving more than one center.

In addition to the eight geographical divisions that were established to implement the city's decentralized recreation programs, the municipal jurisdiction is also divided into nine maintenance districts. The personnel of each district includes a foreman who is responsible for maintaining the parks and playgrounds. The district foreman is, in effect, the maintenance counterpart of the district manager. He is responsible for deploying maintenance equipment to all parks and recreation facilities in his jurisdiction, supervising maintenance personnel, determining the adequacy of maintenance equipment and the need for repairs, and investigating complaints pertaining to facilities. He is directly responsible to the central maintenance division which is located in Griffith Park.

Communication within the park and recreation system is maintained through regular telephone conversations, periodic bulletins issued by central headquarters, and frequent visits to facilities by district recreation directors and foremen. Day-to-day operating decisions remain largely within the province of the immediate supervisor at all levels of the hierarchy.

THE PREDOMINANCE OF PROFESSIONAL PERSONNEL

The employee corps of city and county governments possess a multitude of skills that are similar to those found in the private segment of the economy. Most public agencies, like those in the private sphere, employ both professional and nonprofessional personnel. Investigation indicates that persons in city and county government service who have gained a professional status have relatively greater freedom from central control than do the nonprofessionals. In order to evaluate this relationship between professional status and freedom of action, departments in which attorneys predominate will be examined, that is, the city and county Public Defenders, the District Attorney, and the City Attorney. The city and county health departments, in which physicians exercise the leading roles, are also considered in this context.

THE PUBLIC DEFENDER

The Public Defender represents persons involved in criminal court action who are financially unable to obtain the services of a private attorney. This service is provided by both the city and county governments. The city Public Defender works in cases involving misdemeanors committed within municipal limits; his county counterpart works at all stages of the proceedings over matters tried in Superior Court. The county office performs its work at three branches; the city Defender operates four, in addition to one at traffic court. Each field office is staffed by one deputy. The two Public Defenders have joined the trend toward decentralized provision of services. Citizen convenience, savings in travel time and expenditures, and a subsequent improvement in public relations represent major benefits that have accrued from the establishment of branch offices. However, in the initial stages of development, both faced problems in distributing their available legal manpower, because of the uneven distribution of case loads that was characteristic of the public-defender function. The workload at certain branches tended to fluctuate greatly and, at times, was unusually light, as compared with that at central headquarters. A given deputy might handle as few as two cases a day at a branch office, and his talents could have been used more profitably to ease the heavy volume of business handled at central headquarters. Uneven distribution of workloads among branch offices is still a problem for the county Public Defender, although it no longer exists in the city, where a notable increase in cases has resulted in the fuller utilization of deputies assigned to branch locations. The latter are assigned a large enough number of cases to assure a full working day on a regular basis. Indeed, the city's present problem is that of securing an adequate number of deputies to staff the branch offices.

Unlike many other city and county functions, services provided by the Public Defender are not in steady and consistent demand. While the democratic right to legal aid is beyond question, the average citizen seldom, if ever, requires the services of the Public Defender. This consideration, coupled with the adequate coverage presently afforded the more densely populated areas of the county, makes it unlikely that many additional branches of either the city or county Public Defender will be established in the near future. The value of existing branch facilities, however, and the need for an enlarged staff at these existing sites are testified to by the extensive use made of the services at the branch locations. Of the 27,930 cases coming before the county Public Defender in 1960–61, 4,085 were handled at branch locations; and 124,240 of the 125,624 misdemeanors handled by the city Public Defender in 1959–60 were arraigned at branch offices.[9] Future field expansion will lie in increasing the personnel assigned to these facilities.

---

[9] Of the 124,240 misdemeanor arraignments, 108,682 were handled at the Lincoln Heights branch location in the downtown Los Angeles area.

THE DISTRICT ATTORNEY AND THE CITY ATTORNEY

The District Attorney is responsible for prosecuting all felony cases in Superior Court and all misdemeanors arising in unincorporated areas or in cities with no prosecuting services. The vast extent of the county area has necessitated the establishment of Superior Court Divisions with criminal jurisdiction in areas outside the downtown Civic Center. Through the years, the District Attorney's office has instituted its branches to supply prosecutors for those courts. When a felony is committed in an outlying area, branch-office deputies handle all stages of the prosecution, from issuance of the complaint through the trial. The duties performed by the branch deputies are therefore the same as those conducted by the complaint, preliminary hearing, and trial deputies at the main office. All stages of misdemeanor prosecutions are also conducted in branch offices. The District Attorney's staff now operates through five branch offices and twelve area locations; branches, unlike the area offices, have jurisdiction to try felony complaints. Area offices are mainly concerned with presenting evidence at felony preliminary trials and with prosecuting misdemeanors. It is anticipated that seven new facilities will be opened and increased space will be allotted to many of the branches by 1967.[10]

The City Attorney serves as the legal adviser to elected officials and department heads, represents the municipality in all litigation in which it is involved, and prosecutes misdemeanors cited by city police for violation of the charter, municipal ordinances, and state laws. This office presently operates through five branches for prosecuting criminal cases; all civil matters are handled at central headquarters.

The geographical decentralization of both the City Attorney's and the District Attorney's establishments has inevitably paralleled that of the court system. Decentralization has greatly improved their service to the public by making it possible to solve a variety of problems through informal discussions between the field deputy and the citizen with a problem. Furthermore, field deputies, working in close relationship with law enforcement officers, are in an excellent position to provide police field units with informal advice. Decentralization has not been without its problems, however. In the case of the City Attorney, difficulties have been those minor ones that arise in any organization requiring over-all supervision and coördination of branch operations. Because decentralization in the District Attorney's office

---

[10] See Los Angeles County Chief Administrative Officer, *Proposals for Future Capital Projects, 1957–1967* (Los Angeles, 1957), pp. 174–177.

has been more extensive in nature, however, that office has faced problems that are considerably magnified.

Under present arrangements, all District Attorney's field branches report directly to the chief of branch operations, located at central headquarters. This system has extended the chief's responsibilities beyond the optimum span of control. In view of this, the District Attorney and his advisers have seriously considered designating a number of the branches as regional headquarters and interspersing them between central headquarters and the branch offices. Branch office deputies would report to a regional headquarters, and the three or four regional branch directors would report directly downtown to the chief of branch operations.

Communication is another problem for the District Attorney's office. In the absence of regularly scheduled staff meetings, attended by all branch deputies, headquarters-field communication is conducted on an individual basis. This results in diversity in policies and procedures. An individual moving from one section of the county to another finds the branch offices serving the two areas differ in the kinds of services provided.

THE CITY AND COUNTY HEALTH DEPARTMENTS

The city and county health departments conduct programs of communicable disease control, environmental health, health education, laboratory services, maternal and child care, and vital statistics. Decentralization has been especially necessary for these departments, partly because the public health function requires the performing of services directly for people, and partly because the population growth in their respective jurisdictions has spread over wide geographical areas.

The organizational key for both departments is a district system. Soon after the county Health Department was established in 1913, it was recognized that distance was the greatest obstacle to adequate public health service. The state legislature gave impetus to the decentralization movement in 1919 when it authorized city councils to petition the county to supply basic public health services, as defined by the statute, and to contract for the enforcement of municipal health ordinances. Pomona promptly negotiated a county contract for public health services and, in 1919, the county established its first local public facility in that municipality. By 1924, the county Health Department completed a comprehensive plan for the decentralization of its health facilities, which it submitted to the Board of Supervisors. The crux of this plan was the division of the county area into a number of districts, each comprising several cities and surrounding unincorporated territory, and each provided with a separate health facility. The first of these proposed district centers was established in San Fernando in 1926.

This plan has evolved to the point that there are now fourteen district health centers and nineteen subcenters, serving the entire county except the four cities that maintain independent departments. Each district center is under the supervision of a district health officer who is, in turn, responsible to the county's health officer for the quality of services provided in his jurisdiction. District health centers are designed to handle all public health services encompassed within the county's jurisdiction. Subcenters, on the other hand, need not cover all functions; and in some instances they specialize in particular services that respond to health problems peculiar to the area served. The city Health Department employs a district system that is similar to the county's though it was not fully developed until a later date. Ten districts, encompassing sixteen health centers, are presently maintained by this department.

Both health departments' concepts of district health centers are similar in many respects. Both have created major health centers fully equipped to conduct a fairly complete public health program within their districts, and in both systems each district is headed by a district health officer who is supported by a full public health staff, including nurses, physicians, sanitarians, medical social workers, and medical investigators. All these people are coördinated and directed in functional specialties by various divisional specialists who are housed at central headquarters in downtown Los Angeles. Each district health officer and his executive staff determine policies and plan programs in consultation with the administrative staffs of the districts. The various health centers dispense most direct health services to the public; the few health activities that are performed centrally include preparation of vital statistics, laboratory analyses, industrial health, and general administration. Branches possess limited laboratory facilities for routine analyses. In addition, the city performs selected medical care services, such as maternity, child health, and alcoholic rehabilitation, at the central headquarters; but the county refrains from providing any direct medical-care service at its headquarters. The latter makes a distinct division of responsibility between its central headquarters and branch health centers. Complete responsibility for medical services is delegated to the branches; central headquarters is responsible only for exercising general supervision and providing special technical services to facilitate branch operations.

Those favoring decentralized provision of public health services see it as a means to make service and treatment more accessible to the public, thereby stimulating greater use of the available services. It has also enabled a department to tailor its public health programs to the problems and needs which are characteristic of different communities. Decentralization is an expensive operation, however. Departmental officials believe that the additional expenditures incurred are the direct result of increased demands for services, rather than of decentralization per se. With the exception of expenditures for buildings, decentralization, in and of itself, has not been responsible for larger budgets, since the expenditures would have been incurred in any event, due to increased population and increased service demands.

BRANCH AUTONOMY IN A PROFESSIONAL SETTING

Those departments that are characterized by a predominance of professional personnel have a distinctive strength that permits them to delegate to field personnel a greater degree of authority for operations. The professional status shared by the leading group of the department's personnel assures a common orientation and a certain level of knowledge and competence. The individual professional person is bound by a code of ethics, apart from departmental policies, that tends to prescribe standards and set limits upon his independent action. Professional ethics in themselves serve as an informal supervisory tool, thereby limiting the need for extensive formal supervision by top management. Attorneys and physicians employed by public agencies operate within such an ethical framework, as do their counterparts in the private sphere. This does not mean that such employees are given a completely free hand in performing their official duties as public employees. Deputy public defenders must attend regularly scheduled conferences conducted by the departmental management and are required to file written reports on all cases assigned to them, as well as a daily worksheet indicating the number of cases handled and the amount of time expended. Representatives from central headquarters visit branch offices of the District Attorney and the City Attorney on a regular basis. Headquarters-field communication is achieved in the city and county health departments through regular staff meetings with district directors, periodic field trips, frequent telephone conversations, and numerous reports that are designed to inform headquarters of the various phases of public health program operations conducted in the field.

Despite these techniques of supervision and control, however, wide areas of independent judgment remain available within which the public health physician and attorney may operate freely on the basis of his professional status. Public attorneys are given complete discretion regarding the general strategy and tactics to be used in conducting individual cases. Headquarters rarely interferes, and such interference as exists is generally limited to cases that have created an undue amount of publicity, or in which a branch attorney has reached a decision that conflicts sharply with departmental policies.

Physicians are similarly delegated discretion and encouraged to perform their duties within the bounds of professional doctrine. The relationship between a particular health officer and his patients is certainly one in which the physician is given complete discretion. The major restrictions relate to the eligibility of patients for clinics. Under existing laws, a number of services are provided on the basis of eligibility standards, and it is the medical social worker, not the attending branch physician, who determines whether or not a given patient is eligible to receive treatment.

A "BUSINESS" ENTERPRISE

THE LOS ANGELES CITY DEPARTMENT OF WATER AND POWER

Perhaps the most important characteristic that distinguishes the Department of Water and Power from other public agencies is the degree to which it resembles a private corporation in its orientation. Unlike other city and county departments, it is concerned with making direct sale of services and collecting monthly payments. These considerations have a direct influence upon its pattern of administrative decentralization. Development of branch offices depends largely upon the clientele's habits in paying their bills, with branches being designed to expedite prompt payment for services. Space available for exhibits in branch offices also helps to publicize departmental services and becomes a supplemental advertising device.

This department is a self-sustaining municipal enterprise providing Los Angeles citizens with water and electric energy. It maintains a headquarters office in downtown Los Angeles, three district offices, and twenty branches located at strategic spots throughout the city. This geographic-organizational hierarchy forms the basis for the decentralization pattern currently in use. District and branch offices operate under the jurisdiction of a district and branch offices section, which is located in the main department headquarters building downtown. District offices perform most of the functions assigned to the commercial division whose headquarters is in the central office, and principal functions include: receiving, recording and implementing customers' orders for the connection or discontinuance of light, water, and power services; obtaining credit information and determining applicants' financial responsibility in order to maintain adequate security on all customers' accounts; maintaining records of customers' deposits and services; making meter readings; collecting moneys due the department; and inspecting and adjusting electric and water facilities, equipment, and meters. Each district office, which is headed by a district manager, also performs the regional level of administration and exercises general supervision over branch office operations. Since many records are deposited at the district office, branch personnel can quickly obtain information on a customer's payments record by telephone, teletype, and telautograph communication. In addition, branches forward daily collection reports to the district office, and the latter, in turn, reports periodically to central headquarters and also forwards daily time reports concerning employees of branch and district offices.

Branch offices serve as general informational centers, accept orders and display electrical appliances, and receive bill payments. They also serve as a headquarters for field collectors, servicemen, inspectors, and meter readers. Collectors and meter readers operating in the field represent in themselves a facet of the department's decentralized operations.

Authority to exercise a number of assignments previously performed by central headquarters has been delegated to district and branch personnel. However, the main downtown office continues to perform exclusively such activities as addressographing, maintaining customers' application and order files, billing, key punching, tabulating, and bookkeeping relating to the department's Wire on Time Payment Plan. Branch employees have a wide range of discretion to extend time for payment of bills and determine the amount of deposit required of customers, within general limits set by departmental policies. Duties and responsibilities of branch and district employees alike are carefully set forth in written specifications prepared by the department, however, leaving little choice to local managers.

The department's decentralization program provides its customers with a number of alternative locations at which regular departmental business may be transacted. Its clientele may now pay water and power bills at the central office or at any one of the three district offices or twenty branch offices, as the customer chooses. To further extend this service, the department has instituted a unique type of machine, the Self-Service Payment Depository, which is located in markets and other public places in certain areas where clientele-need is not great enough to warrant establishing a separate branch office.

This department is one of the few agencies characterized by a decrease in decentralization. When first instituted in 1922, branch offices formed part of a long-range plan to facilitate prompt payment of water and power bills. The program was given an additional impetus during the depression period, when adverse economic conditions increased the number of delinquent bills. Changes in economic conditions in recent years and the development of new management practices have produced a decline in the need for branches. Only one office has been constructed during the past ten years, and there are no plans for establishing new ones. This reversal of the trend is the result of procedures that encourage customers to place service orders by telephone and pay bills by personal checks sent through the mail. While the branches' workloads are still sufficient to warrant the continuation of existing offices, there has been some cutback in personnel. Differences in clientele habits have influenced the location and retention of several branch offices. A disproportionately large number currently are in low-income communities, where delinquent bills are relatively frequent and checking accounts are not extensively used. Residents of high-income communities, on the other hand, are more prone to utilize checking accounts in paying their bills, resulting in a concomitant decrease in the need for branch facilities.

In evaluating the decentralization program, departmental administrators refer to a number of benefits that have accrued to both the department and the clientele it is designed to serve. Accessibility and better customer relations are noted as major advantages to the public. From the departmental management point of view, the program has aided recruitment, produced savings in transportation time, and facilitated control and supervision, which are so essential to a large-scale operation of this type. Furthermore, management believes that decentralized operations, coupled with the delegation of reasonable autonomy to branch personnel, have stimulated greater initiative and improved performance.

STAFF FUNCTIONS

Decentralization has not been restricted to the traditional "line" department operations. The staff agencies, Civil Service and Planning, in particular, have been moving in a similar direction. As staff organizations, they have been called upon to give the line, or operating, departments special assistance in creating field organizations and locating regional and district offices. They have now discovered that their own activities may be improved by revamping their organization.

CIVIL SERVICE

Civil Service agencies of the city and county have decentralized their operations by minor degrees for several years, limiting them to utilizing billboard space in other departments' branch facilities, for example, libraries and police and fire stations, to post recruitment announcements. The city Civil Service Department has posted its examination announcements in branch offices of the Water and Power Department for close to twenty years. Serious possibilities of comprehensive decentralization were not considered, however, until the early 1950's. The city Civil Service Department took the first step in 1955 when it opened a branch office in Van Nuys. Subsequently, it also installed a drop-box for applications in the Westchester branch City Hall. Applications were accepted at the San Pedro City Hall and forwarded to central headquarters for processing. Similar arrangements that are now in operation at the West Los Angeles City Hall are planned for other branch civic centers.

An unusually great increase in the number of mail applications for civil service appointments emphasized one need for decentralized operations; applicants were evidently averse to traveling a considerable distance, through heavy traffic, to file applications at the downtown office. The department also assumed that by facilitating the application process, it would encourage a larger number of persons to file for employment, thereby widening the area of competition and improving the quality of personnel hired. The validity of this assumption is difficult to assess empirically but is supported by departmental opinion.

At the present time, the Civil Service Department's branch office in the Van Nuys City Hall is its only field establishment staffed by a full-time employee. This employee receives and passes upon applications, determining applicants' eligibility to file, in accordance with bulletin specifications. This process was formerly conducted exclusively at the departmental headquarters in downtown Los Angeles. The branch facility serves as a general recruiting information center for the community in which it is located, and enables individual citizens to seek city employment near their residence or place of present employment.

The initial decision to establish a branch or an information center has been based, in large part, upon the present location of other municipal offices. The civil service function, according to departmental administrators, is peculiarly suited to decentralization, due to the relative simplicity of the operations involved. Because only a small number of employees are required to staff branch operations, the central headquarters does not run a risk of increasing its own workload with extensive supervision. The civil service function is conducted within the framework of a number of long-established procedures, rules, and regulations governing applications, protests, and related aspects of civil service. These formal rules and regulations have tended to diminish the degree of discretion that branch personnel may exercise. Central supervision now consists of a review of applications forwarded by branch offices, in order to assure the uniform, equitable application of existing standards. The department has also obviated the need for increased expenditures, which usually accompany decentralized operations, by utilizing personnel formerly employed at the central office, and by borrowing employees from other departments, to staff branch offices on a temporary basis. For example, the drop-box at the Westchester branch is presently serviced by a regular employee of the Bureau of Engineering, who distributes application blanks and provides information. Many departments, recognizing the importance of the civil service function to their own recruitment needs, are willing to lend their personnel. The Civil Service Department assures a degree of uniformity of practices by requiring all branch employees, including those assisting from other departments, to complete a brief training period at its application counter in the downtown office.

The county Civil Service Department was motivated by similar considerations of public accessibility and improved recruitment, but its program is characterized by a more significant degree of delegation of duties and responsibilities to branch personnel. It recognized by the 1950's that the central headquarters had an ever-increasing workload of applications and examinations, and experiments with various methods of decentralizing recruitment were made. Application and information centers were established in approximately twenty-five offices of the County Marshal and in all branches of the County Library. A college recruitment specialist was delegated the task of contacting college placement offices, interviewing and selecting candidates on the campuses for engineering and other critically-short types of employment. In some instances, key personnel in line departments were deputized to recruit technical personnel in nationwide recruiting drives. The first branch office, located in Long Beach, was established in 1961. Selection of Long Beach was made because of the distance of this area from the central department in downtown Los Angeles, and the large number of county agencies already located there and thereabouts. The office is staffed by one technical specialist and two clerical workers, all transferred from the central office. Increases in budgeted expenditures were avoided. Assignment of a personnel technician to the field office is significant, because it makes substantive decisions possible at the branch level.

The county Civil Service Commission proceeded cautiously with decentralized procedures, assuming that development of field offices should be preceded by a reappraisal and, if necessary, a reorganization of central headquarters operations. An intensive analysis of these operations resulted in the introduction of a number of innovations, including installation of new tabulating machinery that scores tests in the record time of three seconds per test, conversion of reports on employee performance evaluation and on probation service to tabulating methods, and development of improved standardized test batteries. These newly instituted data-processing methods have had a startling impact upon the entire civil service operation and, therefore, upon the nature of decentralization. Personnel records, dating back to 1913, have been converted to punched cards, and all individual medical test records are being similarly converted. Mechanization has obviated the need for periodic mass testing and the inevitable time lapse between application and appointment so characteristic of traditional civil service techniques. Under the present system, application and testing procedures that formerly required weeks and even months to process are completed within a few hours. Many tests are now administered on a continuous basis and evaluated "on the spot." Today, an individual interested in a position with county government can file his application, complete his written, oral, and medical tests, receive the certification, and be appointed to a department within the space of a few hours!

Data processing, by facilitating the rapid recording and processing of vital data, has been equally beneficial to the administrator. Persons charged with managing the civil service operation are now provided with essential data, presented in precise tabular form. They may determine the number of positions to be filled and the number of applicants available to fill them, the types of skills possessed by employees, the exact number of positions filled at any given time, and numerous other matters. Administrative efficiency is thereby greatly enhanced.

By expediting the free and rapid flow of information, data processing has enabled central headquarters and its branch office to operate as a single coördinated unit. Although the civil service function is performed within the framework of rules and regulations that limit the range of independent judgment on the part of individual employees, there are certain areas in which substantive decisions must be reached in the absence of formally prescribed standards. The decision as to whether a given candidate meets the experience and educational qualifications set forth on a recruitment bulletin, and the ranking of applicants on an oral interview, both represent important decisions that require considerable independent discretion. The county commission has sought to delegate maximum discretion to its branch office, to avoid burdening the central office with excessive supervisory duties and to motivate branch personnel to do optimum work.

The Long Beach branch office has assumed all of the recruitment and examination duties and responsibilities performed at the central office, including testing, application, and certification work. It also handles steps in the continuous examinations. Decisions reached by the technician in charge of this field office, though theoretically subject to review by central headquarters, are, in fact, final; situations requiring headquarters-field consultation regarding specific day-to-day decisions are relatively rare. Applicants may complete the entire process, from testing to appointment, at the Long Beach branch, without any intervention from the downtown office.

Coördinating problems are not yet great, because the commission operates only one branch office. However, plans are in preparation for another, to be set up in the County Building in Santa Monica. Other field offices are contemplated, to tap employment resources in outlying communities and give speedier service to county departments' field establishments. Problems of communication and coördination will inevitably assume a greater magnitude as the number of branch offices is increased. The true potentials of a communication and data processing system as a vehicle to coördinate headquarters-field operations will be realized.

PLANNING

The Los Angeles City Planning Department currently operates four branch offices, in addition to its central office located in the downtown City Hall. The Regional Planning Commission, its counterpart in the county, has two branches. Both planning agencies established these field agencies to facilitate transactions between planners and citizens residing at considerable distance from the downtown Civic Center. The services provided are primarily informational in nature, 75 per cent of the requests relating to some aspect of zoning.

During the initial stages of branch development, the city confined the performance of all technical duties to the central office; branches were limited to providing zoning information, receiving variance requests, and giving instruction in the preparation of exception requests. The concentration of technical services at central headquarters limited field autonomy, since branch employees processing specific requests that required technical knowledge had to refer the cases to the central staff. In later years, however, the department has sought to delegate more and more of the actual technical operations that are local in character. With this thought in mind, it has staffed each branch office with a city planner who is competent in the necessary technical skills. This has raised the field establishments from their former position as mere informational counters and has enabled them to engage in such activities as preparing land maps for their respective jurisdictions. Branch representatives of the Planning Commission are also authorized to exercise certain delegated functions that accrue to the Director of Planning by virtue of statute law. These delegations include such subjects as granting setback modifications and determining compliance with landscaping and parking requirements. Branch employees discuss individual problems with citizens and review the pitfalls as well as the significance of specified requirements before accepting an application for variance or change of zone. However, while they are empowered to confer modifications under specified circumstances, their duties are generally advisory in nature.

The planning and zoning functions are a public responsibility characterized by rigidly detailed rules and regulations. The existence of formally defined procedures and standards that are designed to assure uniformity in the processing of zoning matters, for example, tends to restrict the amount of discretion exercised by field employees.

It has been noted that branch offices of city and county planning agencies serve as extensions of the central office information counter. These branches act as an arm of the central office in yet another respect. Branch personnel, being physically located in various communities and in constant contact with local residents, are in a position to observe community land-use patterns and to implement observation by field studies and verifications. Some field investigations are executed by the central office, but the time and expense involved in traveling between headquarters and the field inevitably reduces the number of possible trips and the intensity of the investigation. Communities served by planning agencies are now subject to a more realistic appraisal than was possible when planners, located in the central office, tended to equate community conditions with symbols on a land-use map. This close coördination between planners and the communities they are assigned to serve has enabled branch personnel to advise central headquarters of the community characteristics and needs. A related benefit is improved public relations. The tremendous population growth has made it difficult for officials at central headquarters to keep abreast of local problems and maintain fruitful relationships with civic leaders. Branch personnel help to close this gap.

Therefore, decentralization has facilitated and improved the planners' work in two respects. First, public inquiries have been encouraged and their response speeded by placing the planning staff in closer proximity to the citizens being served, and public relations activities, conducted by field personnel who are closely identified with the community to which they are assigned, have stimulated greater public interest in the planning agencies' work. Second, the planners are now provided a more realistic picture of community characteristics and needs through information supplied by staff members located in the field.

A STATE AGENCY

THE SUPERIOR COURT

The Superior Court of Los Angeles County shares many of the distinguishing characteristics attributed to other agencies and departments discussed in this chapter. Like the recreation and library departments of city and county government, it represents a "place-oriented" function whose clientele must *go to* the facility in order to utilize its services. It also resembles the administrative legal departments in that its duties and responsibilities are performed within the framework of a professional code of ethics and standards which guides the discretionary actions of persons serving the court. Despite these similarities, however, the Superior Court has many unique features that warrant its consideration apart from the administrative departments. The most obvious distinction is its legal status as an agency of the state. The legislature directs the county to pay a large part of the judges' salaries, to support a substantial portion of court expenses, and to provide courtroom facilities. The county government's support does not alter the legal status of the court as an independent state agency operating under self-established rules, subject to prescriptions by the state constitution, by statutes, and by the rules of the State Judicial Council.

The close relationship between the Superior Court and the regular county government organization is further exemplified by the large number of county employees whose work supports the court operations.

Ninety-eight per cent of the County Clerk's work is done for the court, in his *ex officio* capacity as Clerk of the Superior Court. Establishment of branches of his office has consistently followed the creation of branch courts in outlying areas. Other county departments serving the court include the County Counsel, District Attorney, Public Defender, Probation, and Sheriff. The close working relationships between the court and supporting governmental agencies have important implications for emerging patterns of administrative decentralization. A decision to decentralize courtroom facilities generally precipitates a similar decision by the numerous agencies whose duties are closely allied with court functions.

Organization of the Court. The Superior Court has jurisdiction to hear felonies, misdemeanors (unless otherwise provided for), civil matters involving sums over $5,000, conciliation and domestic relations cases, actions involving title to or possession of real property, and juvenile and adoption cases. The judicial manpower is composed of 120 elected judges, one or more of whom are assigned to special departments, such as civil, probate, pretrial, appellate, domestic relations, conciliation, adoptions, criminal, juvenile and psychopathic.

This extensive judicial system is headed by a Presiding Judge, elected by his colleagues for a one-year term, who organizes the judicial personnel and distributes assignments. In his capacity as the administrative head of the court, he directs the entire judicial operation, with the advice and assistance of several committees. One of his most important duties is assigning judges to specialized divisions and departments to which litigation is distributed, assuring a balanced, equitable distribution of cases among the available judicial manpower. Since 1958, the court has employed an executive officer who works under the supervision of the Presiding Judge, relieving him and the committees of the burden of administrative details. This county's court is the first trial court in the United States to delegate administrative responsibilities to a professional, nonjudicial manager. The executive officer supervises and directs all employees of the court, with the exception of commissioners. He administers the personnel system by implementing appointments, transfers and terminations of service (after consultation with the Presiding Judge and with the judge or supervisor concerned), and by approving sick leaves and vacations; he prepares and administers the budget; maintains accounting records, including payroll; establishes and maintains courtrooms, chambers, and offices; purchases law libraries, supplies, and equipment; and compiles and analyzes statistical data concerning court business. He maintains liaison with county departments serving the courts and with the twenty-three local bar associations, the state legislature, the judicial council, and with civic organizations. He also serves as the Jury Commissioner.

Decentralization of the Court. As early as 1928, it became obvious that Los Angeles County could not be served adequately by a single courthouse. The first branch was established in Long Beach because of the size and location of that city. Nine additional branches of the Superior Court were established by 1950. Until 1959, the decentralization proceeded in an unplanned, piecemeal manner, without due consideration being given to long-range, coördinated development of the system. These deficiencies were analyzed in a Haynes Foundation–supported survey of the trial courts in the Los Angeles metropolitan area.[11] The recommendations produced by this study were implemented by legislation in 1959, limiting the number of branch courts to a maximum of eleven and providing for a redistricting of the entire county. Each judicial district was designed to serve a minimum of three hundred thousand persons. This legislation sought to utilize judicial manpower more effectively by terminating the trend toward single-judge courts and by paving the way for a number of existing facilities to consolidate. District court boundaries, and the location of branch court facilities, were to be determined, finally, by the board of supervisors, provided Superior Court judges had previously approved the proposal. To date, nine districts have been established, and eighteen courthouses have been erected.[12]

Decentralization of the Superior Court has been conducted under vigorous political pressures. Practicing attorneys, whose work causes them to use courtroom facilities on a regular basis, often demand a degree of decentralization that surpasses the optimum point for efficient, economical operations. One such instance occurred in Beverly Hills, where members of the local bar association, local officials, and civic leaders made an unsuccessful attempt to have a courthouse established, contrary to the objectives of a 1949 statute that directed that no branch court be established in a municipality whose city hall was located less than eight miles from that of the nearest branch court. Since existing court facilities in Santa Monica fell within an eight-mile radius from Beverly Hills, the Board of Supervisors was averse to

[11] James C. Holbrook, *A Survey of Metropolitan Trial Courts in the Los Angeles Area* (Los Angeles: John Randolph Haynes and Dora Haynes Foundation, 1956).

[12] The Los Angeles Municipal Court, which has similarly extended its courtroom facilities to outlying areas of the city of Los Angeles, maintains four branch courtrooms outside the Civic Center.

erecting an additional courthouse. Practicing attorneys, on the other hand, based their claim on the unusually large number of their profession practicing in the latter city, and on the large concentration of business and commerce—which made Beverly Hills a primary source of civil litigation. They advocated that the location of Superior Court facilities be determined on the basis of the number of lawyers located in a given area. This criterion would have placed the city, which had more than eight hundred practicing attorneys, high on the priority list for additional courtroom facilities.

There have been other instances of this type, notably in the Southwest District where Inglewood vied with Torrance and finally won designation as a courthouse site by the joint action of the Superior Court judges and the Board of Supervisors in 1961. Courthouse site selection has been partially removed from local political pressures by legislative prescription, adopted in 1959, requiring concurrence of a majority of the Superior Court judges for establishment of any new courthouses or sessions of the court.

The District Courts. Specialization in trial work, accomplished by assigning special court departments, is gradually being extended to the outlying district courts, as their workload increases. Not all branches exercise the same types of jurisdiction, however. District courts in Inglewood, Long Beach, Pasadena, Pomona, and Santa Monica try criminal cases, as well as civil actions. Long Beach and Santa Monica are the only ones authorized to conduct juvenile cases. No district court has jurisdiction over psychiatric cases, however; they are handled by a special psychiatric department, located in the psychiatric unit of county general hospital. All district courts hear civil cases. The establishment of larger, all-purpose district courts served by several judges makes possible the organizing of special departments. When this condition prevails, it will be possible to require that all cases be filed in the court district within which they occur.

Twenty-seven of the one hundred and twenty Superior Court judges perform their duties in district courts. Each district is in the charge of a Presiding Judge, who has administrative supervision over the clerical, secretarial, and professional personnel assigned to his facility. Each judge is assigned, at a minimum, one clerk, a bailiff and a reporter. The jurisdictional responsibility for nonjudicial personnel in the branch courts is complicated, although the presiding judge of the district has primary, operational supervision. The executive officer of the Superior Court system is responsible for discipline of court attachés, but he takes action only after consulting the Presiding Judge of the branch.

The bailiff and the court clerk are employees of the Sheriff and County Clerk, respectively. Over-all administrative control of the countywide judicial system, including assignments of judges, is entrusted to the Presiding Judge of the Superior Court of Los Angeles County.

The status of judges as members of a profession and elected office holders must be considered when analyzing branch autonomy and exercise of discretion. Theoretically, the Presiding Judge is expected to scrutinize the manner in which judges under his jurisdiction perform their duties and responsibilities. Actually, however, his functions are set forth in general terms, and he has no decisive sanctions to assist him in implementing his authority. Therefore, he has been termed an "impressario" in his relations with his Superior Court colleagues.[13] His responsibility for evaluating the suitability of a given judge to handle a specific assignment and persuading the judge to accept it represents exercise of discretion and independent judgment which cannot be formalized in any legislative delegation.

Communication and coördination in Superior Court administration have been conducted in a relatively informal manner. Communication between the Presiding Judge and individual judges has been chiefly by telephone and mail. Former Presiding Judge Louis H. Burke supplemented this type of communication by circulating a monthly newsletter and distributing a comprehensive statistical report apprising the judges of developments in the various court departments and districts. This practice is being continued by his successor. While little emphasis has been placed upon plenary meetings of the court, other types of sessions are held frequently. The advisory committee, which is representative of the entire court and composed of one judge from each group of ten, meets monthly. It has been the Presiding Judge's practice to designate representatives of the branches, as well as of different administrative segments of the Superior Court, to the advisory committee. The court also maintains several other committees, including one on branch courts that advises on interdistrict and central-district relationships. The annual report, prepared by the executive officer, helps inform the administrative and judicial personnel of court developments.

Few would advocate rigid control over the manner in which judges conduct specific cases. It is significant, however, that many individuals, including a large number of Superior Court judges, favor vesting greater authority in the Presiding Judge to supervise judicial working schedules, including the number of hours spent on the bench and the amount of time cases are held under submission. These recommenda-

---

[13] Holbrook, *op. cit.*, p. 54.

tions question the assumption that the judges' professional status justifies their being "answerable only to themselves." [14] This issue has
figured several times in controversies regarding the need for additional
judges and courtrooms. Members of the Board of Supervisors have
questioned whether judicial manpower was being fully utilized. At
the same time, the court administrators have sought to have the court
clerks transferred from the County Clerk's Department and to integrate
all court administration and separate it from the county government's
administrative review.

The Value of Decentralization. Decentralization of the Superior
Court's facilities to suburban areas has facilitated accomplishing the
dual objectives, administrative efficiency and public convenience. From
the official point of view, it has helped to limit the heavy volume of
cases to be filed at the central county courthouse. As the manpower
and jurisdiction of the branches are expanded, the central courthouse
should enjoy even greater relief. Decentralization has also expedited
the judicial process, and thereby has aided the citizens' interest.
Attorneys, litigants, and witnesses, averse to traveling to the downtown
courthouse in connection with cases originating in distant parts of the
county, may now have many types of litigation transacted at a branch
facility situated more conveniently. The objectives of the judicial
process will be even further accomplished when the district courts'
jurisdiction is broadened to cover all types of litigation presently
handled at the courthouse in downtown Los Angeles.

---

[14] Jack W. Keating, "Huge Backlog of Cases Chokes L.A. Courts," Los Angeles
Examiner, Aug. 24, 1958, sec. 1, p. 19.

TWELVE

Decentralization:
Uniformity and Diversity

Decentralized programs in Los Angeles City and Los Angeles County show a mixture of uniformity and diversity. The necessity of servicing an increasing population, spread over a relatively large geographical area, provides the common theme behind them. Yet in actual operation the programs reveal a wide range of diversity in the manner in which they are performed and in the theoretical bases upon which they are formulated. What are the most significant features common to the departmental operations we have examined? What major variations are there in the patterns of decentralization, and why do they occur?

RATIONALE, INITIATIVE, AND SITE SELECTION

Departments of city and county government have been influenced by a myriad of factors that have been classified in three broad categories: demographic and topographical features, administrative needs, and political pressures. As the population grew and spread toward the suburbs, the central governmental headquarters became more and more remote. The local governmental administrators faced innumerable barriers to their attempts to provide efficient, accessible public services to new densely settled population clusters. The citizens, in turn, found it inconvenient to communicate with their public officials. The establishment of branch offices was a reaction to these inadequacies. It should be noted, however, that the increasingly comprehensive nature of governmental duties and responsibilities, reflecting a constantly growing demand for public services, was an unstated premise supporting the need for decentralized administration.

Administrators have played by far the most decisive role as initiators of decentralization. Their influence is evident in both long- and short-range planning. Long-range, coördinated plans were generally the product of analyses and proposals by central staff aides, representing the jurisdiction's planning department and budget or management office. Establishment of branch offices as adjuncts to separate departments, on the other hand, was planned and carried out by departmental administrators who were anxious to foster the program requirements of their respective clienteles. Stimuli of departmental actions were mixed. Professional administrators constantly strove to raise standards of performance for their departments. Those whose departmental status improved, with success in enlarging and perfecting operations, gained personal status and other satisfactions. At the same time, departmental administrators were driven on by a desire for survival. The department whose heads were slow to perceive the direction and nature of demands from the citizens found itself the target of displeasure from the political heads of the city or county. Often departmental decentralization resulted from discussions between administrators and the citizens of particular communities. In some instances, public employees took the lead and encouraged public demand; in others, the interested citizens brought their demands to the governmental representatives.

From the citizen's point of view, the pros and cons of administrative decentralization, if considered at all, are doubtless conceived of as theoretical issues. They acquire practical substance, however, when the citizen is—for example—victimized by a criminal because police protection is far away, or sees his home ravaged by a conflagration before a fire truck can arrive from a distant station. Citizen pressures, though significant in specific instances, tend to be sporadic in nature and selective in their goal. Public demands, often channeled through a county supervisor or city councilman, are usually focused upon the need for a specific branch facility of a particular department. They emanate from special groups whose activities place them in direct contact with public officials in various capacities. The vociferous role played by groups of local attorneys in stimulating the establishment of additional branches of the Superior Court is an excellent example of the influence of special interest groups upon decentralization programs.

Once the decision to decentralize has been reached, a number of equally significant factors enter into the process of site selection. Serious consideration is usually given to establishing a branch facility in an area that is characterized by one or more of the following conditions: a notable population growth; location at a distance from the downtown Civic Center; a sizable clientele group, utilizing the services of a given department on a fairly regular basis; and topographical barriers, such as mountain ranges and drainage channels, that make access to existing public offices relatively difficult. Two other factors frequently have weight. The impact of political pressures upon members of the Board of Supervisors and City Council has already been noted. Availability of transportation facilities, especially freeways or arterial streets, is an equally significant consideration. Areas with traffic congestion or inadequate transportation facilities are usually avoided. These prerequisites merely provide the general framework for site selection, however. Departments vary with respect to their clientele, procedures, techniques, and program objectives.

A number of departments are guided by widely accepted professional standards determining the minimum size of clientele or the level of service deemed sufficient to warrant a separate facility. The county Library Department, for example, estimates a branch library should service no less than seventy-five thousand persons, provide fifteen thousand to twenty thousand books, and have an annual circulation of at least forty thousand items, in order to operate at optimum capacity. The Recreation and Park Department is similarly guided by the National Recreation Association standards for minimum acreage and service coverage for various types of recreation facilities. The prime example of the relationship between site selection and pre-established service standards is the Fire Department's use of the National Board of Fire Underwriters' standards that estimate the number and size of stations required to service areas of prescribed population size.

The Department of Water and Power, on the other hand, expresses a primary concern with locating branch facilities in areas where customers are less likely to have checking accounts and are accustomed to paying bills personally. Library administrators, who are equally concerned with special clientele groups, seek to locate their branches close to schools and shopping centers. It is reasoned that students, and women visiting the library on their way to or from their marketing, are important clientele groups and that library facilities should be located where convenient to them.

Population distribution is an exceedingly important factor in determining branch locations of certain departments, but is of little consequence to others. The work load of the Assessor, for example, depends upon seasonal factors, although population growth and property development affect it too. The County Agricultural Commissioner's work has very little relationship to population growth or distribution. The Department of Public Works uses population growth as a major criterion in selecting branch locations for its engineering bureau, whose responsibilities relate to issuing permits, but the Bureau of Street Maintenance must place its branches according to administrative convenience.

The planners' concept of branch civic centers, grouping a number of city and county offices at a single location, has had a significant impact upon the site selection process, particularly for those departments whose work is closely related to that of other departments or agencies. The County Clerk, for example, has established ten branch offices in buildings that house the same number of Superior Court branches. Most departments tend to favor establishing their branch operations within a decentralized civic center, because it is more convenient for their clientele, and better parking, custodial, and communications facilities are available. The Bureau of Public Assistance, an interesting exception, emphasizes its need to select inconspicuous sites for field offices.

Departmental decentralization programs possess a number of common characteristics when viewed in terms of the rationale behind them, the major forces stimulating their development, and the criteria employed in the selection of specific sites. Yet, there is considerable variation in the actual emphasis given to these characteristics. Let us turn from an examination of the "external" aspects of the decentralization process to a résumé of the manner in which decentralization operates within the departmental hierarchy.

BRANCH AUTONOMY

The essence of the decentralization process rests with the delegation of independent administrative authority and decision-making power to field personnel. At the same time, the scope of public responsibilities and the complexity of activities performed by public agencies often necessitates an equal emphasis upon supervision of branch performance to assure a reasonable degree of uniformity. In surveying the manner in which departments and agencies have sought to reconcile this administrative conflict, it is evident that no single, uniform pattern has emerged. The degree of autonomy exercised by field representatives varies according to the nature of services provided, the philosophy of top management, and the capabilities of branch employees. Yet, one is struck by the fact that relatively little *significant* discretionary authority is left to the field in these two local governments. Major policy is still formulated at the central level of administration and field decisions relevant to it must be referred to central headquarters for consideration and approval. Field employees are consistently subject to formal and informal supervisory techniques employed by the central office.

City and county officials, operating as *public* agents, perform their duties within a legal framework that is designed to prevent usurpation of legally vested authority and to assure uniformity in the application of broad policy decisions. The public official executes programs financed by the taxpayers, and he is bound by legal restrictions whose purpose is to ensure responsibility. He cannot rely exclusively upon his own judgment in determining the degree of authority to be delegated to field agents under his jurisdiction. The insistence upon uniform treatment of citizens is reflected in a series of formal rules and regulations which limit discretionary authority. Decisions relating to zoning are reached within the framework of formally prescribed standards and procedures. Employees receiving civil service applications accept or reject them on the basis of predetermined minimum qualifications for the position. Permits issued at a branch of the Bureau of Engineering must be forwarded to headquarters for approval to prevent arbitrary, though unintentional, variations.

Public employees administering those aspects of local government that do not involve granting permits or licenses, or determining eligibility to receive public funds or employment, are generally permitted greater latitude. Furthermore, those positions that require greater expertise are likely to carry greater freedom from supervision. The technician and the journeyman craftsman have earned their right to perform their duties exempt from close supervision, whether performed in the field or in a central laboratory or shop. The professional person has, in addition to expert knowledge, a code of ethics and a background of training that guarantee a certain degree of knowledge and competence. The need for formalized supervision and control is thereby diminished, since substantive control of behavior is inherent in the ethics of the profession itself. Consequently, a deputy attorney exercises a range of discretion regarding tactics and strategy employed in handling specific cases. Engineers in the Department of Public Works, for example, are allowed a wider range of authority than are nonprofessional employees assigned to the department's street maintenance units. The same distinction applies to public health physicians and nonprofessional attendants working at the admissions desk.

Social case workers are also members of a profession, but they are not permitted the degree of freedom from central control enjoyed by other professional groups. They are expected to implement state and federal assistance programs that are closely circumscribed by highly detailed regulations governing the eligibility of applicants. Adherence to standards and procedures enunciated in these laws places a severe limitation upon the amount of discretion to be exercised by case workers.

The nature of the function being executed is a significant factor affecting the degree of authority exercised by branch personnel. The emergency nature of fire-fighting responsibilities and the primary requirement of speedy suppression of fires, for example, necessitates a considerable degree of freedom on the part of lower-echelon employees at station and battalion levels. The same condition applies to the police function.

Finally, the philosophy adhered to by top management, and the manner in which administrators at the upper levels of the hierarchy interpret the decentralization process, will have an impact upon branch discretion. Administrators who view substantive delegation of authority and responsibility as a means to achieve effective administration will make a strong effort to bestow as much discretion as possible upon branch employees under their jurisdiction. A number of administrators equate employee morale, reflected in improved performance, with authority to make important decisions without close supervision. This philosophy is clearly present in such organizations as the county civil service and probation departments.

In the final analysis, there seems to be a dividing line separating central control from branch autonomy. Central headquarters exercises ultimate authority on matters relating to coördination of the complete enterprise, and of research and planning to determine long-range objectives and the strategy to accomplish them. Branches are predominantly autonomous in short-term research, in providing direct services to the public, and in determining short-range tactics to meet the more immediate program objectives. Within this general framework, branch personnel exercise varied degrees of independent authority, depending upon the legal framework, the professional status of the employees involved, the nature of the function being executed, and the philosophy of top management.

COÖRDINATION, COMMUNICATION, AND CONTROL

In analyzing techniques employed by the city and county administrators to attain the objectives of coördination and control, it is infeasible to divorce supervision from the communication process, for a large number of techniques simultaneously facilitate central control over branch operations and provide effective headquarters-field communications. Obviously an efficient communication system is essential to adequate central supervision and coördination of field operations.

Virtually every decentralized department uses conferences as a means to communicate information, policies, and preferred administrative methods. Meetings between central heads and field representatives, at both the regional and branch levels of administration, are generally conducted at regular intervals, usually weekly or monthly. In some cases, participation is limited to central and regional administrators. In addition to these formal sessions, supplementary conferences may be called from time to time as the need arises. For example, new state legislation or board regulations concerning the Bureau of Public Assistance would warrant a special conference to evaluate effects upon duties and responsibilities. Conferences conducted under the auspices of central-office administrators provide top-level personnel with an opportunity to relay instructions to field directors and discuss administrative problems arising in the field. They also serve as a central control device, especially when branch supervisors are queried about the progress of programs, asked to make specific reports, and given instructions on preferred methods of conduct.

No central headquarters is solely dependent upon the staff conference, however. Most require periodic reports from branch supervisors. Telephone communications take place constantly in local government. Central supervisors often make unscheduled visits to the field office to evaluate performance, stimulate employee morale, and "keep branch personnel on their toes." A number of departments also distribute newsletters and bulletins on a regular basis.

A discussion of central-field communications would not be complete without some reference to the county messenger service. This service was initially established in 1934 to serve the Charities Department and its numerous field offices. It now operates as a division of the Communications Department, which has responsibility for planning, developing, and maintaining all manner of communication systems for the county departments. Operating along eighteen predetermined routes, the messenger service makes twice-a-day deliveries to almost every branch office of all county departments. Making over two hundred stops per day, messengers pick up and deliver materials for inter- and intradepartmental addresses, independent of the U.S. mails. A special trucking service also delivers larger packages.

These communications media keep central authorities apprised of day-to-day performance at the branch levels, facilitate the communication process throughout departmental hierarchies, and help to assure optimum performance, as well as uniformity in the implementation of major policies. However, the effect of these techniques is primarily upon intradepartmental affairs.

The city and county administrative apparatuses are organized in the traditional hierarchy, with formal authority vested at the top of departmental pyramids. Central controls within each department are supplemented by an even greater concentration of authority at a supra-departmental administrative level. Los Angeles City and Los Angeles County have each focused this latter responsibility upon a Chief Administrative Officer.

The importance of the Chief Administrative Officer in the decentralization process cannot be overemphasized, for he alone is in a position to coördinate the myriad of requests for branch facilities. Working through the budget process, this administrator plays a crucial role in evaluating and approving departmental requests for branch needs. In passing upon departmental budget proposals he and his staff decide whether a department has a sufficient workload to warrant granting additional space, personnel authorizations, and expense appropriations. In some instances, the CAO conducts an independent investigation to verify data presented by the department. For example, when the county Probation Department proposed to shift to a more completely decentralized arrangement, which entailed establishing more branches, upgrading some field personnel, and redistributing the workload, the CAO conducted an independent fact-finding study of the department's operations. This study resulted in a considerable modification of the department's original requests.

Using his authority of budgetary review as a wedge for comprehensive investigations of long-range needs, the CAO is in a position to influence the future pattern of branch development. Individual members of the Board of Supervisors or the City Council play a less direct role in this process, although they often work to have branch facilities established in their districts. New parks and recreation areas are more nearly responsive to legislative requests than most field establishments. In all instances, however, budgetary priorities, workloads, and administrative and public convenience figure importantly in decisions to change administrative arrangements by decentralizing.

A FLEXIBLE SYSTEM

Inasmuch as the field establishments of the two governments have been designed to serve a growing population that is in continual flux, they ought to remain flexible and be subject to change. Several departments are considering the feasibility of either establishing additional branches or delegating a greater degree of responsibility to the field. Some previously centralized agencies are currently contemplating decentralizing on an experimental basis. In some cases, it has been discovered that after devolving a specific function on a given branch, related though not identical functions must be similarly decentralized.

The development of the Lakewood Plan has produced still greater need for flexibility in the county administrative system. As county-city contracts have proliferated, the county government has had to establish additional branches of several agencies in close proximity to the contracting cities. In many instances, the contract requires the county to maintain one or more branch facilities within the city. Withdrawals from the system have produced some alterations, and if there were a considerable number of cancellations within an area, the county would have to reorganize its field deployment.

In an important sense, flexibility is being reduced as the two governments plan and construct branch civic centers. The considerable investment made in public buildings, parking facilities, and communications equipment precludes readjustments to respond to population shifts. The desire for administrative convenience and civic beauty, translated into permanent buildings, reduces administrative flexibility. The city Library Department found this to be true in the 1940's when it discovered painfully that library users had moved from the communities in which monumental branch libraries had been built in the 1920's. Nevertheless, branch civic centers tend to become foci of relatively large communities and to assist in stabilizing them.

ASSETS AND LIABILITIES

After analyzing the data, the question that remains is, how well does the system work? What advantages are there in providing local governmental services on a decentralized basis? What problems and inadequacies are inherent? The most obvious advantage is convenience to the users—the public. Decentralization facilitates contacts between the citizens and their public officials and encourages greater utilization of governmental services. It also tends to obviate the criticism that public administrative agencies are remote and distant entities, in relation to the citizens they are designed to serve.

Advantages are not limited to the citizen, however. To the lower echelon employee, decentralization of decision-making means added personal incentive and active interest in his assignments. The branch employee is often in a position to perceive a segment of the entire departmental operation duplicated in his field establishment. To the top-level administrator, decentralization of supervisory responsibility means a change in the type of responsibilities, from overseeing daily work production to planning and coördinating the work program for a more sophisticated organization.

Decentralization has further operated as an aid in recruiting non-professional personnel, overcoming the several disadvantages associated with working in the Los Angeles Civic Center area. With the exception of the relatively few persons who live nearby, the governmental headquarters area is fairly inaccessible for the individual who does not have an automobile. For those who possess a vehicle, traffic congestion and parking are constant problems. For many years, the area surrounding the downtown Civic Center has been characterized by extensive blight and obsolescence. These considerations have tended to discourage a large number of potential job applicants. Decentralization has made county and city employment accessible to a broader geographic cross-section of the population. Personnel officials report greater job satisfaction and lower turnover among nonprofessional employees, resulting from appointment to field establishments nearer the employee's residence.

Improved service and ease of administration have produced support for decentralization from both employees and the administrative hierarchy. Yet, a number of drawbacks are evident. Cost is the most important factor that must be considered at the beginning. The establishment of a branch facility is an expensive operation, in terms of initial construction, continued maintenance, and additional personnel. In a great many instances, however, construction of branches is cheaper than additions to large headquarters structures. Land costs are lower and the unit costs of building are cheaper. Certain intangible benefits, such as citizen convenience and improved administrative efficiency, cannot be stated in dollar terms, so human judgment enters very largely into determining the relative expensiveness of decentralized operations.

A number of concrete administrative dilemmas have been produced that, in a sense, represent contradictions of the advantages. Decentralization may reduce the work volume at central headquarters, but it tends to increase supervisory responsibilities. It invites delegation of authority, but it tends to produce an overhead, supervisory structure. Field establishments enable top officials to comprehend community problems and characteristics, but they create a stepped-up demand for communication techniques and equipment. Construction and maintenance of branch offices may be the cheaper alternative for obtaining improved services, but the total investment in public buildings and appurtenant land becomes a tremendous figure. Decentralization widens the area of employee recruitment and improves the quality of public personnel; yet, it is often difficult to find individuals willing to accept employment at branches located in less-desirable community areas.

Large, complicated, American public administrative organizations generally employ two distinct types of personnel, the generalist who is responsible for over-all coördination and supervision, and the specialist, well-versed in a particular, technical type of endeavor. When the administrative organization decentralizes to the field, specialists are likely to be retained at central headquarters. Costs, as well as a short supply of technicians, usually prevent the duplication of this type of work among the field offices. The generalist-specialist dichotomy, coupled with decentralization, creates two major problems. In the absence of clearly stated lines of communication, branch employees become uncertain as to whether they should report directly to their immediate, generalist supervisor, at the branch facility, or to the central headquarters' subject-matter specialist with whom they are working on a special problem. Furthermore, if branches are staffed solely by generalist-type personnel, they become dependent upon central headquarters for specialized assistance, increasing the central office workload and delaying decisions. There is a belief in some quarters that the smaller branch staff makes a greater burden for central headquarters. It is argued that smaller branches should have sufficient technical personnel available to permit them to perform the majority of their tasks without referring matters elsewhere.

Variation in work volume among branch offices is another condition that may detract from the value of decentralization. For the most part, however, departments adjust service areas to ensure that each field establishment will have a defensible minimum workload. A few, such as the Probation Department, are able to structure the field organization to keep a specific ratio between professional staff and the workload.

Administrative decentralization is neither a dilemma nor a panacea in Los Angeles City and Los Angeles County. Widespread support for this technique would seem to indicate that its problems are out-weighted by accompanying benefits. Although local governmental decentralization is a relatively new concept, the techniques to implement it have been developed rapidly.

IMPLICATIONS FOR THE ORGANIZATION OF LOCAL GOVERNMENT

Both the city and the county have developed the decentralized type of administrative programs to fulfill their missions to a large population distributed over relatively large areas. Without doing so, they could not have retained their roles as potential metropolitan-area governments. To what extent does their experience lend support to proposals for establishing a single metropolitan-wide authority? Administrative decentralization has facilitated the governing process in the Los Angeles metropolitan area but it falls far short of a comprehensive solution.

The contemporary experience of Los Angeles City and Los Angeles County would seem to indicate that if a comprehensive metropolitan government were established in the future, it would have to conduct its operations on a decentralized basis. A public jurisdiction covering a wide geographic area and executing a broad range of public responsibilities *need not* be a remote, unresponsive entity. Los Angeles City and Los Angeles County can readily be categorized as big governments, though their jurisdictions are not metropolitan-wide. Recognizing the dangers of remoteness and unresponsiveness, they have sought to reduce these inadequacies through branch operations. Cannot this same principle be applied to a government enjoying a metropolitan-wide jurisdiction? Cannot a metropolitan-wide government retain a close identity with community areas within its boundaries by rendering public services through field units? Is it not possible for a metropolitan agency whose policies are formulated centrally but whose services are administered at the community level through numerous field establishments, to effect a more responsive system than a municipality which, though smaller in area, concentrates most of its governmental operations at a central point?

The contemporary experience of the city and county may have additional value in demonstrating a basis for the redistribution of functional responsibilities in a federated metropolitan system. An initial problem facing a proposed system of that type centers in the distribution of major functions and segments of major functions, between a metropolitan authority and local units. Are there certain functions that must, of necessity, be performed by a level of government that is easily accessible to the recipients of the services? Conversely, can one, in the interests of uniformity, define other functions that require centralization at the metropolitan level? Carrying this reasoning one step further, is it not possible that those activities performed through decentralized branches by Los Angeles City and Los Angeles County are of such a nature as to warrant their continued performance by *local* units of government in a federated metropolitan system?

Los Angeles' experience is equally significant in its relationship to a borough system of local government based upon the division of large local jurisdictions into a number of constituent political units. Some administrators view branch civic centers as the potential nuclei for such a system, envisaging the ultimate consolidation of all departmental branches within a branch civic center, accompanied by a considerable expansion of branch powers and independence of rigid central control. Branch autonomy would be increased to the point that each branch would have substantial control over its budget preparation and would operate under the guidance of a deputy chief administrative officer who would be responsible for coördinating all branches within his area, much as the present Chief Administrative Officer coördinates the administrative operations of the entire city or county. This system ultimately requires the establishment of local legislative bodies or borough councils.

Numerous similarities may be recognized between decentralized administration of local government and broader, metropolitan-wide reorganization. Perhaps the most potent one rests upon the distinction between limited, short-range improvements that are instituted on a piecemeal basis, and drastic reorganizations designed to provide a broader solution to the problems of governing a whole metropolitan area. Decentralizing local services through field establishments has undoubtedly effected improvements in administration. The relative success of city and county decentralization is a serious deterrent to comprehensive reorganization. It bolsters the existing sense of localism and meets the existing demands.

SUMMARY

Numerous departments and agencies of Los Angeles County and Los Angeles City have established many branch offices in outlying areas to remedy deficiencies inherent in large-scale local government. Departmental decentralization has passed from its initial phase of uncoördinated, piecemeal establishment of field offices to one that is planned and controlled by central management. The branch civic center concept, based upon the grouping of numerous public offices and facilities at a common site, has provided a framework for administrative decentralization in the Los Angeles area.

Headquarters-field relationships have been key problems requiring solution. The decentralization process rests upon the delegation of decision-making authority to field personnel. The degree of independence exercised will vary according to the function performed, the professional status of employees, and the philosophy of top management. The pressures upon large-scale local governments tend to induce responsible administrators to emphasize centralized control and supervision over branch operations.

Administrative decentralization by these two local governments has some important implications for metropolitan governmental reorganization. They have attempted to relate large administrative apparatuses to community and neighborhood needs in order to be responsive to local demands for services. To the degree that they accomplish this objective, the two governments remain major forces in the total government of the metropolitan area. The success of their decentralization programs also indicates that if metropolitan area government were integrated, it would be feasible to administer governmental services in a manner that would assure the citizens relatively easy access.

PART IV
ALTERNATIVE COURSES

THIRTEEN

The Framework for Change

THE SYSTEM of local government in Los Angeles County evolved from an attempt to accommodate to the needs of a rapidly growing urban complex while preserving strong and viable local units of government. Current policies pertaining to the organization and operation of local units are the product of a series of negotiations conducted among representatives of competing groups over a long period of time. The essence of the system has been institutionalized in a legal framework that was established during a period when the metropolitan area was but a dream of the future. This dream has now become reality. Los Angeles, like other metropolitan areas throughout the nation, must candidly appraise the adequacy of its existing system of local government in the light of a rapidly changing urban environment.

CONSTRAINTS UPON CHANGE

Resistance to change is an essential feature common to all forms of society. Every social, political, or economic system that has been institutionalized over a prolonged period of time encompasses both formal and informal safeguards that are designed to sustain the system in its present form and preserve its integrity against forces of change. The Los Angeles system of local government is no exception. Proponents of a substantial reorganization of local governmental structure should be prepared to face resistance from many different quarters. The resistance would be potent, for it would be buttressed by three pillars of argument. Any strategic move for greater governmental integration would have to be waged on *three* fronts. On the philosophi-

cal front, those favoring substantive alterations in the status quo
would be required to present a case strong enough to counterbalance
a long-standing, tenacious fear of big government. On the legal front,
legislation would be needed to implement the modifications and give
them the blessings of legitimacy. On the political front, an active drive
would have to be made to secure the necessary official and popular
backing for any proposed changes. This would require skillful leadership, careful determination of goals, and effective engineering of opinions to gain consent.

THE PHILOSOPHICAL FRAMEWORK

The philosophical opposition to integrative change reflects a mixture
of reverence for localism and fear of big government. It contains a
strong element of majoritarian democratic theory. Although it is based
upon the belief that the mass of citizens have a right to govern themselves and to pass judgment upon the most complicated public issues,
it employs a limited definition of a majority. It emphasizes the local
unit of government as the proper framework for determining the majority interest and declines to accept the broader metropolitan area as the
arena within which to make this determination. This theory assumes
that local government, because it is "close to the people," may be
equated with greater public responsiveness. It is alleged that policies
having a direct bearing upon the interests of particular communities
can best be formulated and executed by local officials familiar with
the people's problems and desires. Because local units of government
comprise smaller geographical areas and deal with less complex matters than those found at state and national levels, public scrutiny of
official actions and decisions is facilitated. The individual citizen is
better able to experience a sense of close personal identification with
a governmental unit that covers a smaller area and executes services
that have a direct impact upon his personal welfare. It is expected that
this identification will be translated into greater citizen interest and
participation in governmental affairs. The smaller the size of a governmental unit, the greater its potential for securing these objectives.

The importance of local government as a vehicle for strengthening
the democratic process has been reëmphasized in recent years. The
growing concentration of power and responsibility at state and national
levels and the increasingly complex nature of the governmental process
have tended to isolate the citizen from the governmental machinery. It
is argued that local government thereby emerges as perhaps the final

remaining outpost of direct citizen participation in government. The strengthening of the neighborhood and community is often posed as an essential protective measure against the overcentralized government so prevalent in our modern society.

The multiplicity of governmental units that forms the essence of the metropolitan problem is a direct outgrowth of this philosophical framework. Every incorporation attempt represents a desire of the inhabitants of the area in question to govern themselves and to keep their government close at hand. Every time a community incorporates successfully, it adds yet another potential pocket of resistance to metropolitan integration. Once the municipality is created, its leaders cherish their autonomy. Those who have an investment in such units are prone to panic at the possibility that a metropolitan "super-government" will be imposed on them and would limit their politicians' power to making decisions affecting the future growth and development of their neighborhood.

Proponents of greater integration are placed in the position of having to modify a belief that is the essence of one branch of democratic theory. Who can rightly challenge the objective of self-determination? Once localism is equated with more responsive government and greater citizen participation, it is clothed with a doctrinal mantle that elicits deep emotion. The question of integration versus localism comes to be viewed in black and white terms. The size of a governmental unit is soon equated with the degree to which its operations conform to this concept of the democratic process. Areawide government conjures up visions of a dictator or an oligarchy seeking to absorb all vestiges of self-determination and impose an arbitrary will upon local areas. Independent municipal units emerge as the protagonists in this ideological battle. They are charged with the mission of retaining responsible democratic government by resisting any movement in the direction of establishing a more centralized, unified government for the metropolitan area.

This is the ideological front on which the battle for greater integration through governmental reorganization predictably will be fought. Despite the emotion-charged presentations and crossfire that characterize the issue of organization integration, however, the battle in no way represents an all-out war between two opposing ideological conceptions of the nature of local government and its role in our society. Even the most avid proponents of comprehensive change in the status quo share their adversaries' belief in the values of localism. Their objective is not to destroy all vestiges of local home rule; rather, it is to modify unrestrained localism in the light of changing urban conditions.

The task, then, is to strike a workable balance between those requirements that are areawide and those having a smaller focus.

THE LEGAL FRAMEWORK

Legislation that is enacted by any society represents the concrete application of the philosophical principles upon which that society rests. The legal framework is designed to legitimize and implement social goals by applying them to specific situations in the form of enforceable legislative enactments. The legislative framework specifies the "rules of the game" or outside limits within which negotiations looking toward adjustments in the status quo take place. However, this legal framework, by its very nature, embodies certain built-in constraints that tend to discourage any abrupt, comprehensive changes in the status quo.

The legal basis for the California system of local government is found in the state constitution and in statutes and legislative codes. Much of this was written during a period when state interference in local affairs was a pressing issue. The state Legislature was prohibited from passing special legislation; the decision to incorporate became a matter of local option; and municipalities, once formed, were given the authority to frame and adopt their own charters. These enactments were based upon the belief that no outside agency should have the power to determine or alter the legal status of a local community. Such matters were to be decided on the basis of local self-determination.

The objectives that initially stimulated the adoption of home rule legislation are still considered to be valid, supportable public goals. However, it is now evident that the continued, unmodified operation of home rule legislation in its new "metropolitan" setting is producing unforeseen consequences that transcend a desire for home rule per se. In practice, the legislative framework governing the operation of local units of government has served to encourage greater fragmentation of government at the expense of comprehensive structural integration.

The incorporation process represents the essence of home rule. The motives behind specific incorporations vary. Some incorporations are defensive measures taken against possible annexation by an adjacent municipality; others are prompted by dissatisfaction with the level of county services available to the area so long as it is unincorporated; and still others are designed to preserve a desired land-use pattern. Despite the variety of motivating factors behind specific incorporations, however, the establishment of *any* municipal corporation indicates a desire to implement the principle of self-determination through local control over municipal affairs.

Significantly, the success of the incorporation process in metropolitan areas is a measure of its power to deter, if not halt, the movement for greater governmental integration. The adverse effect of incorporations upon the drive for governmental consolidation in metropolitan areas does not detract from the substantive values of local home rule, although its present and potential impact upon the face of metropolitan government cannot be ignored. The strength of the incorporation process as a vehicle for hampering comprehensive structural integration can be directly attributed to the legal framework. The absence of any substantive standards, coupled with the exceedingly small population requirement set by the state, has stimulated the formation of a variety of municipalities whose operations in no way resemble those of a "city" in the traditional, accepted sense of the term. Many cities have incorporated, not to provide urban services, but to act as zoning devices in order to preserve a desired land-use pattern. One writer describes the problem in this fashion:

> Cities have been incorporated which have more cows than people, and for the purpose of protecting dairy farms against subdivision and higher levels of municipal taxation. One city's thoroughfares are privately owned, access to which is under guard. Another city consists primarily of cemeteries, has fewer than 300 (living) inhabitants, and derives most of its local revenue from burial fees. Certain cities were able to meet the population requirement for incorporation only by counting persons residing in motels or patients in sanitaria.
>
> Some cities are enclaves of extremely valuable industrial property, whose chief function is the avoidance of taxation and other public responsibilities. Other cities are enclaves of poverty, some having as little as one-third the state-wide average per capita assessed valuation of municipalities. . . .[1]

These incorporations would not have been possible were it not for the open-ended nature of the legal framework governing the establishment of municipalities. Areas considering incorporation are not required to justify their decision to incorporate by meeting any tests of their ability to function as a city. Is the area capable of providing a satisfactory level of service? Does it have an assessed valuation that would permit it to perform essential municipal functions? Would it constitute a "well-rounded" city? Would annexation to an adjacent municipality be a more logical alternative? The burden of providing

---

[1] Stanley Scott, "California Legislation Governing Municipal Incorporation," in Ernest A. Engelbert, ed., *Metropolitan California*, Governor's Commission on Metropolitan Area Problems (Sacramento, 1961), pp. 107–108.

the answers to such questions remains with the localities themselves. Should the localities choose to ignore these questions while reaching a decision to incorporate, they are in no way compelled to do so by the legal framework.

Given the permissive nature of legislation governing incorporation, does this legal framework give equal encouragement to integration through the consolidation of two or more existing municipal corporations? Once a municipal corporation has been formed, its continued existence is protected by state legislation. It can be dissolved only by an action of its residents. Although the legal machinery to produce consolidation of local governments exists, the success of any consolidation proposal is entirely dependent upon the action of the municipal voters. The theory of popular control thereby emerges in practice as a device to retard structural integration by use of an absolute veto. If change is to be accomplished and new perspectives of the metropolitan problems are to prevail, a different method to determine popular will must be sought. Placing the issue before a larger public, one defined on a larger geographic basis, is one method. However, it runs directly counter to the present system. Another method is to develop a legal framework in which the several local units may negotiate to achieve consensus on an areawide basis.

THE POLITICAL FRAMEWORK

The political framework represents the sum total of the various interest groups or countervailing forces that have stakes in the future of Los Angeles local governments. The philosophical framework deals with political theories and concepts; the legal framework is concerned with constitutional provisions and legislative enactments; the political framework deals with people and the power they are capable of exercising in order to facilitate or impede change.

The absence of any unified political leadership is a significant characteristic of the Los Angeles area. Political fragmentation has accompanied jurisdictional fragmentation. Despite this diffusion of political power, however, it is possible to identify three major components of the political framework—the county, the central city and the suburban municipalities. What is their position on the question of governmental integration?

These contenders for leadership in the governmental sphere in the Los Angeles area agree on a number of fundamentals. All strongly support the principle of home rule. They are unified in their opposition toward any political consolidation that would destroy the legal status of a city and transfer all its powers and prerogatives to another agency. They further agree that even more moderate consolidation proposals must depend upon approval by a majority vote in the jurisdictions affected. These are the major areas of unconditional agreement among the countervailing forces. These areas of agreement, in essence, favor continued autonomy of local units of government at the expense of greater political and administrative integration in the metropolitan area.

> The best interest of the people of this state and nation require the maintenance of strong healthy cities which have the right of home rule and which provide local governmental services and perform local governmental and policy-making functions. Local municipal affairs, involving policy making, enforcement of laws and regulatory measures, and governmental activities are not proper subjects for inclusion in regional or metropolitan districts and should be retained by the cities. Any political consolidation of existing local governmental units (cities and/or counties) to form a regional government for any California metropolitan area is basically unsound.[2]

The attitude of existing units toward integration is not entirely negative. Functional consolidation through intergovernmental coöperation is widely supported in principle and practice in Los Angeles County. Many functions have been transferred, in whole or in part, from cities to the county government by voluntary action. The county also administers several specially created, areawide districts such as those conducting air pollution control and flood control. In addition, there are a multitude of formal and informal arrangements between the county and the cities, and between cities, which guarantee mutual coöperation and assistance in such areas as fire fighting and law enforcement.

Functional consolidation has proved to be an acceptable alternative because it is compatible with the principle of home rule. However, even at this relatively low level of integration, considerable controversy has emerged as to the validity of this approach. Municipalities in Los Angeles County have by no means reached a consensus regarding the alternative of functional consolidation through city-county contracts. It would seem that *any* form of integration that goes beyond informal, joint exercise of powers of mutual aid-type agreements executed on a piecemeal basis inevitably produces a degree of controversy. Signifi-

---

[2] Excerpt from *Principles on Metropolitan Government*, adopted by the League of California Cities in February, 1962.

cantly, this controversy always centers around the question of local home rule.

Up to this point, we have been concerned with the official segment of the political framework. It is to be expected that proposal for greater consolidation will inevitably incur the wrath of certain local officials. For some officials, this opposition is based upon a fear that integration will be accompanied by a personal loss of power and prestige; for others, it represents a sincere conviction of the necessity of keeping local government small and close to the people. Official viewpoints, however, represent but one segment of the political framework. How does the citizen fit into this framework?

Most county residents have given little thought to the complex questions of governmental reorganization. Whatever consideration they may have given them, stimulated and informed by newspaper and television presentations, is likely to have been in the broadest terms. The citizen finds it difficult to equate his own welfare with the concerns of so broad a region. Predictably, he will react at such times as he is able to identify specific service deficiencies that have a direct impact upon his personal comfort and well-being.

However, it would be erroneous to conclude that the typical county resident is an entirely passive force in the political framework. Many citizens of Los Angeles County have already expressed a preference for home rule through their participation in the incorporation process. The successful incorporations of seventy-four municipalities, twenty-nine of which occurred during the past eight years, is, in itself, indicative of this preference. Fourteen of the municipalities have framed and adopted their own charters. The absence of any widespread disincorporation or consolidation movements further indicates that even the newer residents of these cities, who did not have an opportunity to vote in the initial incorporation election, are satisfied to maintain the municipal status quo. This substantial group of municipal residents who have been nurtured on self-determination may be expected to react strongly to such symbols as home rule and big government. The question then arises as to whether or not the symbols of integration, coördination, and unification can be used to elicit an equally positive reaction.

Given the nature of the metropolis it is to be expected that public attitudes toward metropolitan government will be nebulous and frequently apathetic. What is notable, however, is the relative absence of definite policy statements emanating from private special-interest organizations. The extreme points of view are well represented. On the one hand, we find a small circle of businessmen and academicians whose members are strongly convinced of the value of integration through areawide government. At the opposite end of the spectrum, there are a number of "anti-metro" groups that view metropolitan government emotionally as a monster that has been concocted by a vast international Communist conspiracy for the purpose of undermining our democratic institutions. Most visible interest groups, however, seem to have adopted the approach of cautious anticipation. The nonpartisan nature of local government in the county has removed the question of metropolitan government from the political party arena. Newspapers, by and large, have not chosen to conduct crusades on behalf of metropolitan government, though they have generally supported less drastic programs of functional consolidation and intergovernmental coöperation. The local chamber of commerce approach toward metropolitan government is a piecemeal one and is characterized by a widespread suspicion of big government, which many chamber managers tend to equate with metropolitan government. The viewpoints of other major interest groups in Los Angeles County have not yet been organized in such a manner as to permit a clear identification of any precise political alignments. In all likelihood, specific policies will only be forthcoming when the issue of metropolitan government has passed from its present speculative phase and is presented in the form of a concrete proposal that must be acted upon, either negatively or affirmatively.

DISCONTENTMENT: THE COUNTERVAILING FORCE

It is evident that the framework for change is basically a negative one, so long as change is perceived as structural revision. It has not produced an environment that is conducive to the acceptance of any comprehensive structural reorganization. On the contrary, it has elevated the principle of home rule to an ideological status and erected an elaborate legal structure that is designed to insure the continued virility of local governments and to protect them from unwanted integration. Political odds are very much in favor of maintaining the status quo. There are no widespread, politically effective drives for governmental integration evident on the Los Angeles scene.

There is one ingredient of political action that, if added to the framework for change, could completely reverse the current picture. That ingredient is widespread discontentment. Mass discontent movements evolve either from a ground swell of frustrations and unhappiness seeking articulation or from a consciously engineered drive to enlarge irritations, identify a scapegoat, and suggest the need for change. In a democracy, dissatisfaction with the accepted way of doing things, if it is strong enough, can virtually move mountains—it can even alter a long-standing traditional belief in certain basic principles. If enough citizens were sufficiently aroused over service deficiencies or the high taxation rates levied by their local governments, they would begin to question the validity of the status quo. If they were further convinced that these problems were the direct outgrowth of overlapping governments, neither philosophical, legal, nor political arguments could prevent some change from taking place. Unrestrained home rule would lose most of its potency as a justification for resisting political integration. Once the philosophical framework had been altered, legislation to facilitate the establishment of a metropolitan government would soon be forthcoming. Official support for "metro" would become a political necessity rather than a political liability.

Dissatisfaction with the performance of local government, if present at all in Los Angeles, is neither widespread nor potent enough to spearhead an active drive for change. Public apathy on questions of metropolitan government reflects more than disinterest—it indicates the absence of substantial complaints and the acceptance of the prevailing way of doing things. To be sure, every citizen, at one time or another, expresses some form of dissatisfaction, whether it pertains to the high tax-rate, a particular service deficiency, or official unresponsiveness to a given problem. However, these complaints are piecemeal and sporadic in nature, and the citizen generally looks for a solution within the existing governmental framework.

The single major campaign for structural reorganization is taking place in the San Fernando Valley section of the city of Los Angeles. Valley residents have become increasingly dissatisfied with the services they receive as part of Los Angeles City. Secession from the city is being discussed extensively and civic leaders are once more studying the possibility of organizing the Valley into a number of borough governments. Significantly, this movement does not represent a demand for greater governmental coördination and unification. On the contrary, it is a reaction to the apparent unresponsiveness of big government. The city has been unable to distribute its resources among sections that are growing at different rates in a manner that satisfies all. The changes that are advocated would, if anything, further complicate an already fragmented governmental structure.

The evolution of Los Angeles County from a sparsely populated agricultural area to a densely settled metropolitan region has not been free from tensions and problems. However, the fact remains that the governments of Los Angeles County have adjusted quite remarkably to the pressures of explosive population growth and economic expansion. A number of factors have been responsible for this ability to forestall the potentially destructive effects of metropolitan development. Los Angeles County is located in a state that has bestowed an unusual degree of freedom on its local governments to experiment with alternative forms of administrative organization and intergovernmental coöperation. Local units of government have taken extensive advantage of the opportunities provided by this permissive legislation.

The government of Los Angeles County has been an important asset in this context. The county has simplified and improved its machinery and operations. Its organization in no way resembles the typical county government, which has been widely condemned for its archaic, cumbersome structure and its long list of independently elected officials. The government of Los Angeles County is a coördinated, truly professional operation that has kept abreast of the most advanced administrative techniques. The number of elected county officers has been reduced to a minimum and all but a very small percentage of county employees have been recruited under civil service. The Chief Administrative Officer, with the aid of a sizable staff of career specialists, has further strengthened the county government to make it a major contender for leadership in the Los Angeles area.

Many people see Los Angeles County as the metropolitan government of the future. It is the largest existing jurisdiction in terms of geographical area, it possesses the necessary skills and facilities, and it has demonstrated its ability to function on an areawide basis. The question of the county's ability or willingness to evolve into a truly areawide government is open to speculation. However, the fact remains that the county has been an effective instrument to introduce coördination and to limit the chaos so inherent in fragmented government. Many regional problems are being attacked on an integrated, coördinated basis through special districts administered by the county. The role of the county as a vendor of municipal-type services for contracting cities is well known. County participation in mutual-aid agreements with municipalities, and in such functions as fire protection and law enforcement, represents yet another example of intergovernmental coöperation in action.

Los Angeles City and the suburban municipalities, taken as a whole, have exhibited an equally strong interest in strengthening their governments in order to insure more effective performance. It is this general high quality of performance that may help to explain the absence of any widespread citizen unrest. The governments within Los Angeles County are essentially effective governments. Most are manned by

professional administrators and are free from the taint of "big city cor-
ruption" that has plagued innumerable other areas. They have succeeded in instituting a notable degree of integration and coördination.
They are, by and large, responsive governments that often anticipate
public dissatisfactions and stem them before they reach serious proportions.

In the final analysis, it would seem that "things are not yet bad
enough" to have stimulated any grass-roots demands for comprehensive reorganization. This does not mean to imply that there are no
serious problems on the Los Angeles scene. Transportation and air pollution represent a few of the thorns that continue to plague both citizens and officials alike. Greater integration of public health services
through consolidation of the Los Angeles City and Los Angeles County
health departments has long been a subject of concern. Fragmented
planning represents yet another area of criticism. Nevertheless, it
would seem that none of these problems has, as yet, reached serious
enough proportions to have made metropolitan government sufficiently
attractive to counterbalance traditional reverence for home rule and
fear of big government.

PARADISE REVISITED?

The relative tranquillity on the Los Angeles scene does not mean that
Los Angeles is a utopia. If this were so, there would be no need to discuss changes in the status quo. This volume would be unique in the
annals of metropolitan studies; it could conclude on a note of blissful
satisfaction and unqualified acceptance of the existing pattern of local
government. Unfortunately, we cannot conclude with so happy an end-
ing. It is estimated that over 460 new residents arrive in Los Angeles
County each day. It is predicted that the county will have to accommodate a population of close to eight million by the year 1970. How
long can the fragmented governments that constitute Los Angeles
County adjust to intensified demands for urban services that require
substantial financial resources or that impinge upon residents of several localities? How long can voluntary intergovernmental coöperation
prevent chaos? How long can "good government" alone replace integrated government?

The conclusion that all is not serene with Los Angeles local governments is attested by the amount of time and effort that has been spent
by series of officials and citizens in analyzing the local governmental
structure. The possibility of achieving more integrated, unified gov-

ernment has been examined for over sixty years.[3] As early as 1903, the Los Angeles Consolidation Commission was formed to explore the question of consolidating certain city and county offices. In 1916, a City–County Consolidation Commission recommended that Los Angeles City consolidate with the county. A further effort to stimulate consolidation was undertaken in 1930 by the Los Angeles Citizens Committee on County Government and Local Autonomy. The committee recommended that Los Angeles City separate from the county and form a consolidated city-county. This recommendation was reiterated two years later by the Los Angeles City Bureau of Budget and Efficiency.

During the 1930's, ten different study groups conducted microscopic analyses of the local governmental structure, with a view toward securing more unified government. Some groups favored governmental consolidation under county auspices. Others opposed this emphasis on the county and recommended that Los Angeles City withdraw from the county. Although these studies formed the basis for the current system of functional consolidation, they failed to provide a solution to the problem of fragmented government.

Intensive analysis of Los Angeles governmental problems was not a feature peculiar to the 1930's. Interim committees of the state Legislature have since published several reports pertaining to the governance of this and other metropolitan areas. The Los Angeles City–County Consolidation Study Commission, organized in 1954, sought to obtain greater functional consolidation between the county and the central city. In 1955, the Bureau of Governmental Research at UCLA published the last in a series of volumes on functional integration in Los Angeles. Two years later, representatives of the county, the central city, and several suburban cities took preliminary steps to organize a Metropolitan Area Study Commission to examine problems of overlapping and duplication. In 1960, Samuel Leask, Jr., and George Terhune, then Los Angeles City Administrative Officer and Assistant Administrative Officer respectively, submitted a proposal for governmental integration in Los Angeles. These experienced city officials recommended the establishment of a Los Angeles Metropolitan Municipal Services District. The district, to be formed by a popular vote, would be responsible for matters having an areawide impact.

This continued interest in governmental reorganization indicates that there is a ferment of ideas and a perception of need. It represents

---

[3] See Edwin A. Cottrell and Helen L. Jones, *Characteristics of the Metropolis* (Los Angeles: Haynes Foundation, 1952), chap. 4.

an effort on the part of selected officials and citizens to offer leadership in anticipation of the time when selective voluntary intergovernmental coöperation will no longer be able to forestall the devastating consequences of metropolitan growth, a time when the costs of overlapping and duplication may become unacceptable.

WHAT OF THE FUTURE?

A pattern for governing a metropolitan area may be analyzed and conceptualized from several approaches. Proposed reorganizations of the present system may take many different forms. They may range from informal coöperative agreements among existing local governments to the establishment of a "super-government" that would absorb all powers and prerogatives of the numerous independent local units that together comprise the metropolitan area.

Proposals for metropolitan reorganization thus far have tended to fall into one of two main schools of thought. One school advocates structural change as the only permanent solution to metropolitan disunity. Proponents of this approach believe that limited devices, such as voluntary intergovernmental coöperation, can only serve to postpone the inevitable creation of a metropolitan government. The political infeasibility of such a course of action, however, has nurtured the growth of another school of thought that subscribes to more gradual integration. It holds that gradual exposure of local governments to small, nonirritating doses of consolidation will eventually instill a metropolitan-wide consciousness that will be conducive to more comprehensive changes in the governmental structure. Until such time as this areawide loyalty develops, functional consolidation through intergovernmental coöperation is the only feasible path to follow.

A third concept is quite relevant within the framework that has been analyzed. This concept is based upon the interplay of countervailing forces. Each of the existing local governments is legally authorized to negotiate with every other government and to operate in concert. Each has experience with joint and coöperative activity. The legal and political framework is characterized by bargaining and competition. If a long-existing but currently limited force, the state government, is employed in a purposeful manner, it can become a positive counterweight stimulating the competitors that are now stalemated to establish new relationships in the governance of the metropolitan area. This concept will be developed more fully in the concluding chapter.

THE STRUCTURAL APPROACH

Structural changes involve legally established shifts in the jurisdictional boundaries and prerogatives of local governments. They are designed to provide formal, institutionalized areawide leadership and coördination, either by expanding the jurisdiction of existing local units or by creating an areawide government empowered to perform services and deal with problems on an areawide basis. Annexation, whereby new territory is added to existing governmental units, is one form of structural change; consolidation of two or more local governments is another.

Municipalities in the Los Angeles area will undoubtedly continue to annex, so long as adjacent unincorporated areas are available. Annexation, as a device to produce integration can be of only limited value in unifying fully developed metropolitan areas. As more and more areas incorporate, the territory remaining to be annexed decreases. Los Angeles City is virtually surrounded by a ring of cities. Piecemeal annexations, conducted either by Los Angeles City or by the suburban municipalities, could never encompass a sufficient amount of territory to bring true integration to the Los Angeles metropolitan area.

Consolidation of existing local units represents another alternative. There are any number of theoretically possible combinations. Los Angeles City could consolidate with the county; suburban municipalities could consolidate with each other and/or with the central city. If carried to the extreme, all of the municipalities within the county, including the central city, could join forces to create a consolidated city-county. Such a consolidated unit would, in effect, be tantamount to a metropolitan government.

The possibility of improving the performance of local government in Los Angeles through consolidation has received a substantial amount of attention over the years. However, political consolidation, because it would destroy the legal status of local units, is viewed by many as a repudiation of the principle of home rule. In order to be effective, such consolidation would have to encompass more than two municipalities; it would have to include an area that is coterminous with the boundaries that define the metropolitan problem. There is little likelihood that a sufficiently large number of municipalities would agree to dissolve their municipal status in order to form a consolidated unit that would be truly metropolitan-wide in scope. Significantly, the 1947 merger of Baton Rouge and East Baton Rouge Parish in Louisiana, and that of Nashville and Davidson County, Tennessee, in 1962, represent the only twentieth-century examples of effective city-county consolidation.

The most comprehensive structural change would be the establishment of a single metropolitan government whose jurisdiction would be restricted only by the outside limits of the metropolitan area. Such a change would require the abolition or merger of all existing local governments. Even the most avid proponents of metropolitan government recognize that this alternative is politically infeasible. The continued existence of local units and their retention of a substantial degree of power are inherent aspects of the political "facts of life." Any attempt to superimpose an areawide governmental authority, without regard to the continued operation of viable local units, would be both unrealistic and unwise.

A *federated* system of metropolitan government surmounts the shortcomings of the other types of structural revision. Under this system, local units are coördinated by a single authority that possesses jurisdiction over matters of metropolitan-wide interest. Existing local units retain control over all activities that are primarily local in nature. Only the metropolitan aspects of certain functions come under the purview of the metropolitan authority.[4] This plan represents a significant compromise between the extremes of an omnipotent supergovernment and unrestrained home rule under the auspices of independent municipal units. Existing local governments would be required to relinquish power over certain functions that formerly fell within their province. Yet, local authority would be protected by retaining municipal control over matters deemed to be of a purely local nature. The successful use of the federated principle in Toronto and Dade County has placed this alternative in a prominent position. However, despite the favorable publicity that has been bestowed upon these two examples of the federated system, no other metropolitan area has adopted this plan. On the contrary, most proposals of this type have never reached a vote, and when they did, they were defeated.[5] The reason is clear. Local units of government cannot be induced to relinquish their legally vested powers and prerogatives to a metropolitan government so long as they have a sufficient financial base adequately to support meaningful services.

---

[4] A system for allocating health, law enforcement, and recreation responsibilities between a hypothetical metropolitan government and existing local units is presented in Beatrice Dinerman, Richard Yerby, and Ross Clayton, *Metropolitan Services: Studies of Allocation in a Federated Organization* (Los Angeles: Bureau of Governmental Research, University of California, 1961).

[5] Proposals for a multipurpose metropolitan-wide district were defeated by voters in Seattle (1958), St. Louis (1959 and 1962), and Cleveland (1961).

The difficulty in securing consensus on a metropolitan-wide authority is well exemplified in Los Angeles. Until recently, the question of "metro" for Los Angeles was limited to theoretical speculation. Then, in 1960, this speculation became more concrete. The Governor's Commission on Metropolitan Area Problems recommended legislation that would permit the establishment of multipurpose districts to conduct functions of regional concern.[6] Establishment of such a district would require an affirmative vote by a majority of residents in the metropolitan area designated for inclusion in the district. The district would be governed by a Metropolitan Council selected by and from the membership of the governing bodies of the cities and counties included in the district. It was further recommended that enabling legislation *must* provide for comprehensive metropolitan planning and one or more of the following functions: metropolitan air pollution, water supply, sewage disposal and drainage, law enforcement, fire protection, urban renewal, civil defense, and any other metropolitan-wide functions requested by members of the proposed district.

Assemblyman Thomas Rees of Beverly Hills introduced a bill that would have permitted the formation of such a district by resolution of the affected cities and counties and a majority of qualified voters in the proposed district. The decision as to what initial functions were to be performed by the district, as well as the inclusion of additional functions in the future, was also to be dependent upon a majority vote. The governing board was to be composed of councilmen and supervisors from the member cities and counties. Costs were to be financed through a formula based upon population and assessed valuation. This Rees Bill was referred to the Assembly Committee on Municipal and County Government for study during the interim between legislative sessions.

Reaction to the bill was predictable. There was an immediate increase in the distribution of "anti-metro" literature. Municipal representatives appeared in large numbers at public hearings to oppose the bill. The League of California Cities officially denounced the "metro government" concept at its annual conference in February, 1962. Scattered newspaper support for the Rees bill was not strong enough to conteract the opposition. Private civic groups failed to take an official stand. Public interest waned to the point that only a handful of individuals were present when hearings on the bill were held in Los Angeles.

---

[6] *Meeting Metropolitan Problems,* report of the Governor's Commission on Metropolitan Area Problems (Sacramento, 1960). The papers prepared for this commission have been compiled and presented in Engelbert, *op. cit.*

The author of the bill attempted to forestall home-rule objections through provisions pertaining to local control over formation of the district and over local representation on its governing board. However, in order to fulfill its main objective of securing greater governmental integration, the bill contained a number of provisions that were interpreted by cities and counties as inroads on home rule. Objections were voiced on a number of grounds. Since costs were to be apportioned throughout the whole area, localities expressed a reluctance to contribute to a district fund that might be used to benefit their neighbors. Objections were also raised to the fact that members of the governing board, though they would be elected to their respective local legislative bodies, would not be elected directly to the Metropolitan Council. It was further alleged that the proposed district would be set up in such a way as to deny localities access to the decision-making process. Since creation of the district, and the addition of new functions, were made dependent upon a majority vote of the *entire* area, it would be impossible for a single city, or a group of cities, to prevent the implementation of decisions agreed upon by the area as a whole. Specific localities would be forced to assume their proportionate share of the financial burden of providing services they might feel their particular communities did not require. Furthermore, a locality would not be permitted to withdraw from the district until it contained over fifty per cent of the district population and was able to secure an affirmative vote of a majority of residents in the district as a whole.

These types of criticisms represent the essence of a variety of problems involved in metropolitan reorganization. In order to be effective, any areawide governmental structure must be organized so that a single jurisdiction cannot thwart the wishes of the metropolitan area as a whole. However, the majority rule principle, upon which the Rees bill was based, was not acceptable to local government leaders. To be sure, every locality upholds the concept of government by the majority, so long as the majority is comprised of those individuals located within the legal boundaries of the local jurisdiction. Localities demand the right to accept or reject any proposed action that will have an impact on their communities. Once this right is granted, however, the interests of specific segments of the metropolis must invariably take precedence over those of the metropolis as a whole.

The Gradual Approach

The municipal approach to a multipurpose district, or any other form of "metro," for that matter, is not entirely negative. Local representatives agree upon the need for greater coördination in certain functional areas. However, they point out that mechanisms already exist for securing this coördination and integration. The county-contract plan and other forms of intergovernmental coöperation have enabled Los Angeles County to achieve an unusual degree of coördination. Regional organizations, such as the Air Pollution Control District, the Flood Control District, the Metropolitan Water District, the Metropolitan Transit Authority, and the County Sanitation Districts have already been created to cope with areawide problems. Municipal officials challenge the assumption that areawide problems cannot be solved within the framework of these organizations.

The system of government now existing and the countervailing forces that operate within its constraints combine to produce a framework within which a number of limited adjustments may be predicted:

1. Municipalities in the Los Angeles area will undoubtedly continue to annex, so long as adjacent, unincorporated areas are available. However, incorporation of cities is also likely to continue as urban communities develop.

2. Functional consolidation will continue to be used, especially when a city can free substantial portions of its budget for other assignment by transferring a function to the county, and provided that acceptable arrangements are made for transferring personnel.

3. Cities will make extensive use of intergovernmental contracts, but may be expected to choose from among an increasing number of contractors, including the county, larger cities, and private enterprisers. As newly incorporated cities increase in population, it may be expected that they will withdraw from contractual arrangements for such functions as police protection, and establish their own services. Cities may also be expected to become more selective in the determination of subfunctions for which they will contract.

4. The county government will continue to perform a significant role in influencing urban development of areas not currently included in any city.

The same framework will condition the alternative for change in the governance of the metropolitan area. Which alternatives develop and ultimately prevail will depend upon which leadership groups are selected and their choice of goals.

FOURTEEN

Prospects for Change in Governance of the Metropolitan Area

PLURALISM of political forces and countervailing balances have been emphasized throughout this book. As we consider the prospects for change in the governance of the metropolitan area, we must consider several alternatives. Many contending forces are involved in the process of change. Significant changes among these major contending groups, either in make-up or in goals, will affect the choice of alternative action that will prevail. In a process of government as fluid as that which prevails in this metropolitan area, several alternative results may be predicted from known information, each consistent with the system that has already developed.

WHO WILL LEAD?

Two essential ingredients of the process of political change are incentive and leadership. What incentives are there for change in the structure of government in the metropolitan area? If such incentives can be identified, who would most strongly respond to them? From what source or sources would leadership likely emerge to identify the incentives and offer a method or route to achieve change? Who would be motivated to spend the resources necessary to change the legal constraints and to engineer opinion in support of a change? What type or types of change would allow these leaders to achieve their goal?

General Incentives for Change

The predominant incentive that produced integration by annexation to Los Angeles City in 1913–1928 was desire to share in the water resources controlled by the city. A concomitant incentive that caused small cities, such as Hyde Park, Wilmington, San Pedro, and Sawtelle, to consolidate with Los Angeles was desire to share in the stronger tax base of the larger city. The incentive that led the prevailing group within the city to share the city's resources was the opportunity to construct a service system that enhanced the economic activities dominant within the metropolis. The myth that bigness of a city was important was undoubtedly a factor as well.

Some of the same deficiencies in resources exist today but other alternatives have been devised in order to prevent the desire to overcome the deficiencies from being channeled into a concerted drive to integrate the governmental structure. Desire for a firm water supply, capable of satisfying present and estimated future needs of a growing population, motivates many communities; yet water district systems, aided by federal and state water programs, supply local needs without demanding general governmental integration. No local governmental agency today has control of a resource comparable to the control over water held by Los Angeles City in the earlier period, therefore none is in a comparably advantageous position to control metropolitan change. Resources that are relevant to metropolitan governmental change are now controlled by the state or federal governments.

Local governmental units with low tax resources today seek to supplement their financial resources with state-collected, locally shared taxes and subventions. New sources of revenue, such as the state-administered local sales tax, have assisted cities and counties alike. The tax and subvention programs have encouraged incorporation of cities. Although these programs have not specifically discouraged annexation, they have provided no weighting in favor of annexation as against incorporation.

Trends in the Los Angeles area in 1954–1962 have also been unfavorable to the equalization of tax resources among local units of government. Areas possessing high property valuations, such as Commerce, Industry, and Irwindale, have incorporated as cities and have sought to withdraw from arrangements that distributed their taxable resources so as to assist less favored communities. Several new cities have supported their municipal services by sales taxes and other revenues, relieving industrial properties of tax responsibilities formerly borne by them when the areas were unincorporated. The city of Commerce threatened to withdraw from the county Consolidated Fire District if property taxes continued to be the source of district revenue; industrial property in Commerce allegedly contributed a greater share of the district revenues than it received in district services. The city negotiated a contract with the district and financed the service by sales-tax revenue.

Numerous cities, when negotiating annexations, bypassed low-valuation residential areas and annexed commercial and industrial properties. Several communities, including Vernon, Maywood, and Bell, have sought to withdraw from the gigantic Los Angeles City School District and form independent districts, partly because their high-valuation industrial property base contributed what they regarded as a disproportionate share of the larger district's revenues. High costs of government services and limited tax revenue resources have combined to motivate local officials and voters to protect their public financial resources in every manner possible, even to following a narrowly selfish policy. In most instances, this reaction has produced further fragmentation of governments rather than unification.

Other incentives to group action remain as possible inducements to change. One reflects metropolitan growth. This is the desire to enjoy the benefits of a publicly provided service that will be shared widely throughout the area and that will require greater resources than any single existing local jurisdiction can afford. Examples of such services are ground transportation, regional airport facilities, and regional outdoor recreational facilities. For a ground transportation system to be feasible in a metropolitan area, its services must be widely utilized. It is generally conceded that the resources required to establish such a system must be greater than any existing local authority can summon for the purpose. Although it has been possible for the central city to provide and operate the region's principal general airport facility, growing air transport requirements and desires of other communities for a greater share in the benefits join in creating a demand for some change. Resource requirements for land and capital, as well as other elements, indicate that some regional organization will be needed to produce the newer type of facilities required. Both transportation systems, ground and airport alike, have wide popular appeal, as well as being significant for economic developments. Outdoor recreational facilities fulfill widely expressed desires of a populace that enjoys a rising standard of living and has become aware of an infinite variety of ways in which to enrich leisure time. Land and water resource, as well as capital, requirements indicate that no existing local jurisdiction can come close to meeting the need. Distribution among several jurisdictions of land resources suitable for recreation uses indicates the need for a regional approach to the program.

An incentive for governmental integration that has often been advanced is the desire to conserve economic resources by reducing duplication of expenditures. The structural change that produced the Toronto Metropolitan Municipality evidently was induced, in part, by a desire to centralize the control of local capital expenditures. Each of the major local governments—municipalities, school districts, and transport authority alike—was placed under the jurisdiction of the metropolitan government for review of its capital expenditure proposals. Competitive forces were squeezed into the allocation mechanism assigned to the Metropolitan Council. The American states, generally, have been content to control the capital outlay of local governments by statutory limits and popular referenda upon bonded indebtedness. California has used the special district to alleviate stringencies produced by the control devices, however. So long as land values rise and population pressures increase, arguments to limit property taxes have less plausibility than when these factors are in equilibrium. Furthermore, the steady shift from property taxes to other local revenue sources based upon sales and income draws off the pressure for the type of reorganization made in Toronto.

Groups whose interests benefit from uniform application of policies and standards throughout an area in which they conduct operations usually favor integration as the best means to guarantee uniformity. In the metropolitan scene, those businesses that suffer from having to obtain licenses in numerous local jurisdictions, and therefore are compelled to conform to a variety of standards, can be expected to favor uniformity and integration. Food vending and distributing businesses, hauling firms, and those doing business door-to-door find multiple licensing a burden. The construction industry and its ancillary businesses and trades find the multiplicity of zoning standards and building-code criteria both frustrating and costly. Several persons in the building industry, particularly large-scale investors and developers, have shown a marked interest at times in having the number of local jurisdictions reduced. Yet, two counterelements are seen with equal frequency. Many in the construction and land development industries find it acceptable or advantageous to have diversity, believing that they gain some freedom thereby. At the same time, local administrators spend much effort attempting to produce greater uniformity in enforcement standards by bringing about coöperative efforts in code drafting. Undoubtedly the pressures for change are strong, yet it is difficult to estimate the degree of change that will result. Ameliorative efforts temper the harsher demands. Furthermore, the restrictions fall upon limited numbers of people and are not generally visible. A concerted drive to publicize examples of one restriction brings amelioration of the irritant rather than demand for a complete revision of local governmental structure.

In the realm of nation-states, small units historically have drawn together to form a stronger union against external influences or competitors that threaten to divide and overwhelm individual units. The analogy does not apply fully to local units in a metropolitan setting because local governments are subject to a degree of legal constraint exercised by the state. Nevertheless, events of recent years illustrate that local government leaders band together in associations to meet current problems, ones that were not applicable to local governments in the first part of the twentieth century. Such associations make it possible for local officials to react to activities of the state and federal governments. In such circumstances, the motive to seek allies to protect a status quo or to strengthen a bargaining position becomes highly relevant.

In the Los Angeles scene, local officials have joined in a variety of associations. Some have been institutionalized, some have been kept more fluid. The purposes of association have been both to negotiate legislation and formal relationships and to demonstrate that independent local governments can meet the tests set by metropolitan-area demands. It may well be, however, that demands for areawide services will induce local officials to go further in institutionalizing intergovernmental relations in order to counter the state and prevent it from taking further direct action in metropolitan affairs. Such an incentive admittedly has led those in the San Francisco region to organize the Association of Bay Area Governments under the Joint Powers Act. Fear of being superseded or downgraded in competition for a significant status in metropolitan-area government may similarly motivate leaders of local governments in the Los Angeles area.

INCENTIVES FOR LEADERSHIP

Efforts to produce change in the pattern of government undoubtedly will depend upon leadership provided by one or more elective officials. For success, such efforts would require at least acquiescence by most elective officials. Opposition from this group would be fatal. What incentives, then, would attract an elective officer to provide the overt leadership for a campaign to integrate or produce greater coördination? Most often, an elective officer is content to operate within the framework of the governmental unit in which his office lies. Under some circumstances, he will seek to enhance his career by trying for office in a larger jurisdiction or endeavoring to win a more prestigeous office. A city councilman moves up the political career ladder by election to the county Board of Supervisors or to the State Legislature. A legislator seeks a statewide office or a seat in Congress.

Political leaders conceivably might be interested in creating some form of metropolitan area government if there were a reasonable possibility that they might fill one of the posts, provided that the new positions carried attractive perquisites. Toronto city officials found the Metropolitan Municipal Board very attractive, although several originally opposed creation of "Metro." The incentive of office is scarcely sufficient alone, however, to motivate political leaders so long as a satisfactory hierarchy and a plentiful number of offices of prestige and power are available. An elective officer can be attracted to take an active part in a program or activity seeking change if it assures him of extensive publicity and an opportunity to establish himself as a public servant who has accomplished a major feat of political leadership. Such an accomplishment may either assure him a successful transition to high office in the state or federal government, or guarantee him a status of great prestige in the local area throughout his lifetime.

These incentives do not operate in a vacuum. Political leaders who are ambitious for elective office tend to engage in those activities and emphasize those issues that will win the support of large segments of the electorate as well as of groups upon whose backing they depend for a nucleus of power. Incentives to group action therefore become equally important as those that attract elective political leaders. However, let us first examine which types of elective offices might yield a potential leader for metropolitan reorganization. Would the mayor of Los Angeles likely be attracted, by reason of his position and its responsibilities? Would a member of the Board of Supervisors, a member of the Los Angeles City Council, or a mayor or councilman of a suburban city be attracted, normally? How about a member of the lower house of the Legislature, elected from a district in the Los Angeles metropolitan area? Would a state senator be a likely leader? Or would the governor of the state predictably offer an influential hand to the most populous metropolitan area in the state? The answer in each case would be influenced, in part, by the scope of the particular office, its access to important sources of power and influence, the relevance of reorganization to the office's constituency, and by the power of the office to influence change.

A mayor of Los Angeles might conceivably be induced to lead some type of reorganization drive, although the odds appear to be rather heavily weighted against this. The position of mayor carries heavy responsibilities, but the city charter does not give the office proportionate authority. Much of the mayor's time is spent in trying to push his programs through an internally complex mechanism. On the other hand, the mayor has access to a very considerable bureaucracy. His words and actions receive immediate attention by the press, radio, and television; he can also gain access to important centers of influence in the community. If a Los Angeles mayor were to seek to achieve any significant role of leadership in the metropolitan area, he would need first to accustom suburban leaders to his working with them to achieve common goals. At present, the jealousies and antipathies expressed towards the central city by suburban leaders spread to include the mayor himself. Also, significantly, no mayor of Los Angeles has yet succeeded in using his office as a springboard to reach higher office.

Mayors and councilmen of suburban cities are under several limitations. They are part-time office holders. Each has limited access to the machinery of his own government, sharing access with other elective officers. None has access to public news media regularly in a manner comparable to the mayor of Los Angeles. This group of municipal officials strongly influences its members on metropolitan questions through participation in the Los Angeles Division of the League of California Cities. Members of the group are heavily committed to opposing integration. Under some circumstances, they might respond to a proposal for voluntary coöperation similar to that undertaken by the Association of Bay Area Governments.

County Supervisor Warren Dorn initiated efforts to form a Metropolitan Area Study Commission in 1958. That activity brought together a considerable percentage of the elective officials of Los Angeles City and the suburban communities, as well as the county board. This group held two organizing meetings, and gave some promise of producing an agenda for future study. The effort was dropped, however, when funds could not be obtained to employ a staff. No specific agenda was ever developed. Those fostering this effort had a basic assumption that it was necessary to involve the elective officials from the various local governments if a plan to produce areawide coördination were to succeed. Yet negative pressures prevailed. The county supervisors have continued to place confidence in county-city contracts and intergovernmental coöperation as the most satisfactory program for the county, and hence for their own political standing.

Some members of the Legislature have shown considerable interest in questions pertaining to metropolitan organization. Being elected by districts, however, Assemblymen have generally shown great cautiousness. Some have been opposed to integration or coördination. On the other hand, Assemblyman Rees, representing a Beverly Hills district, and a close supporter of Governor Brown's administration, chaired a legislative interim subcommittee dealing with metropolitan government and introduced major bills on the subject in the 1959 and 1961 sessions. Chief among the bills was the "multipurpose district act," based upon 1961 recommendations by the governor's Commission on Metropolitan Area Problems. However, Rees had little support from other members of the Los Angeles group in the Assembly and, in the face of strong lobby opposition, was unable to push his bill.

Los Angeles County has only one representative in the State Senate. The incumbent of that position is likely to have a lively interest in metropolitan affairs, for he is the one elective officer who must be concerned about the entire area. The holder of this office is likely to be a pivotal person to legitimize any structural change that may be agreed upon locally. Nevertheless, there are numerous limitations upon the leadership potentials of this office in this matter. This officer cannot afford to support any plan that would favor either the central area or the suburbs at the expense of the other. As a legislator, he has limited resources. The scene of his activities is the Legislature, located over four hundred miles from his constituency. In the interim between sessions he has very limited opportunities for gaining public attention. He has only a small staff. His opportunities for gaining access to the channels of mass communication are much poorer than those enjoyed by an elected executive, such as the mayor of the central city or the governor of the state. During his eight years in office, Senator Richard Richards showed an active interest in metropolitan matters, but estimated that it was not politically advantageous at that time to sponsor legislation to produce organizational change.

Upon taking office in 1959, Governor Brown indicated an interest in utilizing the chief executive office to explore possibilities of metropolitan change. Without waiting for legislative discussion, he appointed a study commission and directed it to study the statewide problem. Although traditions of local home rule would tend to deter a governor from singling out one metropolitan area for attention, he has extensive resources at hand to assist any locally sponsored effort that would seek his aid. The Los Angeles area is the most populous section of the state, and recognition of this fact moves candidates for the gubernatorial office to spend considerable time there wooing votes. The incumbent of the office spends an increasing amount of his time in Los Angeles, conferring with local leaders and relating the programs of state government to issues current in Los Angeles affairs. His speeches, press releases, and plans are given wide circulation. Significantly, most of the administrative departments of state government have field offices in Los Angeles and state administrative heads are regularly involved in the area's affairs. Under several conditions, the governor would have both incentive and facility to exercise a leadership function in metropolitan change.

Restrictive factors, different from those that affect political leaders, but equally limiting, narrow the availability of leaders from the business community. Corporate executives have access to relevant resources; for example, talent, organization, money, and prestige. Nonetheless, corporate officers are responsible to directors, investors, and associates; and the primary responsibility of a business firm is to perform those activities that will yield an income. Many firms are regularly involved in negotiating with local governments in the normal course of conducting business operations. They tend to concern themselves only in those governmental procedures or operations that relate closely to business objectives; other, merely "political" involvement in government is likely to be avoided on the ground that it may expose the firm to unnecessary criticism. Individual officers of business firms engage in these so-called political activities, but usually apart from their responsibilities as corporate executives; activities that are likely to engender controversy may affect adversely the public relations of the firm, and hence are avoided by officers. An increasing number of corporate executives accept responsibilities in fund-raising and organizational work for a variety of civic organizations, which predominantly are concerned with the welfare or cultural affairs of the community. Although a business executive finds that much of this activity drains time and energy from business pursuits, it does not threaten either his status in the community or that of his firm. There is no controversy about the value of the objectives of these organizations; there is little likelihood that they will be involved in an ideological dispute. Nevertheless, executives who enter political activities risk threats of various types, unless a considerable segment of the business community is sympathetic or jointly involved.

The business community has supplied the leaders for some of the officially appointed reorganization commissions. Two of the most publicized commissions, the Governmental Simplification Commission (1934) and the "Little Hoover" Commission (1951), were led by businessmen. Some of the most active leaders were semiretired from business; others were attorneys or were engaged in businesses closely associated with government. Missing from most such commissions were heads of financial establishments and senior executives from large corporate manufacturing, sales, or service firms.

Some situations involving metropolitan area government have aroused segments of the business community in the past. Flood conditions in several areas caused concern for property owners, investors, and those interested in developing residential and commercial tracts. This led to the organization of an areawide program of storm-drain construction. Public disturbance over the air pollution situation moved important segments of the business community to join with political leaders in bringing into being a regional control organization, although many businesses were adversely affected or were required to spend considerable sums for corrective action. Businessmen took an active part in having the Metropolitan Transit Authority created to handle public transportation. In general, leadership recruited from the business community has dealt with specific situations that affected a major section of that community. Situations involving flood damage, polluted air, or transportation need are specific, can be isolated from the routine of events, and can be conceptualized as "problems" to be solved. The solutions that have been offered are reasonably specific in terms of administrative structure, responsibility, and financing. A particular, single-function agency was directed to develop a program and authorized to spend public funds. From the Los Angeles experience, it can be predicted that the business community will most likely react favorably to metropolitan change in those instances in which a single "problem" is identified and a solution can be reached by creating a special-purpose district or government corporation.

A group that is very influential in forming opinions concerning the governance of the metropolitan area comprises the press, radio, and television media. Thus far, each of the central-area newspapers has regarded proposals for change of metropolitan area government as good news-items. Feature stories and editorials on this and related subjects appear often. In recent decades, these papers have seldom supported any specific plan or proposal without qualifications. By the extent and type of coverage given news relating to the county Board of Supervisors, the Los Angeles City government, and the Los Angeles Civic Center development, the *Times* developed an image that is favorable to a metropolitan system whose hub is the downtown business center of Los Angeles. This is offset slightly by four special sections in the Sunday and Thursday editions featuring news of subregional areas. The *Herald-Examiner* focuses attention upon the central area chiefly. The major daily newspapers in Long Beach, Pasadena, Santa Monica, and other suburban communities strongly support the continuance of the local governments in their areas. Attitudes of the dailies are influenced by attitudes and economic interests of their principal advertisers. The community weeklies, eager to build up local reader-ship strength that will bolster their bid for community-centered ad-vertising, emphasize community or local news. They tend to support enterprises that enhance local interest.

Radio and television, like the metropolitan dailies, regard proposals for metropolitan change as good news subjects. By emphasizing prob-lems arising from jurisdictional disputes between local governments and from the multiplicity of local governments, commentators tend to support the attitude that unification and structural change is desirable. Clearly the news media are divided in their attitudes towards govern-mental matters affecting the entire area. Nevertheless, publishers of the daily newspapers and owners of major radio and television stations would be counted in any leadership group seeking a particular change in metropolitan government. Judging by past performance, it is very doubtful if any one of them would undertake to initiate such a move unless an important segment of the business community with which they are associated urged the action.

Other types of groups have not yet demonstrated a leadership inter-est in metropolitan change. The labor movement has confined its local activities chiefly to the traditional range of interests relating to the economic aspirations of the wage earner. Although individual labor union officials have been selected to serve on official commissions and committees, there has been little effort made within labor organizations locally to ascertain if intergovernmental relations or the system of local government in a metropolitan area held any significance for organized labor.

Leaders of minority groups have adapted themselves to the pattern of local government and have sought to articulate the demands of their groups to the makers of existing policy. The Negro community is the most active and largest minority group involved in local government in the Los Angeles area. This community is located in several cities and in portions of unincorporated territory. Only in Los Angeles City are the Negroes sufficiently numerous that they have voiced a demand to elect candidates from their ethnic group to the City Council or to draw council district boundaries to favor them as a group. Shifts in support from incumbent Mayor Poulson to candidate Yorty in the mayoralty election of 1961 indicated that Negro group-voting had become an important factor in central city election politics. In 1963, three Negroes were elected to the City Council. Negro leaders have been active in county government affairs as well as in Los Angeles

City. To date, this group has not articulated an interest with respect to any specific aspect of metropolitan government.

The Mexican-American group is another large group that has become active in local politics recently. It is scattered widely throughout the county, although the principal concentrations are in the Boyle Heights section of Los Angeles, the unincorporated East Los Angeles area, Monterey Park, Montebello, Duarte, Irwindale, and Pico Rivera. One leader from this group has been a member of the Los Angeles City Council for several years; others serve on councils in Duarte and Pico Rivera. After a long period of lethargy towards politics, this group has become articulate and is using group voting to gain influence in local affairs. Mexican-Americans were active in incorporating Duarte and Irwindale. Their community divided over incorporating East Los Angeles, a proposed city that would have had a Mexican-American voting majority. It can be estimated that Mexican-Americans will favor a local government system in which they have an opportunity to make themselves felt, wherein they will not be swallowed by newly constituted majorities. In smaller units they have won some influence. In a larger system, such as Los Angeles City, the present structure is such that they can make use of geographically concentrated voting strength to win a share in the influence system.

Each group, elective officers, business leaders, and minority-group leaders, has certain incentives that will cause it to favor certain alternatives for metropolitan governmental change and to be uninterested or opposed to others. The type of change to be anticipated, then, will be determined largely by which group makes a concerted effort to obtain change at a time favorable to success.

Los Angeles, a relatively young metropolitan area, does not have among its leadership groups individuals whose interests are in a sense detached from interest-group advantage. Some great urban centers, such as New York and Philadelphia, have a cadre of senior statesmen who respond to calls for civic leadership from time to time. Some have "graduated" from the partisan battles or struggles of industry and have considerable wealth as well as personal prestige. Others are members of old families with inherited wealth who possess marked ability in their own right. To say that Los Angeles does not possess either type of potential leader is not to state a value judgment that such leadership is indispensable or that it is to be hoped for in future. One must simply observe that no such types exist here, and that the types present and active will determine the choice of change in government of the metropolitan area, if there is to be change.

WHAT ARE THE ALTERNATIVES?

Four alternatives appear to be legitimate extensions of the governmental system that has developed. Two are institutional and require changes in the formal structure, although neither directly threatens the existing pattern of local governmental institutions. A third is based upon the process of negotiation and compromise, although it will be necessary to create an institution to ensure continuity and to facilitate implementation of the negotiations. The fourth rests entirely upon the process of negotiation, but it employs countervailing forces to obtain more immediate and continuous action than does the third alternative. It rests upon the assumption that the state will choose to use the leverage it possesses as the larger administrative and political unit to influence local governmental action, rather than employ fully the legal powers that it possesses.

The Metropolitan Special District

If it is assumed that the countervailing forces now at work in the metropolitan area are sufficiently equal in strength to maintain the present balance in relationships, a strong possibility exists that additional special districts will be created to satisfy the demand for new areawide services. This assumes too that the existing system of interlocal relations will satisfy most of the demands for governmental functions at the local level, and that the state and federal governments will continue to provide services and subventions comparable to those provided at present.

The district form of government has a number of features to commend it for metropolitan areas. Its complete flexibility is the greatest attraction. The Legislature is under few constitutional restrictions with respect to forming a district, assigning functions to it, and determining its formal structure. Inasmuch as municipal and county governments have become relatively rigid in the midst of metropolitan growth, the special district looms as a means for change. A metropolitan special district can be superimposed, in effect, upon the existing local government structure. Dislocations of existing relationships are therefore confined to specific functions rather than spread over the entire governmental system.

In the metropolitan setting, a basic choice must be made between creating one or more single-purpose districts and creating a multipurpose district. Each alternative has distinctive values not duplicated in the other. The differences are not minor. A proposal to add a second or a third function changes the situation entirely and introduces a host of new problems. Experience in the Los Angeles area indicates that single-purpose districts have an appeal that makes them easier to create than any form of multipurpose government. They have an explicitness and an apparent simplicity that appeals to those who are concerned with a set of events that are viewed as a "problem."

Population increases, technological changes, and changing activities of metropolitan residents combine to produce certain new perceptions of interrelationships among people that create new "problems." Perceptions of needs for such activities as areawide traffic planning, regional airport facilities, a ground transportation system, or regional outdoor recreational facilities grow more intense. The single-purpose district becomes attractive to meet the need when local governments cannot supply an acceptable performance through unilateral or cooperative action, or when the financial requirements of the proposed activities threaten the support of long-established functions.

The favorable features of this type of governmental unit are well known. A grant of taxing power, by the legislative act creating the district, assures a specific source of support and frees the district from the type of restrictions that departments of such multifunction governments as cities or counties are subjected to in the annual budget process. The district's entire staff may concentrate all efforts to perform the function assigned without dissipating attention or energies in satisfying the demands of the central management of a multifunction government. Its policy makers can focus upon the requirements of the single function and devote their entire resources to fulfilling those requirements. By its nature, the single-function district attracts a clientele, comprising users of its service, interested in the service level it will provide and prepared to defend the organization against attacks. To reduce possible antagonisms, the boundaries of a special district may be drawn to exclude property that will not benefit from the service.

If a function has become troublesome or beyond the means of smaller local governments to perform satisfactorily, local officials may well be glad to transfer it to a new agency. A new agency may not jeopardize the public esteem enjoyed by the transferring government, but a transfer to an existing competitor-government would enhance the status of the latter.

Objectionable aspects of special districts are equally well known. Unless a special district is to be financed by new sources of revenue, it adds to the pyramiding of taxes upon real property. A mechanism is lacking to evaluate the various claims upon the property tax and to apportion the resources among the several units of government. A governing board of a general-purpose government, such as a city or county, is able to allocate its revenue among competing claimants by means of the annual budget. When several governments compete for the same source of revenue, however, the responsibility to allocate rests with the voters and they have only a very crude method available to express their choice. The number of special districts existing in the metropolitan area tends to add to the difficulties of the voter in expressing his will upon public policies. He is often less aware of special districts than of general-function governments, and is less clear about the channels by which he may transmit complaints or register a choice on district policies.

Special districts add to the number of governmental units having independent programs, with a consequent lack of coördination. A metropolitan airport district would serve a region more effectively if its air transport facilities were planned to coördinate with ground transportation systems and with zoning and planning for areas surrounding its facilities. A regional outdoor recreation district would need to coördinate its plans with those of local recreation and parks departments, with state and local water agencies, fire authorities, and road authorities. Coördination can be effected between independent jurisdictions, but it is usually accomplished much more easily in a multifunction government, particularly if there is effective central management. The reasons for creating a special district emphasize the district's functional interests and minimize its relations with other organizations.

The multifunction special district is attractive because it brings together under one administrative structure two or more closely related functions but does not require the full array of governmental services that a city or county must legally perform. This was the chief merit that caused the members of the Governor's Commission on Metropolitan Area Affairs to recommend the multipurpose special district as the most desirable mode of bringing about metropolitan simplification. The commission proposed to call a moratorium upon creation of new single-purpose districts in metropolitan areas because this form continued the fragmentation of the governmental pattern.

The California model for those who favor multipurpose districts is the municipal utility district; the most relevant example is the East Bay Municipal Utility District in Alameda County. Originally this district was organized to import a water supply to the East Bay cities. A separate park district was installed later on land owned by the EBMUD for reservoir sites in the hills back of Berkeley and Oakland. More recently the utility district's act was amended to permit it to become the metropolitan sewer authority for the East Bay. Each added function had direct relationship to the district's central function or *raison d'être.* The capability of adding functions, as need arises and public confidence in the district organization grows, makes this model attractive to those who favor the "gradualist" approach to metropolitan unification.

Creation of either a single-function or a multipurpose special district for metropolitan government presents the problem of how representatives are to be selected, which in reality is much the same as when interest-groups represented are to control the governing board, and the decision-making. Therefore, the problem is much more than one of mechanics. Will the mode of representation be determined best by electing the board members? Should the dilemma be avoided by making the members appointive? If so, what office or agency should be given the responsibility for recruiting appointees? Should the existing channels of political influence be tied in with the new organization's decision-making process by designating local elected officials to serve as *ex officio* members of the district board?

Three alternatives are suggested by the examination of existing districts serving the metropolitan area. We find that district board members are either appointed by the governor, are appointed by local governing bodies to represent local units, or are locally elected officials serving *ex officio.* No districts serving areawide constituencies in the Los Angeles area have elected boards. Several reasons are advanced against the use of elected governing bodies for special districts; for example, the added expense of conducting elections for an additional unit of government, the expense involved in mobilizing opinion and conducting campaigns for candidates when a district performs only one or two functions, the difficulty of establishing "meaningful" new constituencies in the midst of numerous long-established electoral districts, the fear that a district with an elected board will become in reality a new, "super-level" of government independent and set apart from the long-established local units.

The Metropolitan Transit Authority and the Sixth District Agricultural District are directed by boards whose members are appointed by the governor. Political interests that prevail in the choice of board members vary from time to time as the governor considers the advice and claims put forward by interested groups.

The flood and air pollution control districts are administered by the Board of Supervisors, serving *ex officio.* Those persons or groups who are influential in electing board members therefore can be influential in district matters. The Metropolitan Water District and the county

Sanitation District System are controlled by large boards comprising representatives of local governments involved in financing the districts and in administering subfunctions related to the districts' program. Board members of MWD are appointed by the chief executive or governing body of the member cities and water districts. Emphasis is given formally to representing taxable real property. Board membership is apportioned among the cities and districts in relative proportion to the amount of taxable property; in addition, voting in board transactions is weighted according to the ratio of taxable property represented. The Sanitary District System board is selected on the basis of representation for each city whose residents are served by the district, with the county representing any unincorporated area served. Each district board is composed of a mayor or councilman from each city served, and one or more supervisors from the county board, all serving *ex officio*. The combined district system is governed by the several district boards meeting in joint assembly.

The choice of a base of representation for a new metropolitan district will depend in large part upon the function or functions assigned. No all-encompassing theory of representation or concept of purpose has controlled the formation of special districts in the past. The basis for each district has been negotiated in the legislative process. The function to be performed, the relationships between contending interested groups, and the goals of these contenders have influenced the choice. Significantly, neither existing metropolitan special agency whose board is appointed by the governor depends upon taxation for financial support. Both administer facilities or enterprises that are revenue producing; both are engaged in activities that are recognized as being largely regional in impact of service. However, in administering the Coliseum and the Sports Arena, the Agricultural District board shares responsibility with the county supervisors and the Los Angeles City government. Strong efforts have been made recently by municipal officials to bring the MTA into close relationship with the governments of those cities in whose territory it operates. On the basis of existing relationships, it seems scarcely predictable that a consensus could be achieved to support creating additional special metropolitan agencies that would be administered by a board appointed by the governor.

Only under special circumstances might it be predicted that the county Board of Supervisors would be chosen *ex officio* governing board of any new metropolitan agency. The conditions are indicated by experience with the two agencies now presided over by the board. When the Flood Control District was formed in 1915, the function assigned was clearly a regional one. Most of the work urgently required was to be performed in unincorporated territory, even though floods had damaged much property within cities. Air pollution was recognized in 1945 as a regional problem. Several cities had tried to deal with it by unilateral action and had been unsuccessful. Furthermore, city governments, as well as private individuals and corporations, were regarded as contributors to air pollution. The district was to regulate municipal incinerators as well as industrial plants and home owners' backyard incinerators.

The federated systems, represented by the MWD and the county Sanitation District System models, appear to be more commensurate with the dominant trend. Both provide a means for linking the existing general-purpose governmental systems of cities and the county in a system that permits decision-making on an areawide function. Both permit general-purpose local governments to perform subfunctions of the areawide function, coördinating the system on a regional framework. The MWD model is somewhat limited in that the basic formula for its organization favors municipalities. When this agency was formed, its function was conceived to be to provide water for urban users. City officials were instrumental in forming the district; municipalities were the original constituent units. No county government was directly involved. On the other hand, the county Sanitation District System was devised to permit the county supervisors and elected city officials to join in directing a program that was regional, serving residents of unincorporated fringe areas as well as those of cities. Both systems provided a framework for decision-making that linked existing general purpose governments and avoided creating an independent new layer of government.

Any institutional plan that proposes to include representatives from all local units of government within the metropolitan area faces a sharp dilemma. Because of the large number of cities that have been permitted to incorporate in Los Angeles County, any plan based upon representation of municipalities will result in a large governing body. However, if a plan proposes to give representation only to selected local governments, those not included cannot participate in the decision-making and will be disinterested in or antagonistic to the district's work. The Leask-Terhune Plan for a Metropolitan Special Service District attempts to meet this dilemma and yet produce a governing board that would be of moderate size. It proposes to group the suburban cities in a series of zones that are to be approximately equal in taxable wealth, and to permit the cities located within each zone to select a designated number of representatives to the district board. The central city would be given representation proportionate to the amount of taxable wealth located within it.

Several reasons can be advanced in favor of constituting a special district board to represent existing municipalities and the county—a federated form of organization. If the function or functions assigned to the new district are to be divided so that the district performs those subfunctions that are regional in impact, and the cities and the county perform subfunctions that are local, the federated system of district organization ensures coördination of interest. The MWD is the model for this system. As a regional wholesaler in water resources distribution, the MWD performs those subfunctions that are essential to gathering and storing the water and bringing it to the general area where it is to be consumed. Cities and water districts serve as retail agencies, drawing allocated shares of water from the MWD and distributing water to the ultimate consumers. This model is based upon the fact that relatively few local government functions are completely area-wide or completely local in nature. Most functions are capable of being divided into categories of subfunctions, some of which are area-wide and others local.[1] Any new federated system of metropolitan area government can be organized to make use of this division of subfunctions. A metropolitan district that is assigned exclusive jurisdiction over a function risks being isolated from the local governmental environment in which it must operate. It is likely to be confronted with antagonism from local government officials whose jurisdiction is being encroached upon or threatened.

If the district's program is to be financed by taxes upon real property, there is a problem of mediating claims against this tax resource. There is, at the same time, a need to balance the representation of units of local government and the tax resource base. If a district board is composed of representatives of local governments, a bloc representing several low tax-resource units could establish a district program and apportion its benefits in a manner that might be detrimental to the interest of the few high-resource areas. Again, the MWD model has much to offer in meeting this problem. Each constituent local government is given representation on the district board, but a balance is achieved by giving wealthier units more members and assigning a weighting to votes in proportion to assessed wealth.

---

[1] Beatrice Dinerman, Richard Yerby, and Ross Clayton, *Metropolitan Services: Studies of Allocation in a Federated Organization* (Los Angeles: Bureau of Governmental Research, University of California, 1961).

The Exercise of Joint Powers

Existing legislation provides another alternative approach to metropolitan government change, one based upon a process of intergovernmental coöperation and a principle of voluntary action to accomplish a purpose that is mutually advantageous. The Joint Powers Act of 1921 authorizes any city, county, or special district to coöperate with any other unit of government to perform jointly any function that any may perform singly. The relationships need not be institutionalized initially, therefore the utmost flexibility is possible.

Although this alternative has already been made legitimate in a legal sense, imaginative leadership will be needed to inaugurate action. To produce by this method a system that will have a meaningful impact upon the Los Angeles metropolitan region will require continued, strong persuasion to bring together a sufficient number of officials from the existing local governments. Current trends in intergovernmental relations indicate a greater likelihood that groupings of local governments of less than regional extent will band together to exercise their powers jointly. For the joint-powers approach to be useful on an areawide basis, a strong, persuasive pressure must be applied. It may be that, as in the San Francisco Bay area, the League of California Cities and the County Supervisors Association will be induced to provide this element.

If the joint-powers approach is attempted, it is conceivable that, for a long period, the only benefit derived will be accustoming officials of the several cities and the county to talking with each other in a semi-formal environment. For many years, the city officials have been accustomed to discussing common interests at meetings of the Los Angeles Division of the League of California Cities and of the statewide League. Officials of individual cities are familiar with meeting the supervisor representing their district on the county board or, occasionally, with the entire board. They are also accustomed to transacting sanitation districts' affairs with the county board members at the joint meetings of the county district system. The Los Angeles Metropolitan Traffic Commission, consisting of members representing cities and the county, has been useful in influencing freeway location and highway master plan development. The County Regional Planning Commission has fostered intergovernmental discussions by establishing area planning committees, comprising city officials and citizens, to aid in developing area plans. Mayors and council members attend meetings of the Board of Supervisors when a specific agenda item concerns their city. However, there is no continuing framework within which city and county elective officers are brought together to discuss matters pertaining to the area as a whole. If intergovernmental coöperation is to achieve truly metropolitan perspective, this type of confrontation of local officials will be necessary.

The Association of Bay Area Governments, organized in the San Francisco–East Bay region, is the prototype of any organization that may be formalized in the process proposed here. A secretariat and a general manager are essential to provide the focus for organizational activity, to prepare agendas for meetings, and to gather information. An executive committee, composed of representatives chosen by each county involved and by the group of municipalities that are members of the association, would provide direction during the interim between general membership meetings and determine the agenda for discussions. Periodically, it would be necessary to convene representatives of all local units belonging to the association in a general assembly.

To inaugurate such an association in Los Angeles, it would be necessary for the organizers to stipulate that as soon as a minimum number of local governments had agreed to join, they would convene the group and start work. It would also be essential to guarantee that other local governments would be permitted to join later and enjoy the same status as original members.

The most important and difficult procedural problem that will likely arise early in the life of an association of this type is to achieve agreement on the selection of topics of basic interest to be explored for possible action programs. Through working together and attempting to achieve this consensus on discussion topics, the participants become accustomed to conducting transactions in a large group and to thinking in terms that range beyond the boundaries of their local jurisdictions. A new modus vivendi could be expected to develop.

After decisions as to the identity and definition of common problems have been reached, there is time to consider what action shall be taken. The conditions under which the joint-powers process develops dictate that there should be flexibility in action programs. It may well be that, after discussing a problem fully and reaching the conclusion that a certain function is regional in its impact, the discussants will agree that each local governmental unit should take action in accordance with a standard approved by the association. It is equally possible that the group may agree to draw a formal contract, assigning administrative responsibility to one of the larger or more appropriately equipped local units to serve as the agent for all. Or, again, it may be that the decision will permit smaller groups within the region to create a coöperative arrangement appropriate to their areas, to be co-ordinated with a region-wide plan or set of standards. Once agreement has been reached as to objectives, many possible combinations of factors may be devised to achieve a plan for action.

Inasmuch as this proposed system depends upon persuasion and mutual interest, there is strong likelihood that something less than a complete number of local governments within the metropolitan area will choose to participate. It is also possible that some governments may enter the discussions in the early stages, but withdraw later if the preponderant number express preference for a program a minority does not accept. Obviously, such are the risks of voluntary processes. A program based upon coöperative action will require the participants to devote considerable time and much ingenuity to developing an activity that will show tangible results. Nevertheless, this activity can be initiated with less formality and expenditure of funds than any approach requiring greater institutional structuring. The most significant result will be the conditioning of local elective officials to talk with each other about region-wide problems.

The greatest liability is inaction. If the process of discussion and negotiation is to be speeded up, some counterpressure or incentive will need to be supplied. A demand, engineered by groups seeking an advantage and based upon popular discontent with the status quo, to create one or more special districts or an integrated metropolitan government would supply such an incentive. Proposals by the state government to take over the performance of functions that are metropolitan in nature would be equally conducive.

State Leadership in Metropolitan Area Affairs

Several alternatives are open to the state to exercise leadership in bringing about change in a particular metropolitan area. Basically, it has the legal authority to legislate changes. It may use the financial, legislative, and administrative resources it possesses to persuade and lead the local governments in a metropolitan area to take joint action. Conceivably, it could propose to move more directly, by means of state administrative action, to deal with metropolitan problems if, after an interim period, the local governments demonstrated themselves unwilling or incapable of taking effective coöperative action.

Legislative revision of the formal structure of government in a metropolitan area, unless consented to by local political leaders, is unrealistic. The home-rule tradition in California politics is too strong. Whatever legislation will be adopted to apply to a specific area will legitimize locally initiated proposals.

The administrative resources of the state are considerable, although they have scarcely ever been used in a coördinated manner to alleviate the problems of metropolitan areas. Over a period of fifty, or more, years the California state government has developed a series of administrative functions that, when exercised in a specific area, have made profound impacts upon its political, economic and social make-up. Included in such functions are highway and freeway location and construction, health protection, mental health care, and water resource development and protection. Until very recent years, the state government performed its functions in a manner that tended to place greater emphasis upon serving rural areas and developing broad intrastate regional relationships. This emphasis was based upon prescriptions of legislative policies. For example, in allocating state highway funds, the Legislature gave priority to highways connecting metropolitan areas, farm-to-market routes, and statewide recreational routes, rather than to highways designed to serve the internal transit needs of specific metropolitan areas. In other words, state highways brought traffic to the edge of the metropolis, but left local governments the problem of providing for the flow of traffic within their borders. State highway policy changed after 1945, and the state administrative heads now plan more explicitly for metropolitan-area traffic needs.

Prior to the adoption of the State Water Plan, state water agencies were chiefly concerned with agricultural water uses, the largest demand upon the state's water resources. The new plan seeks to serve both urban and agricultural users, although the policies for financing the project and the contract with the Metropolitan Water District of Southern California make it more an urban project.

State administrative programs are organized by functional units, for example, highways, health, mental health, employment, institutions, and water resources, as are most governmental systems. This means, then, that coördination of program development and operations is performed at the top of the administrative hierarchies. Various state departments have developed their own individual procedures for establishing liaison with city and county officers concerned with related administrative programs. Each administrator of a state regional office develops informal relations with local governments and with clientele interest groups relevant to the particular department's program. The regional highway engineer gets to know the local road and city administrators, as well as political leaders interested in highway location. Employment office directors become acquainted with major local employers and local agencies. Water resources engineers become well acquainted with local water officials and major users. There is relatively little coördination between state agencies at the local or metropolitan level, however.

Since 1921, governors have been seeking means by which to coördinate the state's administrative activities, and give unity and purpose to the state's performance. Numerous state administrative reorganizations have sought to accomplish this objective. Governor Brown, in 1961, interposed a new level of appointive executive officer, known as the agency administrator, between the department heads and the governor's office, in an effort to strengthen top-level coördination and supervision. These new officers are referred to as assistant governors. However, no serious study has yet been given the concept that state programs might also be coördinated at the metropolitan area level.

If the state's chief executive were to coördinate the planning and performance of the administrative agencies' programs in a metropolitan area, the state would be able to act as an effective metropolitan force, reflecting broader-gauge views than any espoused by a local government. The state spends large sums of money annually and employs a large army of civil servants to perform state functions within the metropolitan area. It operates an extensive number of institutions and public works facilities and makes innumerable decisions that affect the growth and development of the Los Angeles metropolitan area. Its potential for leadership in meeting area problems has not really been developed. Significant beginnings are illustrated by efforts of the state departments of health and mental health, the Highway Commission, and the state Planning Office, in the Finance Department, to work with local officials in planning programs within the metropolitan area. The Local Health Officers Conference, organized by the Department of Health, illustrates an interesting procedure wherein local health officers participate with state health officials in developing standards and plans that are promulgated as state policies and are implemented by both state and local officials. State planning officers assist city and county officials with regional land use planning and zoning when requested. City and county officials have grown accustomed to traveling to Sacramento, as well as to regional offices, to negotiate various local-interest programs with state officials. If the state government were to have a more fully developed set of policies relating to metropolitan area affairs, its principal executive and administrative officers could exercise more leadership in such matters in their relations with local officials.

Traditionally, Americans have divided intrastate matters into a simple dichotomy of state and local. They have insisted, generally, that the state confine itself to matters that are "statewide" in impact, and leave to local governments those matters that are limited in scope. The metropolitan "problem" arises, in part, because the metropolitan area does not fit this simple dichotomy. By reason of its constitutional position, as well as its responsibilities in administrative programs, the state is in a position to bridge that gap if it will extend and coördinate its existing functions.

A concomitant problem, then, is to provide a method by which the state can develop an interrelated set of policies for metropolitan area affairs. Responsibility for developing, as well as directing the performance, of such policies ultimately rests with the governor. Like any political executive in the American system, the Governor requires staff assistance to formulate policy proposals and to direct their implementation. What type of staff assistance is required to assist the governor in developing policies for assisting metropolitan area government and in implementing them, once they are crystallized? There are three types to be considered, two of which are exhibited in a few American states. The governor may appoint a personal assistant to have as extensive responsibilities for advising him on metropolitan area affairs as he chooses. He may further institutionalize such assistance, with the aid of the Legislature, by creating an office of urban affairs in the executive branch to aid him by gathering data, preparing policy plans, maintaining liaison with local officials and their organizations, and drafting and sponsoring legislation pertaining to urban and metropolitan affairs. The Governor of New York, Nelson Rockefeller, has sought to establish this model of institution. A third type is the commission or board for metropolitan area affairs. Such an institution usually comprises a multimember board, whose members are appointed by the governor and serve part-time, and a chairman who has limited executive authority. The board approves subjects for study, develops policy proposals, holds hearings; may act as an administrative tribunal to grant permits and approve proposals; and otherwise enforces legislative policy. Such an institution is usually assisted by a small professional staff. The board is both advisory to the governor and administrative or operational. The extent of its authority and the range of its influence depends upon statutory authority, budgetary resources, and gubernatorial confidence in its usefulness. The state of Minnesota has undertaken an experiment with this type of institution. The Canadian Province of Ontario has had a municipal board for several years.

The simplest method to begin preparing the state for a more active role in urban and metropolitan area affairs is to create a position of assistant or secretary to the governor. Governor Brown was the first

California governor to select an assistant specifically for such an assignment. During his first four-year term, Brown made special assignments of metropolitan topics to various assistants, but just prior to his second inauguration he designated Mr. Sherrill Luke, a former assistant city manager, his assistant for urban affairs. The first responsibilities were to prepare legislative proposals for the Governor's program in the 1963 session. If a governor is to carry on active leadership in metropolitan area affairs, it is essential that he have staff assistance from members of his own office who will have definite, continuing responsibilities. A staff member with duties of this nature should have the kind of access to the state's chief executive that comes with being a member of the official in-group. The assistant should have fully-sponsored access to various executive departments to obtain information and have material prepared for the governor's use. If so equipped, an assistant can be extremely helpful in preparing and helping to implement the governor's legislative program, and in providing liaison with interest groups.

If the urban affairs office is located within an administrative department, such as the Department of Finance, its usefulness to the governor is reduced, and it becomes enmeshed in the internal bureaucratic impedimenta of a large establishment. To be effective in the assignment, a gubernatorial assistant needs to have sufficient experience in local governmental affairs to earn him the respect of those groups with which he must deal. Public-official groups have been opposed generally to the creation of a bureau or office of urban affairs, fearing that such an organization would be given or would seek administrative responsibilities and would acquire authority to encroach upon matters they have long deemed to be "home rule" affairs. A bureau of urban affairs, even though possibly located in the governor's executive offices, tends eventually to acquire some administrative duties, even those peripheral to its main responsibilities.

If the state is to exercise leadership in the sense that it will coordinate and mobilize its existing strengths, now diffused, to persuade and influence local officials and citizens, the governor will require more extensive staff support than a special assistant for urban affairs can provide. By nature of the duties that are commensurate with the status of a bureau or a commission on metropolitan area affairs, choice of either of these alternatives would create a different style of state-local relations.

If, however, the state is to equip itself to make decisions and establish policies respecting metropolitan area government, the commission alternative will be the more rational choice. A commission exercising

statutory authority and chosen by the governor from among leaders
of important segments of the state political environment will have
considerable weight. Given the political support of the governor,
capable leadership, and a knowledgeable professional staff, a commission can become an important instrument to shape policy.

If such a commission were given statutory authority to review proposed annexations and incorporations and the organization of new
single-purpose special districts within any metropolitan area of the
state, it would have significant influence in shaping the governance of
those areas. An important function of such a commission would be as
a forum for testing the validity of claims and proposals made by competing local interest groups. Another would be testing of local political
maneuvers against the criteria of state policy. To perform these types
of functions, the commission would require instruction by the Legislature regarding state policy and criteria. In exercising delegated authority, it could only develop policy within the guidelines laid down
for it by the Legislature and the governor.

Such a commission might well act chiefly through a type of adversary hearing procedure wherein all interested parties that could
show direct interest in a transaction within its jurisdiction would be
permitted to file briefs or statements, present testimony, and test the
claims of proponents. With a professional staff of its own available
to assist it, the commission could test the factual validity of evidence
submitted to it and offer suggestions or counterplans. For example,
if a proposed annexation were opposed by one or more adjacent cities,
by the county, another special district, or by property owners within
the proposed area, the commission could authorize spokesmen for each
group or party to present evidence in an administrative-type hearing
procedure. The commission would be in a position to examine the
evidence and reasoning for and against the specific annexation, incorporation, or district organization proposed. The proceeding, being
an open public hearing before a disinterested public body, would provide greater factual public information for use by officials and citizens
than does the present system.

The commission's decision might be confined to accepting or rejecting the proposed action, or to granting an alternative proposed by an
interested party in the proceeding, stating its reasons for the action in
a written memorandum. In keeping with currently established policy,
an annexation, incorporation, or special district proposal might be
subjected additionally to a popular referendum in the proposed area.
This would permit voters to exercise a final review, after the commis-

sion had indicated that the proposed action met the criteria established by the state in the interest of the people of the entire state.

Hearings and studies by a commission would bring out information regarding situations requiring new legislative policies, and provide the governor and the Legislature with information to guide them. An administrative commission is more likely to inspire confidence in its decisions than a single bureau or department head. Its greatest contribution would be to provide an orderly means for changing the pattern of local government authority, one in which all principal interests can be heard on an equal footing.

IN CONCLUSION

Local governments have established a record of performance that is, by and large, very favorable. The system of government developed in the state as a whole places local governments in a strong strategic position to bargain with those who wish to integrate governments into larger entities. Furthermore, in the Los Angeles area, the locally elected and appointed officers have demonstrated, over a long period of years, that they are able to devise and operate various procedures to achieve coöperative action. The status of the countervailing forces in the contest is not a static one, although none of the contenders have a preponderance of the resources required to dominate the situation.

The need is for a stimulant or an element that will produce even more rigorous efforts to develop coöperative and joint action. Given the present status of the system of government in California, the most effective element likely to produce this action is the state government, and more particularly the executive branch. By means of constitutional and statutory prescription, the state has absented itself for so long from the leadership in local governmental affairs that Californians are accustomed to thinking only in those terms. Yet, the state is obligated, by its position in the American constitutional framework, to concern itself with matters that affect the welfare of considerable segments of its population. Metropolitan problems are of that type.

As the state takes up its responsibilities in this matter, new concepts of its role are required. It has already become an important administrative entity within its own sphere, and it has experimented with several significant relationships with local governments. In no sense should it supplant local governments, nor is it likely to be permitted to do so. Such action would merely replace one majority's view for that of another. By acting as an energized and purposive countervailing force, the state can influence the leaders of local governments to come to grips more emphatically and imaginatively with known problems and to take action. The state acts for interests that are not fully represented by the several local governments that have achieved the present modus vivendi in this metropolitan area.

EPILOGUE

In 1963 official state leadership made the first major concerted effort to cope with the local government problem in the state's metropolitan areas. Governor Edmund Brown prefaced his legislative campaign with several messages relative to these problems. In conjunction with this he sponsored a "package" of four bills on incorporation, annexation, metropolitan affairs, and regional planning, and included funds in his executive budget to implement a continuing study of urban problems. The Legislature approved the program, although it modified the bills substantially, and the Governor signed the measures on July 20.

As originally proposed, the Governor's plan asked that two state commissions be created and that a series of regional planning districts be created to serve under the State Office of Planning. One commission was to be a quasi-judicial body with authority to pass upon proposals for forming cities and special districts and to review proposed annexations. The other was to be an advisory body with responsibility chiefly to analyze conditions and recommend policies relating to local government in growing urban areas to the Governor.

The concept of a state commission with power to act on incorporation and annexation proposals encountered heavy opposition from the local home-rule forces. The County Supervisors' Association especially opposed AB 1662 (Knox *et al.*) which dealt with formation of cities and districts, whereas the League of California Cities objected to the procedures proposed by SB 861 (Nisbet) relating to annexations. The Governor and his staff then agreed to a major change which substituted commissions to be created in each county. In effect, a single five-member commission is created in each county to pass upon formation of cities and special districts, annexations, and to adopt standards and procedures to control these transactions. Each commission is to be composed of two county officials appointed by the Board of Supervisors, two city officials to be chosen by a selection committee composed of the mayors of cities within the county, and a public member, the chairman, to be selected by the other four. Members are to serve for a term of four years. If a commission approves an incorporation, formation of a district, or an annexation, a referendum is held in the area affected, as previously provided by law. If a commission disapproves of a proposal, however, no similar proposition may be initiated within the area for one year.

A state Coordinating Council on Urban Policy, an eighteen-member body to be appointed by the Governor, will study local government problems in the urban areas and propose policies. The Legislature is to review the need for continuing the Council at the 1965 regular session. The Council is to reflect several constituency interests inasmuch as fourteen of the members must be officials: 3 county, 3 city, 2 school district, and 6 state. Local officials are to be appointed from a list of nominees submitted by the County Supervisors' Association, League of California Cities, and State Board of Education, respectively.

A tentative step toward coördinated regional planning is provided by SB 856 (Rees) which authorizes the state Planning Advisory Committee to designate regional planning districts after two-thirds of the counties and cities in an area declare a need for such action. The counties and the cities are to have equal representation on each district board. The act declares the state's interest in coördinating the planning of state public works within the framework of local plans within each region.

The product of this legislative campaign is an advance toward responsible negotiation and definition of policies. Like many group-negotiated products it does not offer the possibility of bold action, but the groups involved are so evenly balanced in resources and are so accustomed to confronting one another that none of the participants desire bold action. With the state taking a more active part, the many groups involved in making local policies will be pushed to act.

APPENDIX TABLES

APPENDIX TABLE 1

LOS ANGELES CITY:
AREA OF ORIGINAL CITY, ADDITIONS AND DETACHMENTS

Original city and additions				
Date	Name	How obtained	Acres	Sq. miles
1880	Original city	Spanish grant	17,924	28.01
Aug. 29, 1859	Southern Extension	Annexation	766	1.20
Oct. 18, 1895	Highland Park	Annexation	904	1.41
April 2, 1896	Western and Southern Addition	Annexation	6,517	10.18
June 12, 1899	University	Annexation	1,134	1.77
June 12, 1899	Garvanza	Annexation	440	.69
Dec. 26, 1906	Shoestring	Annexation	11,931	18.64
Aug. 28, 1909	Wilmington	Consolidation	6,358	9.93
Aug. 28, 1909	San Pedro, Old City and Annex	Consolidation	2,948	4.61
Oct. 27, 1909	Colegrove	Annexation	5,579	8.72
Feb. 7, 1910	Hollywood, Old City and Annex	Consolidation	2,848	4.45
Feb. 28, 1910	East Hollywood	Annexation	7,112	11.11
Feb. 9, 1912	Arroyo Seco	Annexation	4,416	6.90
May 22, 1915	Palms	Annexation	4,672	7.30
May 22, 1915	San Fernando Valley	Annexation	108,732	169.89
June 10, 1915	Bairdstown	Annexation	2,176	3.40
June 14, 1916	Westgate	Annexation	31,149	48.67
June 14, 1916	Occidental	Annexation	666	1.04
Feb. 26, 1917	Owensmouth	Annexation	495	.773
June 15, 1917	West Coast	Annexation	7,942	12.41
Feb. 13, 1918	West Adams	Annexation	380	.59
Feb. 16, 1918	Griffith Ranch	Annexation	149	.23
April 11, 1918	Hansen Heights	Annexation	5,313	8.30
July 11, 1918	Ostend	Annexation	0.98	—
Nov. 13, 1918	Orange Cove	Annexation	146	.23
June 17, 1919	West Lankershim	Annexation	746	1.17
July 23, 1919	Dodson	Annexation	673	1.05
Aug. 6, 1919	Fort MacArthur	Annexation	360	.56
Sept. 10, 1919	Peck Addition	Annexation	286	.45
Sept. 25, 1919	Harbor View	Annexation	112	.175
Feb. 26, 1920	St. Francis Addition	Annexation	33	.05
Sept. 10, 1920	Hill Addition	Annexation	71	.11
Nov. 19, 1920	Chatsworth	Annexation	220	.34
Feb. 22, 1922	La Brea	Annexation	979	1.53
March 2, 1922	Manchester	Annexation	212	.33
June 16, 1922	Melrose	Annexation	430	.67
July 13, 1922	Sawtelle	Consolidation	1,162	1.82
July 27, 1922	Angeles Mesa	Annexation	632	.99
Oct. 5, 1922	Angeles Mesa No. 2	Annexation	216	.34
Oct. 5, 1922	Rimpau	Annexation	90	.14
Jan. 18, 1923	Hancock	Annexation	169	.26
Jan. 18, 1923	Evans	Annexation	85	.13
May 16, 1923	Ambassador	Annexation	1,684	2.63
May 16, 1923	Laurel Canyon	Annexation	8,684	13.57
May 17, 1923	Hyde Park	Consolidation	770	1.20
May 17, 1923	Eagle Rock	Consolidation	2,027	3.17
May 17, 1923	Vermont	Annexation	16	.025
May 17, 1923	Laguna	Annexation	53	.08
May 17, 1923	Carthay	Annexation	243	.38
Dec. 20, 1923	Rosewood	Annexation	395	.62
Dec. 20, 1923	Agoure	Annexation	15	.02
Dec. 20, 1923	Lankershim	Annexation	4,890	7.64
Feb. 4, 1924	Providencia	Annexation	3,085	4.82
Feb. 13, 1924	Annandale	Annexation	435	.68
Feb. 21, 1924	Cienega	Annexation	595	.93
May 31, 1924	Clinton	Annexation	34	.05
Sept. 8, 1924	Fairfax	Annexation	1,203	1.88
Sept. 8, 1924	Wagner	Annexation	600	.94
Jan. 3, 1925	Holabird	Annexation	8	.01
Jan. 8, 1925	Danziger	Annexation	79	.123
Jan. 30, 1925	Hamilton	Annexation	282	.44
April 28, 1925	Santa Monica Canyon	Annexation	109	.17
April 28, 1925	Martel	Annexation	148	.23
Oct. 26, 1925	Beverly Glen	Annexation	521	.81

APPENDIX TABLE 1 (Continued)

Original city and additions

Date	Name	How obtained	Acres	Sq. miles
Nov. 25, 1925	Venice	Consolidation	2,627	4.105
March 18, 1926	Green Meadows	Annexation	2,285	3.57
May 10, 1926	Buckler Addition	Annexation	128	.20
May 29, 1926	Watts	Consolidation	1,081	1.69
Aug. 4, 1926	Sunland	Annexation	3,848	6.01
Nov. 18, 1926	Tuna Canyon	Annexation	4,910	7.67
March 5, 1927	Mar Vista	Annexation	3,190	4.984
April 11, 1927	Barnes City	Consolidation	1,160	1.81
June 11, 1927	Brayton	Annexation	48	.075
Feb. 10, 1928	Wiseburn	Annexation	91	.14
Nov. 10, 1928	White Point	Annexation	6.60	.01
Feb. 17, 1930	Classification Yard	Annexation	263.50	.41
April 17, 1930	Viewpark	Annexation	12.50	.02
Aug. 1, 1930	Sentney	Annexation	6.12	.01
Oct. 17, 1930	Tobias	Annexation	7.52	.01
April 10, 1931	Cole Addition	Annexation	60.28	.09
March 7, 1932	Tujunga	Consolidation	5,568	8.70
Jan. 31, 1933	Lakeside Park	Annexation	81.10	.13
March 14, 1935	Western Avenue Highlands	Annexation	74.40	.12
Aug. 12, 1940	Crenshaw Manor	Annexation	34.80	.054
July 29, 1941	Fairfax No. 2	Annexation	168.12	.263
Aug. 14, 1941	Crenshaw Manor No. 2	Annexation	59.79	.093
Sept. 12, 1941	Woodland Heights	Annexation	8.69	.014
April 13, 1942	Palos Verdes	Annexation	8.41	.013
April 13, 1942	Fairfax No. 3	Annexation	9.52	.015
Dec. 11, 1942	Fairfax No. 4	Annexation	19.81	.031
April 30, 1943	Dominguez	Annexation	284.57	.445
Jan. 7, 1944	Florence	Annexation	47.96	.075
Sept. 25, 1944	Fairfax No. 5	Annexation	15.72	.024
Dec. 1, 1944	Florence No. 2	Annexation	36.35	.057
Dec. 1, 1944	Florence No. 3	Annexation	15.71	.024
Aug. 16, 1945	Lomita Addition	Annexation	10.60	.017
July 19, 1946	Lomita Addition No. 2	Annexation	5.32	.008
Sept. 18, 1946	Mesa Addition No. 3	Annexation	36.07	.056
Oct. 6, 1946	Mar Vista Addition No. 2	Annexation	39.92	.062
Jan. 24, 1947	Angeles Mesa Addition No. 4	Annexation	261.85	.409
Jan. 29, 1947	Mar Vista Addition No. 3	Annexation	131.36	.205
Oct. 14, 1947	Fairfax Addition No. 6	Annexation	46.68	.073
April 6, 1948	Wiseburn Addition No. 2	Annexation	1.56	.002
April 13, 1948	Danziger Addition No. 2	Annexation	2.14	.003
April 22, 1948	Angeles Mesa Addition No. 5	Annexation	633.86	.990
July 23, 1948	Angeles Mesa Addition No. 6	Annexation	41.60	.065
July 26, 1949	Arnaz Addition	Annexation	93.31	.146
Nov. 4, 1949	Fairfax Addition No. 7	Annexation	6.81	.011
May 3, 1950	Lomita Addition No. 4	Annexation	51.74	.081
Nov. 15, 1950	Lomita Addition No. 3	Annexation	1.34	.002
Dec. 20, 1950	Chatsworth Addition No. 2	Annexation	6.96	.011
Oct. 22, 1951	Belvedere Addition	Annexation	1.98	.003
Oct. 24, 1951	Fairfax Addition No. 8	Annexation	3.68	.006
Oct. 24, 1951	Melrose Addition No. 2	Annexation	1.70	.003
Nov. 7, 1951	Lomita Addition No. 5	Annexation	4.03	.006
June 4, 1952	Norman Addition	Annexation	52.59	.083
June 11, 1952	Lomita Addition No. 6	Annexation	9.74	.016
Oct. 14, 1952	Mar Vista Addition No. 4	Annexation	4.86	.008
Jan. 7, 1953	Westgate Addition No. 2	Annexation	40.40	.063
June 3, 1953	Rolling Hills Addition	Annexation	76.60	.120
June 17, 1953	Mar Vista Addition No. 5	Annexation	6.46	.010
Sept. 15, 1953	Fairfax Addition No. 9	Annexation	1.19	.002
Sept. 28, 1953	Keystone Addition No. 1	Annexation	46.34	.073
Oct. 26, 1953	Rolling Hills Addition No. 2	Annexation	34.76	.054
April 26, 1954	Glenoaks Addition	Annexation	3.00	.005
Aug. 11, 1954	Rolling Hills Addition No. 3	Annexation	182.53	.285
Aug. 10, 1954	Rolling Hills Addition No. 4	Annexation	.84	.001
May 9, 1955	Chatsworth Addition No. 3	Annexation	55.58	.087
June 15, 1955	Sunland Addition No. 2	Annexation	21.48	.034
June 23, 1955	Sunland Addition No. 3	Annexation	6.46	.010
July 11, 1955	Sunland Addition No. 4	Annexation	9.09	.015
Aug. 24, 1955	Rolling Hills Addition No. 6	Annexation	127.07	.199

APPENDIX TABLE 1 (Continued)

Date	Name	How obtained	Acres	Sq. miles
Sept. 21, 1955	Rolling Hills Addition No. 7	Annexation	165.79	.256
Oct. 5, 1955	Tuna Canyon Addition No. 2	Annexation	9.27	.015
Feb. 16, 1956	Arroyo Seco Addition No. 2	Annexation	.72	.001
May 9, 1956	Angeles Mesa Addition No. 7	Annexation	22.78	.036
July 23, 1956	Rolling Hills Addition No. 8	Annexation	.23	.001
Sept. 13, 1956	Sunland Addition No. 5	Annexation	28.83	.045
Dec. 12, 1956	Calabasas Addition	Annexation	16.59	.026
Dec. 17, 1956	Tuna Canyon Addition No. 3	Annexation	3.06	.005
April 17, 1957	La Rambla Addition	Annexation	2.22	.004
May 1, 1957	Torrance Addition No. 1	Annexation	1.11	.002
Oct. 9, 1957	Mar Vista Addition No. 6	Annexation	40.92	.064
May 19, 1958	Wiseburn Addition No. 3	Annexation	1.12	.002
May 22, 1958	Palos Verdes Addition No. 2	Annexation	.58	.001
Sept. 12, 1958	Lomita Addition No. 7	Annexation	.33	.001
Oct. 28, 1958	Calabasas Addition No. 5	Annexation	38.95	.061
Nov. 6, 1958	Calabasas Addition No. 6	Annexation	1,116.13	1.744
Feb. 4, 1959	Calabasas Addition No. 2	Annexation	172.53	.270
Feb. 4, 1959	Calabasas Addition No. 3	Annexation	254.15	.338
Feb. 4, 1959	Calabasas Addition No. 4	Annexation	177.05	.277
Feb. 25, 1959	Laurel Canyon Addition No. 3	Annexation	.48	.001
March 9, 1959	Calabasas Addition No. 7	Annexation	61.16	.096
March 11, 1959	Laurel Canyon Addition No. 2	Annexation	10.90	.017
April 1, 1959	Mar Vista Addition No. 7	Annexation	160.74	.252
Sept. 14, 1959	Sunland Addition No. 6	Annexation	60.92	.093
Feb. 29, 1960	Fairfax Addition No. 10	Annexation	.97	.002
Nov. 25, 1960	Palms Addition No. 2	Annexation	3.25	.006
Nov. 29, 1960	Dominguez Addition No. 2	Annexation	.40	.001
Jan. 13, 1961	Laurel Canyon Addition No. 4	Annexation	.10	—
March 17, 1961	Fairfax Addition No. 11	Annexation	.35	.001
June 1, 1961	Calabasas Addition No. 8	Annexation	.49	.001
Total area (before deducting detachments):			293,621.07	458.691

Detachments

Date	Name	Acres	Sq. miles
March 1, 1948	Burbank Detachment	285.13	.446
Dec. 28, 1948	Beverly Hills Detachment No. 1	6.13	.009
Dec. 28, 1948	Beverly Hills Detachment No. 2	.14	—
Dec. 16, 1949	Culver City Exclusion	4.09	.006
Jan. 21, 1950	San Fernando Detachment	33.10	.051
Oct. 17, 1950	Beverly Hills Detachment No. 3	2.63	.004
Jan. 12, 1951	Beverly Hills Detachment No. 4	8.56	.013
Aug. 28, 1952	Culver City Detachment No. 1	8.32	.013
Aug. 14, 1953	Inglewood Detachment No. 1	17.29	.027
Dec. 21, 1953	Burbank Detachment No. 2	5.56	.009
June 25, 1954	Beverly Hills Detachment No. 5	4.75	.007
Aug. 19, 1954	Burbank, Exclusion No. 1	81.00	.127
Aug. 16, 1955	Burbank Detachment No. 3	12.12	.019
Oct. 19, 1955	Burbank Detachment No. 4	7.19	.011
Jan. 4, 1957	Torrance Detachment No. 1	1.11	.001
Sept. 3, 1957	Beverly Hills Detachment No. 6	7.46	.011
Oct. 14, 1957	Culver City (Frawley No. 1)	1.92	.003
Feb. 4, 1959	Burbank Detachment No. 5	35.13	.054
Dec. 11, 1959	El Segundo Detachment	26.44	.041
Feb. 29, 1960	Beverly Hills Detachment (Clifton Way)	.91	.001
Total area detached		548.98	.853
Totals		293,072.09	457.838

Source: Los Angeles City, Controller, *Annual Report* (Los Angeles, 1961).

APPENDIX TABLE 2

RANK OF CITIES BY PER CAPITA SALES TAX REVENUE[a]

Rank no.	City	Population (1960 census)	Gross sales tax revenue (1959–60)	Per capita sales tax revenue (1959–60)
66	Bradbury	618	$ 1	$ 0.002
65	Rolling Hills	1,664	759	0.46
64	Lawndale	21,740	33,909	1.56
63	Palos Verdes Estates	9,564	23,349	2.44
62	La Verne	6,516	17,871	2.74
61	Rosemead	15,476	54,341	3.51
60	Walnut	934	3,569	3.82
59	Claremont	12,633	53,040	4.20
58	Sierra Madre	9,732	48,170	4.95
57	Baldwin Park	33,951	171,402	5.05
56	Duarte	13,962	72,769	5.21
55	Rolling Hills Estates	3,941	21,823	5.54
54	La Puente	24,723	137,565	5.56
53	Manhattan Beach	33,934	196,877	5.80
52	Glendora	20,752	132,680	6.39
51	Norwalk	88,739	581,630	6.55
50	Pico Rivera	49,150	335,252	6.82
49	Monterey Park	37,821	278,093	7.35
48	Artesia	9,993	75,143	7.52
47	South Pasadena	19,706	164,861	8.37
46	Torrance	100,991	994,672	9.85
45	Paramount	27,249	285,503	10.48
44	Azusa	20,497	216,367	10.56
43	Maywood	14,588	160,399	11.00
42	San Marino	13,658	153,091	11.21
41	West Covina	50,645	624,504	12.33
40	Arcadia	41,005	515,047	12.56
39	Montebello	32,097	412,118	12.84
38	Lakewood	67,126	866,346	12.91
37	Lynwood	31,614	408,353	12.92
36	Gardena	35,943	467,047	12.99
35	Downey	82,505	1,125,528	13.64
34	Long Beach	344,168	4,794,771	13.93
33	Bell	19,450	277,846	14.29
32	Redondo Beach	46,986	680,662	14.49
31	Bellflower	45,909	682,408	14.86
30	Pomona	67,157	1,074,819	16.00
29	San Gabriel	22,561	371,934	16.49
28	Hawthorne	33,035	552,687	16.73
27	Monrovia	27,079	453,428	16.74
26	Compton	71,812	1,214,711	16.92
25	Los Angeles	2,479,015	43,335,386	17.48
24	Burbank	90,155	1,598,174	17.73

APPENDIX TABLE 2 (Continued)

Rank no.	City	Population (1960 census)	Gross sales tax revenue (1959–60)	Per capita sales tax revenue (1959–60)
23	Dairy Valley	3,508	62,470	17.81
22	Alhambra	54,807	991,319	18.09
21	Glendale	119,442	2,270,074	19.01
20	South Gate	53,831	1,066,603	19.81
19	Inglewood	63,390	1,286,621	20.30
18	Hermosa Beach	16,115	334,056	20.73
17	Santa Monica	83,249	1,856,549	22.30
16	Covina	20,124	456,267	22.67
15	Avalon	1,536	36,868	24.00
14	Whittier	33,663	834,062	24.78
13	Pasadena	116,407	2,938,940	25.25
12	Sante Fe Springs	16,342	416,550	25.49
11	San Fernando	16,093	459,232	28.54
10	Culver City	32,163	1,016,837	31.62
9	Huntington Park	29,920	1,005,914	33.62
8	El Segundo	14,219	561,667	39.50
7	South El Monte	4,850	201,532	41.55
6	El Monte	13,163	675,219	51.30
5	Signal Hill	4,627	250,686	54.18
4	Beverly Hills	30,817	1,736,998	56.36
3	Irwindale	1,518	418,427	275.64
2	Industry	778	397,366	510.75
1	Vernon	229	1,923,173	8,398.14
	Total	4,911,585	$84,866,335	

Source: State Controller, California, *Annual Report of Financial Transactions Concerning Cities of California, 1959–60* (Sacramento, 1960), pp. 22–68.
a Average per capita (gross sales divided by population): $17.28.
Mode: $10.01–15.00 range.
Range categories: $ 0.00–$ 5.00 = 9
                    5.01–   10.00 = 12
                   10.01–   15.00 = 15
                   15.01–   20.00 = 11
                   20.01–   25.00 = 6
                   25.01–   30.00 = 3
                   30.01–   35.00 = 2
                   35.01–   40.00 = 1
                   40.01–   45.00 = 1
                   45.01–   50.00 = 0
                   50.01–   55.00 = 2
                   55.01–   60.00 = 1
                   60.01– 280.00 = 1
                  280.01– 515.00 = 1
                  515.01– 8,400.00 = 1

APPENDIX TABLE 3

Per Capita Assessed Valuation and Density of Population of Cities in Los Angeles County[a]

City	Area[b] in sq. mi. (Dec., 1961)	Population[c] estimate (Jan., 1962)	Population density per sq. mi.	Rank by population density	Total assessed valuation[d] (1961)	Per capita assessed valuation	Rank by per capita assessed valuation	Total levy (1961)
Alhambra	7.484	57,272	7,652.6	19	$ 103,703,070	$ 1,810.71	27	$1,749,374
Arcadia	11.222	44,339	3,951.1	47	99,304,770	2,239.67	20	1,166,894
Artesia	1.614	10,397	6,441.8	28	9,398,080	903.92	64	No levy
Avalon	1.210	1,560	1,289.3	62	5,019,980	3,217.94	13	96,037
Azusa	6.919	21,909	3,166.5	53	33,320,480	1,520.86	37	540,394
Baldwin Park	6.275	37,747	6,015.5	30	30,438,595	806.38	68	41,943
Bell	2.814	20,681	7,349.3	22	20,798,140	1,005.66	62	316,731
Bellflower	6.159	48,915	7,942.0	15	54,184,250	1,107.72	59	No levy
Beverly Hills	5.684	32,385	5,697.6	34	205,241,420	6,337.55	6	2,122,576
Bradbury	1.996	646	323.6	67	2,377,640	3,680.56	11	20,470
Burbank	16.941	92,206	5,442.8	37	232,072,930	2,516.90	15	4,011,673
Claremont	4.070	13,978	3,434.4	52	19,453,620	1,391.73	45	297,009
Commerce	6.485	9,986	1,539.9	60	180,308,500	18,056.13	3	No levy
Compton	8.257	73,314	8,879.0	11	81,971,190	1,118.08	58	917,336
Covina	4.325	22,251	5,144.7	40	39,254,430	1,764.16	29	616,149
Cudahy	1.060	11,425	10,778.3	4	8,455,265	740.07	70	No levy
Culver City	4.101	32,406	7,902.0	17	75,558,570	2,331.62	18	1,771,510
Dairy Valley	8.755	3,578	408.7	66	17,993,830	5,029.02	8	No levy
Downey	12.766	89,055	6,976.0	23	132,051,935	1,482.81	39	451,880
Duarte	6.695	14,248	2,128.2	57	12,798,010	898.23	65	No levy
El Monte	6.137	32,273	5,258.8	39	37,798,985	1,171.23	56	389,444
El Segundo	5.516	14,895	2,700.3	54	106,740,420	7,166.19	5	1,181,725
Gardena	4.421	38,494	8,700.1	12	49,854,160	1,295.12	50	447,913
Glendale	29.240	122,976	4,205.7	46	202,755,615	1,648.74	34	2,772,563
Glendora	5.312	24,210	4,557.6	43	30,610,430	1,264.37	51	441,607

City								
Hawthorne	4.495	37,592	8,363.1	14	65,564,780	1,744.12	30	745,188
Hermosa Beach	1.360	16,718	12,292.6	2	24,827,940	1,485.10	38	288,349
Huntington Park	2.832	30,998	10,945.6	3	55,324,040	1,784.76	28	625,910
Industry	10.908	813	74.5	70	34,036,700	41,865.56	2	No levy
Inglewood	8.817	78,291	8,879.6	10	121,181,050	1,547.83	36	1,441,221
Irwindale	9.493	1,540	162.2	68	13,370,230	8,681.97	4	No levy
Lakewood	7.461	68,177	9,137.8	8	72,091,460	1,057.42	61	309,800
La Mirada	4.775	23,822	4,988.9	41	31,222,350	1,310.65	49	No levy
La Puente	3.389	26,332	776.7	64	22,367,995	849.46	67	No levy
La Verne	5.266	6,871	1,304.8	61	8,246,380	1,200.17	55	149,072
Lawndale	2.242	23,281	10,384.2	6	16,335,480	701.67	71	No levy
Long Beach	46.326	352,385	7,606.6	20	517,497,140	1,468.56	42	
Los Angeles	457.773	2,572,616	5,619.9	35	4,329,736,290	1,683.01	31	99,868,285
Lynwood	3.886	32,854	8,454.5	13	46,351,080	1,410.82	44	294,935
Manhattan Beach	3.810	34,748	9,120.2	9	39,382,525	1,133.38	57	583,415
Maywood	1.138	14,895	13,088.8	1	13,297,735	892.77	66	151,326
Monrovia	13.501	28,035	2,075.1	58	45,556,340	1,624.98	35	912,155
Montebello	7.463	36,232	4,854.9	42	71,670,800	1,978.11	23	1,108,572
Monterey Park	7.078	42,125	5,951.5	31	56,983,300	1,352.72	46	987,699
Norwalk	9.219	91,495	9,924.6	7	73,193,047	799.97	69	No levy
Palos Verdes Estates	4.737	10,594	2,236.4	56	31,565,670	2,979.58	14	358,609
Paramount	4.285	28,527	6,657.4	27	37,722,250	1,322.33	48	47,749
Pasadena	22.588	119,034	5,269.8	38	227,157,170	1,908.34	25	
Pico Rivera	7.853	49,906	6,355.0	29	60,391,135	1,210.10	53	No levy
Pomona	18.383	71,792	3,905.3	48	101,680,930	1,416.33	43	2,232,114
Redondo Beach	6.200	49,122	7,922.9	16	96,400,595	1,962.47	24	1,341,987
Rolling Hills	2.953	1,781	603.1	65	7,759,060	4,356.57	9	74,109
Rolling Hills Estates	1.249	4,498	3,601.3	50	10,511,410	2,336.91	17	15,013
Rosemead	2.364	16,122	6,819.8	25	17,337,710	1,075.41	60	No levy
San Dimas	8.225	7,587	922.4	63	9,180,340	1,210.01	54	33,967
San Fernando	2.362	16,451	6,964.9	24	24,222,480	1,472.40	41	438,895
San Gabriel	3.505	23,414	6,680.2	26	38,739,205	1,654.53	33	552,741
San Marino	3.750	13,777	3,673.9	49	51,025,400	3,703.67	10	788,948

APPENDIX TABLE 3 (Continued)

City	Area[b] in sq. mi. (Dec., 1961)	Population[c] estimate (Jan., 1962)	Population density per sq. mi.	Rank by population density	Total assessed valuation[d] (1961)	Per capita assessed valuation	Rank by per capita assessed valuation	Total levy (1961)
Santa Fe Springs	8.591	16,341	1,902.1	59	57,738,610	3,533.35	12	337,770
Santa Monica	8.100	86,628	10,694.8	5	159,780,945	1,844.45	26	3,069,309
Sierra Madre	2.943	10,304	3,501.2	51	15,182,175	1,473.43	40	240,059
Signal Hill	2.140	4,816	2,250.5	55	24,683,110	5,125.23	7	227,339
South El Monte	1.124	4,890	4,350.3	44	11,535,270	2,358.95	16	No levy
South Gate	7.324	56,067	7,655.2	18	113,081,378	2,016.90	21	770,095
South Pasadena	3.470	20,490	5,904.9	32	33,957,120	1,657.25	32	666,030
Temple City	3.604	26,944	7,476.1	21	33,394,880	1,239.42	52	No levy
Torrance	19.909	109,969	5,523.6	36	218,429,390	1,986.28	22	2,964,680
Vernon	4.981	221	44.4	71	182,068,810	823,840.77	1	355,824
Walnut	7.875	988	125.5	69	2,290,670	2,318.49	19	14,129
West Covina	12.820	54,668	4,264.3	45	73,675,600	1,347.69	47	753,340
Whittier	11.041	63,612	5,761.4	33	63,646,880	1,000.55	63	1,073,530
Total	969.075	5,259,509			$9,152,859,170			

SOURCE: [b] County Engineer's Office, Los Angeles County.
[c] Los Angeles County, Regional Planning Commission, *Population and Dwelling Units*, Bull. 75 (Jan., 1962).
[d] Los Angeles County, Auditor-Controller, *Taxpayers' Guide*, 1961.
[a] Average population density per sq. mi. = 5,427.3; average assessed valuation per capita = $1,740.25.

APPENDIX TABLE 4

Change in Area of Incorporated Cities in Los Angeles County, 1947–1953 and 1954–1961

City	Area in sq. mi., April 3, 1947	Area in sq. mi., Dec. 31, 1953, or on incorporation	Net change, 1947–1953	Area in sq. mi., Dec. 31, 1961	Net change, 1954–1961
Alhambra	6.700	7.410	0.710	7.484	0.074
Arcadia	10.580	10.595	0.015	11.222	0.627
Artesia[a]		1.614		1.614	None
Avalon	1.210	1.210	None	1.210	None
Azusa	4.130	4.173	0.043	6.919	2.746
Baldwin Park[a]		6.127		6.275	0.148
Bell	1.570	1.570	None	2.814	1.244
Bellflower[a]		6.074		6.159	0.085
Bell Gardens[a]		2.398		2.398	None
Beverly Hills	5.030	5.061	0.031	5.684	0.623
Bradbury[a]		1.996		1.996	None
Burbank	16.280	16.726	0.446	16.941	0.215
Claremont	3.370	3.370	None	4.070	0.700
Commerce[a]		6.367		6.485	0.118
Compton	5.260	7.817	2.557	8.257	0.440
Covina	0.930	1.926	0.996	4.325	2.399
Cudahy[a]		1.060		1.060	None
Culver City	3.250	3.991	0.741	4.101	0.110
Dairy Valley[a]		8.600		8.755	0.155
Downey[a]		11.785		12.766	0.981
Duarte[a]		6.492		6.695	0.203
El Monte	1.560	2.141	0.581	6.137	3.996
El Segundo	5.360	5.360	None	5.516	0.156
Gardena	3.040	4.104	1.064	4.421	0.317
Glendale	20.190	29.119	8.929	29.240	0.121
Glendora	2.240	2.598	0.358	5.312	2.714
Hawthorne	2.250	2.969	0.719	4.495	1.526
Hermosa Beach	1.360	1.360	None	1.360	None
Hidden Hills[a]		1.254		1.254	None
Huntington Park	2.810	2.829	0.019	2.832	0.003
Industry[a]		6.541		10.908	4.367
Inglewood	7.060	7.359	0.299	8.817	1.458
Irwindale[a]		9.477		9.493	0.016
Lakewood[a]		6.994		7.461	0.467
La Mirada[a]		4.749		4.775	0.026
La Puente[a]		3.204		3.389	0.185
La Verne	1.750	1.818	0.068	5.266	3.448
Lawndale[a]		1.897		2.242	0.345
Long Beach	34.060	40.549	6.489	46.326	5.777
Los Angeles	452.645	453.902	1.257	457.773	3.870
Lynwood	3.430	3.705	0.275	3.886	0.181
Manhattan Beach	3.810	3.810	None	3.810	None
Maywood	1.140	1.140	None	1.138	−0.002
Monrovia	8.100	8.241	0.141	13.510	5.269
Montebello	7.420	7.420	None	7.463	0.043
Monterey Park	4.800	6.244	1.444	7.078	0.834
Norwalk[a]		9.095		9.219	0.124
Palos Verdes Estates	4.730	4.730	None	4.737	0.007
Paramount[a]		4.285		4.285	None
Pasadena	21.140	22.540	1.400	22.588	0.048
Pico Rivera[a]		7.604		7.853	0.249
Pomona	13.260	14.817	1.557	18.383	3.566
Redondo Beach	6.040	6.078	0.038	6.200	0.122
Rolling Hills[a]		2.953		2.953	None
Rolling Hills Estates[a]		1.249		2.273	1.024
Rosemead[a]		2.241		2.364	0.123
San Dimas[a]		5.464		8.225	2.272
San Fernando	2.310	2.362	0.052	2.362	None
San Gabriel	3.340	3.340	None	3.505	0.165
San Marino	3.720	3.731	0.011	3.750	0.019
Santa Fe Springs[a]		6.522		8.591	2.069

APPENDIX TABLE 4 (Continued)

City	Area in sq. mi., April 3, 1947	Area in sq. mi., Dec. 31, 1953, or on incorporation	Net change, 1947–1953	Area in sq. mi., Dec. 31, 1961	Net change, 1954–1961
Santa Monica	8.100	8.100	None	8.100	None
Sierra Madre	2.940	2.943	0.003	2.943	None
Signal Hill	2.140	2.140	None	2.140	None
South El Monte[a]		1.124		1.430	0.306
South Gate	7.090	6.988	−0.102	7.324	0.336
South Pasadena	3.470	3.470	None	3.470	None
Temple City[a]		3.604		3.604	None
Torrance	18.880	18.879	−0.001	19.909	1.030
Vernon	4.160	4.160	None	4.981	0.821
Walnut[a]		7.737		7.875	0.138
West Covina	8.730	9.086	0.356	12.820	3.734
Whittier	3.920	5.222	1.302	11.041	5.819
Total	735.305	767.103	31.798	974.057	68.446[b]

Source: County Engineer, Los Angeles County.

[a] Incorporated after December 31, 1953.

[b] This net total represents the area added by annexations during this period. In addition, the amount of territory under municipal control was increased by incorporations totaling 138.508 square miles. Thus, the gross total added during this period was 206.954 square miles.

BIBLIOGRAPHY

Bibliography

BOOKS, REPORTS, AND MONOGRAPHS

Antieau, Chester James. *Municipal Corporation Law.* New York: Matthew Bender, 1958. Vol. 1.

Beebe, James L., *et al. Proceedings of Metropolitan Government Symposium.* Los Angeles: Los Angeles Chamber of Commerce, State and Local Government Committee, 1958.

Bemis, George W., and Nancy Bashé. *From Rural to Urban—the Municipalized County of Los Angeles.* Los Angeles: Haynes Foundation, 1947.

Bigger, Richard. *Flood Control in Metropolitan Los Angeles.* University of California Publications in Political Science, vol. 6. Berkeley and Los Angeles: University of California Press, 1959.

Bigger, Richard, and James D. Kitchen. *How the Cities Grew.* Los Angeles: University of California, Bureau of Governmental Research, 1952.

Bigger, Richard, *et al. Metropolitan Coast—San Diego and Orange Counties, California.* Los Angeles: University of California, Bureau of Governmental Research, 1958.

Bromage, Arthur W. *Political Representation in Metropolitan Agencies.* Michigan Governmental Studies no. 42. Ann Arbor: University of Michigan, Institute of Public Administration, 1962.

Bollens, John C. *Appointed Executive Local Government—The California Experience.* Los Angeles: Haynes Foundation, 1952.

———. *Special District Governments in the United States.* Berkeley and Los Angeles: University of California Press, 1957.

———. *The States and the Metropolitan Problem.* Chicago: Council of State Governments, 1956.

Bollens, John C., and Stanley Scott. *Local Government in California.* Berkeley and Los Angeles: University of California Press, 1951.

Bureau of Governmental Research, University of California, Los An-

geles. *County Government in California.* Sacramento: County Supervisors Association of California, 1958.

California. Citizens Legislative Advisory Commission. *Standing and
Interim Committees of the California Legislature.* Report prepared
by Jay Doubleday and published under the authority of the Rules
Committee for the Assembly of the State of California. Sacramento:
State Printing Office, 1959.

California. Governor's Commission on Metropolitan Area Problems.
Meeting Metropolitan Problems. Sacramento, 1960.

————. ————. *Metropolitan California.* Sacramento, 1961.

California Commission on County Home Rule. Final Report. *County
Government in California.* Sacramento, 1931.

California Legislature. Assembly. Interim Committee on Conservation,
Planning, and Public Works. *A Metropolitan Multipurpose District
for California—Report of the Subcommittee on Planning.* Assembly
Interim Committee Reports, 1957–1959, vol. 13, no. 24. Sacramento,
1959.

————. ————. Interim Committee on Municipal and County Government. *Financing Local Government in Los Angeles County.* Sacramento, 1952.

————. ————. ————. *Preliminary Report Covering Fringe Area
Problems in the Counties of Sacramento, Napa, Kern, and Alameda.*
Sacramento, 1952.

————. ————. ————. *Preliminary Report Covering Fringe Area
Problems in the County of Los Angeles.* Sacramento, 1953.

————. ————. ————. *Final Report Covering Fringe Area Problems
in the State of California.* Sacramento, 1953.

————. ————. ————. *Special Report on Fire Services in Los Angeles
County.* Assembly Interim Committee Reports, 1955–1957, vol. 6, no.
6. Sacramento, 1957.

————. ————. ————. *Concepts in Metropolitan Government.* Assembly Interim Committee Reports, 1957–1959, vol. 6, no. 9. Sacramento, 1959.

————. ————. ————. *Functional Consolidation of Local Government.* Assembly Interim Committee Reports, 1957–1959, vol. 6, no. 10.
Sacramento, 1959.

————. ————. ————. *Special Districts in the State of California:
Problems in General and the Consolidation of Sewer and Fire District Acts.* Assembly Interim Committee Reports, 1957–1959, vol. 6,
no. 12. Sacramento, 1959.

————. ————. ————. *Fire Grading and Rating.* Assembly Interim
Committee Reports, 1959–1961, vol. 6, no. 14. Sacramento, 1961.

————. ————. Interim Committee on State and Local Taxation. *The
Borough System of Government for Metropolitan Areas.* Report
prepared by Wendell Maccoby. Sacramento, 1951.

————. ————. Joint Judiciary Committee on Administration of Justice. *Second Partial Report on the Operation of the Courts.* Sacramento, 1959.

———. Senate. Interim Committee on State and Local Taxation. *Report. Part Two: State and Local Sales and Use Taxes in California.* Sacramento, 1953.

———. ———. ———. *Report. Part Four: A Legal History of Property Taxation in California.* Sacramento, 1953.

———. ———. ———. *Report. Part Six: Property Assessments and Equalization in California.* Sacramento, 1953.

———. ———. ———. *Report. Part Seven: Fiscal Problems of Urban Growth in California.* Sacramento, 1953.

———. ———. Senate Fact Finding Committee on Local Government. *Report.* Sacramento, 1961.

Case, Fred E., *et al. The Impact of the Growth of the Los Angeles Metropolitan Region on the Demand for Outdoor Recreation Facilities in Southern California, 1976 and 2000.* Washington, D.C.: Outdoor Recreational Requirements Review Commission, 1963.

Chapin, F. Stuart. "The Protestant Church in an Urban Government," in *Cities and Society,* ed. Paul K. Hatt and Albert J. Reiss, Jr. Glencoe: Free Press, 1957.

Cottrell, Edwin A., and Helen L. Jones. *Characteristics of the Metropolis.* Los Angeles: Haynes Foundation, 1952.

———. *The Metropolis: Is Integration Possible?* Los Angeles: Haynes Foundation, 1954.

Crouch, Winston W. *Intergovernmental Relations.* Los Angeles: Haynes Foundation, 1954.

———. *State Aid to Local Government in California.* Publications of the University of California at Los Angeles in Social Sciences, vol. 6, no. 3. Berkeley: University of California Press, 1939.

Crouch, Winston W., *et al. California Government and Politics.* 2d ed. Englewood Cliffs, N. J.: Prentice-Hall, 1960.

Dahl, Robert A. *Who Governs?* New Haven: Yale University Press, 1962.

Dana, Samuel T., and Myron Krueger. *California Lands.* Washington, D.C.: American Forestry Association, 1958.

Dillon, John F. *Treatise on the Law of Municipal Corporations.* Chicago: James Cockcroft, 1872.

Dinerman, Beatrice. "Community Coördinating Councils in Los Angeles County." Unpublished manuscript at the Bureau of Governmental Research, University of California, Los Angeles, 1960.

———. *Hospital Development and Communities.* Los Angeles: Bureau of Governmental Research, University of California, 1960.

Dinerman, Beatrice, *et al. Metropolitan Services: Studies of Allocation in a Federated Organization.* Los Angeles: Bureau of Governmental Research, University of California, 1961.

Dvorin, Eugene P., and Judith Norvell Jamison. *Tax Exemptions and*

Local Self-Government. Los Angeles: Bureau of Governmental Research, University of California, 1958.

Earle, Howard H. *Contract Law Enforcement Services by the Los Angeles County Sheriff's Department*. Los Angeles: School of Public Administration, University of Southern California, 1960.

Engelbert, Ernest A., ed. *Transportation and Metropolitan Planning*. Vol. III. Southern California Planning Institute. Berkeley and Los Angeles: University Extension, University of California, 1956.

Fesler, James W. *Area and Administration*. University, Alabama: University of Alabama Press, 1949.

Fordham, Jefferson B. *A Larger Concept of Community*. Baton Rouge: Louisiana State University Press, 1956.

Gold, Thompson, and Company. *Economic Analysis of the Proposed City of Commerce*. South Pasadena, 1959.

Gove, Samuel K. *The Lakewood Plan*. Urbana: Institute of Government and Public Affairs, University of Illinois, 1960.

Government Affairs Foundation. *Metropolitan Surveys: A Digest*. Chicago: Public Administration Service, 1958.

Gulick, Luther Halsey. *The Metropolitan Problem and American Ideas*. New York: Alfred A. Knopf, 1962.

Harris, Joseph P. *California Politics*. Stanford: Stanford University Press, 1955.

Harris County Home Rule Commission. *Metropolitan Harris County*. Houston: Harris County Home Rule Association, 1957.

Hawley, Amos. *Human Ecology*. New York: Ronald Press, 1950.

Hichborn, Franklin. *Story of the Session of the California Legislature of 1909*. San Francisco: James H. Barry, 1909.

———. *Story of the Session of the California Legislature of 1911*. San Francisco: James H. Barry, 1911.

———. *Story of the Session of the California Legislature of 1913*. San Francisco: James H. Barry, 1913.

———. *Story of the Session of the California Legislature of 1921*. San Francisco: James H. Barry, 1922.

Higgins, Edwin. *California's Oil Industry*. Los Angeles: Chamber of Mines and Oil, 1928.

Hirshleifer, Jack, *et al. Water Supply—Economics, Technology, and Policy*. Chicago: University of Chicago Press, 1960.

Holbrook, James G. *A Survey of Metropolitan Trial Courts Los Angeles Area*. Los Angeles: University of Southern California, 1956.

Holmes, Jack D. L. *A Selected and Annotated Bibliography of Shopping Centers*. Austin: Bureau of Business Research, University of Texas, 1957.

Janowitz, Morris. *The Community Press in an Urban Setting*. Glencoe: Free Press, 1952.

Jones, Victor. *Metropolitan Goverment*. Chicago: University of Chicago Press, 1942.

Kaufman, Herbert. *The Forest Ranger*. Baltimore: Johns Hopkins Press, 1960.

Key, V. O., and Winston W. Crouch. *The Initiative and the Referendum in California*. Publications of the University of California at Los Angeles in Social Sciences, vol. 6, no. 4. Berkeley: University of California Press, 1939.

Koiner, C. Wellington. *History of Pasadena's Municipal Light and Power Plant*. Pasadena: City of Pasadena, 1925.

League of California Cities, Los Angeles County Division. County-City Relations Committee. *Report*. Los Angeles, 1951.

Leask, Samuel, Jr., and George Terhune. *Metropolitan Government for Los Angeles: A Workable Solution*. Los Angeles: City Administrator's Office, 1961.

Lee, Eugene C. *The Politics of Nonpartisanship—A Study of California Elections*. Berkeley and Los Angeles: University of California Press, 1960.

Lee, Rose Hum. *The City*. New York: Lippincott, 1955.

Los Angeles Central City Committee and Los Angeles City Planning Department. *Centropolis, 1980*. Los Angeles: City of Los Angeles, 1961.

Los Angeles City Bureau of Budget and Efficiency. *A Study of a Proposed City and County Government of Los Angeles within the Present City Limits*. Los Angeles: City of Los Angeles, 1932.

———. *A Study of Local Government in the Metropolitan Area within Los Angeles County*. Los Angeles: City of Los Angeles, 1935.

Los Angeles City Planning Commission. *Branch Administrative Centers*. Los Angeles: City of Los Angeles, 1950.

Los Angeles County. Bureau of Efficiency. *Problems Involved in the Proposed Separation of Los Angeles City from the County of Los Angeles*. Los Angeles: County of Los Angeles, 1932.

———. Charter Study Committee. *Recommendations of the Charter Study Committee Presented to the Board of Supervisors*. Los Angeles, 1958. (Mimeographed.)

———. Chief Administrative Officer. *Proposals for Future Capital Projects, 1957–1967*. Los Angeles: County of Los Angeles, 1957.

———. Committee on Governmental Simplification. *Final Report*. Los Angeles: County of Los Angeles, 1935.

———. Department of Community Services. *Staff Produced Administrative Studies*. Los Angeles: County of Los Angeles, 1960.

———. Department of Parks and Recreation. *Yesterday and Today*. Los Angeles: County of Los Angeles, 1960.

Mangore Corporation. *Community Attitudes towards Governmental and Educational Services in Four Southeast Cities*. Los Angeles, 1959.

Martin, Roscoe C., et al. *Decisions in Syracuse*. Metropolitan Action Studies, no. 1. Bloomington: Indiana University Press, 1960.

May, Samuel C., and James M. Fales, Jr. *The State's Interest in Metropolitan Problems.* Berkeley: Bureau of Public Administration, University of California, 1955.

Mezirow, Jack D. "The Coordinating Council Movement in Los Angeles County." Unpublished Ph.D. dissertation, University of California, Los Angeles, 1955.

Morden, Margaret Gorsuch, and Richard Bigger. *Cooperative Health Administration in Metropolitan Los Angeles.* Los Angeles: Bureau of Governmental Research, University of California, 1948.

Nadeau, Remi A. *The Water Seekers.* Garden City, N.Y.: Doubleday, 1950.

Ostrom, Vincent. *Water and Politics: A Study of Water Policies and Administration in the Development of Los Angeles.* Los Angeles: Haynes Foundation, 1953.

Park, Robert E., Ernest W. Burgess, and Roderick D. McKenzie. *The City.* Chicago: University of Chicago Press, 1925.

Perry, Everett R. *Handbook of Branch Libraries.* Los Angeles: City Library, 1928.

Peterson, Lorin. *The Day of the Mugwump.* New York: Random House, 1962.

Public Administration Service. *The Government of Metropolitan Miami.* Chicago: Public Administration Service, 1954.

———. *The Government of Metropolitan Sacramento.* Chicago: Public Administration Service, 1957.

Redinger, David H. *The Story of Big Creek.* Los Angeles: Angelus Press, 1949.

Reining, Henry, Jr., and Frank P. Sherwood. *Government Alternatives in Paramount.* Los Angeles: University of Southern California, 1956.

Robinson, W. W. *Land in California.* Berkeley and Los Angeles: University of California Press, 1948.

Robson, W. A., ed. *Great Cities of the World.* Winston W. Crouch and Dean E. McHenry. *Los Angeles.* London: George Allen and Unwin, 1954.

Sacramento Metropolitan Area Advisory Committee. *Final Report.* Sacramento, 1957.

Sayre, Wallace, and Herbert Kaufman. *Governing New York City.* New York: Russell Sage Foundation, 1960.

Scott, Mel. *Metropolitan Los Angeles: One Community.* Los Angeles: Haynes Foundation, 1949.

Scott, Stanley. *Major Metropolitan Studies and Action Programs in California.* Berkeley: Bureau of Public Administration, University of California, 1959. (Mimeographed.)

Scott, Stanley, ed. *Metropolitan Area Problems.* Report of the Pacific Coast Conference on Metropolitan Problems. Berkeley: University Extension and Bureau of Public Administration, University of California, 1960.

Scott, Stanley, and Willis Culver. *Metropolitan Agencies and Concurrent Office Holding: A Survey of Selected Districts and Authorities.* Berkeley: Bureau of Public Administration, University of California, 1961. (Mimeographed.)

Scott, Stanley, and Lewis Keller. *Annexation? Incorporation? A Guide for Community Action.* Berkeley: Bureau of Public Administration, University of California, 1959. 3d ed.

Shevky, Eshref, and Marilyn Williams. *Social Areas of Los Angeles.* Los Angeles: Haynes Foundation, 1949.

Southern California Research Council. *The Southern California Metropolis—1980.* Claremont: Pomona College, 1959.

Staniford, Edward F. *Business Decentralization.* Los Angeles: Bureau of Governmental Research, University of California, 1960.

Studenski, Paul. *The Government of Metropolitan Areas in the United States.* New York: National Municipal League, 1930.

Sweeney, Stephen, and George S. Blair, eds. *Metropolitan Analysis.* Philadelphia: University of Pennsylvania Press, 1958.

Swisher, Carl B. *Motivation and Technique in the California Constitutional Convention 1878–79.* Claremont: Pomona College, 1930.

Taxpayers' Association of California. *City and County Consolidated for Los Angeles.* Los Angeles: Taxpayers' Association of California, 1917.

The California Assembly. *California State Government—Its Tasks and Organization.* Stanford: Stanford University, in coöperation with The American Assembly of Columbia University, 1956.

Thompson, Warren S. *Growth and Changes in California's Population.* Los Angeles: Haynes Foundation, 1955.

Tilton, L. Deming, and George W. Robbins, eds. *Los Angeles: Preface to a Master Plan.* Los Angeles: Pacific Southwest Academy, 1941.

Town Hall. *Pay Policies for Public Personnel.* A Report of the Municipal and County Government Section of Town Hall. Los Angeles: Town Hall, 1961.

U.S. Congress. House of Representatives. 87th Cong., 1st sess. *Governmental Structure, Organization, and Planning in Metropolitan Areas: A Report by the Advisory Commission on Intergovernmental Relations.* Washington, D.C.: Government Printing Office, 1961.

———. ———. ———. *Government in Metropolitan Areas: Commentaries on a Report by the Advisory Commission on Intergovernmental Relations.* Washington, D.C.: Government Printing Office, 1961.

Vieg, John A., *et al. California Local Finance.* Stanford: Stanford University Press, 1960.

Warren, Robert. "Religious Organization and the Development of the Urban Community." Unpublished manuscript at the Bureau of Governmental Research, University of California, Los Angeles, 1959.

Wood, Robert C. *Suburbia: Its People and Their Politics.* Boston: Houghton Mifflin, 1959.

Zierer, Clifford M. *California and the Southwest.* New York: John Wiley and Sons, 1956.

ARTICLES

Arnold, S. J. "General Managers' Report," *Tax Digest* (March, 1960), 57–63.

Bigger, Richard, and James D. Kitchen. "City Managers and Metro," *National Civic Review,* XLIX (March, 1960), 120–126.

Brewer, Michael F. "Local Government Assessment: Its Impact on Land and Water Use," *Land Economics,* XXXVII (Aug., 1961), 207–217.

Crouch, Winston W. "The Government of a Metropolitan Region," *University of Pennsylvania Law Review,* 105 (Feb., 1957), 474–488.

Dinerman, Beatrice. "Chambers of Commerce in the Modern Metropolis," *BGR Observer* (Sept., 1958) (Bureau of Governmental Research, University of California).

Foley, Donald L. "The Use of Local Facilities in a Metropolis," *American Journal of Sociology,* 56 (Nov., 1950) 238–246.

Harris, Chauncey D., and Edward L. Ullman. "The Nature of Cities," *Annals of the American Academy of Political and Social Science,* 242 (Nov., 1945), 7-17.

Hawley, Amos. "The Incorporation Trend in Metropolitan Areas, 1900–1950," *Journal of the American Institute of Planners,* XXV (Feb., 1959), 41–45.

Huckshorn, Robert J., and Charles E. Young. "Study of Voting Splits in City Councils in Los Angeles County," *Western Political Quarterly* (June, 1960), 479–497.

Hutchins, Wells A. "California Ground Water: Legal Problems," *California Law Review,* 45 (Dec., 1957), 688–697.

Jones, Victor. "Cooperation Pattern," *National Civic Review,* LI (June, 1962), 302–308.

———. "The Organization of a Metropolitan Region," *University of Pennsylvania Law Review,* 105 (Feb., 1957), 538–552.

Lee, Eugene C. "Home Rule Appraised," *National Civic Review,* LI (Oct., 1962), 486–488.

Moskovitz, Adolphus. "Quality Control and Re-Use of Water in California," *California Law Review,* 45 (Dec., 1957), 586–603.

Ostrom, Vincent, *et al.* "The Organization of Government in Metropolitan Areas," *American Political Science Review,* LV (Dec., 1961), 831–842.

Peppin, John C. "Municipal Home Rule in California, I" *California Law Review,* XXX (Nov., 1941), 1–45.

————. "Municipal Home Rule in California, II," *California Law Review*, XXI (March, 1942), 273–332.

————. "Municipal Home Rule in California, III," *California Law Review*, XXXII (Dec., 1944), 341-393.

————. "Municipal Home Rule in California, IV," *California Law Review*, XXXIV (Dec., 1946), 644–694.

Quinn, James A. "The Burgess Zonal Hypothesis and its Critics," *American Sociological Review*, 5 (April, 1940), 210–218.

Schnore, Leo F. "The Timing of Metropolitan Decentralization," *Journal of the American Institute of Planners*, 25 (Nov., 1959), 200–206.

Smith, Stephen C. "Legal and Institutional Controls in Water Allocation," *Journal of Farm Economics*, XLII (Dec., 1960), 1345–1358.

————. "The Rural-Urban Transfer of Water in California," *Natural Resources Journal*, 1 (March, 1961), 64–75.

Index